HOUSTON JUNIOR LEAGUE
COOKBOOK

The Junior League of Houston, Inc.
1811 Briar Oaks Lane
Houston, Texas 77027

Foreword

This is the original HOUSTON JUNIOR LEAGUE COOKBOOK with a beautiful new cover to commemorate the book's 35th anniversary. First published in 1968, more than 130,000 copies have been sold by The Junior League of Houston, Inc.

The Junior League of Houston, Inc. is an organization of women committed to promoting voluntarism, developing the potential of women, and improving communities through the effective action and leadership of trained volunteers. Its purpose is exclusively educational and charitable. The sale of this book and others promotes the mission and contributes to the charitable endeavors of The Junior League of Houston, Inc.

Also by The Junior League of Houston, Inc.:
Peace Meals: A Book of Recipes for Cooking and Connecting (2008)
Sweet Dreams Douglas (2002)
Stop and Smell the Rosemary: Recipes and Traditions to Remember (1996)
The Star of Texas Cookbook (1983)

Any inquiries about this book or orders for additional copies should be directed to:
The Junior League of Houston, Inc.
1811 Briar Oaks Lane
Houston, Texas 77027
713.871.6608
www.juniorleaguehouston.org

Cover design courtesy of Panhandle-Eastern Corporation.
"Plantation Pineapple" fabric courtesy of Brunschwig & Fils.
Cover photography by J. Michael Martinez,
Temple Webber Photography, Houston, Texas.

Manufactured by
Ⅲ Favorite Recipes® Press
An imprint of

FRP®INC

P. O. Box 305142
Nashville, Tennessee 37230
800-358-0560

HOUSTON JUNIOR LEAGUE COOKBOOK COMMITTEE

CHAIRMAN

Mrs. Lorenzo Boykin Taylor

CO-CHAIRMEN

Mrs. John H. Lindsey

Mrs. Richard R. McKay

Mrs. H. Edward Maddox, III

EDITORIAL ASSISTANTS

Mrs. Robert B. Crouch

Mrs. John L. Hamilton

ARTIST

Mrs. R. L. "Pete" Hawk

Mrs. George N. Allen, Jr.

Mrs. Bruce E. Barnett

Mrs. Ben A. Brollier

Mrs. Lewis A. Brown

Mrs. Douglas S. Craig

Mrs. Robert J. Holley

Mrs. George V. Kane, Jr.

Mrs. John H. Meyers

Mrs. Kline McGee

Mrs. Rotan McGown

Mrs. J. Howard Park, III

Mrs. William M. Thorsell, Jr.

Mrs. Charles B. Williams

Table of Contents

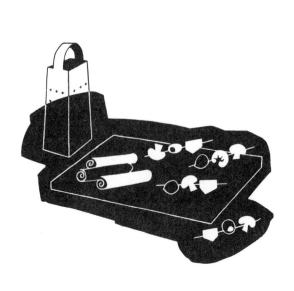

APPETIZERS

BEVERAGES

Hints

Popcorn heated with garlic butter.

Potato chips sprinkled with Parmesan cheese and broiled lightly.

Pecan halves spread with sharp cheese and put together in pairs.

Canned mushrooms, marinated in French dressing, chilled, drained, and served with toothpicks.

Cubes of honeydew melon and thin slices of imported ham, on toothpicks.

Plum tomatoes, halved, with a smoked oyster inserted between halves, put together with toothpicks.

Beef or cheese fondue served "do it yourself" style.

Charcoal broiled shrimp, served with sweet and sour sauce.

Many recipes found elsewhere in this book would make excellent appetizers served in smaller quantities.

BEVERAGES

TO CLEAR CLOUDY TEA: Add a little boiling water and the clear amber color will return. Never refrigerate hot brewed tea, for the refrigerator may cause it to cloud, although its flavor will not be impaired.

TO MAKE CLOUDLESS ICED TEA: Combine 1/4 cup tea leaves (or 12 tea bags) and 3 cups cold water in a glass or china container. Cover, and refrigerate for 12-24 hours. Strain; serve over ice.

TO MAKE COLORFUL ICE CUBES: Freeze fruit juices in ice trays; or add a little food coloring to water before freezing in ice trays.

TO MAKE DECORATIVE ICE CUBES: Fill ice cube tray about 2/3 full with freshly boiled water (to insure clear ice cubes). Let freeze. Place one of the following decorations in each cubicle, then gently pour on just enough water to cover. Continue freezing. Suggested decorations: sprigs of mint; slices of lime, lemon or orange; red or green maraschino cherries, with stems; pineapple chunks; whole fresh strawberries.

TO DECORATE PUNCH BOWL (AND CHILL PUNCH): Freeze water or fruit juice, and fruit, in alternate layers in a large bowl or ring mold. Unmold and float in punch bowl.

Garden Cheese Dip

1 large package (8 oz.)
  cream cheese
2 tablespoons Roquefort cheese
2 tablespoons grated carrots
1/2 tomato, peeled
1 tablespoon minced green
  pepper

1/2 cucumber, peeled
1/2 teaspoon minced onion
1/2 teaspoon lemon juice
1/8 teaspoon salt
1 tablespoon mayonnaise, or
  more for right consistency

Combine all ingredients in blender and blend. If mixture is too thick for dipping, add a little milk. Makes approximately 2 cups.

To use as salad, hollow out center of a large head of lettuce. Stuff lettuce with cheese mixture, being careful not to split lettuce. Refrigerate about 6 hours. To serve, cut in slices or wedges.

Mrs. Frank C. Smith, Jr. (Sally McQueen)

Shrimp Dip

1 large package (8 oz.)
  cream cheese, softened
1 cup Brockles Special Dressing
  (a Thousand Island type
  dressing)
1/2 cup mayonnaise
2 pimientos, minced
1 small onion, grated

1/4 cup minced green onions
3-6 teaspoons Tabasco
1 tablespoon Lawry's
  seasoned salt
1 tablespoon horseradish
2 pounds cooked, shelled shrimp,
  chopped

Cream softened cheese with dressing and mayonnaise. Stir in remaining ingredients. Makes about 3 pints.

Mrs. William A. Bramley (Kay Borden)

Neptune Cheese Dip

1 1/2 pounds cooked, shelled
  shrimp, cut in small pieces
6 large packages (8 oz. each)
  cream cheese, softened
1 large onion, grated

Juice of at least 3 lemons
6 tablespoons Durkee's sauce
1 teaspoon (or more) Tabasco
1 teaspoon salt
1/2 cup milk, to thin if necessary

Mix together all ingredients. Makes over 2 quarts.

Mrs. James A. Reichert (Betsy Calhoun)

Clam Dip

1 envelope Knorr cream of
leek soup
1 pint sour cream

1 can (7½ oz.) clams,
drained and minced

Pulverize dried soup in a bowl. Mix in sour cream. Add clams. Serve on your favorite crackers. Makes approximately 3 cups.

Miss Holly Willis

Green Chile Dip

1 can (4 oz.) green chiles,
chopped
1 large package (8 oz.)
cream cheese

Mayonnaise to soften cheese
1 teaspoon grated onion
Lemon juice, to taste

Mix all ingredients; taste, and correct seasoning. Refrigerate for a few hours. Serve with tostados. Makes approximately 1-1/2 cups.

Mrs. Harry H. Hudson (Carolyn Brock)

Black Bean Dip

2 small packages (3 oz. each)
cream cheese
1 can condensed black bean soup
1 small onion, finely chopped

Salt and pepper
2 tablespoons minced parsley
2 tablespoons mayonnaise
4 teaspoons Worcestershire sauce

Mash cream cheese until smooth. Add other ingredients and blend until smooth. Chill at least 3 hours before serving. This can be prepared ahead as it keeps well in the refrigerator for several days. Makes about 2-1/2 cups.

Mrs. Eugene A. Ellingson (Louise Pincoffs)

Avocado Dip

1 can (10 oz.) Rotel tomatoes and
green chilies, drained
1 envelope onion soup mix
2 small packages (3 oz. each)
cream cheese, softened

3 avocados, mashed
1 tablespoon minced onion
2 teaspoons Worcestershire sauce
Squeeze of lemon juice
Salt

Mash tomatoes; add all other ingredients. Beat well. Serve with tostados. Makes about 3-1/2 cups.

Mrs. Holcombe Crosswell (Emily Attwell)

Avocado-Jalapeño Dip

1 avocado, mashed
2 teaspoons grated onion
2 teaspoons jalapeno juice
1 teaspoon minced jalapeno pepper

2 teaspoons mayonnaise
Dash of Worcestershire sauce
Salt and pepper

Place all ingredients in bowl and mix well. Place avocado seed in the dip until serving time to retain color. Serve with Fritos. Makes about 3/4 cup.

Mrs. John A. Beck (Audrey Louise Jones)

Guacamole Dip

2 medium avocados
½ cup sour cream
2 tablespoons lemon juice
1 tablespoon grated onion

¾ teaspoon salt
Dash freshly ground pepper
Tabasco

Puree peeled avocados in a sieve or blender. Mix in all other ingredients. Makes approximately 1-1/2 cups.

Mrs. Marvin V. Cluett (Lollie Lauderdale)

Caviar Dip for Artichokes

½ cup mayonnaise (homemade preferably)
1 tablespoon lemon juice
½ - ¾ of a 2-ounce jar domestic whitefish caviar

Mix all ingredients. This amount will serve as a dip for the leaves and hearts of 2 artichokes which have been cooked and chilled. (Be sure to remove the choke portion before serving.)

Mrs. Harry H. Hudson (Carolyn Brock)

Curry Dip

1 cup mayonnaise
1 teaspoon curry powder
1 teaspoon garlic salt

1 teaspoon tarragon vinegar
1 teaspoon horseradish
1 teaspoon grated onion

Mix all ingredients together in a blender; cover and refrigerate. Serve with carrot strips, celery sticks, cauliflowerets or cucumber sticks. Makes about 1 cup.

Mrs. Richard L. Parry (Molly McCloud)

Cucumber Dip

1 cucumber, peeled and
finely grated
1 teaspoon grated onion
2 packages (3 oz. each)
cream cheese
2 teaspoons mayonnaise

Generous pinch Lawry's
seasoned salt
½ teaspoon sugar
1 or 2 drops green food
coloring (enough to turn
dip a pale, pale green)

Quarter the cucumber lengthwise and remove seeds before grating. Drain off juice. Blend with other ingredients. Chill and serve with potato chips, crackers, or as a dip for vegetables. Makes about 1 cup.

Mrs. William A. Bramley (Kay Borden)

Easy Liver Pâté

¾ pound calf liver, sliced
½ cup butter
1 medium onion, chopped
3 tablespoons sherry or
brandy

1 can (3½ oz.) mushroom
pieces and juice
1 teaspoon salt
Dash Tabasco
1 teaspoon Worcestershire sauce

Saute sliced liver in butter with onions until done. Cut in chunks and put in blender, adding sherry, juice from mushrooms, salt, Tabasco and Worcestershire sauce. Blend. If too thick add a little mayonnaise. Stir in mushroom pieces, which have been coarsely chopped. Pour into crock and refrigerate. It will thicken when cold. Serve in the crock with toast squares. Or, may be spread on toast and topped with small pieces of truffle. Makes about 2 cups.

Miss Margaret E. Biehl

Chicken Liver Pâté

4 tablespoons soft butter
1 small onion, chopped
½ pound chicken livers
2 tablespoons brandy
¼ teaspoon dry mustard

⅛ teaspoon mace
⅛ teaspoon powdered cloves
½ teaspoon salt
¼ teaspoon pepper
Good dash cayenne

Melt 2 tablespoons butter in frying pan. Saute onion for 2 minutes. Add chicken livers and saute about 5 minutes more, turning livers to cook evenly. Put liver and onions in blender and puree until smooth. Deglaze frying pan with brandy and pour over livers in blender. Add all seasonings and remaining 2 tablespoons of butter. Blend again, but for a very short time. Pack into a 1-1/2 cup mold and refrigerate. Garnish with parsley and serve on bread rounds.

Mrs. James Howard Park, III (Bette Naylor)

Liver Pâté and Consomme

1 can (4¾ oz.) Sell's liver pate,
or 1 can (4¾ oz.) Underwood's
liverwurst spread
1 package (3 oz.) cream cheese
Pinch salt
Few drops Worcestershire sauce

1 can beef consomme
1 teaspoon gelatin, softened
in the consomme
3 tablespoons bourbon
Truffles and pimientos (optional)
Parsley for garnish

Mix the liver pate, cream cheese, salt and Worcestershire sauce into a soft paste. Bring to a boil the consomme and gelatin. Let it cool. Add bourbon to the jelly when it starts to set. (If you desire to use truffles and pimientos for decoration, arrange them attractively in a small amount of jelly mixture and allow decorative layer to set before proceeding with mold.) Pour half of the jelly into a 2-1/2 cup mold. When set, spread on the pate, then add remaining jelly; do not let the pate touch the sides of the mold. Chill until firm. Unmold and garnish with parsley. Serve as a spread for crackers. Makes approximately 2 cups.

Mrs. Thomas F. Hudgins, Jr. (Carlys Ann King)

Hot Broccoli Dip

½ cup chopped onion
½ cup chopped celery
½ cup chopped mushrooms
3 tablespoons butter
1 package frozen chopped broccoli,
cooked and drained

1 can condensed mushroom
soup
1 package (6 oz.) garlic
cheese, diced
Generous squeeze of lemon
juice

Saute onion, celery and mushrooms in butter until tender. Add to broccoli. Mix in mushroom soup and the cheese; cook over low heat until cheese is melted and well blended. A squeeze of lemon juice helps to retain the nice green color. Serve in chafing dish with tostados, Fritos or toast rounds. This can be prepared ahead of time but do not heat until the last minute. May also be frozen. Makes about 1 quart.

Mrs. Richard W. Burns (Peggy Kirksey)

7

Texas Bean Dip

½ pound butter
⅓ pound sharp cheese, grated
2 jalapeno peppers, chopped,
  plus a little juice

1 small onion, grated
1 clove garlic, crushed
1 can (15 oz.) Ranch Style beans
  (or beans in chili-seasoned
  sauce)

Heat all ingredients, except beans, in double boiler until cheese melts. Add beans which have been pureed in blender. Serve hot in a chafing dish with tostados. Makes about 1 quart.

Mrs. Robert E. Clemons (Grayson Reed Cecil)

Chafing Dish Oyster Dip

4 strips bacon
2 tablespoons bacon drippings
1 bunch green onions or
  shallots, finely chopped
3 tablespoons flour
1 cup oyster liquor (add water if
  necessary to make 1 cup)

1 pint oysters, chopped
1 tablespoon finely chopped
  parsley
1 tablespoon butter
Salt, pepper and cayenne
5 or 6 soda crackers, crushed
  (if needed)

Fry bacon in heavy skillet; remove and crumble. Saute onions in bacon drippings. Add flour and stir well. Add oyster liquor. (Mixture will be very thick.) Add oysters, parsley, butter, salt, pepper and cayenne. Cook slightly over hot water, stirring occasionally. Add bacon. If mixture is too thin, add crumbled crackers. Serve in chafing dish with crackers or toast rounds. Serves 8-10.

Mrs. Charles B. Moore (Mary Alice Bone)

Hot Crabmeat Spread

½ cup sliced almonds
¼ cup butter, melted
1 can (6½ oz.) crabmeat

¼ cup remoulade sauce
1 teaspoon Worcestershire
  sauce

Brown almonds in butter. Add other ingredients. Mix well and heat. Serve as a hot spread with Euphrates crackers. Makes approximately 2 cups.

Mrs. Henry Hamman (Ann Hufendick)

Shrimp Superbe

40 raw shrimp	1 tablespoon chopped chives
5 tablespoons butter	1 tablespoon chopped parsley
1 tablespoon flour	Anchovy paste (a dab the size
1 tablespoon tomato paste	of a pea)
2 ounces dry vermouth	Salt and pepper
1 pint cream	

Boil shrimp with your favorite seasonings. Drain, shell and dice. (If you must use canned shrimp, drain and rinse well.) Saute the shrimp in 4 tablespoons of the hot melted butter for 5 minutes. Add flour; blend and cook 3 minutes. Add tomato paste and blend; then add vermouth, cream, chives, parsley and anchovy paste which has been mixed with the remaining tablespoon of butter. Cook a few minutes and season with salt and pepper. Serve hot as a dip. May also be served on split and toasted English muffins for a luncheon dish. Will serve 12 as an appetizer or 6 as a luncheon entree.

Mrs. Frederick M. Schall, Jr. (Belen Wagner)

Oysters Ernie

24 select oysters	Flour
Salt and pepper	Butter

Sprinkle oysters with salt and pepper; dredge in flour. Saute in butter until crisp and brown on both sides. Place oysters on hot serving plate and top with Ernie's Sauce.

ERNIE'S SAUCE

2 tablespoons melted butter	2 tablespoons Worcestershire
1/4 cup lemon juice	sauce
1/2 cup sherry	2 tablespoons flour
1 cup A-1 steak sauce	3 tablespoons water

Mix all ingredients, except flour and water, together in saucepan; warm over low heat. Blend flour and water and stir into sauce. Do not let boil. Adjust seasoning to taste, adding more A-1 if too thin, more wine if too thick or too highly seasoned. Pour over oysters. Serve with toothpicks. Sauce may be saved, strained, reheated and used again.

Mrs. John L. Hamilton (Ann Lowdon)

9

Oyster Roll

1 large package (8 oz.) cream cheese	1 can (3¾ oz.) smoked oysters
1 tablespoon mayonnaise	Parsley, finely chopped
	Dash red pepper (optional)

Soften cream cheese, mix with mayonnaise and spread mixture to edges of a piece of wax paper (8" x 11"). Place paper on a cookie sheet and refrigerate for at least 6 hours. Drain and finely chop the oysters. Remove cream cheese from refrigerator and keep at room temperature about 15 minutes. Then carefully spread chopped oysters over the cream cheese and roll in jelly-roll fashion starting on the long side. You may use a spatula to help; but once started, it is fairly easy. Serve immediately or rewrap and refrigerate for 24 hours. Decorate with parsley and a little red pepper if desired. Slice and serve with crackers or toast rounds. Serves 8.

Mrs. Frank J. McGurl (Mary Martin)

Olé Molé Hamburgers

3 pounds ground beef	2 teaspoons salt
1½ cups dried bread crumbs	2 teaspoons pepper
1 medium-large onion, minced	½ pound butter
1 tablespoon cornstarch	2 tablespoons flour
¼ teaspoon ground allspice	2 cans beef consomme
1 cup milk	Mole seasoning powder to taste
1 cup cream	½ cup dry red wine (optional)
	Small buns

Mix ground beef, bread crumbs, onion, cornstarch, allspice, milk, cream, salt and pepper, but do not handle too much. Roll into balls the size of a walnut, then flatten. Brown in butter, a few a time; keep warm. Blend flour with butter remaining in pan. Add consomme. Add mole seasoning powder to taste. Return hamburgers to pan and simmer 45 minutes. (If sauce should taste bitter after simmering, add a little sugar.) Add wine before serving, if desired. Serve from a chafing dish with small buns. Makes 45-50 small hamburgers.

Mrs. Garrett Stuart Livingston, Jr. (Mary Ann Ransom)

Pickled Shrimp

1¼ cups salad oil	1 clove garlic, crushed
¾ cup white vinegar	2 pounds cooked, shelled shrimp
1½ teaspoons salt	3 medium onions,
2½ teaspoons celery seed	thinly sliced
2½ tablespoons capers,	Several bay leaves
with juice	Several whole cloves

Make a marinade sauce by mixing together the first 6 ingredients; chill. In a shallow refrigerator dish arrange shrimp and onions in layers, sprinkling broken bay leaves and cloves throughout. Pour the marinade sauce over all. Cover and refrigerate for 24 hours, turning shrimp occasionally. Will keep for several weeks in the refrigerator.

Mrs. Boykin Craig (Lorenza Boykin)

Anchovies Piquant

1 can anchovy fillets	3 finely chopped shallots or
3 tablespoons olive oil	green onions
3 tablespoons chopped parsley	1 tablespoon tarragon vinegar
	Triscuit crackers

Drain fillets well and place on small serving dish. Mix remaining ingredients together into a thick paste. More onion or parsley may be added to thicken, if desired. Pour sauce over anchovies and marinate for at least one hour before serving. Serve with Triscuit crackers. This Swedish snack serves 4.

Mrs. Mervyn Lea Rudee (Betsy Eager)

Nachos

Doritos or tostados	Old English or Cheddar cheese,
Refried beans or bean dip	grated
(canned is fine)	Slices of jalapeno pepper

Spread Doritos (or tostados) with the mashed beans. Sprinkle cheese over beans. Top with a small slice jalapeno pepper. (A small dab of sour cream may also be added.) Bake at 350° for 10-15 minutes, or until cheese melts.

Mrs. William Graham Guerriero (Margaret Ann White)

Cheese Roll

1¼ pounds sharp Cheddar cheese, grated	1 medium onion
1 large package (8 oz.) cream cheese	½ to ¾ cup chopped pecans
	½ cup poppy seeds

Mix cheeses together well, kneading with your hands. Grate onion over cheese and knead again. Add pecans and mix well. Form into 2 medium-sized rolls or balls, and roll in poppy seeds. Wrap in wax paper and then in foil. May be kept in refrigerator for weeks, or frozen. Makes 2 rolls, about 8'' long.

Mrs. William Thomas Crittenden, Jr. (Betty Lou LaMaster)

Easy Cheese Ball

1 package (6 oz.) bacon and cheese roll	1 jar (5 oz.) Old English cheese
1 package (6 oz.) jalapeno cheese roll	1 large package (8 oz.) cream cheese
1 package (6 oz.) garlic cheese roll	1 tablespoon chili powder
1 jar (5 oz.) Rokachell cheese	½ cup chopped parsley
	¾ cup walnuts (optional)

Let all cheese stand at room temperature until soft, then mix. Form into two balls. Refrigerate several hours. Roll the balls in a saucer of chili powder, then in a saucer of parsley or chopped walnuts. Freezes well.

Mrs. William G. Guerriero (Margaret Ann White)

Beer Cheese Spread

1 pound sharp Cheddar cheese	3 tablespoons Worcestershire sauce
1 pound mild Cheddar cheese	1½ cups beer (approximately)
1 can (6 oz.) tomato paste	
1 teaspoon garlic salt	

Grate cheeses and mix well with other ingredients into a smooth, spreadable paste. Add more beer if necessary to give proper consistency. Serve with crackers or rye bread rounds. Mixture may be spread between 2 slices of bread and grilled for hot sandwiches. Makes about 3 pints.

Mrs. A. J. Hurt, Jr. (Patty Parrish)

Wine Cheese Spread

1 large package (8 oz.)
  cream cheese
2 ounces Roquefort or Blue cheese
½ cup port wine

½ pound sharp cheese, grated
½ teaspoon Worcestershire sauce
½ teaspoon salt
Dash cayenne

Mash cream cheese and Blue cheese; gradually blend in wine. Mix together grated cheese, Worcestershire sauce, salt and cayenne. Combine both cheese mixtures. Pack into 6" (3-cup) ring mold, or shape into mound, and chill thoroughly. Serve with assorted crackers. Makes about 3 cups.

Mrs. Roger G. Stotler (Nance Fruit)

Mystery Cheese Ball

½ pound New York State
  sharp cheese, grated
5 jars (5 oz. each) Blue cheese
  spread

4 tablespoons grated onion
2 teaspoons Worcestershire sauce
½ to 1 cup finely chopped pecans
¼ cup finely chopped parsley

Have all cheeses at room temperature; mix together in a mixer at low speed. Add onion and Worcestershire sauce and mix thoroughly. Place in a tightly covered container and refrigerate. Allow to season for 3 or 4 days. When ready to serve shape into a ball; roll in chopped pecans and parsley until well covered. Serve with crackers. Makes one large or two small cheese balls. Will keep 2 weeks or longer tightly wrapped in the refrigerator. May also be frozen with success.

Mrs. Thornton Greer (Ann Trimble Painter)

Pecan Cheese Rounds

1 pound margarine (do
  not use butter)
1 pound New York sharp
  cheese, grated

4 cups flour
Salt to taste
Cayenne to taste
Pecan halves

Cream margarine. Add grated cheese and blend well. Add flour, salt and cayenne. Roll into 1" balls. Press pecan half on top of each. Refrigerate overnight before baking. Bake at 250° approximately 60 minutes or until light brown and crisp. Freezes well. Makes 10-12 dozen.

Miss Harriet Jean Turner

Mother's Cheese Straws

1 cup grated sharp Cheddar
  cheese
½ cup butter (do not substitute)
1 cup flour

1 egg yolk
½ to 1 teaspoon salt
Cayenne
Paprika

Mix together all ingredients except paprika. Chill. Roll out dough to approximately 1/8" thick. Slice into strips. Bake on cookie sheet at 400° for about 10 minutes. When done, sprinkle with paprika. Let cool on wire racks. Store in a tightly covered tin box and they will keep for weeks. Makes approximately 75 (1/2" x 2") cheese straws.

Mrs. Dick Hoskins Gregg (Katherine Red Parker)

Cheese Thins

½ pound Old English cheese,
  grated
½ pound butter
1 cup pecans, finely chopped

1 teaspoon red pepper
1 teaspoon salt
2½ cups sifted flour

Blend cheese and butter thoroughly. Add remaining ingredients. Make four rolls about 8" long. Wrap in wax paper or foil. Place in refrigerator overnight, or until ready to bake. Slice 1/8" thick and place on lightly greased cookie sheet. Bake at 350° until lightly browned, about 20 minutes. Makes 8 dozen.

Mrs. Thomas E. Kelly (Jane Moore)

Hotsy-Totsies

Sliced salt-rising bread
  (whole wheat, or thin rye
  may be used)
Butter

Salt
Cayenne
Grated Parmesan cheese

Butter bread slices on both sides and fit onto a cookie sheet. Salt well and sprinkle with cayenne. Cover with Parmesan cheese and cut into about 1/2" squares. Bake at 200° for 1 hour. If crisp but not brown, turn oven up briefly, but watch or they will burn. (One slice of bread makes 12 cubes.) Serve with cocktails, salad or soup. Keeps well in covered containers, or freezes successfully.

Mrs. Ben A. Calhoun (Katherine Seymour)

Hot Cheese-Olive Puffs

48 small pimiento-stuffed olives
½ pound sharp cheese, grated
½ cup soft butter

½ teaspoon salt
1 cup sifted flour
1 teaspoon paprika
Cayenne

Drain olives on paper towels. Blend cheese and butter. Sift salt, flour and paprika together. Combine with cheese and butter mixture. Wrap dough around olives, using about 1 teaspoon of mix per olive. These may be frozen at this point. Bake on an ungreased cookie sheet 15 minutes at 400°. If frozen, bake 20 minutes. For a variation small cocktail onions may be substituted for olives. Makes 4 dozen.

Mrs. Herbert E. Smith (Barbara Hartung)

Blue Cheese Puffs

1 egg yolk, beaten
1 tablespoon mayonnaise
Dash salt
Dash red pepper

1 egg white, stiffly beaten
16 Ritz crackers
Blue cheese spread

Mix together beaten egg yolk, mayonnaise, salt and red pepper. Fold in stiffly beaten egg white. Spread crackers with Blue cheese spread. Pile egg mixture on top. Bake at 350° for 13 minutes. Makes 16.

Mrs. Claude C. Cody, III (Muriel Fursteneau)

Swiss Cheese Tarts

Pastry dough
¼ cup grated onion
2 tablespoons butter
½ pound Swiss cheese, grated
3 eggs

1½ cups cream
⅛ teaspoon dry mustard
1 teaspoon salt
Black pepper
Cayenne

Make enough pastry for 4 pie crusts (9"). Roll dough 1/8" thick. Cut into rounds and fit into 2" tart cups or muffin tins. Saute onion in butter. Remove from heat. Add cheese and stir well. Beat eggs until foamy. Beat in cream and mustard. Add salt, black pepper and cayenne. Stir this mixture into the cheese-onion mixture and pour into the pastry cups. Bake at 400° for 20 minutes, or until golden. Serve hot. These tarts freeze well. Makes 4 dozen.

Mrs. Marvin V. Cluett (Lollie Lauderdale)

15

Hamburger Stroganoff Dip

1½ pounds lean ground beef
2 medium onions, finely chopped
½ pound fresh mushrooms, chopped
¼ cup butter
1 cup beef broth

3 tablespoons catsup
1 teaspoon salt
3 tablespoons flour
½ teaspoon caraway seeds (optional)
2 cups sour cream

Brown ground beef, onions and mushrooms in butter. Add broth, catsup and salt; simmer, covered, for 30 minutes. Mix flour and caraway seeds with sour cream; add to meat mixture. Stir, over low heat, until thickened; do not allow to boil. Serve in a chafing dish as a dip with crisp toast triangles or corn chips; or serve over noodles as a main course. Makes approximately 1-1/2 quarts dip, or serves 6 as a main course.

Mrs. H. Edward Maddox, III (Donna Gray)

Sausage Squares

1 pound bulk sausage ("hot" if preferred)
½ cup chopped onion
¼ cup grated Parmesan cheese
½ cup grated Swiss cheese
1 egg, beaten

¼ teaspoon Tabasco
1½ teaspoons salt
2 tablespoons chopped parsley
2 cups Bisquick
⅔ cup milk
¼ cup mayonnaise
1 egg yolk

Cook sausage and onion over low heat until meat is browned. Drain off excess fat. Add cheeses, whole egg, Tabasco, salt and parsley. Make Bisquick dough by mixing it with milk and mayonnaise. Spread half of dough over bottom of well-greased 8" square pan. Cover with sausage mixture. Spread remaining dough over sausage mixture. Brush with beaten egg yolk. Bake 25-30 minutes at 400°. Cut in squares and serve hot. May also be served for a brunch or a coffee. Makes 16 squares.

Mrs. Frank M. Wozencraft (Shirley Cooper)

Mushroom-Sausage Canapes

16 large fresh mushrooms

1 pound bulk sausage
16 buttered toast rounds

Wash and stem large mushrooms. Stuff mushroom caps with sausage. Place on broiler tray. Broil under low heat about 20 minutes. Serve hot on buttered toast rounds. Serves 8.

Mrs. Robert Mosbacher (Jane Pennybacker)

Sausage Pastries

1 cup butter
2 packages (8 oz. each)
   cream cheese
2 cups flour

½ teaspoon salt
1 pound "hot" bulk sausage
   (do not pre-cook)
Paprika

Combine butter and cream cheese in mixer; beat until very smooth. Add flour and salt. Blend well. Divide dough into two balls and flatten with hands to about one-half inch in thickness. Cover with wax paper and refrigerate overnight. This will keep for several days. Let pastry stand at room temperature for 30 minutes before rolling (it will be stiff). Roll pastry thin on a lightly-floured board or pastry cloth. Then cut into rounds with small biscuit cutter. Put a dab of the ground sausage on each round. Moisten edges of pastry rounds with water, fold over, crimp with fork tines. Sprinkle with paprika. Bake on ungreased cookie sheet at 425° for about 15 minutes, or until golden. Serve hot. May be frozen before baking. Serves 20.

Mrs. John T. Currie (Dorothy Peek)

Tequeños

Shortening or oil for deep
   fat frying
4 cups flour
1¼ teaspoons salt
¼ teaspoon powdered thyme
¼ teaspoon powdered marjoram
⅛ teaspoon white pepper

1 cup bite-sized shredded
   wheat cereal, crushed
1 egg, beaten
½ cup soft butter
1 cup warm milk
1 pound sharp Cheddar cheese,
   cut into strips 1" x ⅛"

Heat fat to 400°. Sift together the flour and seasonings. Stir in cereal crumbs. Add egg, butter and milk. Mix until smooth. Knead several times on floured board, then divide dough into thirds. Roll and stretch until thin, cut into 1/2"-wide strips. Wrap dough strips tightly around cheese strips in spiral form, overlapping dough slightly to cover and completely seal in cheese. Fry 1 minute or until brown; drain on absorbent paper. Tequenos may be frozen before baking. If so, thaw 1 hour at room temperature before frying. Or, fry a day ahead and reheat in a 400° oven for 5 minutes before serving. These are a favorite in Venezuela. Makes 6-7 dozen.

Mrs. Gordon R. West (Josephine Morrow)

Bacon and Mushroom Canapes

1 pound bacon
½ pound fresh mushrooms,
　finely diced

Mayonnaise
Melba toast rounds

Fry bacon until crisp; drain and crumble in small pieces. Combine bacon and mushrooms with just enough mayonnaise to hold together and moisten. Spread on toast rounds and bake at 400° for about 10 minutes. Leftover mixture may be spread on toast and broiled. Serves 12.

Mrs. Frank J. McGurl (Mary Martin)

Brazilian Canapes

1 slice of thin-sliced bread
1 layer of butter, softened
1 thin slice of white part small
　green onion (white onion
　may be used)

4 teaspoons mayonnaise
Parmesan cheese

Trim crust from bread; cut into 4 squares. Spread with softened butter, place a slice of onion on top of the butter. Place a scant teaspoon of mayonnaise in a blob on top and sprinkle with lots of Parmesan cheese. Bake in 350° oven for 10-15 minutes until puffy and brown. Makes 4 canapes.

Mrs. Raleigh W. Johnson, Jr. (Marjorie Bintliff)

Sardine Canapes

1 can sardines, packed in
　olive oil
1 tablespoon mayonnaise
Few dashes Tabasco
Few dashes Worcestershire
　sauce

1 teaspoon onion juice
Dash lemon juice
Cayenne and black pepper
12 slices day-old sandwich bread
Hard-cooked egg or grated
　sharp cheese for topping

Mash sardines well. Stir in mayonnaise, Tabasco, Worcestershire sauce, onion juice, lemon juice, cayenne and black pepper. Cut rounds out of bread. Toast on one side only. Spread untoasted side with additional mayonnaise. Heap sardine spread on rounds. Sprinkle sieved hard-cooked egg on top and serve well chilled. To serve hot, sprinkle grated sharp cheese on top of canapes instead of hard-cooked egg. Place in oven until cheese is melted. Makes 12 canapes.

Mrs. Hughes Fleming (Mildred Blair Hughes)

Boots' Shrimp

Raw shrimp
Melted butter

Progresso seasoned bread
crumbs

Peel raw shrimp, leaving the tails on. Dip each shrimp in melted butter, then roll in bread crumbs. Place on a cookie sheet and bake at 500° for about 10 minutes. These shrimp may be served as an entree as well as an hors d'oeuvre. A seafood sauce or garlic butter may accompany the shrimp but is not at all necessary.

Mrs. James B. Thompson (Sandra Settegast)

Water Chestnuts Wrapped in Bacon

2 cans (5 oz. each) water
chestnuts, drained
2-3 tablespoons soy sauce

Pepper
2 teaspoons brown sugar
8 slices bacon

Soak water chestnuts in soy sauce, pepper and brown sugar for at least 2 hours. Drain. Wrap 1/3 to 1/2 slice bacon around each nut and secure it with a toothpick. Bake in 350° oven until bacon is done. Makes about 16 hors d'oeuvres.

Mrs. W. K. King (Rosalie Meek)

Stuffed Mushrooms

12 large fresh mushrooms
2 tablespoons olive oil
1 small onion, chopped
½ clove garlic, crushed
4 anchovy fillets, chopped
1 tablespoon chopped
parsley

¼ teaspoon salt
½ teaspoon pepper
1 slice bread, soaked in water
and squeezed dry
1 egg
2 tablespoons bread crumbs
1 tablespoon olive oil

Rinse and stem mushrooms. Chop stems and cook in olive oil with onion and garlic for 5 minutes. Add anchovies, parsley, salt and pepper. Cook 5 minutes longer over high heat. Remove from heat. Add bread and egg; mix until smooth. Fill each mushroom cap with stuffing, piling high. Place in greased baking dish. Sprinkle with bread crumbs, then with oil. Bake in 400° oven for 20 minutes. This hot hors d'oeuvre doubles as a garnish for meat. Makes 12 stuffed mushrooms.

Mrs. Latane Temple (Josephine Bond)

Hawaiian Tidbits

Slices of bacon, halved; or slices of ham, cut in strips
Pineapple chunks

Wrap strips of bacon or ham around pineapple chunks and secure with toothpicks. Broil until meat is crisp. Goes well with rum drinks in the summer.

Mrs. W. Bryan Trammell, Jr. (Ann Gordon)

Party Pizzas

1 can (6 oz.) tomato paste
⅓ cup olive oil
1½ teaspoons oregano
Salt and pepper
1 cup pimiento-stuffed olives

7 brown and serve rolls
Slices of Monterrey Jack or
   sharp American cheese
Parsley, minced (or dry flakes)

Mix together tomato paste and olive oil. Add oregano, salt and pepper. Slice olives; add to tomato mixture. Cut rolls in half. Spread tomato paste mixture on rolls. Put slice of cheese on top of pizza. Sprinkle a little parsley on top. Bake in 450° oven only a few minutes. Serve immediately. These little pizzas may be frozen for future use. Makes 14.

Mrs. Donald A. Moffitt (Bonner Baker)

Individual Pizzas

English muffins, split in half
Butter
Tomato paste

Oregano
"Hot" sausage, cooked
   and crumbled
Grated cheese of your choice

Split muffins; heat under broiler. Do not toast. Spread with butter, then with tomato paste. Sprinkle with oregano, then crumbled "hot" sausage, and last of all, grated cheese. Broil until meat is thoroughly heated. Serve piping hot. Ideal at cocktail suppers, or as a family treat. Make plenty—they go like popcorn.

Mrs. Gleaves M. Love (Betsy Riggle)

Cheese Pocketbooks

2 pounds Cheddar cheese, grated
½ pound Blue cheese
2 packages (8 oz. each) cream cheese
2 tablespoons Worcestershire sauce
¼ teaspoon Tabasco

1 clove garlic, crushed
Salt, Accent, red pepper, and paprika to taste
2-3 tablespoons fresh lemon juice
1-2 tablespoons mayonnaise
4 loaves extra-thin sliced bread
Butter

Let cheese soften and then combine with all ingredients except bread and butter. Cut crusts from bread. Butter one side. Flip over and place a spoonful of cheese mixture in center of bread slice and fold the four corners to the center to form a pillow-shaped "pocketbook." These may need to be secured with a toothpick. Bake 12-15 minutes at 400°. May be frozen and baked straight from the freezer. If so, add 5-10 minutes to baking time. Serve hot. Makes 96 pocketbooks. Also nice to accompany a fruit plate or bowl of soup for a light meal. The cheese mixture alone may be used as a sandwich spread. This recipe makes 2 quarts cheese spread.

Mrs. Herbert E. Smith (Barbara Hartung)

Open-Faced Anchovy Round

1 slice bread
Anchovy paste
Slice of tomato

Hard-cooked egg slices
Thousand Island dressing

Cut a slice of bread with the top of a glass to make a large round. Toast it on both sides. Spread a thin layer of anchovy paste on top. On this place a slice of tomato and a few slices of hard-cooked egg. Pour dressing over all.

Mrs. James A. Walsh (Harriet Brady)

Grilled Mushroom Sandwiches

½ pound mushrooms, chopped
2 tablespoons butter
2 tablespoons flour

¾ teaspoon salt
Cayenne
16 slices white bread

Saute mushrooms in melted butter in saucepan over low heat about 5 minutes. Sprinkle flour, salt and cayenne over mushroom mixture; stir until thick. Use large biscuit cutter to make rounds from bread slices. Spread mixture between two rounds. Spread soft butter on outside of sandwiches and grill on both sides. Makes 8 sandwiches.

Mrs. Lorenzo B. Taylor (Marilyn Dubach)

Poolside Sandwich Tray

SALAMI SANDWICHES

Party rye bread
Cream cheese, flavored with horseradish
Imported hard salami (sliced wafer thin)

Spread bread first with softened, flavored cream cheese; then add salami.

CUCUMBER SANDWICHES

Cucumbers, thinly sliced   White thin-sliced bread
Wine vinegar   Mayonnaise

Soak cucumber slices in wine vinegar and ice for 2 hours. Spread bread with mayonnaise and add drained cucumbers.

SHRIMP SALAD SANDWICHES

Shrimp, cooked and shelled   White, thin-sliced bread
Celery, coarsely chopped   Parsley, finely chopped
Mayonnaise

Cut cooked shrimp in half lengthwise. Mix with celery and mayonnaise. Spread generously on bread and sprinkle with parsley before adding top slice of bread. These may be served as hors d'oeuvres; or, in larger portions, as a light luncheon.

Mrs. Robert A. Johnston, Jr. (Carol Smith)

Imperial Sandwiches

Black or French bread   Minced onion
Scraped or ground raw beef   Capers
Caviar (fresh if available)   Hard-cooked egg, chopped
                                  Lemon wedges

On pieces of black bread, French bread or toasted French bread, spread 1/3" of raw beef. Top with 2/3" caviar. Garnish with minced onion, capers, chopped hard-cooked egg and lemon wedges. Serve with cold vodka, champagne or beer.

Mrs. George A. Hill, III (Gloria Lester)

Open-Faced Shrimp Sandwiches

½ pound shrimp, cooked
and shelled
¼ cup chopped chives
5 tablespoons Dijon or
Dusseldorf mustard
1-2 tablespoons chopped
capers
3 tablespoons mayonnaise
1 can (5 oz.) water chestnuts, drained and chopped

Salt and freshly ground
black pepper
1 teaspoon lemon juice
Tabasco
8 slices white or dark bread
Slices of hard-cooked egg
Watercress
Pimiento-stuffed olives

Chop the shrimp coarsely and combine with the chives, mustard, capers, mayonnaise, water chestnuts, salt, pepper and lemon juice. Add more mayonnaise if necessary to make a spreadable mixture. Add Tabásco and blend well. Spread the mixture on the bread and garnish with egg slices, watercress and olives. Makes 4 sandwiches. May also be served on crackers.

Mrs. John B. Carter, Jr. (Sue Browne)

Texas Avocado Sandwich

1 ripe avocado (medium size)
½ teaspoon lemon or onion
juice
2 tablespoons chopped,
toasted almonds

2 tablespoons crisp,
crumbled bacon
Dash black pepper
Dash cayenne
Dash chili powder

Mash avocado; add lemon or onion juice. Stir in almonds and bacon; add seasonings. Mix to a creamy smoothness and spread between thin slices of white bread. Serve immediately. Serves 2 generously.

Mrs. William F. Yeoman (A. J. Vance)

Pimiento Cheese

8 ounces sharp Cheddar cheese
1 large onion, or less
1 can (4 oz.) pimiento, plus liquid

Mayonnaise
Red pepper
Salt

Into a bowl grate cheese and onion. Add pimiento and enough mayonnaise to make mixture as moist as desired. Season with red pepper and salt. Allow to remain in refrigerator for 24 hours for a mellow taste. This sandwich spread, refrigerated, will keep for days. Makes 1 pint.

Mrs. Baxter Adams (Carol Nash)

Citrus Cooler

1 large can (46 oz.)
grapefruit juice
4 cups fresh or frozen
reconstituted orange juice

1 pint orange sherbert
2 small bottles (7 oz. each)
carbonated water, chilled
Pineapple and lime sherbet balls

Mix juices with orange sherbet. Chill in punch bowl. Add chilled carbonated water. Scoop pineapple and lime sherbet balls into bowl just before serving. Popular for teen-age party. Makes 20-24 cups.

Mrs. Thomas L. Carter (Maudie Russell Bowen)

Fruit Punch

1 large can (12 oz.) frozen
orange juice concentrate
1 small can (6 oz.) frozen
lemonade concentrate

1 cup sugar
8 cups water
Mint

Combine all ingredients except mint; boil until syrupy. Stir in a "handful" of mint. Let cool. Serve over crushed ice. Makes about 3 quarts.

Mrs. William A. Bramley (Kay Borden)

Summer Drink

2 cups sugar
2 cups water
1 cup fresh lemon juice

2 cups fresh orange juice
Ginger ale
Mint

Bring sugar and water to a boil; allow to cool. Add lemon juice and orange juice; chill. Put ice in glasses and fill 1/3 full with the mixture. Then fill to top with ginger ale. Put a sprig of mint in each glass. Makes 1 quart.

Mrs. Roger G. Stotler (Nance Fruit)

Hot Fruit Punch

9 cups cranberry juice
9 cups unsweetened pineapple
juice
4½ cups water

1 scant cup brown sugar
4 cinnamon sticks (broken up)
4 teaspoons whole cloves
¼ teaspoon salt

Put cranberry juice, pineapple juice, water and brown sugar in a 30-cup electric percolator. In the basket put cinnamon sticks, cloves and salt. Perk as usual. Serve hot. Great as a hot cocktail before lunch or for afternoon tea on a cold day. Makes 30 punch cups.

Mrs. Richard R. Nelson, Jr. (Marjorie Shepherd)

Spiced Apple Cider

1 cup brown sugar	1 gallon apple cider
1 small can (6 oz.) frozen lemonade concentrate	1 teaspoon ground nutmeg
	1 tablespoon whole cloves
1 small can (6 oz.) frozen orange juice concentrate	1 tablespoon whole allspice
	24 cinnamon sticks

Combine brown sugar, lemonade concentrate, orange juice concentrate, cider and nutmeg in large saucepan. Tie cloves and allspice in a cheesecloth bag and add to mixture. Simmer, covered, for 20 minutes. Remove and discard bag. Place a cinnamon stick in each cup, pour in cider, and serve hot. This is nice at Christmas time. It is also good for teen-age parties and can easily become witches' brew at Halloween. Makes about 5 quarts.

Mrs. George N. Allen, Jr. (Bonnie Blades)

Iced Tea Punch

6 cups water	8 sprigs fresh mint
¾ to 1 cup sugar	½ cup fresh lemon juice
6 small tea bags	½ cup fresh orange juice

Bring water to a boil; add sugar, tea bags and mint. Steep 5 minutes. Remove tea bags and mint. After tea mixture has cooled, add fruit juices. Chill well before serving. Makes approximately 2 quarts.

Mrs. John H. Meyers (Alice Baker Jones)

Coffee Punch

1 gallon strong coffee, allow to cool	1 pint vanilla ice cream
½ gallon coffee ice cream	1 pint heavy cream, whipped
	Nutmeg or cinnamon

Blend coffee and half of the coffee ice cream to a fairly thick consistency and chill in a punch bowl in refrigerator. When ready to serve, mix in ice cream balls made with the remaining quart of coffee ice cream and the vanilla ice cream. Top with heaps of whipped cream. Sprinkle with nutmeg or cinnamon. A refreshing change from coffee or tea for warm weather entertaining. Makes about 20-30 cups.

Mrs. Thomas L. Carter (Maudie Russell Bowen)

Cranberry Daiquiri for Children

1 bottle (16 oz.) cranberry juice   Juice of 1 lemon
1 box (10 oz.) frozen strawberries   Crushed ice

Put cranberry juice, frozen berries and lemon juice in blender. Fill with crushed ice. Turn on blender a few seconds until well mixed. Pour into glasses. If a more frozen consistency is desired, make ahead and store in freezer. Fun and festive to have for the children, especially at Christmas time. Makes 1 quart.

Mrs. Richard R. McKay (Emily Ann Finch)

Instant Spiced Tea Mix

1 cup instant tea   1½ cups sugar
   (unsweetened)   1 teaspoon ground cloves
1 cup Tang   1 teaspoon cinnamon

Mix all ingredients together. Put one heaping teaspoon of mix in each cup and fill with hot water. Store mix in a tightly closed container and keep on hand to brighten dreary winter days. Makes approximately 1 quart mix.

Mrs. George N. Allen, Jr. (Bonnie Blades)

Cafe Au Cacao

1 gallon cold coffee   ½ fifth creme de cacao
1 gallon chocolate ice cream,   ½ pint heavy cream, whipped
   softened

Combine coffee, ice cream and creme de cacao. Mix well. Fold in whipped cream. Makes 20-30 punch cups.

Mrs. Marvin H. McMurrey, Jr. (Laura Sue Henderson)

Eggnog

6 eggs, separated   1 cup milk
6 tablespoons sugar   2 cups heavy cream,
1 cup bourbon   lightly whipped
   Freshly ground nutmeg

Beat egg yolks and sugar thoroughly. Slowly add bourbon and milk. Fold in stiffly beaten egg whites and whipped cream. Sprinkle nutmeg on top. A Christmas tradition in my family for generations. Serves 8.

Mrs. David J. Braden (Jane White)

Elizardi's Eggnog

1 dozen eggs, separated
½ teaspoon salt
2¼ cups sugar (in all)
2 cups (or more) bourbon
1 jigger (2 oz.) rum

3 pints heavy cream
1 quart milk
1½ tablespoons vanilla
Nutmeg to sprinkle on top

Beat egg yolks and salt; add 1-1/2 cups sugar. After sugar has dissolved, gradually add bourbon and rum to the mixture, stirring constantly. Beat egg whites until stiff, slowly adding 1/2 cup sugar. Whip cream; stir in 1/4 cup sugar. Add milk and vanilla to the yolk mixture, stirring constantly. Fold in beaten egg whites. Taste; add more whiskey if desired (mixture should be a little strong at this point). If not sweet enough, add more sugar. If too thick, add more milk. Fold whipped cream into eggnog, sprinkle nutmeg on top and serve immediately. Makes approximately 20 punch cups.

Mrs. Edward W. Kelly, Jr. (Ellen Elizardi)

Bloody Mary

4 cups V-8 juice
1½ cups vodka
1½ teaspoons salt
Juice of 1 lemon

10 shakes Tabasco
1 tablespoon Worcestershire
sauce
Lime slices for decoration

Mix first 6 ingredients. (This can be done early in the day and stored in the refrigerator.) When ready to serve, pour mixture into double Old-Fashioned glasses filled with ice. Squeeze a slice of lime in each glass and drop the slice into the glass. Makes 6 drinks.

Mrs. Frank J. McGurl (Mary Martin)

Mexican Maria

2 ounces tomato juice
2 ounces tequila
Juice of ½ lime

Dash Tabasco
¼ teaspoon salt
Slice of lime

Blend all ingredients together until well mixed. Pour over ice in an Old-Fashioned glass and garnish with a slice of lime. Ole! Makes 1 drink.

Mrs. Rotan McGown (Charlotte Rotan)

Glendorn Orange Fandango

2 ounces gin   1-2 teaspoons sugar
3 tablespoons orange juice

Mix and pour over crushed ice. Powerful. Makes 1 drink. Can also be made in quantity and served from a punch bowl.

Mrs. David F. Dorn (Julia Leary)

Freezer Milk Punch

1½ gallons vanilla mellorine   2 fifths bourbon
   (not ice cream)   1 fifth rum
1 gallon milk   1 cup white creme de cacao

Let 1 gallon mellorine thaw until mushy. Mix soft mellorine, milk, bourbon, rum and creme de cacao thoroughly. Place in freezer. Allow to thaw for 2 hours before serving. Mix well and pour over remaining 1/2-gallon mellorine in punch bowl. This milk punch may be made several days in advance of a party and any leftover may be frozen and re-frozen. Makes approximately 50 cups of punch.

Mrs. James A. Reichert (Betsy Calhoun)

Mint Crush

1 small can (6 oz.) frozen   ¾ cup gin, vodka or rum
   limeade concentrate   12-15 fresh mint leaves

Mix all ingredients in blender. Add enough cracked ice to thoroughly chill. Pour into cocktail glasses. Serves 4-6.

Mrs. Hughes Fleming (Mildred Blair Hughes)

Schiffbauer Special

1 small can (6 oz.) frozen   1 can (8½ oz.) crushed
   lime-lemonade concentrate   pineapple
2¼ cups pineapple juice   Crushed ice
                                      2 cups light rum

Mix lime-lemonade concentrate, pineapple juice and crushed pineapple together in pitcher. Fill blender 2/3 full with crushed ice. Add 1 cup of the pineapple mixture and 1/2 cup rum. Turn on blender and blend to count of ten. (Drink should be the consistency of a frozen daiquiri.) Serve in large champagne glasses or small Old-Fashioned glasses, garnished with tiny sprigs of mint, if desired. What a refreshing, sneaky cooler. This recipe makes 16 cocktails.

Mrs. John H. Lindsey (Sara Houstoun)

Harrison Ranch "Machina"

1 jigger cointreau   1 jigger lime juice
1 jigger vodka

Mix all ingredients. For a tart, refreshing drink, serve over crushed ice in tall frosted glass. Or may be served over ice cubes in Old-Fashioned glass. Makes 1 drink.

Mrs. James Howard Park, III (Bette Naylor)

Albritton Deepfreeze Daiquiri

2 small cans (6 oz. each) frozen   1 fifth light rum
   pink lemonade concentrate   6 lemonade-cans water
1 small can (6 oz.) frozen
   limeade concentrate

Put half of the above (1 can pink lemonade, 1/2 can limeade, 1/2 bottle rum and 3 cans water) in blender and blend thoroughly. Pour into large, heavy glass jar with top. Put other half of ingredients in blender and blend thoroughly. Pour into same glass jar and stir. Put top on jar, put jar in deepfreeze, and let mixture freeze for at least 12 hours. Approximately 30 minutes before serving, remove jar from freezer and stir. When ready to pour into cocktail glasses, stir again. Mixture should be icy. Any portion not used may be re-frozen again and again. This mixture never freezes solid and is a very refreshing, tasty drink to have on hand. This recipe makes about 2 quarts or 20-25 cocktails.

Mrs. John H. Lindsey (Sara Houstoun)

Velvet Hammer

1 package (10 oz.) frozen   Juice of 2 lemons (little less
   sliced strawberries   than 1/2 cup)
1 cup light rum   Crushed ice

Put strawberries, rum and lemon juice in blender and turn on for a few seconds. Add enough crushed ice to almost fill blender (approximately one tray of ice, crushed). Blend until mixture is of icy, mushy consistency. Pour into daiquiri glasses. Festive enough for a ladies' luncheon, but has enough zip to please the men. Makes 6-8 drinks.

Mrs. James Howard Park, III (Bette Naylor)

Instant Martini

18 ounces gin
3 ounces dry vermouth
5 ounces water

Combine all ingredients and store in freezer. Serve without ice, but add onion or olive if desired. This recipe was given to me by an inspired friend—and is a very dangerous thing to have on hand. Makes 8-10 drinks.

Mrs. Frank J. McGurl (Mary Martin)

Hot Toddy for One

1 teaspoon sugar
2 tablespoons hot water
2 ounces bourbon
Juice of ¼ lemon

½ stick cinnamon
Lemon slice
4 whole cloves
¾ cup boiling water
Nutmeg

In a heavy mug dissolve sugar in hot water. Add bourbon, lemon juice and cinnamon stick. Stick lemon slice with 4 cloves and put in mug. Pour boiling water over all. Sprinkle with nutmeg. The perfect ending to a frosty day. Serves 1.

Mrs. Phillip B. Sherwood (Mary Alexander)

Winter Wine Cup

4 cups dry red table wine
3 orange slices
¼ cup sugar
½ teaspoon ground cloves
2 cinnamon sticks

½ teaspoon ground allspice
½ teaspoon cinnamon
¼ cup orange juice
4 ounces vodka (optional)

Combine all ingredients except vodka and simmer 10 to 15 minutes. Add vodka if desired. Serve in thick mugs on a cold, wintry day for a warm feeling inside. Makes 4 drinks.

Mrs. Richard R. McKay (Emily Ann Finch)

Hot Buttered Rum

2 tablespoons brown sugar
1 tablespoon butter
Allspice, cloves, nutmeg and
   cinnamon (all ground)

6 cinnamon sticks
6 cups milk, heated
6 jiggers (2 oz. each) rum

Make a paste of brown sugar, butter and spices. For each drink, place 1 cinnamon stick and 1 heaping teaspoon spice paste in mug. Add hot milk and 1 jigger rum. Stir well. Makes 6 drinks.

Mrs. Richard R. Nelson, Jr. (Marjorie Shepherd)

Champagne Punch

2 cups sugar
2 cups water
Juice of 6 lemons
2 cups apricot nectar
1 can (6 oz.) frozen
   orange juice concentrate

2 cans (12 oz. each)
   apple juice
2 cups pineapple juice
2 bottles (12 oz. each)
   ginger ale
2 fifths champagne

Boil sugar and water for 1 minute and cool. Add juices. Freeze. Thaw 1 to 1-1/2 hours before serving. Add ginger ale and champagne. Serve over block of ice in punch bowl. Makes approximately 6 quarts punch.

Mrs. James A. Reichert (Betsy Calhoun)

Fish House Punch

1 cup sugar
1 cup water
1 fifth rum
1 fifth cognac

1½ ounces peach brandy
1 fifth tea
1½ cups fresh lemon juice
Ginger ale

Boil the sugar and water together and mix with remaining ingredients except the ginger ale. Do this the day before and refrigerate. To serve, put equal parts of punch base and ginger ale in the punch bowl. Makes about 3 quarts punch base.

Mrs. Robert E. Clemons (Grayson Reed Cecil)

Anniversary Punch

3 fifths champagne
1 fifth sherry
1 fifth brandy
2¼ cups carbonated water

2½ ounces orange Curacao
2½ ounces White Maraschino
liqueur

Chill ingredients, mix together and pour over block of ice in punch bowl.
Makes approximately 35 punch cups.

Mrs. Phillip B. Sherwood (Mary Alexander)

Champagne Bowle

1 fifth dry champagne
1 fifth sauterne wine
5 ounces Curacao

8 ounces brandy
1 quart carbonated water

Pour all ingredients over a block·of ice in punch bowl. For any festive occa-
sion and certain to please even non-punch lovers. Makes about 20 punch
cups.

Mrs. James Douglas McMurrey (Odette Hemenway)

Sangria

1 small can (6 oz.) frozen
limeade concentrate
3 cups water

2 cups dry red wine
8 slices of orange, lime
or lemon

Combine limeade concentrate, water and wine. Serve iced cold with a slice of
fruit in each glass. (May also be served in punch bowl with fruit slices float-
ing on top.) Cooling and different for a picnic. Makes 1-1/2 quarts.

Mrs. Lyon L. Brinsmade (Susannah Tucker)

SOUPS

GUMBOS

Hints

IN MAKING MEAT-STOCK SOUPS, use aged meat for richer flavor; always add salt to water in which meat is simmered, as salt draws out more flavor.

TO REMOVE FAT FROM BROTH OR STOCK: Skim off fat with metal spoon; or lay paper towel on surface of soup and, when saturated, remove and replace with fresh towel; or wrap piece of ice in paper towel and skim across surface of soup; or refrigerate broth overnight, and remove congealed fat the following day.

TO MAKE SOUP FROM LEFTOVER VEGETABLES: Puree vegetables in blender; add milk (or stock) and seasonings. Serve hot or cold.

TO SPRUCE UP CANNED SOUP: Combine several varieties of canned soups and add a dash of sherry, vermouth or lemon juice. Season well.

IF SOUP IS TOO SALTY: Add half of a peeled raw potato. If still too salty, add the other half.

GARNISHES FOR SOUP

Slices or tiny cubes of avocado.

Salted, buttered popcorn.

Brown onion rings.

Slivered almonds or chopped salted nuts.

Grated or sliced hard-cooked egg.

Finely chopped watercress, parsley or chives.

Strips of pimiento, raw mushrooms, carrot, green onion or green pepper.

Paper-thin slices of lemon, orange or lime.

Sliced or chopped olives, green or ripe.

Grated or crumbled cheese.

Sour cream mixed with lemon juice.

Whipped cream, seasoned with horseradish or catsup.

Croutons, dipped in melted butter, rolled in Parmesan cheese, then toasted.

Curried Avocado Soup

1 avocado, sliced
2 cups chicken broth
1 cup milk or cream
2 tablespoons light rum
1 teaspoon (or less)
    curry powder

1 teaspoon Spice Islands
    Beau Monde Seasoning
Generous dash white pepper
Generous pinch dehydrated
    green onions
1 lime for garnish

Mix all ingredients, except lime, in blender. Serve cold in chilled cream soup bowls with thin lime slice on top. Serves 6-8.

Mrs. James Howard Park, III (Bette Naylor)

Black Bean and Sherry Soup

2 pounds beef soup bones
1 pound dried black beans
3 medium onions, chopped
3 ribs celery, chopped
3 medium potatoes,
    peeled and diced
1½ teaspoons salt

½ teaspoon pepper
1 teaspoon crushed garlic
½ teaspoon thyme
4 bay leaves
½ teaspoon chervil
1 cup cream sherry

Put all ingredients, except sherry, in 4 quarts water; simmer 1-1/2 hours or until beans have lost their shape. Remove bones and bay leaves. Puree soup in blender, or put through fine sieve. Add sherry and correct seasoning. Serves 12 generously.

Mrs. Louis Chapin (Ann Trumbull)

Famous White Bean Soup

1 pound (2 cups) small,
    white dried beans
3 quarts cold water
3 medium potatoes, peeled,
    boiled and mashed
6 ribs celery, finely cut

¼ cup chopped parsley
2 onions, minced
2 cloves garlic, crushed
2 pounds ham hock
Salt and pepper

Soak beans in water overnight; drain. Place beans in large soup kettle, cover with fresh water, and cook for about 1 hour or until beans are tender. Drain. Add the 3 quarts water, mashed potatoes, celery, parsley, onions, garlic and ham hock. Cook slowly for 2 hours, stirring occasionally. Remove ham hock. Pull meat from bones and cut into small pieces. Return meat to soup. Season to taste with salt and pepper. Freezes well. Makes 3 or more quarts.

Mrs. John H. Lindsey (Sara Houstoun)

Borscht

4 cups beef broth or water	1 cup chopped celery
2 cups beef consomme	¼ cup lemon juice
2 cups chopped cooked beets	2 teaspoons salt
(canned or fresh)	¼ teaspoon white pepper
½ cup chopped onion	Sour cream

Combine broth and consomme; add beets, onion and celery. Simmer 30 minutes. Mash through strainer. Add lemon juice, salt and pepper. Serve hot or cold topped with teaspoon sour cream. Serves 8.

Mrs. W. P. Hobby (Oveta Culp)

Snappy Onion Soup

6 onions, thinly sliced	7 cups water
6 tablespoons butter	Salt and pepper
6 bouillon cubes	

Saute sliced onions in butter until golden brown. Add bouillon cubes and water. Simmer, covered, for 1 hour. Season with salt and pepper. This is an easy version of an old favorite. Serves 8.

Mrs. Garrett Stuart Livingston, Jr. (Mary Ann Ransom)

The People's Broth

3 medium onions, chopped	1 medium head cabbage
½ cup butter	1 heaping tablespoon
6 small carrots	chopped parsley
2 small potatoes	¼ teaspoon savory
2½ quarts seasoned	¼ teaspoon marjoram
chicken broth	2 teaspoons monosodium
2 teaspoons (or more) salt	glutamate
½ teaspoon pepper	Grated Parmesan cheese

Saute onions in butter. Scrape carrots and cut into 2" lengthwise strips. Peel potatoes and cut into large cubes. Add carrots, potatoes, chicken broth, salt and pepper to onions. Bring to a boil; cook 10 minutes. Save several outer leaves of cabbage. Cut remaining cabbage into fairly large chunks, add to broth, and cook 10 minutes longer. Stir in parsley, savory, marjoram and monosodium glutamate. Taste and correct seasoning if necessary. Keep warm for 5-10 minutes before serving. (This soup must cook quickly to taste very fresh.) Arrange reserved cabbage leaves in soup tureen before pouring in the soup. Accompany with Parmesan cheese to be sprinkled over each serving. Serves 8 generously as a main dish.

Mrs. Lorenzo B. Taylor (Marilyn Dubach)

Broccoli Soup

2 cups milk
2 tablespoons flour
2 tablespoons butter
1 teaspoon salt
Dash pepper

½-¾ cup cooked, chopped
broccoli (fresh or frozen)
4 sprigs parsley
½ cup celery leaves
1 thin slice onion
Paprika for garnish

Combine all ingredients, except paprika, in blender. When well blended, heat in double boiler, stirring occasionally. Ladle into soup cups and sprinkle with paprika. Serves 4.

Mrs. John H. Lindsey (Sara Houstoun)

Corn Chowder

¼ cup chopped onion
3 tablespoons shortening
3 cups peeled, cooked, diced
potatoes
3 cups canned creamed corn
1 quart milk

1 large can (8 oz.) mushroom
stems and pieces
1½ teaspoons salt
⅛ teaspoon pepper
Dash cayenne
6 small crackers, crumbled
Parsley (optional)

Saute onions in butter until delicate brown. Discard onion. Add remaining ingredients, except parsley, to butter in pan. Bring to a boil. Ladle into soup cups. Garnish with chopped parsley, if desired. Serves 6-8.

Mrs. Charles W. Moody, Jr. (Patti Hunter)

Cream of Corn Soup

3 cups milk
1 can (1 lb.) creamed corn
1 small onion, minced
2 tablespoons butter
1 heaping tablespoon flour
1 egg

½ cup heavy cream
1 teaspoon chopped chives
1 teaspoon chopped parsley
Salt and pepper
1 sweet red pepper,
chopped (optional)

Combine milk and corn in top of double boiler. Saute minced onion in butter a few minutes (do not brown); add flour. Add to corn mixture and cook 15-20 minutes. Mash through strainer. Just before serving, add well-beaten egg, cream, chives, parsley, salt and pepper. Reheat. Serve hot and garnish with chopped red pepper. Serves 6-8.

Mrs. Hughes Fleming (Mildred Hughes)

Tomato Corn Soup

1 medium onion, chopped	1 teaspoon salt
2 tablespoons butter	½ teaspoon pepper
1 tablespoon flour	1 scant tomato-can water
2 bay leaves	1 cup canned creamed corn
10 peppercorns	½ cup milk or cream
1 can (1 lb.) tomatoes	Croutons or parsley,
1 tablespoon sugar	for garnish

In saucepan, saute onion in butter; add flour. Mix in bay leaves and pep-percorns. Slowly cook 2 minutes, stirring constantly. Add tomatoes, sugar, salt, pepper and water. Simmer 20 minutes. Add corn; cook 10 minutes longer. Force through sieve until only corn skins, peppercorns and bay leaves are left in sieve. Add milk to soup and heat. (Do not boil, for it will curdle.) Serve hot, topped with croutons or parsley. Serves 4.

Mrs. Thornton Greer (Ann Painter)

Cucumber Vichyssoise à la Willie

2 potatoes, peeled and diced	2 cucumbers, peeled, coarsely
1 cup chicken bouillon	grated
1 cup dry white wine	1 teaspoon grated onion
1 cup heavy cream	1 teaspoon salt
	Pepper

Cook potatoes in bouillon and wine for 15 minutes, uncovered. Cover; con-tinue cooking until potatoes are tender. Remove from heat; let stand covered for 10 minutes. Mix potatoes in blender with a little of the cream. Stir in remaining cream, cucumbers, onion, salt and pepper (do not blend again). Chill at least 6 hours before serving. Serves 6-8.

Mrs. Wallace M. Davis, Jr. (Barbara Sterrett)

Soup Superb

2 cans clear green turtle soup	1 bay leaf
1 can consomme	½ pint heavy cream, whipped
2 cans condensed	1 teaspoon horseradish
cream of pea soup	Toasted Parmesan cheese
1 soup-can water	

Combine all soups, water and bay leaf; heat. Remove bay leaf. Add horse-radish to whipped cream. Top each serving with a spoonful of whipped cream mixture. Sprinkle with toasted Parmesan cheese. Soup may be served hot or cold. Serves 8.

Mrs. Harmon Whittington (Dolores Welder)

Dilled Potato Soup

2 cans frozen cream of potato soup (undiluted)	1 teaspoon dried dill
1¾ cups milk	⅛ teaspoon salt
1½ cups water	Dash white pepper
	1 cup sour cream

Thaw soup; combine with milk and water. Add dill, salt and pepper. Warm over low heat, stirring to mix thoroughly. Just before serving, add sour cream and mix well. Serves 6.

Mrs. George C. Lee (Grace Sullivan)

Southern Okra Soup

1 soup bone	1 large onion, finely chopped
1 pound boneless soup meat	½ cup chopped celery
1 bay leaf	1 green pepper, chopped
2 pounds fresh okra, sliced; or 3 packages frozen okra	4 ears fresh corn, cut from cob; or 2 packages frozen corn
2 cans (1 lb. each) tomatoes	Salt and pepper
1 package frozen baby lima beans	Worcestershire sauce (optional) Tabasco (optional)

Cover soup bone and meat with water; simmer 2 hours. Add bay leaf and okra; continue to simmer until okra softens. Add all remaining ingredients, except Worcestershire sauce and Tabasco; cook slowly until vegetables are tender. Remove bay leaf. When ready to serve, correct seasoning. Season with Worcestershire sauce and Tabasco if desired. Better if made the day before—may be frozen. Serves 10-12.

Mrs. Thomas B. Eaton, Jr. (Margot Teague)

Spinach Vichyssoise

1 package frozen spinach	1 carrot, peeled and chopped
4 leeks, white part, finely sliced	1 quart chicken stock
¼ cup finely chopped onion	1 teaspoon (or more) salt
¼ cup butter	2 cups milk
5 medium Idaho potatoes, peeled and cubed	3 cups cream
	White pepper

Slightly cook spinach; drain, puree, and set aside. Saute leeks and onion in butter until yellow. Add potatoes, carrot, chicken stock and salt. Bring to a rapid boil, cover, reduce heat, and simmer until vegetables are soft. Puree in blender or mash through sieve. Add milk, cream and spinach. Season with white pepper. Chill. Serves 14.

Mrs. Macrery B. Wheeler, Jr. (Elma Landram)

Spinach Soup

1 package frozen chopped spinach	1 cup boiling water
3 tablespoons melted butter	1 cup milk
2 teaspoons chopped onion	1 cup cream
1 teaspoon lemon juice	Pepper
1½ heaping tablespoons powdered	¼ teaspoon nutmeg
chicken stock base	Parmesan cheese (optional)

Cook spinach in lightly salted water. Drain thoroughly. In blender place spinach, butter, onion, lemon juice, chicken stock base and boiling water and blend thoroughly. Add milk, cream, pepper and nutmeg. Serve hot with Parmesan cheese on top. (May also be served cold). Serves 4-6.

Mrs. Richard R. McKay (Emily Ann Finch)

Mushroom - Mint Soup

8 medium onions, chopped	4 quarts chicken stock
2 cloves garlic, crushed	3 cups light cream
½ pound butter	1 cup heavy cream
2 pounds fresh mushrooms	½ cup chopped fresh mint
4 teaspoons lemon juice	Dry sherry
¼ cup flour	Salt and pepper

Slowly saute onion and garlic in butter 3-4 minutes. Add mushrooms and lemon juice; cook very slowly about 10 minutes. Chop mixture coarsely in blender. Return to pan; stir in flour and stock. Cook over low heat until slightly thickened. Add cream and mint. If necessary thin with a little water. Season with sherry, salt and pepper. Do not boil at any time when cooking or reheating. May be kept in refrigerator several days. Serves 24.

Mrs. Sanford E. McCormick (Balene Cross)

Madrilène with Caviar

1 can (13 oz.)	1 jar (4 oz.) red caviar
consomme madrilene	Homemade mayonnaise

Chill consomme until slightly thickened; spoon into 4 soup cups. Divide caviar equally into soup cups; fold gently into consomme. Chill 4-6 hours. Serve with generous tablespoon mayonnaise on top. Serves 4.

Mrs. Gentry Kidd (Winifred Crawford)

Winter Soup Bowl

½ cup chopped celery
2 tablespoons bacon drippings
1 tablespoon cornstarch
⅓ cup water
3 tablespoons chopped
    green onion

1 can (1 lb.) tomatoes
2½ cups well-seasoned
    chicken broth
½ cup dry white wine
1 tablespoon lemon juice
Dash curry powder

Saute celery in bacon drippings until tender. Dissolve cornstarch in water; add with other ingredients to celery. Simmer slowly 20 minutes, stirring occasionally. Serves 4-6.

Mrs. Richard R. McKay (Emily Ann Finch)

Watercress Soup

2 bunches watercress
2 thick slices of onion
1 rib celery, 3" long
1 tablespoon cornstarch
1 tablespoon sugar

1 teaspoon salt
3 cups chicken bouillon
1 can (13 oz.)
    evaporated milk
2 tablespoons butter

Into blender put watercress leaves, onion, celery, cornstarch, sugar, salt and 2 cups of the bouillon; blend until smooth. Pour into saucepan; add remaining bouillon and bring to a boil. Reduce heat; cook 10 additional minutes, stirring constantly. Add evaporated milk and butter; simmer 5 minutes. Serves 6.

Mrs. P. G. Bell, Jr. (Sue Ledbetter)

Cream of Tomato Soup

½ cup chopped onion
3 cups canned tomatoes
    with juice
1½ cups water
½ teaspoon soda
2 tablespoons butter

1 tablespoon flour
2 cups milk
¼ teaspoon thyme
1 teaspoon salt
Pinch of coarsely ground
    pepper

Cook onion and tomatoes in water until onion is tender; strain. Mix 1 heaping tablespoon of the onion-tomato mixture with strained liquid. Discard remaining onion-tomato mixture. Add soda. Set aside. Melt butter and stir in flour. Add milk and cook until thickened. Add thyme, salt and pepper. Combine with tomato mixture; heat. Freezes well. Serves 8.

Mrs. Thomas W. Moore (Lila Godwin)

Bayou Tomato

6 cups peeled and finely
  chopped tomatoes
1 medium onion, grated
¾ cup lemon juice
1 teaspoon vinegar

1 teaspoon celery seed
Salt
6 tablespoons mayonnaise
Curry powder
Chopped parsley

Combine tomatoes, onion, lemon juice, vinegar and celery seed. Mix well.
Season with salt. Pour into freezer tray and freeze to a mush (about 1 hour).
Serve half-frozen, topped with mayonnaise which has been seasoned with
curry and chopped parsley. Serves 6.

Mrs. Olive D. Hershey (Olive Duncan)

Coronado Gazpacho

½ cup olive oil
¼ cup lemon juice
6 cups tomato juice
½ cup finely minced onion
2 tomatoes, peeled and chopped
2 cups finely minced celery
⅛ teaspoon Tabasco

2 teaspoons salt
¼ teaspoon freshly ground
  pepper
2 green peppers, finely
  chopped
2 cucumbers, peeled and diced
Croutons

Beat olive oil and lemon juice together. Stir in tomato juice, onion, tomatoes,
celery, Tabasco, salt and pepper. Taste; add more seasoning if desired.
(The mixture should be highly seasoned.) Chill at least 3 hours before
serving. The green peppers, cucumbers and croutons should be served
separately as an accompaniment for the soup. Serves 8-10.

Mrs. Harmon Whittington (Dolores Welder)

Gazpacho Madrid

8 medium tomatoes
1 slice bread
3 tablespoons olive oil
1½ teaspoons vinegar

1 tablespoon salt
1 teaspoon pepper
1 small clove garlic

Peel and quarter tomatoes. Remove crust from bread and tear into pieces.
Place all ingredients in blender; add water to cover and blend well. Serve
with any or all of the following: peeled, diced tomatoes, diced cucumbers,
chopped green peppers, chopped onions, toasted bread cubes. Serves 8.

Mrs. Edward W. Kelley, Jr. (Ellen Elizardi)

Vegetable Soup

1 large soup bone, cracked
2 pounds lean stew meat
4 chicken necks, uncooked
4 chicken backs, uncooked
5 quarts water
1 teaspoon salt
¼ teaspoon pepper
1 clove garlic, crushed
⅓ cup barley
2 cans (1 lb. each) tomatoes
1 package frozen baby lima beans
1 package frozen cut string beans
3 carrots, peeled and sliced
1 large onion, diced
1 package frozen green peas

1 green pepper,
 finely diced
1 package frozen yellow corn
2 potatoes, peeled and diced
1 turnip, peeled and diced
3 ribs celery, sliced
2 cups water
1 tablespoon gravy or
 Worcestershire sauce
1 tablespoon paprika
3 dashes Tabasco
Salt and pepper
Garlic salt
Onion salt
Celery salt

Put soup bone, stew meat, and chicken pieces into large soup kettle; add 5 quarts water, salt, pepper and garlic. Simmer slowly all day, or at least 6 hours, until meat falls from bones. If necessary, add water to keep meat covered at all times. Pour into a colander and drain off all stock into a large bowl. Store stock in refrigerator overnight. Remove all usable meat (chicken and beef) from colander and place in separate covered bowl in refrigerator.

The next day, skim off and discard all fat on stock. Return stock to soup kettle. In a separate pan, boil barley in 4 cups water for 1 hour; drain. Set aside. Heat soup stock to boiling and add vegetables in order given, allowing time between additions so that vegetables with longer cooking times will get a head start. When soup is ready, all vegetables should be tender but none mushy. When soup is nearly done, add 2 cups water (or more for desired consistency); add reserved meat, cooked barley, gravy, paprika, Tabasco, salt and pepper to taste. (If portion of soup is to be frozen, substitute 3/4 cup uncooked, broken vermicelli in place of potatoes, as it freezes better.) Makes approximately 7 quarts.

Mrs. John H. Lindsey (Sara Houstoun)

43

Grace's Crab Bisque

1 can condensed cream of
mushroom soup
1 can condensed cream of
asparagus soup
1 soup-can milk
½ pound King crabmeat

2 tablespoons sherry
Cayenne
Whipped cream, with a
little salt added
Parsley (optional)

Mix soups and milk in blender until smooth; combine with crabmeat, which has been cut into small pieces. Add sherry and cayenne; heat. Serve piping hot, topped with a spoonful of whipped cream and a sprig of parsley if desired. This soup takes only 5 minutes to prepare, and no one would guess that it is a real quickie from your shelf. Serves 4-6.

Mrs. Douglas S. Craig (Alice Picton)

Martha Washington's Crab Soup

2 hard-cooked eggs
1 tablespoon butter
1 tablespoon flour
1 quart milk
1½ pounds lump crabmeat
½ cup heavy cream

Salt and pepper
Dash nutmeg
½ teaspoon mushroom sauce
½ teaspoon A-1 steak sauce
⅓ cup cream sherry

Mash hard-cooked eggs; combine with butter and flour. Bring milk to boil; gradually stir into egg mixture. Add crabmeat and simmer 5 minutes. Add cream; bring to boiling point. Add salt, pepper, nutmeg, sauces and sherry. Serves 6-8.

Mrs. John B. Carter, Jr. (Sue Browne)

Soup for the Gods

1 can (5-6 oz.) King crabmeat
or lobster
2-3 tablespoons dry sherry
1 can condensed cream of pea soup

1 can condensed tomato soup
2¼ cups light cream
Whipped cream or
chopped parsley

Pour sherry on crabmeat and marinate 2 hours in refrigerator. Combine soups with cream. Heat; do not boil. Add crab and sherry; bring to the boiling point. Top with whipped cream or chopped parsley. Serves 6.

Mrs. Whipple S. Newell (Louise Parkinson)

44

Left - Over Turkey Soup
STOCK

Bones and meat from
leftover turkey
8 white peppercorns
1 bay leaf
1 teaspoon thyme

6 whole cloves
6 sprigs parsley
1 medium onion, diced
3 ribs celery, diced
1 carrot, peeled and diced

Bring all ingredients to a boil in 4 quarts cold water. Reduce heat at once; simmer 2-1/2 to 3 hours, or until reduced by half. Strain. Cool uncovered and refrigerate until ready to use. Remove fat. The heated broth may be served as is, used as turkey stock or used as the base for turkey soup.

TURKEY SOUP

3 large onions, finely chopped
3 ribs celery, finely chopped
2 carrots, peeled and chopped
½ pound butter
1½ cups flour

3 quarts turkey stock
1 pint cream
Salt and pepper
¼ cup finely diced, cooked turkey
¼ cup cooked rice

Cook onions, celery and carrots in a little water 20 minutes, or until tender. Set aside. In a large heavy pan melt butter; thoroughly blend in flour. Heat turkey stock and cream; add very gradually to butter-flour mixture, stirring until lumps disappear. Add vegetables, water in which they were cooked, and seasonings. Stir and cook over low heat 10 minutes. Correct seasoning. Add turkey and rice. Serve in large bowls. Makes about 3 quarts soup. Serves 12-16.

Mrs. J. Rorick Cravens (Mary Cullinan)

Easy Oyster Stew

2 cups milk, or half milk
and half cream
1 can condensed cream of
celery soup

¼ cup butter
1 pint fresh oysters
Salt and pepper

Heat milk and soup in saucepan. Add butter, then oysters. Simmer until edges of oysters curl. Season with salt and pepper. Serves 4-6.

Mrs. F. Fox Benton (Ann Temple)

Meat Ball Chowder

2 pounds ground lean beef	3 tablespoons flour
2 tablespoons milk	¼ cup finely chopped parsley
2 teaspoons salt	⅓ cup fine cracker crumbs
⅛ teaspoon pepper	1 tablespoon salad oil
2 eggs, slightly beaten	

To make meatballs combine all ingredients except oil; mix thoroughly. Form into balls about the size of walnuts (40-50 balls). Heat oil and brown balls lightly.

CHOWDER

6 cups water	2-3 cups peeled, diced potatoes
1 tall can (46 oz.) tomato juice	(about 3)
6 beef bouillon cubes	¼ cup uncooked rice
4-6 onions,	1 tablespoon sugar
cut into eighths	2 teaspoons salt
3 cups sliced carrots	2 bay leaves
(about 6)	1 teaspoon marjoram (optional)
3-4 cups sliced celery	2 cans (12 oz. each) Mexicorn

In an 8-10 quart kettle bring all ingredients except Mexicorn to a boil. Reduce heat and simmer 30 minutes, adding Mexicorn for last 10 minutes. Add browned meat balls. Makes 6-7 quarts.

Miss Janet Woods

Senegalese

1 chicken hen	1 or 2 apples,
1 quart chicken broth	peeled and chopped
1 or 2 onions, chopped	2 to 4 tablespoons curry powder
2 ribs celery, chopped	2 tablespoons flour
2 tablespoons butter	1 pint cream

Cook chicken in seasoned water, reserving 1 quart chicken broth. Chill overnight; remove chicken fat from broth. Strain broth. Saute onions and celery in butter 10 minutes. Add apples; cook 5 minutes longer. Mix curry powder and flour together; stir into onion mixture. Add chicken broth; simmer over low heat 40 minutes. Mash through sieve. When cool, add cream and salt if needed. Chill. Serve in chilled bouillon or cream soup bowls. Put 1 tablespoon chopped white meat of chicken in each serving. Serves 12.

Mrs. Pete Gardere (Nancy Penix)

Oyster Soup

2 tablespoons minced green onions with tops	1 jar (12 oz.) fresh oysters
2 tablespoons minced parsley	3½ cups milk, heated
2 tablespoons butter	1 scant teaspoon salt
2 tablespoons flour	Several dashes cayenne
	Paprika

Saute onions and parsley in butter until tender. Add flour and blend. Drain oysters, reserving liquor. Cut oysters into pieces and add to flour mixture. Cook a few minutes until edges of oysters curl. Stir in reserved oyster liquor; continue stirring while slowly adding hot milk, salt and cayenne. Do not boil. Add a dash of paprika to each serving. Serves 4-6.

Mrs. Douglas S. Craig (Alice Picton)

Bouillabaisse

1 pound medium raw shrimp	6 whole cloves
1 quart water	½ teaspoon thyme
Salt and pepper	½ teaspoon marjoram
3 bay leaves	2 cans (1 lb. each) tomatoes (or
Celery leaves	4 large tomatoes, peeled
1 red snapper (about 3 lbs.)	and chopped)
2 cups water	1 pound fresh lump crabmeat
¼ cup butter	2 cans (4 oz. each) sliced
2 cloves garlic, minced	mushrooms
2 large onions, finely chopped	2 pinches saffron
3 tablespoons dried parsley flakes	1 cup dry white wine
1 cup uncooked rice	

Cook shrimp in 1 quart of water which has been seasoned with salt, pepper, bay leaves and celery leaves. Save broth from shrimp. Shell and clean shrimp. Poach red snapper in 2 cups water seasoned with salt and pepper; reserve broth. Let fish cool and cut in large pieces, discarding skin and bones. In a large heavy pan melt butter. Saute slowly the garlic and onion until soft and slightly yellow. Add rice, parsley, cloves, thyme, marjoram, tomatoes and the reserved broth from shrimp and fish. Cover and cook slowly for about 20 minutes or until rice is done. Add fish, shrimp, crab, mushrooms, saffron and wine. Correct seasoning. Bring soup to a boil and serve in soup plates. Serves 10.

Mrs. Elbridge H. Gerry (Barbara Eisner)

Booz's Seafood Gumbo

3 quarts water
2 cans (1 lb. each) tomatoes
1 can (10 oz.) Rotel tomatoes
  and green chiles
½ cup catsup
2 tablespoons Worcestershire
  sauce
1 tablespoon (or more) salt
½ teaspoon Tabasco
Cayenne
½ teaspoon black pepper
5-6 drops Louisiana hot sauce
1 pound salt pork

2 cloves garlic, peeled and
  chopped
1½ cups flour
½ cup butter
2-3 large onions, coarsely
  chopped
1 large green pepper, chopped
1 cup chopped celery
½ cup chopped parsley
1 pound fresh okra, sliced
1 pint oysters
2 pounds raw shrimp, shelled
1 pound fresh crabmeat
  (or 12 fresh crabs)

In a large deep pot combine water, tomatoes, catsup, Worcestershire sauce, salt, Tabasco, cayenne, black pepper and Louisiana hot sauce. Simmer slowly about 1 hour. Meanwhile, chop salt pork in very small pieces. Put in skillet with chopped garlic and fry until brown. Remove all pieces of pork. Discard all but 1-1/2 cups fat. Add flour and brown slowly in the fat. Stir constantly over low heat until mixture turns a deep mahogany color about 30 to 40 minutes. Set aside to cool. In another large skillet, fry onions, green pepper, celery, parsley and okra. Add the roux and sauteed vegetables to the tomato mixture and simmer at least 1 hour. Return salt pork to gumbo if desired. Add seafood and simmer 30 more minutes. Makes 6 quarts.

Mrs. J. Harvey Suttles, Jr. (Lida Picton)

Goose Gumbo
STOCK

1 wild goose and giblets
  (or ducks)
3 quarts water
1 onion, chopped

2 ribs celery, chopped
1 tablespoon salt
1 teaspoon pepper
1 bay leaf

Simmer goose and giblets in water with onion, celery and seasoning, for 1-1/2 to 2 hours, or until tender. Remove goose from stock; strain stock and reserve. When goose is cool, bone and cut into large pieces; chop giblets.

Continued on next page

GOOSE GUMBO

1 cup flour
1 cup bacon drippings
3 medium onions, chopped
4 ribs celery, chopped
2 cloves garlic, crushed
Stock from goose plus water
    to make 3 quarts, heated
1 small can (8 oz.) tomato sauce

1 package frozen cut okra
2 tablespoons Worcestershire
    sauce
½ teaspoon Tabasco
1 tablespoon salt
1 tablespoon pepper
Goose meat

In a heavy pot, brown slowly the flour in fat until it is walnut-colored, stirring constantly to prevent scorching. When roux is browned, quickly add the chopped onion, celery and garlic. Cook over medium heat for 5 minutes, stirring occasionally. Add hot stock, a little at a time, stirring until smooth. Add tomato sauce, okra, Worcestershire sauce, Tabasco, salt and pepper. Add goose meat. Simmer for about 1 hour. Serve over rice. People who don't like wild goose or duck will like this gumbo. Makes about 4 quarts.

Mrs. William G. Reymond (Madeline Noland)

Chicken Ham Gumbo

1 pound fresh okra
2 tablespoons butter
Salt and pepper
2 tablespoons cooking oil
4 large chicken breast halves
1 meaty ham hock, or
    2 cups chopped ham

2½ cups canned tomatoes
1 onion, diced
3 sprigs parsley, chopped
1 bay leaf, crushed
3 quarts boiling water
Salt
Cayenne

Wash, stem and cut okra into 1/2" pieces. Fry okra in butter until brown, being careful not to scorch. Season with salt and pepper. Pour cooking oil into deep soup pot. When hot, add chicken and ham; let cook about 10 minutes. Chop tomatoes and reserve juice. Add tomatoes, onion and parsley to meat mixture, stirring frequently. Add fried okra, juice of tomatoes, bay leaf and boiling water. Let simmer, stirring occasionally, for about 1 hour. Remove chicken and ham, discard all skin and bones. Shred chicken and ham meat, return to gumbo. Add more salt and cayenne to taste. Serve piping hot. Freezes well. Makes about 4 quarts.

Mrs. John H. Lindsey (Sara Houstoun)

49

SALADS

DRESSINGS

Hints

SALADS

FOR CRISP SALADS: Wash greens thoroughly under cold running water. Wrap in a clean towel. Store in refrigerator in towel or plastic bag. Add dressing just before serving.

TO PEEL ORANGES AND GRAPEFRUIT: Place fruit in hot water for 5 minutes, then peel and section. Using this method, no membranes adhere to segments.

TO MOLD GELATIN: Rinse mold in cold water, or grease lightly with oil, before spooning gelatin mixture into mold.

TO UNMOLD GELATIN: Dip mold into warm (not hot) water for just a second, or wrap mold in hot cloth. Loosen edges slightly. Place serving dish on mold; invert, and carefully remove the mold.

SALAD GARNISHES:
    Hard-cooked eggs, quartered, sliced or grated.
    Tomato slices, dipped in chopped parsley or chives.
    Stuffed or ripe olives, sliced or grated.
    Cooked beets, cut in cubes, strips or slices.
    Green or red bell peppers, sliced in rings.
    Crumbled crisp bacon.
    Croutons.

TO MAKE CROUTONS: Trim crusts from slices of bread; cut bread into 1/3 inch cubes. Saute in melted butter until golden brown on all sides. Or, toss cubes in melted butter and brown in a 300° oven. (Garlic may be added to the butter if desired.)

SALAD DRESSINGS

If mayonnaise separates, or Hollandaise sauce curdles, gradually beat it into a well-beaten egg yolk until it is thick.

To help "bought" mayonnaise taste homemade, stir in a little olive oil and lemon juice.

To vary basic oil-and-vinegar dressing, add herbs, cheese, catsup or mayonnaise. Lemon juice may be substituted for vinegar.

Candied Apple Salad

1 jar (15 oz.) applesauce
3 tablespoons red hots
1 envelope unflavored
  gelatin

2 tablespoons water
¼ cup sugar
1 tablespoon lemon juice
¼ teaspoon ground nutmeg

Bring the applesauce and red hots to a boil. When red hots are melted, remove from heat. Add gelatin which has been softened in water and stir until gelatin has dissolved. Then add sugar, lemon juice and nutmeg. Spoon into 6 individual molds. Chill until firm. Serves 6.

Mrs. Mary K. Logan (Mary Kay Kleinecke)

Cinnamon Apples
with Cream Cheese Filling

6 tart apples
1½ cups water
2 cups sugar
¾ cup red hots
Red food coloring (optional)
1 small package (3 oz.)
  cream cheese

Orange juice to soften cheese
1 tablespoon grated orange rind
½ cup broken toasted pecans
½ cup sliced ripe olives
  (optional)
Salt

Core and peel apples. Make a syrup of water, sugar and red hots. Boil syrup in heavy skillet for 10 minutes or until thickened. Add food coloring if desired. Place apples in gently boiling syrup; baste and turn until tender, about 25-30 minutes. Carefully remove apples from skillet. Drain thoroughly and chill. Stuff with Cream Cheese Filling.

To make Cream Cheese Filling, mash softened cream cheese and add small amount of orange juice until it is a good consistency to stuff apples. Add orange rind, pecans and olives. Season with salt to taste. Fill cavities of the cinnamon apples and chill before serving. Serves 6.

Mrs. James H. Weyland (Alta Jean McConathy)

Citrus Avocado Ring

2 envelopes unflavored gelatin
½ cup cold water
1 cup hot water
½ cup sugar
¼ teaspoon salt
1 cup fresh grapefruit juice

½ cup fresh lemon juice
1½ cups pureed avocado
   (3-4 avocados)
1½ cups fresh grapefruit sections
1½ cups fresh orange sections

Soften gelatin in cold water. Add hot water and stir until dissolved. Stir in sugar, salt and fruit juices. Chill until mixture is thickened. Fold in avocado puree. Rinse a 6-cup ring mold with cold water and fill with gelatin mixture. Chill until firm. Unmold and fill center with grapefruit and orange sections. Serves 10-12.

Mrs. Rotan McGown (Charlotte Rotan)

Creamy Avocado Mold

1½ envelopes unflavored gelatin
1 cup cold water
¾ cup boiling water
2 tablespoons lemon juice
1¼ teaspoons salt

1 teaspoon grated onion
2 or more dashes Tabasco
2½ cups mashed ripe avocado
1 cup sour cream
1 cup mayonnaise

Soften gelatin in cold water; dissolve in boiling water. Add lemon juice, salt, onion and Tabasco. Let cool to room temperature. Stir in avocado, sour cream and mayonnaise. Pour into a 6-cup ring mold. Chill until firm (5 to 6 hours or overnight). Serves 12.

Mrs. George N. Allen, Jr. (Bonnie Blades)

Cranberry Delight

1 large package (6 oz.)
   raspberry-flavored gelatin
2 cups boiling water
1 cup cold water
1⅓ cups drained Mandarin
   orange segments

1 cup drained crushed pineapple
2 cans (1 lb. each) whole
   cranberry sauce
⅓ cup chopped pecans
Sour cream or mayonnaise
   for topping

Dissolve gelatin in boiling water. Add cold water; chill until partially set. Stir in orange segments, pineapple, cranberry sauce and pecans. Spoon mixture into 16 individual molds. Chill until firm. To serve, top with sour cream or mayonnaise. Serves 16.

Mrs. George V. Kane, Jr. (Alafair Benbow)

Frozen Cranberry Salad

1 cup fresh cranberries
2 medium apples, peeled, cored and chopped
1 cup diced marshmallows

½ cup sugar
1 cup heavy cream, whipped
½ cup chopped pecans
Red food coloring

Chop cranberries in blender or mince by hand. Mix cranberries, apples, marshmallows and sugar together and chill for at least 1 hour. Fold in whipped cream, nuts and one drop of food coloring. Place in freezer overnight. Keeps well for several days if covered with foil. Holiday pretty! Also appropriate as a dessert. Serves 8.

Mrs. Gleaves M. Love (Betsy Riggle)

Green Grape Salad

2 small packages (3 oz. each) cream cheese
3 tablespoons mayonnaise or celery seed dressing

1½ pounds seedless green grapes
Lettuce leaves (red tip is attractive)

Combine cream cheese (softened to room temperature) and mayonnaise or dressing. Add grapes to cheese mixture; refrigerate for at least 3 hours. Serve on lettuce leaves. May be topped with sliced fresh peaches. Light and refreshing served with chicken. Serves 6.

Mrs. Frank J. McGurl (Mary Martin)

Orange Sherbet Salad

2 cans (11 oz. each) Mandarin orange segments
1 small package (3 oz.) orange-pineapple-flavored gelatin

½ cup boiling water
¾ cup reserved juice from oranges
1 pint orange sherbet, softened

Drain oranges, reserving juice. Dissolve gelatin in boiling water. Add the orange juice and sherbet. Mix thoroughly and chill. When gelatin mixture is slightly thickened, fold in orange segments. Pour into individual molds or into shallow pan. Chill until firm. Cut into squares to serve. This is a favorite with children. Serves 8.

Mrs. Raymond Thornton (Dee Ann Minnis)

Pacific Salad

12 large oranges or
  2 cans(11 oz. each) Mandarin
  orange segments

4 large white onions
3 ripe avocados
Poppy seed or French dressing

Peel oranges and slice into cartwheels, saving juice; or, drain Mandarin orange segments, reserving juice. Slice onions and separate into rings. Peel and slice avocados and toss thoroughly in reserved orange juice. Drain. Mix all ingredients lightly with desired salad dressing. Refrigerate at least 45 minutes before serving. Serves 12-16.

Mrs. Raymond Thornton (Dee Ann Minnis)

Mandarin Orange Salad with Ginger Dressing

2 small packages (3 oz. each) orange-flavored gelatin
3 cans (11 oz. each) Mandarin orange segments (reserve liquid)
2 cans (5 oz. each) water chestnuts, drained, sliced paper thin

Prepare gelatin using juice from the oranges plus enough water to total 3 cups of liquid. Cool mixture and combine with orange segments and water chestnuts. Chill until set. Serve with Ginger Dressing. Serves 10-12.

GINGER DRESSING

4 ounces cream cheese, softened
½ cup fresh orange sections,
  chopped

½ cup crystallized ginger,
  very finely chopped
¼ cup cream

Combine ingredients except cream and mix well. Add cream until dressing is the consistency of mayonnaise.

Mrs. George McCullough Thompson (Julia Eddleman)

Peach Supreme

1 can (28 oz.) sliced peaches
1 cup syrup from peaches, heated
1 small package (3 oz.)
  lemon-flavored gelatin

⅔ cup creamed cottage cheese
½ cup chopped pecans
  (optional)
½ cup heavy cream

Drain sliced peaches, reserving 1 cup syrup. Dissolve gelatin in hot syrup; allow to cool. Add peaches, cottage cheese and pecans. Whip cream to medium consistency; add to gelatin mixture. Pour into a 6-cup serving dish and chill well. Salad will not be firm enough to unmold. Serves 6.

Mrs. Holcombe Crosswell (Emily Attwell)

Green Gage Plum Salad

2 cans (15 oz. each)
Green Gage plums
1 small package (3 oz.)
cream cheese, softened
1¾ cups liquid (juice from
plums plus water)

1 small package (3 oz.)
lime-flavored gelatin
2 teaspoons unflavored gelatin
2 tablespoons water
1 teaspoon lemon juice
1 cup pecans, chopped

Drain plums, reserving juice. Mash plums; combine with cream cheese; mix well. (Blender may be used.) Heat diluted plum juice and pour over lime-flavored gelatin; stir to dissolve. Soften unflavored gelatin in cold water; add to warm lime-flavored mixture and stir. Add lemon juice; stir in plum-cheese mixture; fold in pecans. Pour into a 1-1/2 quart mold or individual molds. Chill until set. Serves 8-10.

Mrs. R. L. Hawk (Peggy Parker)

Green Plum and Grape Salad

1 large package (6 oz.)
lemon-flavored gelatin
1 cup hot water
1 small can (6 oz.) frozen
lemonade concentrate

1 can (1 lb., 14 oz.) Green Gage
plums, drained
1 can (1 lb.) crushed pineapple,
drained
1 cup halved fresh green grapes
1 cup sour cream

Dissolve gelatin in hot water. Stir in lemonade until it is thawed. Mash plums. Add plums, pineapple, grapes and sour cream to gelatin mixture. Mix well. Pour into a 2-quart mold and chill until firm. Garnish with small bunches of green grapes or wedges of fresh pineapple. Serves 10-12.

Mrs. Lorenzo B. Taylor (Marilyn Dubach)

Creamy Frozen Fruit Salad

2 cups sour cream
2 tablespoons lemon juice
¾ cup sugar
⅛ teaspoon salt
1 banana, sliced

1 can (8½ oz.) crushed
pineapple, drained
¼ cup sliced maraschino
cherries
¼ cup chopped pecans

Blend sour cream, lemon juice, sugar and salt. Stir in remaining ingredients. Pour into a 1-quart mold or 6 individual cupcake papers in muffin tin. Place in freezer until firm. Serve on crisp lettuce with mayonnaise if desired. Serves 6.

Mrs. Bruce E. Barnett (Ann Poyner)

Fruit Nectar Salad

1 envelope unflavored gelatin	½ cup water
2 tablespoons sugar	10 whole cloves
¼ teaspoon salt	1 tablespoon lemon juice
1 can (12 oz.)	1½ cups any drained fruit
apricot nectar	(fresh or canned)

Thoroughly mix gelatin, sugar and salt in a small saucepan. Add nectar, water and cloves. Place over low heat and stir until gelatin is dissolved. Simmer 5 minutes. Remove from heat and discard cloves. Add lemon juice. Chill until thickened, then add fruit of your choice. Pour mixture into 3-cup mold, chill until firm. Serves 4-6.

Mrs. David F. Dorn (Julie Leary)

Marian Nye's Strawberry Salad

2 small packages (3 oz. each)	2 packages frozen strawberries
strawberry-flavored gelatin	1 small can (8 oz.) crushed
2 cups boiling water	pineapple
3 bananas, mashed	½ pint sour cream (at room
	temperature)

Dissolve gelatin in boiling water. Let cool. Add bananas, undrained strawberries and pineapple. Pour half of mixture (approximately 2 cups) into 9'' x 9'' Pyrex dish. Chill until congealed. (Do not refrigerate remaining half of mixture.) Carefully spread sour cream onto congealed layer. Cover sour cream layer with remaining strawberry mixture, being very careful not to mix the two layers. Chill until firm. Cut into squares to serve. Serves 9.

Mrs. C. Pharr Duson, Jr. (Betty Tomforde)

Fruit and Gingerale Salad

1 can (1 lb.) pitted	1 cup cold water
Royal Anne cherries	2 cups juice from fruit
2 cans (1 lb. each)	1 bottle (28 oz.) gingerale, chilled
pineapple tidbits	Juice of 1 lemon
4 envelopes unflavored	3 ounces slivered almonds
gelatin	(optional)

Drain fruit, reserving juice. Slice cherries. Soften gelatin in water. Heat over boiling water until gelatin is dissolved. Add dissolved gelatin to 2 cups of the reserved fruit juice. Add gingerale and lemon juice. Refrigerate until partially thickened. Add cherries, pineapple and almonds. Pour into a 3-quart salad mold. A light, refreshing salad. Serves 12.

Mrs. Dean Emerson, Jr. (Martha Vinson)

Summer Salad

2 small packages (3 oz. each)
lime-flavored gelatin
1¼ cups boiling water
2 cups apple juice

1 can (1 lb.) pear halves, drained
3 large oranges, peeled and
sectioned
4 ounces Danish Blue cheese,
cut in small cubes

Dissolve gelatin in boiling water. Add cold apple juice and stir well. Cool until syrupy. Pour 3 tablespoons of the gelatin mixture into a 2-quart mold. Tip and rock the mold until the entire inside is coated. Chill until set. Dip orange sections into remaining gelatin mixture and arrange in a pattern in the mold. Chill until set. Dip pear halves into gelatin mixture; arrange them in the mold; chill until set. Combine remaining gelatin and Blue cheese chunks; carefully pour into mold. Chill several hours. Serves 10.

Mrs. G. Huckins Morris (Glory Huckins)

Versatile Fruit Salad

2 eggs, beaten
2 tablespoons vinegar
2 tablespoons lemon juice
¼ cup sugar
2 tablespoons butter

2 cups miniature marshmallows
2 cups diced fresh fruit
2 cups canned pineapple tidbits,
drained
1 cup heavy cream, whipped

Cook eggs, vinegar, lemon juice and sugar in double boiler until thick. (Mixture will thicken quickly.) Remove from heat; while still hot add butter and marshmallows and stir until marshmallows melt. Allow to cool. Fold in fresh fruit of your choice, pineapple and whipped cream. Turn into individual molds or a glass serving bowl and chill overnight. Suggested combinations of fresh fruit—strawberries, green grapes and peaches in summer or orange sections and bananas in winter. Canned fruit, well drained, will also give good results. Serves 8.

Mrs. Paul F. McBride, Jr. (Pattie Cunningham)

Best Ever Fruit Salad

1 can (1 lb.) pineapple slices
1 can (1 lb.) pears
1 can (8 oz.) pitted
Royal Anne cherries

12 large marshmallows,
cut in half
1 can (3½ oz.) coconut
1 cup sour cream

Thoroughly drain fruit and cut into bite-sized pieces. Mix fruit, marshmallows and coconut with sour cream. Refrigerate for 12 hours. Serves 8.

Mrs. Lewis A. Brown (Sidney Walsh)

Artichoke Aspic

2 envelopes unflavored gelatin	¼ teaspoon (or more)
½ cup cold water	grated onion
2 cans beef consomme	Salt and pepper
Juice of 2 lemons	1 can (15 oz.) artichoke
Few drops Tabasco	hearts, drained

Soften gelatin in cold water. Add consomme which has been heated; stir to dissolve gelatin. Add lemon juice, Tabasco, onion, salt and pepper. Cut artichoke hearts into small pieces; add to gelatin mixture. Spoon into 1-1/2 quart mold or individual molds. Chill until firm. Serve with curried mayonnaise. Serves 8.

Mrs. Richard R. McKay (Emily Ann Finch)

Artichoke Salad with Roquefort Dressing

8 lettuce cups	2 tablespoons lemon juice
8 tomato slices (¼" thick)	1 teaspoon salt
8 large artichoke bottoms,	1 teaspoon sugar
canned or fresh	½ small onion, quartered
2 hard-cooked eggs, grated	1 cup salad oil
2 ounces black domestic	2½ ounces Roquefort cheese
caviar, drained	

Place ingredients on individual plates in the following order: lettuce cup, tomato slice, artichoke bottom, spoonful of grated egg, and a dab of caviar. To mix dressing, place lemon juice, salt, sugar, onion and salad oil in blender and blend at low speed. Add cheese and blend until cheese is chopped. (Be very careful not to blend too long.) Serve Roquefort dressing over salad. This is an elegant dinner party salad. Serves 8.

Mrs. Harry H. Hudson (Carolyn Brock)

English Pea Salad

1 can (8 oz.) tiny English peas	¼ teaspoon curry powder
1 tomato, peeled and chopped	Cracked black pepper
1 medium onion, chopped	Salt
3 tablespoons mayonnaise	

Drain peas. Mix all ingredients and chill thoroughly. Serves 4.

Mrs. Robert L. Baker (Ann McAshan)

Artichokes à la Grecque

2 cans (1 lb. each) small artichoke
   hearts and liquid
¼ cup vinegar
1 bay leaf, crushed
4 sprigs celery leaves, chopped
¼ teaspoon thyme
1 clove garlic, crushed

1 medium onion, chopped
¼ teaspoon pepper
1 teaspoon salt
2 slices of lemon
½ cup olive oil
1 tablespoon Worcestershire
   sauce

Drain artichokes, reserving liquid. Simmer artichoke liquid and all other ingredients except artichoke hearts for 15 minutes. Strain hot mixture, discarding vegetable pulp remaining in the strainer; pour liquid over artichoke hearts. Cool. Marinate 3-4 hours in refrigerator. Drain artichokes before serving as salad or appetizers. Serves 8.

Mrs. John M. Hopper (Tany Pollard)

Mustard Ring

4 eggs
½ cup vinegar
½ cup water
½ cup sugar
Salt and pepper

½ teaspoon turmeric
3 tablespoons dry mustard
1 envelope unflavored gelatin
½ cup cold water
½ pint heavy cream, whipped

Beat eggs in top of double boiler. Add vinegar, 1/2 cup water, sugar, salt, pepper, turmeric and dry mustard. Cook over hot water until thick, stirring constantly. Add gelatin which has been softened in 1/2 cup cold water and stir well. Remove from heat; place pan in cold water to hasten cooling. When mixture is cool, fold in whipped cream. Spoon mixture into a 2-quart ring mold. Chill until firm. Serve with cole slaw, shredded raw cabbage, or other chilled raw vegetables placed in center of ring. Serves 12.

Mrs. Paul F. McBride, Jr. (Pattie Cunningham)

Martha's Salad

1 jar (8 oz.) preserved
   kumquats

2 pounds tender young spinach
Wishbone Italian dressing

Remove seeds from kumquats and cut into halves or slices. Toss broken spinach leaves and kumquats with dressing until well-coated. Serves 8.

Mrs. Terry H. Keith (Betty Ann Warner)

Asparagus Salad Ring
with Vinaigrette Dressing

2 cans (1 lb. each)	2 tablespoons minced onion
green asparagus	1 cup heavy cream, whipped
2 envelopes unflavored gelatin	1½ teaspoons salt
½ cup cold water	Few dashes Tabasco
2 cups liquid (juice from	2 tablespoons parsley flakes
asparagus plus water)	3 tablespoons lemon juice
¾ cup mayonnaise	1½ cups slivered almonds

Drain asparagus, reserving juice. Soften gelatin in cold water. Heat asparagus juice (and water to make 2 cups liquid). Dissolve gelatin in juice; refrigerate. When mixture is partially set, add mayonnaise, onion, whipped cream, salt, Tabasco, parsley flakes and lemon juice. Cut asparagus into small pieces and add to gelatin mixture. Add almonds and mix well. Spoon mixture into individual molds or into a 2-quart ring mold. Chill until firm. Serve with Vinaigrette Dressing spooned over salad. Serves 12.

VINAIGRETTE DRESSING

3 tablespoons finely chopped celery	1 teaspoon (or more) salt
1½ tablespoons chopped chives	Coarsely ground black pepper
1½ tablespoons chopped parsley	3 drops Tabasco
1 tablespoon chopped pimientos	Few dashes Worcestershire
1 tablespoon chopped	sauce
sweet red pepper	3-4 tablespoons red wine vinegar
½ clove garlic, crushed	¾ cup olive oil

In a pint jar, combine all ingredients except olive oil; mix thoroughly. Add oil; shake vigorously. Shake dressing before serving. Makes 1-1/2 cups.

Mrs. Hughes Fleming (Mildred Hughes)

Mother Safford's Spaghetti Salad

1 package (7 oz.) spaghetti,	1 jar (3-4 oz.) pimiento-
broken and cooked	stuffed olives, sliced
4 hard-cooked eggs, chopped	1 large onion, grated
2 large ribs celery, chopped	Mayonnaise (enough to
1 green pepper, minced (optional)	moisten salad well)
	Salt

Combine all ingredients and mix well. Serve cold. Serves 6-8.

Mrs. H. R. Safford, Jr. (Betty Howard)

Pickled Beets; Beet Red Eggs

3 pounds small fresh beets or 3
    cans (1 lb. each) baby beets
1 teaspoon whole allspice
1 stick cinnamon

6 whole cloves
2 cups vinegar
½ cup water
½ cup sugar

If using fresh beets, boil until tender, drain and remove skins. If using canned beets, drain. Tie allspice, cinnamon and cloves in cheesecloth bag. Heat vinegar, water, sugar and spice bag to boiling point. Add beets and boil 5 minutes. Remove spice bag and chill beets well before serving. Beets may be packed and sealed with pickling liquid in sterilized jars. Makes 3 pints.

To make Beet-red Eggs, pour juice from pickled beets over whole, shelled, hard-cooked eggs, covering them with juice. Let stand 2 days. The eggs become a beautiful color and have an excellent flavor. Serve as appetizers with crisp celery hearts, or slice for sandwiches or salads.

Mrs. George McCullough Thompson (Julia Eddleman)

Dressed Green Beans

3 cans (1 lb. each) green beans
1 tablespoon salad oil
1 tablespoon vinegar

1 onion, thinly sliced
Salt
Cracked pepper

Drain beans. Mix together all other ingredients and pour over beans. Cover and marinate for at least 2 hours. Before serving, cover with Anchovy Cream Dressing.

ANCHOVY CREAM DRESSING

1 cup sour cream
½ cup mayonnaise
1 teaspoon lemon juice
¼ teaspoon dry mustard
1 tablespoon horseradish

Small amount onion juice
2 teaspoons chopped chives
    (optional)
1 teaspoon anchovy paste
    (optional)

Mix all ingredients together. This dressing may be made ahead and will last for several days. Makes 1-1/2 cups.

Mrs. Kline McGee (Adrian Rose)

Stuffed Beets

2 cans (1 lb. each) tiny whole
beets and liquid
1 cup vinegar
½ cup sugar

¼ teaspoon salt
1 teaspoon pepper
1 tablespoon whole cloves

Drain beets; reserve liquid. Combine liquid, vinegar, sugar, salt, pepper and cloves. Bring to a boil. Put beets in jar or deep dish, cover with hot liquid and chill. Remove centers of beets and fill with Cream Cheese, Pineapple-Pecan Filling or Chive Filling. Makes at least 50 stuffed beets.

PINEAPPLE - PECAN FILLING

2 packages (3 oz. each)
cream cheese, softened
1 teaspoon Miracle Whip
salad dressing

1 cup finely chopped pecans
1 can (8 oz.) crushed pineapple,
well drained

Mash cream cheese; add salad dressing and mix well. Stir in pecans and pineapple. Fill centers of beets. (Any extra filling may be used to fill apricot, peach or pear halves for fruit salad.)

CHIVE FILLING

2 packages (8 oz.) cream cheese
with chives, softened

2 teaspoons Miracle Whip
salad dressing

Combine cream cheese with chives and salad dressing. Fill centers of beets. Serve as salad or for appetizers. (Any extra filling may be used for a spread with crackers.)

Mrs. John C. Goss (Jacqueline Ehlers)

Endive and Spinach Salad

1 small clove garlic, crushed
¼ cup olive oil
1 teaspoon sugar
¾ teaspoon oregano
1 teaspoon salt
⅛ teaspoon pepper

1 tablespoon wine vinegar
2 tablespoons lemon juice
6 slices bacon
1 head Belgian endive
¼ pound fresh spinach

Make a dressing of garlic, oil, sugar, oregano, salt, pepper, vinegar and lemon juice. Let stand at least 30 minutes before using. Meanwhile, fry bacon crisp and crumble. Pour dressing over cold, crisp, torn endive and spinach; toss well. Sprinkle bacon over salad. (This dressing is quite tart.) Serves 6.

Mrs. Fred T. Spangler (Zillah Mae Ford)

Frosted Green Bean Salad

6 tablespoons vinegar
¾ cup salad or olive oil
2 medium onions, minced
Salt and pepper
3 cans (1 lb. each) Blue Lake
   green beans, drained

6 tablespoons mayonnaise
4 teaspoons additional vinegar
2 teaspoons prepared mustard
Salt
8 hard-cooked eggs, chopped
8 slices bacon, fried crisp

Combine 6 tablespoons vinegar, oil, onions, salt and pepper. Pour over beans and chill several hours or overnight. Drain and heap marinated beans in salad bowl. Make frosting for beans by combining mayonnaise, 4 teaspoons vinegar, mustard, salt and hard-cooked eggs; mix well. Pour over marinated beans. Garnish with crumbled bacon just before serving. Serves 10-12.

Mrs. William A. Bramley (Kay Borden)

Broccoli Salad

2 packages frozen chopped broccoli
¾ cup beef consomme
2 envelopes unflavored gelatin
2 tablespoons Worcestershire
   sauce
1 teaspoon (or less) Tabasco

1 teaspoon salt
2 tablespoons lemon juice
2 teaspoons grated onion
⅔ cup mayonnaise
4 hard-cooked eggs

Cook broccoli. Drain and chop finely. Soften gelatin in 1/4 cup consomme. Heat remaining consomme; add Worcestershire sauce, Tabasco, salt, lemon juice and onion. Add softened gelatin to hot consomme mixture; stir until dissolved. Combine broccoli and mayonnaise. Add consomme mixture to broccoli mixture. Slice eggs and arrange in ring mold. Spoon broccoli mixture carefully over sliced eggs. Chill until firm. Serves 8-10.

Mrs. Richard R. McKay (Emily Ann Finch)

Carolyn's Marinated Slaw

1 medium head cabbage
1 medium onion
1 green pepper
½ cup salad oil

¼ cup sugar
¼ cup tarragon vinegar
Salt and pepper

Grate, **do not chop**, cabbage, onion and green pepper; mix together. Combine oil, sugar and vinegar. Stir well. Pour over the slaw. Season with salt and pepper. Mix well and refrigerate for 24 hours. Drain before serving. Serves 8-10.

Mrs. Gleaves M. Love (Betsy Riggle)

Golden Slaw

1 medium head cabbage, finely chopped	1 tablespoon additional sugar
1 medium onion, finely chopped	1 tablespoon salt
¾ cup sugar	1 tablespoon prepared mustard
1 cup vinegar	1 tablespoon celery seed
	1 cup salad oil

Alternate layers of cabbage and onion in large bowl. Sprinkle 3/4 cup sugar over all. Boil vinegar, 1 tablespoon sugar, salt, mustard and celery seed a few minutes. Add salad oil and bring to a boil again, stirring constantly. Pour over cabbage and onion layers. Cover and refrigerate overnight. Drain before serving. Will keep in refrigerator for several days. This is an unusual version of an old stand-by. Serves 8.

Mrs. Joseph T. Painter (Ann Hill)

Celery Victor

4 hearts of celery	½ cup French dressing
1 cup chicken broth	(oil and vinegar)
¼ teaspoon monosodium glutamate	Anchovies
	Tomato wedges

Wash celery thoroughly without separating ribs. Cut off leafy tops. Simmer celery in pan with broth and monosodium glutamate. Cook until tender, remove and drain. Cut lengthwise into 2 or 4 pieces, depending on size. Place warm celery in a shallow dish, pour dressing over. Marinate for 1 hour or more as it cools. Chill thoroughly. Turn. Arrange celery on salad plates with two strips anchovies over each serving. Garnish with tomato wedges or water cress and serve on lettuce. Serves 6-8.

Mrs. J. Rorick Cravens (Mary Cullinan)

Cucumber Salad

3 medium cucumbers	3 tablespoons vinegar
¾ teaspoon salt	1 teaspoon mustard
¼ cup sour cream	Salt and pepper
½ onion, chopped	Chopped parsley and chives
1 teaspoon lemon juice	(optional)

Peel cucumbers and slice paper-thin. Add 3/4 teaspoon salt. Let stand in colander to drain for at least 30 minutes. Press in colander until all water is removed. Make dressing by mixing sour cream, onion, lemon juice, vinegar, mustard, salt and pepper together. Combine cucumbers and dressing; chill. Sprinkle with chopped parsley or chives if desired. Serves 6.

Mrs. Harmon Whittington (Dolores Welder)

Cucumber Ring Mold

4 medium cucumbers,
  peeled
1 green pepper
1 onion
2 ribs celery

1 large package (6 oz.)
  lime-flavored gelatin
2 cups hot water
Lots of salt and white pepper
½ cup sour cream
1 tablespoon lime juice

Puree all vegetables in blender. Dissolve gelatin, using only 2 cups water. Stir pureed vegetables into gelatin; add salt, pepper, sour cream and lime juice. Pour into lightly oiled 1-1/2 quart mold and chill until firm. When using a ring mold, I fill the center with Sour Cream Cucumbers. Serves 8-10.

Mrs. Lorenzo B. Taylor (Marilyn Dubach)

Sour Cream Cucumbers

2 medium cucumbers,
  thinly sliced
½ onion, chopped
1 cup sour cream

¼ cup lemon juice
3 tablespoons sugar
Salt and pepper,
  to taste

Mix together all ingredients. Chill for an hour before serving. These cucumbers may be served as a relish or used to fill the center of Cucumber Ring Mold.

Mrs. Lorenzo B. Taylor (Marilyn Dubach)

Crowning Glory Salad

2 small packages (3 oz. each)
  lime-flavored gelatin
1½ cups hot water
2 tablespoons lemon juice
1½ medium cucumbers
  (do not peel)

1 large onion
1 pint creamed cottage cheese
1 cup sliced almonds
2 cups mayonnaise

Dissolve gelatin in hot water. Add lemon juice and cool. Grind cucumbers and onion; strain off juice. To the gelatin mixture add cucumbers and onion, cottage cheese, almonds and mayonnaise; mix well. Pour into a 2-quart mold. Chill until firm. Serves 10-12.

Mrs. Ralph Ellis Gunn (Esme Patterson)

Vegetable Medley

⅓ cup brown sugar
⅔ cup tarragon vinegar
⅔ cup salad oil
Garlic salt
Salt and pepper
Tabasco

1 can (1 lb.) Blue Lake
  green beans
1 can (12 oz.) Mexicorn
1 large onion, sliced
2 cucumbers, sliced
1 or 2 tomatoes, peeled and
  sliced

Combine brown sugar, vinegar and salad oil. Season with garlic salt, salt, pepper and Tabasco. Pour dressing over vegetables which have been drained and mixed together. Refrigerate and marinate in dressing for at least 24 hours. Will keep about 2 weeks in refrigerator. Makes approximately 2 quarts. Serves 10-12.

Mrs. Robert B. Crouch (Nancy Wencke)

Red and White Salad Mold

WHITE LAYER

4 hard-cooked eggs
  (optional)
1 envelope unflavored gelatin
½ cup cold water
1 teaspoon salt
2 tablespoons lemon juice

2 teaspoons Tabasco
1 cup mayonnaise
1½ teaspoons grated onion
½ cup diced celery
¼ cup diced green pepper
½ cup diced pimiento

If desired arrange slices of hard-cooked eggs attractively in a 2-quart mold. Soften gelatin in cold water; then dissolve it over hot water. Add salt, lemon juice and Tabasco. Combine gelatin mixture and mayonnaise; add onion, celery, green pepper and pimiento; mix well. Pour gently over the sliced eggs. Chill until firm.

RED LAYER

1 envelope unflavored gelatin
½ cup cold tomato juice
1¼ cups heated tomato juice

1 tablespoon lemon juice
¼ teaspoon salt
Black pepper

Soften gelatin in cold tomato juice; then add to the hot tomato juice; stir until dissolved. Add lemon juice, salt and pepper. Chill until consistency of unbeaten egg whites. Then pour over white layer and chill to set. Serves 10.

Mrs. Joseph R. Crump (Ruth Grace)

Mrs. Chubb's Buffet Salad

Variety of vegetables
French dressing (oil and vinegar)

Marinate vegetables of your choice, some cooked, some raw, in French dressing for at least 24 hours. (Suggestions: peas, lima beans, green beans, beets, cauliflower, squash, carrots, avocados, cucumbers, tomatoes.) Drain and arrange with lettuce on platter or individual salad plates and serve with Cheese Dressing.

CHEESE DRESSING

1 pint dry cottage cheese
1¼ ounces Roquefort cheese
2 packages (3 oz. each) softened cream cheese
1 clove garlic, crushed

2 tablespoons onion juice
½ cup mayonnaise, or enough to thin to proper consistency
Salt

Combine all ingredients and serve with chilled, marinated vegetables. Makes approximately 3-1/2 cups dressing, enough for about 14 cups vegetables.

Mrs. William Buck Arnold (Lucy Gray)

Tomato Aspic

3 envelopes unflavored gelatin
4 cups tomato juice
1 tablespoon dried crab boil
3 green onions, sliced
1 rib celery, sliced
1 can beef consomme
1 teaspoon lemon juice

6 dashes Louisiana hot sauce or Tabasco
Salt
½ cup green olives, sliced
1 can (1 lb.) tiny green peas, drained
2 carrots, grated (optional)

Soften gelatin in 1/2 cup tomato juice. Simmer 1-1/2 cups tomato juice with crab boil, onions and celery for about 20 minutes. Strain and discard vegetables. Dissolve softened gelatin in warm tomato juice. Add remaining 2 cups tomato juice, consomme, lemon juice, hot sauce and salt. Refrigerate until mixture begins to thicken. Then add olives, peas and carrots. Mixture may be put into a 9'' x 12'' dish and cut into squares, or congealed in a 2-quart ring mold. Hot and tangy! Sometimes I use avocado, shrimp and hard-cooked eggs in place of carrots, peas and olives. Serves 12 generously.

Mrs. Charles B. Moore (Mary Alice Bone)

Sunday Night Supper Salad

1 head iceberg lettuce
5 hard-cooked eggs
5 strips bacon
½ cup chopped pickled beets

½ cup grated Parmesan cheese
1 can (2½ oz.) shoestring
potatoes
½ large onion, sliced crosswise

Tear lettuce into bite-sized pieces. Chop eggs coarsely. Cook bacon until crisp and crumble. Make layers in salad bowl of all ingredients in order listed. Add Spicy Dressing and toss well. Serves 2-4 for Sunday night supper or 10-12 as a dinner salad.

SPICY DRESSING

1 clove garlic, crushed
½ teaspoon dry mustard
¼ teaspoon thyme
½ teaspoon marjoram
2 tablespoons vinegar

2 teaspoons chili powder
½ teaspoon Tabasco
1 thin slice of onion
½ cup salad dressing or
mayonnaise

Combine all ingredients in blender and blend thoroughly. Makes about 3/4 cup dressing.

Mrs. Donald J. Douglass (Shirley Engelhardt)

Caesar Salad

2 cups bread cubes
½ cup butter
2 cloves garlic, crushed
Juice of 2 lemons
½ cup olive oil
¼ cup vinegar
1 tablespoon Worcestershire
sauce

2 whole garlic cloves, peeled
3 heads romaine lettuce
2 heads leaf lettuce
2 eggs
¼ cup grated Parmesan
cheese
1 can anchovy fillets
Salt and pepper

Make croutons by sauteeing bread cubes and crushed garlic in butter until bread is crisp. Remove and set aside. To make dressing, shake lemon juice, olive oil, vinegar, Worcestershire sauce and garlic cloves together in a jar; chill. Tear romaine and lettuce into bite-sized pieces. Toss together the greens and croutons. Break eggs over greens and add cheese, anchovies, salt and pepper. Remove garlic from dressing. Pour dressing over salad; toss thoroughly. Serves 12.

Mrs. Henry Hamman (Ann Hufendick)

Hawaiian Caeser Salad

2 tablespoons olive oil
Salt
1 large clove garlic, peeled
2 tomatoes, peeled
2 heads romaine lettuce (or any
  mixed salad greens)

¼ cup chopped green onion
½ cup grated Romano cheese
½ cup (or more) crisp,
  crumbled bacon
½ cup croutons

Pour olive oil into large wooden bowl, sprinkle with salt and rub with garlic. Remove garlic and place tomatoes, cut in eighths, in bowl. Add romaine which has been torn into pieces. Add onion, cheese and bacon. Pour Mint Dressing over salad. Add croutons and toss. Serves 6-8.

MINT DRESSING

¾ cup olive oil
Juice of 2½ lemons
½ teaspoon freshly ground pepper

¼ teaspoon chopped fresh mint
¼ teaspoon oregano
1 coddled egg

Put olive oil, lemon juice, pepper, mint and oregano into a small bowl. Add coddled egg and whip vigorously. (To coddle egg, break egg into boiling water. Remove from heat and let stand uncovered for 8 minutes.)

Mrs. Lorenzo B. Taylor (Marilyn Dubach)

Patio Salad

1 can (1 lb.) kidney beans
2 cups diced fresh tomatoes
1 cucumber, peeled and diced
½ cup chopped green pepper
½ cup chopped green onion

2 cups diced sharp cheese
¼ to ½ cup mayonnaise
Salt and pepper
Lettuce leaves
2 slices bacon, fried crisp
3 hard-cooked eggs

Drain beans and diced tomatoes. Combine beans, tomatoes, cucumber, green pepper, onion, cheese and enough mayonnaise to moisten. Season with salt and pepper; chill. Arrange in lettuce-lined bowl and sprinkle with crumbled bacon and sliced eggs. Serves 8.

Mrs. Roger G. Stotler (Nance Fruit)

SALADS

Tossed Green Salad

2 quarts mixed salad greens
3 tomatoes, peeled
1 can (15 oz.) artichoke hearts,
drained
¼ cup (or more) toasted
sesame seeds

½ cup grated Romano or
crumbled Blue cheese
Salt and pepper
Blue cheese salad dressing
(oil and vinegar type)

Tear (do not cut) greens into bite-sized pieces. Place in salad bowl and add tomatoes and artichokes, both of which have been cut in chunks. At serving time, sprinkle with sesame seeds and cheese. Season with salt and pepper. Toss with dressing until each leaf is thoroughly coated. Serves 8.

Mrs. John L. Hamilton (Ann Lowdon)

Kane Patch Salad

4 strips thick-sliced bacon
1 hard-cooked egg
1 medium tomato, peeled
6 cups mixed salad greens (iceberg, Boston, red tip lettuce)

3 heaping tablespoons
mayonnaise
2 tablespoons cider vinegar
Salt
Coarsely ground pepper

Cook bacon until crisp; crumble. Dice egg; cube tomato. Tear greens into bite-sized pieces. Add bacon, egg and tomato to greens. Combine mayonnaise and vinegar; season with salt and pepper. Add to salad and toss well. Serves 6.

Mrs. George V. Kane, Jr. (Alafair Benbow)

Frozen Tomato Mayonnaise

1 envelope unflavored gelatin
2 tablespoons cold water
1 cup Snap-e-Tom or
tomato juice

1 cup mayonnaise
1 tablespoon Worcestershire
sauce
½ tablespoon onion juice

Soften gelatin in cold water; place over hot water until gelatin is dissolved. Combine all ingredients, mix well, and pour into ice tray. Freeze. Serve frozen in avocado halves or on lettuce. Serves 6-8.

Mrs. A. S. Vandervoort, Jr. (Mary Porter Kirkland)

Spinach and Bacon Tossed Salad

6 cloves garlic, peeled and
   quartered
¾ cup French dressing (oil
   and vinegar type)

1 pound fresh spinach
3 hard-cooked eggs, chopped
8 slices bacon, fried crisp

Add garlic to French dressing and refrigerate for 2 hours before serving. Wash spinach and tear into bite-sized pieces. Refrigerate. At serving time place spinach in large salad bowl; sprinkle with eggs and crumbled bacon. Remove garlic from dressing and toss salad with enough dressing to thoroughly coat greens. Serves 6.

Mrs. Henry Hamman (Ann Hufendick)

Fresh Mushroom Salad

¼ pound fresh mushrooms
¼ cup red wine vinegar
¾ cup olive oil
1 teaspoon lemon juice

Salt and pepper
Lettuce leaves
Chopped chives and
   parsley

Wash and thinly slice mushrooms; do not peel. Combine vinegar, olive oil, lemon juice, salt and pepper; pour over mushrooms. Marinate for at least 1 hour. Chill. Serve on lettuce and sprinkle with chopped chives and parsley. Serves 4.

Mrs. Bass C. Wallace (Julia Picton)

Bean Salad

⅓ cup apple cider vinegar
⅓ cup sugar
2 tablespoons olive oil
2 tablespoons soy sauce
Celery salt
1 can (1 lb.) green beans, drained

1 can (1 lb.) kidney beans,
   drained
1 medium purple onion,
   thinly sliced
1 can (5 oz.) water chestnuts,
   drained

Make a marinade of vinegar, sugar, olive oil, soy sauce and celery salt. Marinate beans, onion and water chestnuts several hours or overnight. Serves 6-8.

Mrs. Wallace S. Wilson (Mary Malone)

Green Bean and Potato Salad

1 package frozen French-cut green
    beans, cooked and drained
4 medium potatoes, boiled, peeled
    and diced
1 medium onion, chopped
4-6 tablespoons bacon drippings

3-5 tablespoons vinegar
Salt and pepper
½ to ¾ cup mayonnaise
1 small can (8 oz.) tiny
    whole beets or sliced
    beets (optional)

Mix warm beans, warm potatoes and onion. Add 4 tablespoons bacon drippings and 3 tablespoons vinegar. Taste for seasoning. Add salt, pepper, more bacon drippings or vinegar as needed. Let stand at room temperature for about 1 hour. (Bacon fat will congeal if salad is refrigerated too soon.) Then refrigerate salad. Just before serving, mix in mayonnaise. Garnish with drained beets if desired. A good change from potato salad. Serves 8.

Mrs. Harry H. Hudson (Carolyn Brock)

Picnic Potato Salad

6 medium boiling potatoes
2 small onions, minced
3 sweet pickles, minced
1 jar (2 oz.) pimientos,
    drained and minced

Salt and pepper
Mayonnaise
1 teaspoon prepared
    mustard

Boil unpeeled potatoes until just tender. When cool, peel and cut into bite-sized pieces. Combine with onions, pickles, pimientos, salt and pepper. Flavor the mayonnaise with mustard and mix enough into the potato mixture to bind it. Serves 8.

Miss Ellen Ketchum

Creamy Potato Salad

7 large boiling potatoes
2 tablespoons bacon drippings
1½ tablespoons white vinegar
1 cup mayonnaise

1 cup sour cream
6 hard-cooked eggs, grated
2 medium onions (or less), grated
Salt and pepper
7 slices bacon, fried crisp

Boil potatoes until tender; peel and cut into bite-sized pieces. Mix bacon drippings and vinegar and pour over hot potatoes; let cool. Mix mayonnaise and sour cream together. Add eggs, onions, salt and pepper to potatoes. Fold in the mayonnaise mixture. Crumble bacon over top. May be served hot or cold. Serves 8-10.

Mrs. H. L. Murchison (Lynn Lyles)

Gloria's Hot Potato Salad

6 slices bacon	1 teaspoon prepared mustard
6 potatoes	1½ teaspoons (or more) salt
¼ cup bacon drippings	Pepper
1½ teaspoons flour	2 ribs celery, chopped
1 cup cold water	2 small onions, chopped
⅓ cup white vinegar	Fresh parsley, finely chopped
1 tablespoon sugar	Sliced radishes for garnish

Fry bacon crisp and crumble. Boil, peel and dice potatoes. Blend bacon drippings and flour in skillet. Stir in water. Add vinegar, sugar, mustard, salt and pepper. Bring to a boil, stirring constantly. Add celery, onions, parsley, potatoes and bacon. Toss and garnish with sliced radishes if desired. Serves 6-8.

Mrs. Lyon L. Brinsmade (Susannah Tucker)

Bermuda Salad Bowl

1 small head cauliflower	⅔ cup Good Seasons Old
1 small head lettuce	Fashion French Dressing
½ large Bermuda onion	3 ounces Blue cheese,
½ cup sliced stuffed olives	crumbled

Separate cauliflower into flowerets and slice thin, lengthwise. Tear lettuce into small pieces. Slice onion paper-thin. Combine all ingredients in salad bowl; toss lightly. Serves 6 generously.

Mrs. Platt W. Davis, Jr. (Janet Houstoun)

Rice Salad

1 cup uncooked rice	2 tablespoons grated onion
1 package frozen cut	Salt and pepper
green beans	Onion salt
½ cup mayonnaise	1 tablespoon lemon juice
¼ cup Blue cheese salad dressing	2 tablespoons crumbled
(olive oil base)	Blue cheese
½ cup chopped dill pickles	4 hard-cooked eggs, sliced

Cook rice; slightly undercook green beans and drain. Mix with mayonnaise, salad dressing, pickles and onion. Season with salt, pepper, onion salt and lemon juice. Mix lightly with fork and chill. Before serving, add cheese and 3 of the eggs, mixing lightly. Garnish with remaining sliced egg. Serves 6-8.

Mrs. A. Baker Duncan (Sally Witt)

Crabmeat Salad

1 cup chili sauce	1½ ounces cream cheese
1 cup mayonnaise	1 teaspoon Worcestershire sauce
1 teaspoon anchovy paste	4 Holland Rusks or toast rounds
1 teaspoon grated onion	Lettuce
1 teaspoon vinegar	4 tomato slices
Tabasco	4 avocado slices
Salt and pepper	1 pound lump crabmeat

To make sauce, combine chili sauce, mayonnaise, anchovy paste, onion, vinegar, Tabasco, salt and pepper. Mix well and set aside. Soften cream cheese with Worcestershire sauce; spread on Holland Rusks. On each of 4 salad plates, arrange lettuce, Holland Rusk, slice of tomato, slice of avocado and crabmeat. Spoon sauce over each salad. Makes 4 servings.

Miss Harriet Jean Turner

Crab Salad with Louis Dressing

⅔ cup slivered almonds	1 large potato, peeled, cooked
Butter for sauteing	and diced (optional)
4 cups (2 lbs.) fresh	1 cup halved fresh mushroom caps
lump crabmeat	1 cup shredded curly endive

Saute almonds in a little butter. Combine crabmeat, potato, mushrooms, endive, and 1/2 cup of the almonds. Add the Louis Dressing and toss very lightly. If desired, garnish salad with pickled beets, ripe olives and finely chopped parsley. Sprinkle remaining almonds over all. Chill well. Serves 6.

LOUIS DRESSING

1 cup mayonnaise	2 or 3 dashes Tabasco
½ cup chili sauce	Salt
¼ cup dry sherry	

Mix mayonnaise with chili sauce. Stir in sherry and Tabasco; season with salt. Blend well.

Mrs. Ford Hubbard, Jr. (Patricia Peckinpaugh)

West Indies Salad

1 medium onion, finely chopped
1 pound fresh lump crabmeat
Salt and pepper

½ cup salad oil
⅓ cup cider vinegar
½ cup ice water

Layer half of onion in large mixing bowl. Arrange crabmeat on onion layer. Sprinkle remaining onion over crabmeat. Season with salt and pepper. Pour over salad in this order: salad oil, vinegar, ice water. Cover and allow to marinate from 2-12 hours (the longer, the better). When ready to serve, toss lightly but do not stir. Serves 4.

Miss Harriet Jean Turner

Curried Shrimp Salad

1 pound shrimp, cooked,
  shelled and chilled
1 cup sliced celery
3 green onions, chopped
½ cup mayonnaise

½ cup sour cream
Juice of 1 lemon
1½ teaspoons curry powder
1½ teaspoons salt
Pepper

Cut shrimp in half, lengthwise; add celery and green onions. Mix remaining ingredients together to make a sauce. Stir sauce into shrimp mixture until it is of desired consistency. Serve on salad greens. This salad also can be used to fill avocado halves or rosette tomatoes. Lump crabmeat can be substituted for shrimp. The curry sauce alone is a good dip for cherry tomatoes, celery sticks, carrot sticks and cauliflowerets. Serves 4.

Mrs. Suzanne S. Braden (Suzanne Schmidt)

Shrimp and Cauliflower Salad

½ cup uncooked rice
2 cups cooked and shelled shrimp
1½ cups uncooked
  cauliflower buds
½ teaspoon salt
Pepper
2 tablespoons lemon juice

¼ cup French dressing
  (oil and vinegar type)
2 tablespoons chopped onion
2 tablespoons chopped
  pimiento-stuffed olives
¼ teaspoon dry mustard
Mayonnaise
Whipped cream

Cook rice; let cool. Mix all remaining ingredients together adding mayonnaise plus a little whipped cream until salad is of desired consistency. Serves 12.

Mrs. Lorenzo B. Taylor (Marilyn Dubach)

Salmon Salad

1 can (1 lb.) red salmon	2 sour pickles, chopped
2 hard-cooked eggs, chopped	1 teaspoon Worcestershire
1 tablespoon cider vinegar	sauce
1 tablespoon lemon juice	2 tablespoons chopped onion
½ teaspoon salt	2 ribs celery, chopped

Mix all ingredients together and chill for several hours before serving. Serve with mayonnaise. Serves 3-4.

Mrs. Fletcher H. Etheridge (Carolyn Smith)

Lobster Mousse

½ cup minced celery	1 envelope unflavored gelatin
2 cups cooked, chopped lobster	½ cup heavy cream, whipped
1 tablespoon chopped green onion	½ cup mayonnaise
2 tablespoons lemon juice	Worcestershire sauce
2 tablespoons lime juice	Salt and pepper

Combine celery, lobster and green onion. Add lemon and lime juice. Soften gelatin in 3 tablespoons cold water; place over hot water until gelatin is dissolved. Mix whipped cream and mayonnaise together and add dissolved gelatin. Add to lobster and season with Worcestershire sauce, salt and pepper. Pour into 1-quart mold. Chill until set. This mousse can be served as main course for luncheon, or unmolded and served with crackers as an hors d'oeuvre. Individual molds may be used as a first course for dinner. I mold this salad in a fish mold and serve it for cocktail buffet suppers. Serves 4-6.

Mrs. Richard R. McKay (Emily Ann Finch)

Seafood Salad Alcorn

1 cup cooked lobster meat	1 cup mayonnaise
1 cup lump crabmeat	1 teaspoon grated onion
3 cups cooked and shelled	3 tablespoons lemon juice
shrimp	Pepper
2 ripe avocados	1 cup diced celery

Cut seafood into bite-sized chunks. To make dressing, mash avocado pulp; add mayonnaise, grated onion, lemon juice and pepper. Toss seafood and celery in dressing. Spoon salad onto lettuce leaves. Garnish with asparagus spears, tomato wedges and ripe olives if desired. Serves 6 as a main course.

Mrs. Lorenzo B. Taylor (Marilyn Dubach)

Seaside Salad

1 small package (3 oz.) lime-flavored gelatin	Thin cucumber and pimiento slices
1¼ cups hot water	1 can (7 oz.) tuna fish (or chicken)
5 tablespoons vinegar	1 cup peeled, chopped cucumber
½ teaspoon Worcestershire sauce	1 tablespoon chopped onion
½ teaspoon salt	2 tablespoons chopped pimiento
	½ cup mayonniase

Add hot water to lime-flavored gelatin and stir until dissolved. Add vinegar, Worcestershire sauce and salt. Measure 1/4 cup of the mixture into a 1-quart mold and chill. When nearly firm, place cucumber and pimiento slices attractively on gelatin and chill again. Add tuna or chicken, chopped cucumber, onion, pimiento and mayonnaise to the remaining gelatin mixture. Cool. When slightly thickened, spoon onto firm gelatin layer in mold. Chill again until firm. An easier version of this salad may be made by mixing all ingredients together and pouring into mold to chill until firm. Serves 8.

Mrs. Frank C. Smith, Jr. (Sally McQueen)

Molded Neptune Salad

1 can condensed tomato soup	½ cup finely chopped green pepper
2 small packages (3 oz. each) cream cheese	2 cans (7-8 oz. each) lobster, shrimp or tuna; or 1 can (1 lb.) red salmon
2 envelopes unflavored gelatin	
½ cup cold water	½ teaspoon Worcestershire sauce
½ cup mayonnaise	½ teaspoon salt
1 tablespoon finely chopped onion	¼ teaspoon pepper
1 cup finely chopped celery	

Stir tomato soup and cream cheese in top of double boiler. Soften gelatin in cold water and add to soup mixture. Mix well and heat over boiling water until gelatin dissolves. Add remaining ingredients in order listed. Mix well. Chill until firm. Serves 6-8.

Mrs. Edward H. Patton, Jr. (Anne Berry)

Eggs in Consomme with Seafood Sauce

6 hard-cooked eggs
1 teaspoon anchovy paste
Salt and pepper
1 teaspoon Worcestershire sauce

2 envelopes unflavored gelatin
2 cups cold water
1 can beef consomme

Cut eggs in half. Mash yolks with anchovy paste, salt, pepper and Worcestershire sauce. Fill egg whites with yolk mixture. Soften gelatin in 1/2 cup of the water. Add heated consomme and stir until gelatin is dissolved. Add remaining water. Pour a small amount of the mixture into a 9" x 12" dish and chill until partially set. Arrange stuffed eggs in chilled consomme. Carefully pour the remaining consomme over eggs. Chill until firm. Serve with Seafood Sauce. Serves 12.

SEAFOOD SAUCE

½ pound cooked and shelled
    shrimp (or crab)
1 tablespoon chopped green onion
1 tablespoon chopped green pepper

½ teaspoon anchovy paste
1 hard-cooked egg,
    chopped (optional)
1 cup mayonnaise

Mix shrimp, onion, green pepper, anchovy paste and hard-cooked egg together. Combine with mayonnaise. Makes about 2 cups sauce.

Mrs. John H. Meyers (Alice Baker Jones)

Tallahasse Chicken Salad

5-pound chicken hen
1 whole stalk celery,
    finely chopped
1 pint mayonnaise

½ of a 9-ounce jar Crosse and
    Blackwell Chow Chow pickles
    (with mustard sauce)
Salt and cayenne
Lemon juice

Cook hen slowly until tender and cool in broth. For salad, cut into bite-sized pieces; for sandwiches, cut up very finely. Measure 4 cups chicken and 2 cups chopped celery in a bowl. Add mayonnaise. Grind pickles and with mustard sauce, gently fold into the salad. Season with salt, cayenne and lemon juice. Better if made the day before using. Spread top with thin layer of mayonnaise to keep it moist and cover with wax paper. Refrigerate. Makes over 2 quarts salad.

Mrs. Jack Bowman (Margaret McMullen)

Cold Curried Chicken Salad

2 cups uncooked rice
1 cup uncooked cauliflower,
cut into 1/4" slices
1 bottle (8 oz.) creamy
French dressing
1 cup mayonnaise
1 tablespoon curry powder
1 tablespoon salt
1 1/2 teaspoons pepper
1/2 cup milk
6-7 cups cooked chicken or
turkey, cut in large pieces
1 cup thin strips green pepper
2 cups diagonally sliced celery
1 cup thinly sliced red onions

Cook rice until just tender and chill. Toss chilled rice with cauliflower and French dressing. Refrigerate at least 2 hours. In another large bowl combine mayonnaise, curry powder, salt and pepper. Slowly stir in milk. Add chicken and toss. Refrigerate at least 2 hours. When ready to serve, combine both mixtures; add green pepper, celery and onions. Serve with the following condiments: flaked coconut, slivered almonds, pineapple cubes, currant jelly, chutney, crumbled bacon, chopped hard-cooked eggs. Serves 12-15.

Mrs. Joseph T. Painter (Ann Hill)

Chicken à la Can Salad

2 cans (5 oz. each)
boned chicken
Bite-sized pieces of lettuce
(about 2 cups)
2 tomatoes, peeled and diced
8 slices crisp bacon, crumbled
1/2 cup mild-flavored Thousand
Island dressing

Toss all ingredients together and serve as salad. (Also good as sandwich filling.) Serves 4.

Mrs. Robert J. Hogan (Mary Burke)

Danish Beef Salad

2 tablespoons garlic vinegar
1/4 cup salad oil
1/2 teaspoon salt
1/8 teaspoon pepper
1/2 teaspoon dry mustard
Monosodium glutamate
4 cups cooked and diced
roast beef
1 small onion, chopped
4 ribs celery, finely diced
1 tablespoon minced parsley
1 small can anchovies,
drained and chopped

Combine vinegar, oil, salt, pepper, dry mustard and monosodium glutamate to make a marinade. Mix beef, vegetables and anchovies; marinate for at least 4 hours, stirring once or twice. Serves 4.

Mrs. Frank J. McGurl (Mary Martin)

Oil and Vinegar Dressing

6 tablespoons Spice Islands
    eschalot wine vinegar
½ teaspoon dry mustard
½ teaspoon seasoned salt
½ teaspoon salt

Freshly ground black pepper
1 clove garlic, crushed
¼ cup salad oil
¼ cup olive oil

Combine all ingredients except oils in pint jar and stir well. Add both kinds of oil and shake vigorously. You may vary this dressing to suit your own taste. Lemon juice may be used for all or a part of the vinegar; all olive oil or all salad oil may be used instead of the combination of oils. Herbs may be added if desired. Blue cheese or sieved hard-cooked egg may be crumbled into dressing. Makes about 1 cup.

Mrs. Richard R. McKay (Emily Ann Finch)

Balinese French Dressing

½ cup salad oil
1 teaspoon (or more) fresh
    onion juice
1 tablespoon lemon juice
1 egg white

¾ teaspoon salt
¼ teaspoon white pepper
¼ teaspoon monosodium
    glutamate

Pour 2 tablespoons of the oil in blender; add all other ingredients. Turn blender on and slowly pour in the remaining oil. Turn off blender. Dressing will have the consistency of sour cream. (Even if this dressing separates, it is good.) Makes about 1/2 cup.

Mrs. Vernon L. Miller (Lois DuBose)

Lionel's Flame Room Dressing

1 egg
1 teaspoon dry mustard
½ teaspoon prepared mustard
½ teaspoon salt
½ teaspoon pepper

2 cups salad oil
2 tablespoons white vinegar
2 teaspoons lemon juice
4 tablespoons onion juice
4 or 5 tablespoons ice water

Combine egg, dry mustard, prepared mustard, salt and pepper. Add oil gradually, beating constantly. Add vinegar, lemon juice and onion juice. Thin with ice water to desired consistency. Makes 1 pint.

Mrs. James A. Walsh (Harriet Brady)

Sweet French Dressing

1 cup salad oil	1 teaspoon paprika
⅔ cup red wine vinegar	1 teaspoon salt
2 tablespoons Worcestershire sauce	5 or 6 cloves garlic, peeled
1 tablespoon soy sauce	¼ cup sugar

Mix all ingredients in a jar. Shake well to dissolve sugar. Store in refrigerator. (Flavor improves with age.) Use on citrus fruit or green salad. Makes 1 pint.

Mrs. James P. Jackson (Sarah Faulkner)

Low Calorie French Dressing

1 small onion, sliced	2 tablespoons Worcestershire sauce
1 clove garlic, peeled	
1 can condensed tomato soup	10 drops Sweeta liquid sugar substitute
½ cup red wine vinegar	1 envelope Good Seasons Old Fashion French Dressing Mix

Put onion and garlic in a jar. Add all other ingredients. Shake well and refrigerate at least 24 hours. Remove garlic before serving. Makes 1 pint.

Mrs. F. Fox Benton (Ann Temple)

Roquefort Salad Dressing

5 ounces Roquefort cheese	½ teaspoon garlic powder
2 tablespoons warm water	1 pint mayonnaise
1 tablespoon pepper	

Mash cheese with warm water. Mix in pepper, garlic powder and mayonnaise. Blend until smooth. Keeps indefinitely in refrigerator. Makes 3 cups.

Mrs. Jack T. Currie (Dorothy Peek)

Blue Cheese Salad Dressing

1 cup white vinegar	1½ cups salad oil
Garlic powder	Salt and pepper
4 ounces Blue cheese	

Measure half of the vinegar into bowl. Add garlic powder and stir well. Add Blue cheese and blend with fork. Pour into jar. Add remaining vinegar, oil, salt and pepper. Shake well and serve. Makes 3 cups.

Mrs. Eric W. Strom (Jane De Marse)

Creamy Blue Cheese Dressing

2 tablespoons wine vinegar
4 ounces Blue cheese
1 cup sour cream
3 tablespoons mayonnaise
½ teaspoon salt
1½ teaspoons onion juice
½ teaspoon dry mustard

In saucepan, combine vinegar and cheese and heat until cheese has melted. Remove from heat and add remaining ingredients. Mix well and refrigerate. Serve dressing on tossed green salad. Can also be used as a dip for raw vegetables. Makes 1 pint.

Mrs. Paul F. McBride, Jr. (Pattie Cunningham)

Green Goddess Dressing

1 egg yolk
2 tablespoons tarragon vinegar
1 tablespoon anchovy paste
½ to 1 teaspoon salt
1 cup salad oil
¼ cup cream
1 tablespoon lemon juice
1 teaspoon grated onion
½ clove garlic, crushed
2 tablespoons chopped chives
2 tablespoons chopped parsley

Combine egg yolk, vinegar, anchovy paste and salt in bowl. Beat in the salad oil, 2 tablespoons at a time. Stir in cream, lemon juice, onion, garlic, chives and parsley. Serve on tossed green salad. May also be served with shrimp or crab salad. Makes about 2 cups.

Mrs. Ford Hubbard, Jr. (Patricia Peckinpaugh)

David's Thousand Island Dressing

2 hard-cooked eggs
1 pint Miracle Whip
   salad dressing
½ cup catsup
1 tablespoon chili sauce
1½ teaspoons minced onion
2 dashes white pepper
2 dashes garlic powder
5 dashes onion salt
4 drops Worcestershire sauce

Finely chop eggs and mix all ingredients together. Makes 1-1/2 pints.

Mrs. David M. Underwood (Lynda Knapp)

Thousand Island Dressing

1 hard-cooked egg
¼ medium onion
10 or 12 pimiento-stuffed olives
8 or 10 capers
2 tablespoons creamy orange-
colored French dressing

1 teaspoon India relish
¾ cup mayonnaise
Salt and pepper
Celery salt
Garlic powder

Grate egg, onion and olives. Mash capers through the finest holes in grater. Add French dressing, relish and mayonnaise. Mix well. Season with salt, pepper, celery salt and garlic powder. Thin with a little cream if too thick. Refrigerate at least 1 hour before serving. Can be used on open-faced club sandwiches or on tossed green salad. Makes about 1 cup.

Mrs. H. Edward Maddox, III (Donna Gray)

Mixer Mayonnaise

4 egg yolks
1 quart salad oil, chilled
3 tablespoons lemon juice

1½ teaspoons salt
Several dashes Tabasco
Paprika to color

Beat egg yolks until thick. Beating constantly, slowly add about half of the oil. Add lemon juice, salt, Tabasco and paprika. Continuing to beat, slowly add the remaining oil. Makes 1 quart.

Mrs. Robert E. Clemons (Grayson Cecil)

Blender Mayonnaise

1 egg
2 tablespoons lemon juice
½ teaspoon dry mustard

1 teaspoon salt
1 cup salad oil

Put egg, lemon juice, mustard and salt in blender. Add 1/4 cup of the oil. Cover and blend thoroughly (about 5 seconds). Without stopping blender, gradually pour in remaining oil. Makes 1-1/4 cups.

Mrs. Gleaves M. Love (Betsy Riggle)

Versatile Creamy Salad Dressing

1 quart mayonnaise
1 pint creamy orange-colored
    French dressing
2½ teaspoons anchovy paste

2 or 3 cloves garlic,
    peeled
1 can (2 oz.) grated
    American cheese

Mix all ingredients in blender. Serve on tossed green salad. May also be used as dip for raw vegetables. Keeps indefinitely in refrigerator. Makes 1-1/2 quarts.

Mrs. Richard R. Nelson, Jr. (Marjorie Shepherd)

Gallagher Ranch Salad Dressing

1½ cups salad oil
1 cup cream
2 teaspoons chopped onion
2 teaspoons chopped parsley
1 teaspoon crushed garlic

1 tablespoon mustard seed
1 teaspoon celery seed
2 teaspoons salt
¼ cup tarragon vinegar
Juice of 1 lemon

Combine all ingredients in a large jar and shake well. Keeps almost indefinitely in refrigerator. Makes about 1 quart.

Mrs. James L. Whitcomb (Mary Hill Brown)

Fiesta Salad Dressing

1 clove garlic, peeled
1 fresh, hot red pepper
    (about 3" long)
Salt
Dash sugar
3 tablespoons olive oil

1 tomato, peeled
2 tablespoons vinegar
Juice of 1 lemon
6 pimiento-stuffed olives,
    chopped
6 ripe olives, chopped

Mash garlic clove, hot pepper, salt and sugar with olive oil into smooth paste. (Remove some of the pepper seeds before crushing pepper if a milder dressing is desired.) Mash tomato to a pulp and add. Add vinegar, lemon juice and chopped olives. Mix well. Makes enough dressing for 4 tossed green salads.

Mrs. Lorenzo B. Taylor (Marilyn Dubach)

Egg Dressing for Raw Spinach Salad

3 hard-cooked eggs
1 tablespoon prepared
    horseradish
1-2 teaspoons tarragon vinegar

Salt and pepper
Dash Tabasco
¾ cup mayonnaise
1 teaspoon prepared mustard

Grate eggs and combine with other ingredients. Serve over fresh spinach leaves. Makes 1 cup.

Mrs. Robert E. Clemons (Grayson Cecil)

Tootsie's Fruit Salad Dressing

1 egg, beaten
¼ cup sugar
1 tablespoon lemon juice
2 tablespoons orange juice

1 small package (3 oz.)
    cream cheese
6 marshmallows
1 cup heavy cream, whipped
¼ cup chopped nuts

Combine egg, sugar, lemon juice and orange juice; cook until thick. Add cream cheese and marshmallows; stir until melted. Let cool. Fold in whipped cream and nuts. Serve over fruit salads. Can also be used as topping for cobbler or other desserts. Makes about 1 quart.

Mrs. William G. Godfrey (Dineen Schuhmacher)

May's Dressing for Fruit Salad

1 teaspoon flour
¼ teaspoon sugar
¼ teaspoon salt
1 cup pineapple juice

2 tablespoons lemon juice
½ cup orange juice
2 eggs, separated
1 large package (8 oz.)
    cream cheese

Mix flour, sugar and salt together in saucepan. Add fruit juices and cook for 5 minutes. Remove from heat and add beaten egg yolks. Cook 5 more minutes, stirring constantly. Add cream cheese and beat until blended. Fold in stiffly-beaten egg whites. Serve over fruit salad. This dressing can also be used as the base for frozen fruit salad. Keeps well in refrigerator. Makes about 3 cups.

Mrs. H. E. Daniels (Gayle Garth)

Celery Seed Dressing

½ cup sugar
1 teaspoon dry mustard
1 teaspoon salt
½ medium onion, grated

⅓ cup vinegar
1 cup salad oil
1 tablespoon celery seed

Combine sugar, mustard, salt, onion and a little of the vinegar. Mix well. Beating vigorously (using electric mixer, preferably), add oil alternately with remaining vinegar. Stir in celery seed. Cover and store in refrigerator. Serve over fruit salad. Makes approximately 2 cups.

Mrs. Wilson Breiel (Nancy Buford)

Poppy Seed Dressing

⅔ cup honey
1 teaspoon salt
⅔ cup vinegar

2½ cups salad oil
5 tablespoons poppy seeds

Put all ingredients except poppy seeds in blender and blend until mixture is thick and oil disappears. Turn off blender. Add poppy seeds and stir with a long-handled spoon until seeds are evenly distributed. Pour into quart jar and refrigerate. If an oniony flavor is desired, add a slice or two of onion to the ingredients before blending. Makes 1 quart.

Mrs. John H. Lindsey (Sara Houstoun)

CHEESE

EGGS

Hints

CHEESE

To keep cheese fresh, wrap it in a vinegar-soaked rag and refrigerate.

1/4 pound cheese makes about 1 cup grated cheese.

Melt cheese over low heat; high heat will make it stringy.

EGGS

BEATING EGGS:

Slightly beaten eggs are eggs beaten just until whites and yolks are combined.

Beaten eggs are eggs beaten until whites and yolks are well blended.

Well-beaten eggs are eggs beaten until whites and yolks are completely blended and look light and fluffy.

Beating egg whites: Egg whites cannot be stiffly beaten if there is even a trace of yolk in the whites. When separating an egg, if egg yolk gets into the white, remove it with a piece of egg shell. (Yolk will adhere readily to shell.)

COOKING EGGS:

To hard-cook eggs: Completely cover eggs with water, add 1/2 teaspoon salt. Bring to a boil. Take pan off heat, cover, and let stand 20 minutes. Cool immediately by plunging eggs into cold water, to prevent yolks from discoloring.

When poaching eggs, add some vinegar to the water to keep the whites from spreading.

When baking eggs, or cooking scrambled eggs, always use a low temperature. (High temperature toughens eggs.)

STORING EGGS:

To store whole raw egg yolks: Place yolks in jar with tight-fitting lid. Cover with water. Refrigerate, covered, until ready to use. Drain before using. Do not keep longer than 3 days.

To store raw egg whites: Refrigerate egg whites in jar with tight-fitting lid until ready to use. Egg whites remain fresh for a week to 10 days.

Snappy Cheese Bake

2 cans (4 oz. each) green
   chile peppers
1 pound mellow Cheddar
   cheese, grated

6 eggs
1½ cups Bisquick
1 quart milk

Butter a large shallow baking dish. Split and seed green chilies; spread flat in bottom of dish. Cover green chilies with cheese. In large bowl, beat eggs, and add Bisquick and milk. Beat well. Pour egg mixture over peppers and cheese. Bake at 350° for 1 hour. Great with steaks or as a brunch or supper dish. Serves 8.

Mrs. E. Robert Seal (Joan Mulligan)

Cheese Fondue Casserole

12 slices white or French
   bread
3 cups milk, scalded
3 eggs

Salt and pepper
2 dashes Tabasco
¾ pound sharp cheese
¼ cup butter

Cut crusts from bread; place bread, stacked double, in greased oblong baking dish. Combine scalded milk and slightly-beaten eggs; add salt, pepper and Tabasco. Cut cheese in small pieces and melt with butter in top of double boiler. Add cheese mixture to egg mixture and blend well. Pour over bread. Place baking dish in pan of water and bake at 350° about 25 minutes, or until firm. If desired, serve with mushroom sauce. Casserole may be prepared the day before and refrigerated until ready to bake. Serves 6.

Mrs. David R. Park (Jane Burrill)

Individual Cheese Soufflé

1 egg yolk
⅓ cup grated Cheddar cheese
¼ cup milk
¼ teaspoon salt

Dash freshly ground pepper
Dash cayenne
2 egg whites

Beat egg yolk with fork. Add cheese, milk, salt, pepper and cayenne; mix well. Beat egg whites until stiff; fold into cheese mixture. Pour into individual baking dish and bake in 450° oven for 12 minutes. Serves 1.

Mrs. George F. Neff (Anne Lummis)

Cheese Soufflé

3 tablespoons butter	1 cup milk
3 tablespoons flour	1 cup grated New York or
Salt and pepper	other sharp cheese
	4 eggs, separated

Melt butter over low heat in saucepan. Blend in flour, salt and pepper, stirring constantly. Add milk and continue to stir until mixture is smooth and thick. Remove from heat. Add cheese to the hot mixture and stir until melted. Let cool. Add beaten egg yolks; mix well. Fold in stiffly beaten egg whites. Pour into ungreased souffle or baking dish, or into 4 individual dishes. Place souffle dish in pan of warm water and bake at 325° for 50-60 minutes. If individual dishes are used reduce baking time to 30 minutes. (This recipe may be doubled, increasing baking time to approximately 1-1/2 hours.) Serves 4.

Mrs. Dean Emerson, Jr. (Martha Vinson)

Cheese Custard
with Mushroom Sauce

6 eggs, well beaten	1 cup milk
¼ teaspoon salt	1 cup grated Velveeta
¼ teaspoon dry mustard	cheese

Combine eggs, salt, dry mustard, milk and cheese and pour into greased 1-1/2-quart baking dish. Set in pan of water and bake at 350° for 45 minutes, or until set. Serve with Mushroom Sauce. Serves 6.

MUSHROOM SAUCE

2 tablespoons butter	1 cup cream
1½ tablespoons flour	5 tablespoons grated cheese
Salt and pepper	1 can (4 oz.) mushrooms, drained

Melt butter in saucepan; stir in flour, salt and pepper. Add cream slowly, stirring constantly. Cook 2 minutes. Stir in grated cheese and mushrooms. Heat thoroughly. Spoon sauce over Cheese Custard. Makes approximately 1-3/4 cups sauce.

Mrs. Fletcher B. Emerson (Ann Craddock)

Quiche Lorraine à la Versailles Picnic

1 baked 10-inch pastry shell	4 paper-thin slices (4"x8" each)
4 slices bacon	Swiss cheese
1 large onion, sliced	3 eggs
1 tablespoon bacon drippings	¼ teaspoon dry mustard
1 cup boiled or baked ham,	1 cup cream, heated
shredded	Nutmeg

Broil bacon until crisp. Crumble and sprinkle over bottom of pie shell. Saute onion rings in bacon drippings until soft. Arrange over bacon. Place half the shredded ham and 2 slices of cheese over onions. Repeat layers of ham and cheese. Beat eggs and mustard together; add to warm cream and beat again. Pour into pie shell and let stand 10 minutes. Sprinkle on enough nutmeg to cover top. Bake in a pre-heated 350° oven for 35 minutes. This quiche will keep for about 3 days, and can be warmed successfully if covered with foil. May also be served cold. Serves 4 generously.

Mrs. Frank A. Lawson (Virginia Cronin)

Cheddar Quiche Lorraine
CRUST

1 cup sifted flour	½ cup grated Cheddar cheese
¼ teaspoon salt	1 teaspoon caraway seeds
¼ cup butter	⅓ cup cream

Sift flour and salt into mixing bowl; cut in butter. Stir in cheese and caraway seeds. Add cream and stir with fork until dough holds together. On lightly-floured board, roll dough to a circle 1-1/2" larger than inverted 9-inch pie plate. Fit loosely into pie plate.

FILLING

½ pound Cheddar cheese	5 eggs
1 can (3½ oz.) French fried onions	2 tablespoons Mister mustard
½ cup finely chopped celery	1¾ cups milk
⅓ cup finely chopped green pepper	¾ cup grated Cheddar cheese

Cut cheese into 6 or 8 slices, 3" x 4" x 1/2". Cover bottom of pie shell with cheese, overlapping slices. Set aside 1/2 cup French fried onions; sprinkle remainder over cheese. Sprinkle in celery and green peppers. Beat eggs and mustard until well blended. Add milk; stir thoroughly. Pour into pastry shell. Sprinkle reserved French fried onions and grated cheese on top. Bake at 325° for approximately 1 hour, or until firm.

Mrs. George McCullough Thompson (Julia Eddleman)

Blue Cheese Quiche

1 9-inch pastry shell,
partially baked
2 small packages (3 oz. each)
cream cheese, softened
3 ounces Blue cheese
2 tablespoons butter, softened

3 tablespoons heavy cream
2 eggs, slightly beaten
½ teaspoon minced onion or
½ tablespoon minced chives
Salt and pepper

Mash and blend cheeses. Add butter, cream, eggs, onion, salt and pepper and mix well. Pour into pastry shell; bake at 375° for 30 minutes or until quiche has puffed up and is golden brown on top. Serve hot for hors d'oeuvres or first course. May be served hot or cold as luncheon entree.

Mrs. Louis Chapin (Ann Trumbull)

Sunshine Eggs

4 hard-cooked eggs
2 tablespoons butter
2 tablespoons flour
Salt and pepper

1 cup milk
4 slices Canadian bacon,
lightly broiled
4 slices toast

Crumble egg yolks and set aside; chop whites and set aside. To make cream sauce, melt butter in saucepan over low heat. Mix in flour, salt and pepper. Gradually add milk, stirring constantly. Continue to cook and stir until mixture is smooth and thick. Remove from heat. Add chopped egg whites to cream sauce. Place a slice of Canadian bacon on each slice of toast; top with 1/4 cup creamed mixture. Sprinkle crumbled egg yolks over top. Serves 4.

Mrs. Tom Ball, Jr. (Doris Chambers)

Best Ever Stuffed Eggs

4 hard-cooked eggs
1 teaspoon minced onion
⅛ teaspoon dry mustard

⅛ teaspoon salt
Dash Tabasco
¼ cup mayonnaise

Cut eggs in halves, lengthwise. Remove yolks; force through sieve into bowl. Add remaining ingredients (use more seasoning if desired). Fill centers of egg whites with yolk mixture; chill. Makes 8 halves.

Mrs. P. Michael Wells (Page Thomson)

Party Eggs

8 hard-cooked eggs
1 package frozen chopped
   spinach, cooked
½ teaspoon grated onion
1 teaspoon Worcestershire sauce
Tabasco
2 teaspoons lemon juice

2 tablespoons melted butter
Salt and pepper
1 can condensed cream of
   mushroom soup
1 small jar (8 oz.) Cheez Whiz
Buttered bread crumbs
Parmesan cheese

Slice eggs in half, lengthwise, and remove yolks. Mash yolks. Combine yolks, spinach, onion, Worcestershire, Tabasco, lemon juice, melted butter, salt and pepper. Mix well. Mound yolk mixture into egg whites. Place in a buttered shallow baking dish. Heat soup and Cheez Whiz in double boiler. Pour over stuffed eggs. Cover with buttered bread crumbs, sprinkle with Parmesan cheese and bake in 350° oven until bubbly.

Mrs. Robert E. Clemons (Grayson Cecil)

Eggs Noel

3 eggs
1 tablespoon Durkee's
   sauce

1 tablespoon milk, cream
   or sour cream
Salt and pepper
1 tablespoon butter

Combine eggs, Durkee's, milk, salt and pepper; beat thoroughly. Melt butter in skillet; add egg mixture and scramble. Serve on toast rounds or English muffins, or as scrambled eggs. Serves 2.

Mrs. James Noel (Virginia Grubbs)

Tennessee Eggs

6 large or 8 small
   hard-cooked eggs
1 tablespoon butter
1 tablespoon flour

1 pint heavy cream
Salt and pepper
Buttered bread crumbs

Grate whites and yolks of eggs separately. Melt butter over low heat and stir in flour. Gradually add cream, stirring constantly until sauce thickens. Season with salt and pepper. Mix grated whites with cream sauce and pour into buttered 1-1/2-quart round casserole. Cover with layer of buttered bread crumbs. Add grated yolks and top with another layer of buttered crumbs. Bake in 350° oven for 30-45 minutes. Serves 6.

Mrs. E. Voss Cooksey (Evelyn Dietze)

Shirred Eggs

For each serving:

1 slice bacon	1 teaspoon butter
1 teaspoon bacon drippings	Salt and pepper
1 egg	2 small salted crackers
1 teaspoon milk or cream	Paprika

Fry amount of bacon needed until almost done. While bacon is still limp, line teflon muffin cups with 1 slice bacon each. For each cup add bacon drippings and carefully break in 1 egg. Top each egg with milk, butter, salt and pepper. Crumble crackers over all and sprinkle with paprika. Bake at 350° for about 15 minutes, or until egg whites are set and cracker crumbs toasted. Shirred eggs are ideal for house guests because they can be stored overnight in the refrigerator and baked quickly the next morning. Serve 1 shirred egg per person.

Mrs. R. L. Hawk (Peggy Parker)

Eggs Florentine

1 box frozen chopped spinach	1 cup medium cream sauce
2 tablespoons butter	1½ teaspoons grated onion
2 teaspoons lemon juice	Pinch nutmeg
¼ teaspoon celery salt	6 eggs
Salt and pepper	1 cup grated Swiss cheese

Cook spinach and drain well. Season with butter, lemon juice, celery salt, salt and pepper. Add cream sauce, grated onion and nutmeg to spinach and mix thoroughly. Place in shallow 1-1/2-quart baking dish. Break eggs over spinach mixture. Sprinkle cheese over eggs. Bake at 325° for 15-20 minutes, or until eggs are set. Serves 4-6.

Mrs. Richard R. McKay (Emily Ann Finch)

Eggs au Beurre Noir

4 eggs
2 tablespoons butter
2 tablespoons capers

Butter 2 shirred-egg dishes and place 2 eggs in each. Bake in 325° oven until firm but not hard, about 15 minutes. Brown butter in skillet on top of stove. When almost black, add capers (do not drain). Pour butter and capers over shirred eggs and serve. Serves 2.

Mrs. Pete Gardere (Nancy Penix)

MEAT

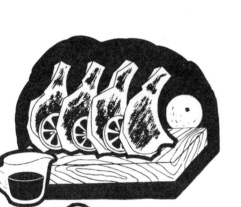

BEEF

PORK

LAMB

VEAL

Hints

MARINADE FOR TENDERIZING MEAT: Combine 1 cup garlic French dressing and 1 tablespoon mixed dried herbs. Soak meat in marinade for several hours before cooking.

TO MAKE BASIC MEAT GRAVY: Lift roast from pan; pour off all but 1/4 cup drippings. Stir in 3 tablespoons flour to make a smooth mixture; brown slightly over low heat, stirring. Gradually stir in 2 cups water or beef bouillon. Add 1/2 teaspoon salt and dash of pepper. Color with Kitchen Bouquet if desired. Stir gravy until smooth and bubbly. If necessary, strain before serving. Makes 2 cups gravy.

MEAT GARNISHES:
Parsley, watercress, mint
Mushrooms, sauteed or stuffed
Roasted potatoes, roasted carrots, broiled tomatoes, pickled beets
Sliced lemons, dipped in chopped parsley
Sliced oranges, topped with mint, currant or cranberry jelly
Sauteed pineapple slices, garnished with jelly or maraschino cherries
Baked apples, cinnamon apples, glazed apple rings, apple sauce
Peach or apricot halves, filled with jelly or mincemeat
Prunes, stuffed with cheese, soaked in sherry
Chilled melon slices, cubes or balls
White grapes, split, seeded, stuffed with Roquefort cheese

HAM GLAZES:
Mix equal parts of jelly and prepared mustard
Combine 2 cups cranberry sauce and 1/2 cup brown sugar
Mix 1/2 cup honey with 1 cup brown sugar and 1/2 cup orange juice
Mix 1 cup honey with 1/2 cup orange marmalade
Combine 1 cup brown sugar and 1/2 cup syrup from canned spiced crab apples. Garnish with heated crab apples.

TO HEAT FRANKFURTERS (SIMMERED): Drop frankfurters into a kettle of boiling water. Cover; remove from heat, or keep heat so low the water never boils. Heat 5-8 minutes. Remove with tongs; never break skins with a fork.

Beef Fillet Sauté

8 slices beef tenderloin, ½" thick
3 tablespoons butter
½ pound fresh mushrooms, sliced
2 tomatoes, peeled and coarsely chopped

2 teaspoons arrowroot
1 tablespoon powdered beef stock base
1 cup hot water
⅔ cup dry red wine
Chopped parsley

Saute meat slices in butter in heavy skillet, about 3 minutes on each side. Remove to a warm platter. Add more butter to skillet if necessary. Saute mushrooms and tomatoes. Combine arrowroot, beef stock base and water; add to skillet. Add wine and stir over low heat. Pour sauce over beef slices. Sprinkle with chopped parsley and serve immediately. Serves 4-6.

Mrs. Richard R. McKay (Emily Ann Finch)

Steak de Burgo

2 tablespoons butter
1 clove garlic, minced
1 tablespoon basil

2 slices beef tenderloin
Salt and pepper

Melt butter in heavy skillet over high heat. Add garlic and basil. Cook mixture quickly until garlic is clear but not brown. Sprinkle meat with salt and pepper, cook in seasoned butter. For rare, cook about 4 minutes on each side. Serves 2.

Mrs. Jack L. Maxwell (Nancy Nelms)

Steak au Poivre

2-2½ pounds boneless top sirloin steak, cut 1" thick
Coarse black pepper
Salt
4-6 tablespoons butter

3 tablespoons olive oil
⅓ cup meat stock
¼ cup dry white wine
2 tablespoons Cognac

Divide steaks into 4 equal pieces. Trim excess fat. Press ground pepper into steaks on both sides, adding just a pinch of salt to each side. Brown steaks quickly on both sides in butter and olive oil. Reduce heat and cook to desired degree of doneness. Place on a hot, buttered platter. Add stock, wine and Cognac to skillet. Stir thoroughly, correct seasoning, and pour over steaks. Serves 4.

Miss Frances Heyck

Rib Roast "Unattended"

1 standing rib roast, any size
Salt and pepper

At noon, pre-heat oven to 375°. Season roast with salt and pepper. Put roast, uncovered, in pre-heated oven. After 1 hour turn off oven and **do not open the door.** Forty minutes before serving, turn oven on again to 375°. Roast will be medium-rare in center and well-done around edges. So convenient for company when you don't know exactly when serving time will be.

Mrs. Terrence G. McGreevy (Beth Connelly)

Roast Calypso

4-5 pound sirloin tip or	1 cup olive oil
rump roast	3 or 4 tablespoons brown sugar
Kitchen Bouquet	½ cup rum
Flour	Dash Worcestershire sauce
4 or 5 limes, juice and rind	1 teaspoon cracked pepper

Rub roast with Kitchen Bouquet and flour. Combine lime juice, lime rind, olive oil, brown sugar, rum, Worcestershire sauce and pepper; bring to a boil. Baste roast every 15 or 20 minutes as it is being cooked over charcoal or in oven. Serves 8-10.

Mrs. H. Irving Schweppe, Jr. (Laura Randall)

Sauerbraten

1 boneless beef chuck roast	2 bay leaves
or top round (about 3 lbs.)	1 teaspoon peppercorns
Water and wine vinegar,	Bacon drippings
in equal parts, to cover meat	5 or 6 gingersnaps, crushed
	Salt

Place meat in a crock or bowl and cover with a marinade of water and wine vinegar. Add bay leaves and peppercorns. Cover tightly and allow to marinate for at least 48 hours in refrigerator. (Roast may be marinated as long as a week.) To prepare roast for cooking, remove from crock, and drain; reserve marinade. (Do not wipe dry.) Brown meat on all sides in bacon drippings over low heat. Drain off grease and add marinade to pan. Cover and cook slowly over low heat, as you would a pot roast, until tender. Remove meat from pan and discard bay leaves. Add gingersnaps to thicken gravy. Season with salt and allow gravy to simmer until it is the desired consistency. Slice meat, reheat it in the gravy, and serve piping hot. Serves 6-8.

Mrs. Rotan McGown (Charlotte Rotan)

Spiced Beef

Juice and rind of 2 lemons
1½ cans beef consomme
1½ cups dry red wine
½ teaspoon pepper
2 teaspoons ground allspice
3 bay leaves, crumbled
2 teaspoons ground cloves
1 teaspoon sage
½ teaspoon thyme
1 teaspoon salt
1 teaspoon monosodium
glutamate
1 beef pot roast (5-6 lbs.)
2 onions
6 carrots
¼ cup olive oil

Peel lemons with vegetable peeler and chop rind. Make marinade by mixing consomme, wine, spices, salt, monsodium glutamate, lemon juice and lemon rind in saucepan. Heat almost to boiling. Pour over roast and refrigerate 24 hours. The next day, let meat come to room temperature; remove meat from marinade and wipe dry. Heat marinade to just boiling and let simmer while preparing onions and carrots. Scrape carrots and quarter lengthwise; chop onions. Brown both in olive oil in large Dutch oven or heavy iron skillet. Put vegetables in pan with marinade. Brown the roast quickly in the same oil. Pour marinade over roast, and bake, covered, approximately 4 hours in 325° oven. Serve on platter garnished with carrots. Strain gravy and thicken with flour to desired consistency. (Leg of lamb or beef brisket may also be prepared by this method.) Serves 10-12.

Mrs. Joseph T. Painter (Ann Hill)

Scallopini Marsala

1½ pounds baby beef, or milk-fed
veal (eye of round or sirloin,
sliced ¼" thick)
½ cup flour
⅓ cup Parmesan cheese
1 teaspoon salt
¼ cup butter
¼ pound fresh mushrooms, sliced
2 green onions with tops,
chopped
½ cup consomme or beef broth
1-2 tablespoons lemon juice
¼ cup Marsala wine
Chopped parsley

Trim meat and cut into 3" or 4" pieces. Pound very thin between sheets of wax paper. Combine flour, cheese and salt. Dredge meat pieces in flour mixture, shaking off as much as possible. In half the butter, brown each slice of meat for about 1 minute on each side. Set aside and keep warm. Add remaining butter to skillet and saute mushrooms and onions until tender. Add consomme, lemon juice and wine. Stir well. Return meat to the skillet and simmer until done, about 30 minutes. (If veal is used, simmer only 10 minutes.) To serve, pour pan juices over meat and sprinkle with parsley. Good with buttered thin spaghetti. Serves 6.

Mrs. H. Edward Maddox, III (Donna Gray)

Beef Brisket

1 beef brisket, boned and trimmed	Garlic salt
Unseasoned meat tenderizer	3 tablespoons Figaro's
Lawry's seasoned salt	liquid smoke
Celery salt	¼ cup Worcestershire sauce

Sprinkle both sides of brisket with meat tenderizer. Sprinkle liberally with seasoned salt, celery and garlic salts. Pour liquid smoke and Worcestershire sauce over roast. Cover and refrigerate for 24 hours. Bake, covered, in 225° oven for 6-8 hours. Drain off pan juices before serving. May be served hot or cold. Roast may be refrigerated, wrapped in foil, and rewarmed very successfully.

Mrs. John L. Hamilton (Ann Lowdon)

Beef Roulades

2½ pounds round steak, ⅛" thick	3 tablespoons butter
¾ pound ground pork	1½ pounds whole, small white
1 teaspoon poultry seasoning	onions, peeled
¾ teaspoon salt	⅓ cup flour
½ clove garlic, crushed	1 tablespoon meat extract paste
2 tablespoons finely	1 can beef bouillon, undiluted
chopped onion	2½ cups red wine
¼ pound salt pork, sliced	1½ pounds fresh mushrooms
thinly into 8 slices; or	1 bay leaf
8 slices bacon	1 tablespoon chopped parsley

Wipe beef with damp paper towels; cut into 8 pieces (approximately 4" x 6"). Combine ground pork, poultry seasoning, salt, garlic and chopped onion. Toss lightly to mix well. Place about 2 tablespoons of mixture on each piece of beef; roll up, starting roll on short side of steak slice. Wrap each roll with a thin strip of salt pork or bacon and tie with a heavy thread. In hot butter in a Dutch oven, brown the roulades on all sides, removing them as they brown. Add the whole onions and brown on all sides. Remove pan from heat. Stir in flour and meat extract paste. Gradually stir in bouillon and wine. Bring to boiling point, stirring constantly. Return roulades to Dutch oven. Add mushrooms and bay leaf. Bake, covered, in a 350° oven for 2 hours, or until meat is tender. If sauce seems thick, thin with a little more wine. To serve, discard bay leaf and remove thread from roulades. Arrange in center of a large heated platter. Surround with the onions and mushrooms. Sprinkle with chopped parsley. Allow 1 or 2 roulades per person. Makes 8 roulades.

Mrs. Frank C. Smith, Jr. (Sally McQueen)

Buffet Beef

2 large onions, sliced
½ pound butter
2 sirloin steaks (about 2 lbs. each) moderately thick
Accent
Salt and pepper

½ teaspoon basil
½ teaspoon marjoram
2 cans (3½ oz. each) browned-in-butter mushrooms, with liquid
1 cup dry red wine

Set electric fry pan for 250°-300°. Saute onions in butter until pale gold and tender; remove and set aside. Bone steaks, remove fat, and cut beef into long, thin strips. Brown steak strips in butter, a few at a time, so each is well browned. When all meat is browned, return to fry pan. Add onions; season generously with Accent, salt, pepper, basil and marjoram. Add mushrooms and just enough mushroom liquid to begin simmering meat. Cover fry pan and let cook until meat is tender, adding mushroom liquid as needed until all is used. When meat is tender, add wine, and let simmer a few more minutes. Although ideally suited for an electric fry pan, this can be prepared on top of the stove. Serve with fluffy, well-buttered white rice tossed with salted cashews or shelled pistachio nuts. Serves 6-8.

Mrs. John L. Hamilton (Ann Lowdon)

Beef Bourguignonne

2 pounds beef (chuck, round, or sirloin) cut in 1" cubes
Salt and pepper
1½ cups Burgundy wine
3 tablespoons cooking oil
1 tablespoon tomato paste
3 tablespoons flour

1 cup rich beef stock
1 clove garlic, crushed
½ bay leaf, crushed
½ pound bacon, diced
16 tiny white onions, or
16 green onions
16 large mushrooms, cut in half

Season beef well with salt and pepper; marinate in wine for about 4 hours. Remove beef, draining well; save marinade. Brown beef cubes on all sides in oil in heavy skillet. Add half of reserved marinade to meat in skillet; simmer until liquid evaporates. Remove meat and keep warm. Add tomato paste to skillet and stir for 1 minute on low heat. Add flour and continue to stir for 2 minutes. Add remaining marinade slowly, stirring until thick. Thin with beef stock to consistency of rich gravy. Add garlic and bay leaf. Season with salt and pepper. Return beef to sauce and cook slowly, covered, for about 1 hour. In separate pan, fry bacon to golden brown, not crisp. In the same pan, saute onions and mushrooms over low heat for 10-15 minutes. Skim off bacon fat. Season with salt and pepper. Mix with beef and sauce just before serving. Serves 4.

Mrs. H. Edward Maddox, III (Donna Gray)

Emerald Isle Stew

½ pound salt pork
2 pounds beef round, or venison
Seasoned flour
12 peppercorns
3 whole cloves
1 bay leaf
1½ cloves garlic, crushed
1 can (8 oz.) tomato sauce

1 cup bouillon
1 large onion, chopped
¼ cup chopped parsley
½ cup dry sherry or dry
  white wine
6 medium potatoes, peeled
  and quartered
6 carrots, scraped and quartered
1 rib celery, chopped

Blanch salt pork by boiling in water a few minutes; slice and saute slowly in Dutch oven. Cut beef into 1" cubes. Discard pork and brown beef in pork drippings. Pour off most of fat. Sprinkle browned meat with well-seasoned flour. Make a spice bag by tying peppercorns, cloves and bay leaf in a piece of cheesecloth. Combine spice bag, garlic, tomato sauce, bouillon, onion and parsley; heat to boiling and pour over meat. Simmer, tightly covered, for at least 2-3 hours (or up to 8 hours, if time allows), or until meat is very tender. Add hot water in small amounts while simmering, if necessary. During last hour of cooking, add wine, potatoes, carrots and celery. This stew is much better if made ahead and allowed to season. Serves 6-8.

Mrs. Fred Spangler (Zillah Mae Ford)

Round Steak Le Blanc

2 large beef round steaks
  (1½-2 lbs. each)
Cooking oil
2 large onions, thinly sliced
6 tablespoons butter
6 tablespoons flour
Salt and pepper

4 tomatoes, sliced; or 1 can
  (1 lb.) tomatoes
2 cups water
2 cloves garlic, crushed
Bay leaf, crushed
⅓ cup chopped parsley
⅓ cup chopped celery

Cut meat into serving-size pieces. Sear meat on both sides in small amount of cooking oil. Remove to plate, reserving oil and juice. In heavy pot, saute onions slightly in butter. Add flour and stir until smooth. Add tomatoes and continue stirring. Add reserved oil and juice. Stir a moment. Add water, garlic, bay leaf, parsley, celery, salt and pepper. Return meat to pot and let come to a boil. Turn heat very low and simmer until tender (at least 1 hour, depending on the meat). Serve with rice, mashed potatoes, grits or noodles. This is even better the second day and freezes well. Serves 6.

Mrs. Henry G. Safford, Jr. (Georgia Howard)

Round Steak with Gingersnap Gravy

2 pounds beef round steak
Seasoned flour
Bacon drippings
2 onions, finely chopped
2 fresh tomatoes, peeled and
  chopped; or 2 cups canned
  tomatoes, well drained

Salt and pepper
2 bay leaves
6 peppercorns
4 whole cloves
2 cups beer
6 gingersnaps, crushed
2 or 3 tablespoons lemon juice

Cut steak into cubes or bite-sized strips. Dredge in seasoned flour and brown on all sides in small amount of bacon drippings. Add onions, and saute until soft. Add tomatoes, salt and pepper. Tie bay leaves, peppercorns and cloves in a cheesecloth bag and add to beef. Stir in beer. Cover and simmer slowly 2-3 hours, or until beef is tender. Thicken gravy with crushed gingersnaps; add lemon juice. Serve with buttered noodles. Serves 4-6.

Mrs. H. Edward Maddox, III (Donna Gray)

Chinese Beef

1 flank steak (about 2 lbs.)
2 tomatoes, peeled
2 green peppers
2 tablespoons olive oil or
  cooking oil
1 clove garlic, crushed
1 teaspoon salt

Dash pepper
¼ teaspoon powdered ginger
¼ cup soy sauce
½ teaspoon sugar
1 tablespoon cornstarch
¼ cup water
1 can (1 lb.) bean sprouts,
  drained

Cut steak in thin strips across the grain of meat. Cut tomatoes in quarters. Remove seeds and ribs from peppers; cut in big chunks. Heat oil in large skillet. Add beef, garlic, salt, pepper and ginger. Sear over high heat until brown on all sides. Add soy sauce and sugar. Cover tightly and cook slowly 5 minutes. Add tomatoes and peppers; bring to a boil, cover, and cook briskly for 5 minutes. Make a smooth paste of cornstarch and water. Add to beef and cook until sauce thickens slightly. Stir in bean sprouts and serve. Serves 6.

Mrs. W. K. King (Rosalie Meek)

Beef Kwangtung

3 tablespoons cooking oil
1 clove garlic, crushed
½ teaspoon powdered ginger
1 cup sliced, fresh mushrooms
1 small celery root, peeled
   and sliced in strips; or 1 cup
   diagonally sliced celery
½ cup sliced green onions

1 pound sirloin steak, cut in thin
   strips across the grain
1 package frozen snow peas
¼ cup soy sauce
2 tomatoes, peeled and cut in
   wedges
2 tablespoons cornstarch
1 cup chicken broth
Rice or Chinese noodles

Heat oil in large skillet. Add garlic, ginger, mushrooms, celery and green onions; saute 2 minutes. Add beef strips and snow peas; cook 3 minutes or until meat browns. Stir in soy sauce and tomatoes. Combine cornstarch and broth; add to mixture in skillet. Cook until sauce is clear and thick. Do not overcook. Serve on rice or Chineese noodles. (French-cut beans may be substituted for the snow peas. Serves 4-6.

Mrs. John E. Chapoton (Sally Eastham)

Pizza Pie

1 package cheese pizza mix
1½ tablespoons cooking oil
1 pound bulk sausage or
   1 pound ground beef

4 ounces Romano cheese
1 can (3 oz.) sliced mushrooms,
   drained
½ teaspoon oregano

Prepare crust as directed on package. Pour cooking oil on 14" pizza pan and spread evenly over pan. Place dough in center of pan, coat well with oil, and flatten out to about 1/2" thickness. Let stand for 15-20 minutes, flatten again, pushing dough out toward edges of pan. Repeat process several times; the more often you let dough rise, the more tender crust will be. (Sounds like more trouble than it is.) Meanwhile, crumble and brown sausage in skillet. Drain and set aside. Grate cheese; set aside. Twenty minutes before serving time, flatten dough over bottom and up sides of pan. Spread pizza sauce from package over dough, stopping within 1/2" of edge of dough. Arrange mushrooms on top of sauce. Sprinkle cheese from package over mushrooms. Sprinkle sausage evenly over top and cover with grated Romano cheese. Sprinkle with oregano. Bake for 20 minutes at 425°. Remove from oven and run spatula under pie to loosen from pan. Cut into wedges, using kitchen scissors. Serves 4.

Mrs. Suzanne S. Braden (Suzanne Schmidt)

Italian Meatballs and Spaghetti

MEATBALLS:

1 ½ pounds ground round steak
2 eggs
1 teaspoon salt
1 medium onion, finely
chopped
⅓ cup Parmesan cheese
1 teaspoon parsley flakes
4 slices bread
Olive oil for browning

1 package (7 oz.) thin
spaghetti, cooked

SAUCE:

5 cups canned tomatoes,
chopped, with juice
2 cans (6 oz. each) tomato paste
2 tomato-paste cans water
3 or 4 cloves garlic, crushed
2 cans (4 oz. each) mushrooms,
with liquid
1 teaspoon basil
1 teaspoon parsley flakes
2 teaspoons sugar
2 teaspoons salt
2 small bay leaves
½ cup dry red wine

Put all meatball ingredients, except bread, into large bowl. Cover bread with water and soak for 1 minute; squeeze out water, and add to meatball ingredients. Mix well. Shape into balls the size of golf balls. Brown quickly on all sides in hot olive oil in Dutch oven. (About 10 can be browned at once, as they brown quickly.) Turn them with a spoon so they won't break. When meatballs are browned, remove and set aside. Combine all sauce ingredients in same pan and simmer 1/2 hour, covered. Remove bay leaves. Add meatballs to sauce, and simmer 30 minutes more. Serve over cooked spaghetti. Serves 6 generously.

Mrs. H. Edward Maddox, III (Donna Gray)

Italian Spaghetti

4 slices bacon
1 onion, chopped
2 small cloves garlic,
crushed
1 green pepper, chopped
2 ribs celery, chopped
1 pound ground beef
1 can condensed tomato soup
1 can (6 oz.) tomato paste
1 tomato paste-can water
1 can (3 oz.) mushrooms,
with liquid
1 teaspoon salt
Pepper
½ teaspoon oregano
2 tablespoons Parmesan cheese
1 package (10 oz.) thin
spaghetti, cooked

Fry bacon crisp; remove and crumble. To the bacon drippings, add onion, garlic, green pepper and celery. Add meat and brown. Add soup, tomato paste, water, mushrooms, salt, pepper, oregano, cheese and crumbled bacon. Simmer slowly 30 minutes. Serve over hot spaghetti. Serves 6.

Mrs. Garry S. Dundas (Barbara Bering)

Spaghetti with Meat Sauce

¼ cup chopped onion
1 clove garlic, crushed
½ cup chopped celery
½ cup chopped green pepper
2 or 3 tablespoons bacon
   drippings or olive oil
1 pound ground beef
1 bay leaf
2 teaspoons salt

1 teaspoon B.V. meat extract
Tabasco
1 teaspoon Worcestershire sauce
2 cans (8 oz. each) tomato sauce
1 can (3 oz.) mushrooms
   with liquid
1 package (10 oz.) spaghetti,
   cooked

Slightly saute onion, garlic, celery and green pepper in oil. Remove vegetables from skillet; add meat and brown. Stir in sauteed vegetables, bay leaf, salt, meat extract, Tabasco, Worcestershire sauce, tomato sauce and mushrooms. Simmer 1-1/2 hours, covered. Remove bay leaf. Skim off excess fat if necessary. Serve sauce over spaghetti. Serves 6.

Mrs. Fletcher H. Etheridge (Carolyn Smith)

Lazy Lasagne

2 pounds ground round steak
1 teaspoon salt
1 envelope Lawry's spaghetti
   sauce mix
2 cans (1 lb. each) tomatoes
1 can (15 oz.) tomato sauce

½ teaspoon basil
Grated Parmesan cheese
1 package (8 oz.) lasagne
   noodles
2 packages (6 oz. each) sliced
   Mozzarella cheese

In Dutch oven or large saucepan, brown meat in salt. Add spaghetti sauce mix, tomatoes, tomato sauce, basil and a generous sprinkling of Parmesan cheese. Simmer 30 minutes. Cook lasagne noodles just until tender. In 9" x 11" casserole, layer meat sauce, noodles, and Mozzarella cheese. Sprinkle with Parmesan cheese. Repeat layers, saving enough meat sauce to pour over top layer. Bake in 300°-325° oven for 20 minutes. This is a simplified version of lasagne, yet has an authentic taste; better by far if made the day before or at least early in the morning, and then baked just before serving. Serves 6-8.

Mrs. John L. Hamilton (Ann Lowdon)

Lasagne

2 cans (1 lb. each) tomatoes	2 pounds ground beef chuck
4 cans (8 oz. each) tomato sauce	2 teaspoons monosodium
2 tablespoons sugar	glutamate
2 teaspoons salt	1 can (6 oz.) tomato paste
1 tablespoon oregano	1 tomato paste-can water
¼ teaspoon pepper	1 pound lasagne noodles
2 teaspoons onion salt	2 egg whites, slightly beaten
1 can (4 oz.) mushrooms,	1½ pounds Ricotta cheese
drained	1½ cups grated Parmesan
½ cup olive oil	cheese
2 cups minced onion	1 pound Mozzarella cheese,
2 cloves garlic, crushed	thinly sliced

Combine tomatoes, tomato sauce, 1 tablespoon sugar, salt, oregano, pepper, onion salt and mushrooms; simmer uncovered for 10 minutes. Pour olive oil into heavy skillet and saute onions, garlic and meat. Add monosodium glutamate, tomato paste and water. In large heavy pan, combine tomato mixture with meat mixture; simmer slowly 2-3 hours, or until thick. Meanwhile, cook lasagne noodles in salted water and drain. Combine egg whites, remaining 1 tablespoon sugar and Ricotta cheese. In large, deep rectangular casserole, layer noodles, Ricotta cheese mixture, meat sauce, Parmesan cheese, and Mozzarella cheese. Repeat layers. Cover casserole and bake at 350° for 1 hour. Uncover for last 15 minutes of baking. Let stand for 15 minutes before serving. This casserole may be prepared ahead and baked just before serving. Serves 10-12.

Mrs. Bass C. Wallace (Julia Picton)

Fandango

1 pound lean, ground beef	1 can condensed cream of
1 medium onion, chopped	celery soup
1 can (8 oz.) mushrooms, drained	1 cup sour cream
1 or 2 cloves garlic, crushed	1 tablespoon uncooked rice
1 teaspoon oregano	Salt and pepper
2 packages frozen chopped	1 package (6 oz.) sliced
spinach, thawed	Mozzarella cheese

Brown meat, onion, mushrooms, garlic and oregano. Spoon into 2-quart casserole. Stir in spinach, soup, sour cream, rice, salt and pepper. Put cheese (grated, or cut in strips) on top of casserole. Bake in 350° oven for 35-45 minutes. Serves 4.

Mrs. Richard R. Nelson, Jr. (Marjorie Shepherd)

Hamburger Stroganoff

½ cup minced onion
1 clove garlic, crushed
¼ cup butter
1 pound ground beef
2 tablespoons flour
2 teaspoons salt
¼ teaspoon pepper

1 can (8 oz.) sliced mushrooms, drained
1 can condensed cream of chicken soup
1 cup sour cream
2 tablespoons minced parsley
Rice or Chinese noodles

Saute onion and garlic in butter over medium heat. Add meat and brown. Add flour, salt, pepper and mushrooms. Cook 5 minutes. Add soup and simmer, uncovered, 10 minutes. Stir in sour cream and heat thoroughly. Sprinkle with parsley. Serve over rice or Chinese noodles. Meat mixture may be cooked early in day. Do not add sour cream and parsley until reheating for serving. Serves 4.

Mrs. F. Tarrant Fendley, Jr. (Mary Ann Elliott)

Tallarene George

1 pound ground round steak
1 onion, chopped
2 tablespoons cooking oil
5 cans (8 oz. each) tomato sauce
6 ounces (3½ cups) uncooked noodles

1 can (1 lb.) creamed corn
1 can (6 oz.) pitted ripe olives, halved
Salt and pepper
½ pound Swiss cheese, grated

Brown meat and onion in oil in Dutch oven. Add tomato sauce and noodles; cook, covered, until noodles are tender, stirring occasionally. Add corn and olives. Season with salt and pepper. Spoon into casserole, and top with grated cheese. (If deep casserole is used, make 2 layers of meat mixture and cheese.) Bake at 350° for about 30 minutes, until bubbly. Serves 6.

Mrs. John H. Lindsey (Sara Houstoun)

Mardi - Gras Hash

6 strips bacon	1 can (6 oz.) tomato paste
1 package (5 oz.) noodles	1 can (1 lb.) green peas, drained
⅓ cup chopped onion	2 cans (3 oz. each) mushrooms,
⅓ cup chopped green pepper	drained
⅓ cup chopped celery	1 teaspoon Worcestershire sauce
1½ pounds lean ground beef	Salt and pepper
1 pound American cheese, grated	1 cup soft bread crumbs

Fry bacon crisp; crumble and set aside. Reserve bacon drippings. Cook noodles just underdone in boiling salted water, and drain. Saute onion, green pepper, celery and meat in bacon drippings until brown. Add half of the grated cheese and stir until melted. Mix in tomato paste, green peas, mushrooms and Worcestershire sauce. Add cooked noodles; season with salt and pepper. Put in 2-quart baking dish. Sprinkle with remaining cheese, cover with bread crumbs, and sprinkle bacon over all. Bake in 300° oven for 45 minutes. Serves 6-8.

Mrs. Victor F. Grima (Chlotille Cole)

Italian Casserole

8 ounces small uncooked noodles	1 large package (8 oz.) cream
1 tablespoon butter	cheese, softened
1 pound ground chuck	¼ cup sour cream
2 cans (8 oz. each) tomato	⅓ cup sliced green onions
sauce	1 tablespoon minced green
Salt and pepper	pepper
1 cup creamed cottage cheese	2 tablespoons butter, melted

Cook noodles and drain. Saute meat in 1 tablespoon butter until browned. Stir in tomato sauce. Season with salt and pepper. Remove from heat and set aside. In a bowl combine cottage cheese, cream cheese, sour cream, green onions and green pepper. Spread half of the noodles in a 2-quart casserole. Cover with cheese mixture. Add remaining noodles. Pour 2 tablespoons melted butter over noodles. Spread meat mixture over all. Bake, covered, in 350° oven for 30 minutes. This casserole may be prepared early in the day, refrigerated, and baked just before serving. Serves 6.

Mrs. Ormonde Smith, Jr. (Margaret Plunkett)

Five Spice Beef 'N Rice

1 pound ground beef
1 tablespoon olive oil
¾ cup finely chopped onion
1½ teaspoons salt
Dash pepper
⅛ teaspoon garlic powder
⅛ teaspoon thyme
⅛ teaspoon oregano

1 small bay leaf
1 can condensed cream of
  mushroom soup
1 can (1 lb.) tomatoes
1 cup uncooked rice
2 or 3 slices American cheese,
  cut into ½" strips
Sliced, stuffed olives, for garnish

Brown meat in oil; add onion and cook until tender. Stir in seasonings, soup and tomatoes. Cook rice until almost done, drain, and add to beef mixture. Bring to a boil, reduce heat, simmer 5 minutes. Stir occasionally. Spoon into a 1-1/2 quart baking dish. Crisscross cheese on top. Broil until cheese melts. Garnish with olives. Serves 6.

Mrs. C. Pharr Duson, Jr. (Betty Tomforde)

"Top-of-Stove" Stuffed Peppers

2½ pounds ground lean chuck
1 medium onion, chopped
1 can condensed black bean soup
1½ teaspoons chili powder
1 teaspoon sugar
1 teaspoon pepper
2 tablespoons Worcestershire
  sauce or A-1 sauce
2 tablespoons dry red wine

1 teaspoon salt
½ teaspoon garlic powder
  (optional)
½ teaspoon ground celery seed
2 tablespoons chopped parsley
4 large bell peppers, halved
  lengthwise
Catsup

Brown meat and onion together without additional fat in large Dutch oven. Drain fat from meat. Add other ingredients, except bell peppers and catsup. Cover, and cook slowly for 10-15 minutes. Stir occasionally. Wash and cut peppers in half, lengthwise. Remove and discard seeds, veins and stems. Heap meat mixture into peppers. Decorate tops with dabs of catsup. Cover bottom of Dutch oven with 1/4" water. Carefully place stuffed peppers in water. Cover tightly with heavy lid, and steam over medium heat for 10-12 minutes, until peppers are tender but not soft (much better if they are slightly crisp). Meat filling can be made a day ahead and re-heated before filling peppers. Allow 1 or 2 stuffed pepper halves per serving.

Mrs. Carroll E. Church (Jean-Marie Ormondroyd)

Stuffed Peppers

½ cup uncooked rice
6 large green peppers
1 pound ground beef
1 medium onion, chopped
1 cup finely diced celery
2 tablespoons bacon drippings
1½ cups grated Cheddar cheese
1½ teaspoons celery seed

½ to ¾ can Rotel tomatoes and
green chilies (10 oz. can)
Salt and pepper
1 can condensed tomato soup
1 soup-can water, or
a little more
1 can (8 oz.) tomato sauce

Cook rice until tender. Cut tops off peppers, remove seeds, and boil pepper cases for 5 minutes. Drain. Saute beef, onion and celery in bacon drippings. Add rice, 1 cup grated cheese, celery seed and tomatoes. Season with salt and pepper. Stuff pepper cases with mixture and place in greased, or foil-lined, baking dish. Make a sauce by mixing soup, water, tomato sauce and remaining 1/2 cup grated cheese; pour over peppers. Bake, uncovered, in 350° oven for about 45 minutes. Baste several times during cooking. The stuffed peppers can be frozen before cooking. Freeze separately in plastic bags with a generous amount of sauce over each pepper. Serves 6.

Mrs. H. D. McCament (Margaret Lester)

Horton Hamburger Hash

1 eggplant
3 ripe tomatoes
2 large onions
½ cup butter
(more needed later)

¾ cup flour
1 teaspoon salt
1 teaspoon coarsely ground
pepper
1 pound ground beef

Peel eggplant, tomatoes and onions; slice into 1/4" rounds. Heat butter in heavy skillet. Combine flour, salt and pepper. Dip eggplant slices in flour mixture and saute in butter until lightly browned. Remove eggplant from skillet and place in bottom of baking dish. Dip tomato slices in flour mixture and saute in more butter until lightly browned. Remove tomatoes from skillet and place in casserole over eggplant. Saute onion slices in more butter until lightly browned. Remove onions from skillet and place in casserole. Saute ground beef in same butter (adding more, if necessary), until lightly browned. Sprinkle meat over top of casserole. Bake in 300°-325° oven for 1 hour, or until brown on top. Can be made ahead of time and heated before serving; is even better reheated. Serves 4-6.

Mrs. J. L. Coffman (Glenn Errol Horton)

Stuffed Cabbage Leaves

8 large cabbage leaves
⅓ cup uncooked rice
1 pound ground beef
1 clove garlic, crushed
1 onion, finely chopped

2 tablespoons minced parsley
1 teaspoon salt
⅛ teaspoon pepper
⅛ teaspoon cayenne

Cook cabbage leaves in boiling, salted water for 5 minutes. Drain and cut out thick center spines. Cook rice until tender. Combine meat, rice, garlic, onion, parsley, salt, pepper and cayenne. Place a generous, rounded spoonful of meat mixture on each cabbage leaf. Fold leaf around filling, secure with toothpicks. Arrange in casserole, folded side down. Cover with the following sauce:

SAUCE

1 clove garlic; crushed
2 medium onions, chopped
2 tablespoons butter
1 large can (35 oz.) tomatoes
  with liquid
½ cup beef broth
½ cup brown sugar
1 tablespoon tarragon vinegar

2 tablespoons lemon juice
1½ teaspoons salt
¼ teaspoon pepper
1 bay leaf
¼ teaspoon thyme
1 teaspoon caraway seeds
2 tablespoons honey
2 tablespoons sour cream

Saute garlic and onions in butter until lightly browned. Add tomatoes, broth, brown sugar, vinegar, lemon juice, salt, pepper, bay leaf, thyme and caraway seeds. Simmer for 10 minutes. Spoon sauce over cabbage rolls. Bake in covered casserole at 350° for 1 hour. Uncover; stir honey and sour cream into sauce. Bake 30 minutes more. This casserole can be frozen successfully. If preparing for freezer, cool, wrap, and freeze before adding honey and sour cream. On serving day, uncover casserole and heat at 350° for 1 hour, stirring in honey and sour cream after 30 minutes. Serves 4.

Mrs. Jane B. Pinckard (Jane Burton)

Supper Sensation

2 tablespoons butter
1 large onion, chopped
2 pounds ground round steak
2 cans (1 lb. each) tomatoes
2 cans condensed tomato soup
¼ teaspoon basil
1 teaspoon paprika
¼ teaspoon cayenne

1 bay leaf, crushed
3 tablespoons chili powder
⅛ teaspoon garlic powder
2 teaspoons salt
2 cans (1 lb. each) kidney
   beans, with liquid
Corn bread or rice

Melt butter, add onion and meat; cook until brown, stirring often. Add tomatoes, soup, basil, paprika, cayenne, bay leaf and chili powder. Simmer 1 hour. Stir garlic powder, salt and beans into mixture. Heat thoroughly. Serve on lightly buttered squares of hot corn bread or on rice. Serves 10.

Mrs. John L. Hamilton (Ann Lowdon)

Beef - Zucchini Italienne

3 tablespoons butter
3 tablespoons flour
¾ pound ground round steak
1 can (16 oz.) tomatoes,
   chopped
½ green pepper, chopped

2 green onions with tops, minced
½ teaspoon basil
1 bay leaf, crushed
Salt and pepper
5 or 6 small zucchini
1 cup grated cheese (optional)

Melt butter and blend in flour. Add all other ingredients, except zucchini and cheese. Cook slowly for about 8 minutes, breaking up meat well. Slice zucchini thin; do not peel. Parboil 2-3 minutes and drain well. Arrange zucchini in shallow, buttered casserole and pour meat sauce over it. Sprinkle with grated cheese, if desired. Bake 30 minutes at 350°. Serves 4.

Mrs. Frank C. Smith, Jr. (Sally McQueen)

Onion Meat Loaf

½ pound ground beef
½ pound ground veal
½ pound ground pork or sausage
1 can (1 lb.) tomatoes

1 envelope onion soup mix
1 onion, chopped
1 cup dry cereal (cornflakes,
   Rice Krispies, etc.)

Mix all ingredients together and blend well. Shape into loaf, and bake at 350° for about 1 hour. Serves 6-8.

Mrs. Robert B. Crouch (Nancy Wencke)

Meat Loaf

3 pounds ground chuck
1 large potato, peeled and grated
1 large green pepper, finely chopped
1 large onion, finely chopped
4 ribs celery, finely chopped
2 cloves garlic, crushed

1 can (1 lb.) tomatoes, drained and chopped
1 egg, beaten
Salt and pepper
Accent
3 strips bacon
1 can (8 oz.) tomato sauce

Mix together all ingredients, except bacon and tomato sauce. Shape into a long oval loaf. Top with strips of bacon. Bake at 325° for about 30 minutes. Skim off fat. Spread tomato sauce over meat loaf and continue baking for 1 hour. Serves 10-12.

Mrs. Jack T. Currie (Dorothy Peek)

Beef Pie Surprise

1 unbaked 9-inch pastry shell
1 can (1 lb.) Italian style tomatoes, well drained
½ cup (scant) tomato paste
½ cup raisins
½ teaspoon oregano
½ teaspoon paprika

1 teaspoon salt
¼ teaspoon allspice
¼ teaspoon pepper
1 onion, finely minced
2 tablespoons butter
1 pound ground beef
4 ounces Blue cheese, crumbled

Pre-bake pastry shell for 5 minutes in 425° oven. Combine tomatoes, tomato paste, raisins and seasonings. Brown onion slightly in butter and add to tomato mixture. Brown beef in same pan. Add tomato mixture to beef and simmer slowly for 1-2 hours. Add cheese and stir thoroughly. Pour into pastry shell. Bake in 425° oven for 30 minutes. Serves 6.

Mrs. O. Strother Simpson (Betty Eastham)

Hamburger Quiche

1 unbaked 9-inch pastry shell
½ cup chopped onion
¼ cup chopped green pepper
1 tablespoon cooking oil
1 pound lean ground beef
1 can condensed tomato soup
½ cup soft bread crumbs

1 cup (or more) grated
   Cheddar cheese
1 egg, beaten
½ teaspoon salt
¼ teaspoon pepper
½ teaspoon basil
1 large fresh tomato, peeled

Saute onion and green pepper in oil until soft. Add beef and brown well. Remove pan from heat. Combine soup, bread crumbs, 1/2 cup cheese, egg, salt, pepper and basil; add to meat and stir until well blended. Pour mixture into pastry shell. Bake at 375° for 30-40 minutes, or until pie crust is done and a little browned. Cut the tomato into eighths and arrange in a circle over top of pie. Sprinkle remaining grated cheese over all and return to oven for 3-5 minutes to melt cheese. Serves 4-6.

Mrs. Mervyn Lea Rudee (Betsy Eager)

Barbecued Hash

2 tablespoons chopped onion
2 tablespoons chopped green
   pepper
1 small clove garlic, crushed
Bacon drippings or oil
Leftover gravy

2 cups diced, leftover roast
1½ cups diced potatoes
1 teaspoon chili powder
1 tablespoon Worcestershire
   sauce
3 tablespoons catsup
Salt and pepper

Saute onion, green pepper and garlic in small amount of bacon drippings or oil. Add leftover gravy plus water to make about 1-1/2 cups liquid. Add all other ingredients and simmer in a covered skillet for about 30 minutes, or until potatoes are done. Serves 3-4.

Mrs. Charles W. Dabney, Jr. (Julia Vinson)

Foursome Favorite

4 Pepperidge Farm puff
   pastry shells
1 can (1 lb.) artichoke hearts,
   drained
2 packages (3 oz. each)
   smoked beef

1 cup sour cream
1 can condensed cream of
   mushroom soup
1 can (4½ oz.) chopped ripe
   olives, drained
Sherry to taste

Bake pastry shells. Combine remaining ingredients in large saucepan. Simmer, do not boil, until thoroughly heated. Serve in pastry shells. Serves 4.

Mrs. William C. Braden, Jr. (Dorothy Jane Reed)

Corned Beef Hash

1 small onion, chopped	1 can (12 oz.) corned beef
2 tablespoons bacon drippings	1 can (4 oz.) mushroom stems
1 medium potato, boiled in	and pieces, drained
jacket	1 cup cream

Saute onion in bacon drippings until transparent, but not brown. Peel and dice potato; add to skillet. Add corned beef (break it up well), mushrooms and cream to skillet. Mix well. Heat slowly over low heat, stirring occasionally, until cream thickens. This will take about 30 minutes. No salt or pepper is necessary. Good for supper or breakfast. Serves 4.

Mrs. Thomas W. Moore (Lila Godwin)

Spanish Sweetbreads

2½-3 pounds sweetbreads	¾ cup consomme
¼ cup white vinegar	1 teaspoon salt
2 cups sliced carrots	Pepper
2 cups chopped celery	2 tablespoons powdered
2 cups chopped onions	horseradish
Vegetable oil	Butter
1 can (1 lb.) tomatoes	1 package (10 oz.) egg or
1 can (6 oz.) tomato paste	spinach noodles
	Parsley for garnish

To prepare sweetbreads for cooking, cover with ice water for at least 1 hour. Drain. Cover with fresh water and add vinegar. Bring to a boil; cover. Boil 3-5 minutes. Plunge into ice water. Remove membranes and connecting tissue.

Cook carrots, celery and onion, separately, in small amount of vegetable oil, in order to retain color, shape and flavor. (Cook onion only until transparent.) Transfer vegetables to top of large double boiler. Mash tomatoes and add to vegetables; add tomato paste and consomme. Add salt and pepper. Cook over boiling water for 1 hour (or a little longer). Add most of the horseradish, but be sure to taste, as horseradish varies in strength. (It is the most important ingredient in this recipe.) Cut sweetbreads into bite-sized pieces. Fry in butter until browned. Add to tomato mixture, re-heat and serve. (Sweetbreads will become soggy if allowed to sit in tomato mixture.) To serve, mound cooked noodles in center of platter, surround with sweetbread mixture, and garnish with parsley. Serve with bowl of grated Parmesan cheese. Serves 6-8.

Mrs. Ralph Ellis Gunn (Esme Patterson)

Sausage - Liver Loaf

1 pound calf liver, finely chopped	1 tablespoon lemon juice
½ pound bulk pork sausage	1 teaspoon salt
1 medium onion, chopped	⅛ teaspoon pepper
1 cup dry bread crumbs	1 teaspoon celery salt
1 teaspoon Worcestershire	2 eggs, beaten
sauce	4 slices bacon

Mix all ingredients except bacon and form into small loaf. Top with bacon strips, and bake in 350° oven for 45 minutes. Serves 6-8.

Mrs. Lewis N. White (Amelia Duncan)

Tongue

1 calf tongue	2 tablespoons butter
1 carrot, quartered	2 tablespoons flour
1 onion, quartered	½ can condensed mushroom soup
1 rib celery, with leaves	1 medium onion, diced
1 bay leaf	Sherry

In salted water to cover, boil tongue with carrot, onion, celery and bay leaf until tender. Remove tongue; strain and reserve broth. Skin and slice the tongue. Make sauce with butter, flour and about 1 cup broth. Stir in soup and add diced onion. Heat 20 minutes; add sherry to taste. Serve sauce over tongue slices. This is even enjoyed by people who think they don't like tongue. Serves 4.

Miss Harriet Jean Turner

Saucy Tongue

1 calf tongue	Whole cloves
Salt	1 jar (10 oz.) blackberry jelly
1 tablespoon pickling spice	plus 1 cup water, OR
(optional)	1 jar (10 oz.) currant jelly
2 bay leaves	plus 1 cup dry red wine
2 ribs celery with tops	Juice of 1 lemon

In salted water to cover, boil tongue with pickling spice, bay leaves and celery. When tender, skin and trim tongue, and stick well with cloves. Place tongue in buttered baking dish. Melt blackberry jelly with water or currant jelly with wine. Pour over tongue. Squeeze lemon juice over all. Bake 20 minutes in 350° oven, basting frequently with pan juice. Serves 4.

Mrs. John Harris Meyers (Alice Baker Jones)

Pork Roast

1 pork loin roast (4-5 lbs.)	Garlic powder
2 tablespoons dry mustard	1 cup sherry
2 teaspoons thyme	¾ cup Kikkoman soy sauce
1 teaspoon salt	4 cloves garlic
½ teaspoon pepper	2 teaspoons ground ginger

Place roast in shallow dish and rub well with mixture of dry mustard and thyme. Punch holes about 4" apart in the roast and fill with salt, pepper and a little garlic powder. Combine sherry, soy sauce, garlic and ginger; pour over meat. Let stand 3-4 hours at room temperature, or overnight in refrigerator, turning at least once. Place roast on rack in shallow roasting pan. Bake, uncovered, at 325° for 2-1/2 to 3 hours, or until meat thermometer registers 185°. Serve with currant sauce. Serves 6-8.

CURRANT SAUCE

1 jar (10 oz.) currant jelly
1 tablespoon soy sauce
2 tablespoons sherry

Melt jelly, add soy sauce and sherry. Simmer for 2 minutes. Serve with pork roast.

Mrs. James A. Baker, Jr. (Bonner Means)

Pork Tenderloin

2 pork tenderloins (2-3 lbs. each)	6 small white onions
½ clove garlic, slivered	Melted butter
Salt and pepper	2 tablespoons (or more) orange marmalade

Make slits in meat and insert slivers of garlic. Place meat in 8" x 10" baking pan. Salt and pepper generously. Arrange onions around meat. Insert meat thermometer in largest tenderloin and roast at 325° until thermometer registers 185° (or allow 40 minutes per pound). Turn onions occasionally and brush them with butter. After 30 minutes spread meat liberally with orange marmalade. Serves 6.

Mrs. H. Edward Maddox, III (Donna Gray)

Florida Pork Loin

1 pork loin roast (3-4 lbs.)   1 cup orange juice
2 teaspoons salt   1 cup water
½ teaspoon Tabasco   1 lemon, thinly sliced
¼ cup finely chopped onion

Rub roast with salt and Tabasco. Place in skillet with onion, and brown on all sides. Remove roast to baking dish. Bake, uncovered, at 300° for 2 hours or until done. Baste frequently with orange juice and water. During last 30 minutes of baking, arrange lemon slices over roast. (This pork is also good cold, made into sandwiches using raisin bread.) Serves 4-6.

Mrs. Walter Browne Baker (Adelaide Lovett)

Pork Chops

6 pork chops   6 teaspoons brown sugar
Salt and pepper   1 cup water
6 slices apple   2 tablespoons vinegar
6 slices onion   ½ cup raisins

Brown pork chops. Season with salt and pepper. Arrange in baking dish. On top of each chop place an apple slice, an onion slice, and a teaspoon brown sugar. Stir water, vinegar and raisins into skillet with pork chop drippings. Bring to a boil; pour over chops. Bake, uncovered, in 350° oven for 1 hour, or until tender. Makes 6 servings.

Mrs. J. Philip Wandel (Priscilla Rodman)

Baked Pork Chops

4 very thick, center cut, pork chops   ½ cup cooking oil
Flour   ½ cup apple jelly
Salt and pepper   1 cup dry white wine

Heavily dredge pork chops in flour seasoned with salt and pepper. Brown chops on both sides in cooking oil; drain. Arrange in baking dish. Heat apple jelly; add wine. Pour over chops, cover, and bake at 325° for 3 hours. Serves 4.

Mrs. Gentry Kidd (Winifred Crawford)

Chili Pork Chops

4 lean pork chops
1 can (20 oz.) creamed corn
½ teaspoon salt
2 teaspoons chili powder
⅛ teaspoon pepper

1 teaspoon instant minced
  onion
¼ cup sweet pepper flakes
½ cup bread crumbs
2 tablespoons melted butter

Trim excess fat from pork chops. Rub each side with a little salt and pepper. Brown chops in melted pork fat. Place in casserole. Combine corn, salt, chili powder, pepper, onion and pepper flakes; spoon over chops. Cover casserole and bake 35 minutes in 350° oven. Blend bread crumbs with melted butter; sprinkle over casserole and bake, uncovered, 15 minutes longer. Serves 4.

Mrs. Sam E. McHard, Jr. (Lois Vincent)

Pork Chops Creole

6 loin pork chops, 1" thick
Flour
1 medium onion, chopped
1 can (1 lb.) tomatoes
½ green pepper, chopped

1 teaspoon salt
¼ teaspoon pepper
1½ teaspoons Worcestershire
  sauce
1 cup uncooked rice

Dust pork chops on both sides with flour. In a lightly greased skillet, saute pork chops on each side until golden brown. Remove and keep warm. Drain excess fat from skillet if necessary and saute onion until tender. Add tomatoes, green pepper, salt, pepper and Worcestershire sauce. Return pork chops to tomato mixture and simmer, covered, 1 hour or until tender. Meanwhile, cook rice. Arrange pork chops on a heated platter. Cover chops with hot fluffy rice; then pour the tomato sauce over all. Makes 6 servings.

Mrs. Charles B. Williams (Bobbie Ruth Richardson)

Yankee Barbecued Spareribs

4 pounds meaty pork ribs
Salt and pepper
1 lemon, thinly sliced
1 large onion, chopped
1 teaspoon chili powder
1 teaspoon celery seed

¼ cup brown sugar
¼ cup vinegar or lemon juice
1 tablespoon Worcestershire
  sauce
1 cup catsup
2 cups water

Continued on next page

Spread ribs, meaty side up, in roasting pan. Sprinkle with salt and pepper. Arrange lemon slices on ribs and brown, uncovered, in 450° oven for 45 minutes. Mix remaining ingredients together to make sauce. Pour over ribs. Reduce heat to 350° and continue baking for 1-1/2 hours. Do not cover, but baste and turn ribs occasionally. If sauce gets too thick, add a little water. Serves 4.

Mrs. W. S. Perkins (Sue Scott)

Fruited Sweet-and-Sour Pork

1½ pounds pork, sliced in
  thin strips
2 tablespoons butter
1 can (13½ oz.) pineapple
  tidbits with syrup
½ cup bottled Russian dressing
¾ cup water

2 tablespoons cornstarch
1½ tablespoons soy sauce
1 teaspoon vinegar
¼ teaspoon salt
1 medium green pepper,
  thinly sliced
½ cup thinly sliced onion

Saute pork in butter for 2-3 minutes, until meat is browned. Drain pineapple, reserving 3/4 cup syrup. Combine syrup, Russian dressing, water, cornstarch, soy sauce, vinegar and salt. Pour over meat and stir until thickened. Cover and simmer over low heat 30 minutes, or until meat is tender. Add green pepper, onion and pineapple tidbits. Cover and heat 5 minutes. Serve over rice. Serves 6.

Mrs. Pete Gardere (Nancy Penix)

Quick Chop Suey

2 cups cubed cooked pork, veal,
  chicken or beef
Butter
½ cup sliced onion
½ cup sliced green pepper
1 cup diagonally sliced celery
1 can (1 lb.) bean sprouts, drained
1 can (5 oz.) water chestnuts,
  drained and sliced

1 can (5 oz.) bamboo shoots,
  drained
1 cup liquid reserved from
  canned vegetables
1 tablespoon cornstarch
½ teaspoon salt
2 tablespoons soy sauce
Mushrooms and almonds
  (optional)

Brown meat quickly in a little butter. Add onion, green pepper and celery; cook 3 minutes. Combine reserved liquid from vegetables with cornstarch. Add to meat, stirring until thickened. Add bean sprouts, water chestnuts, bamboo shoots, salt and soy sauce. (Add mushrooms or almonds if desired.) Heat; serve with rice. Serves 6.

Mrs. Lewis N. White (Amelia Duncan)

Ham Loaf

2 eggs, beaten	Milk
1 pound ground fresh pork	¼ cup vinegar
1 pound ground ham	½ cup brown sugar
1 cup bread crumbs	6 tablespoons currant jelly

Mix well-beaten eggs, pork and ham. Soften bread crumbs in small amount of milk; add to meat mixture and mix well. Form into loaf. Make basting sauce by stirring vinegar, brown sugar and jelly over low heat until jelly melts; add water for desired consistency. Bake ham loaf in 350° oven for 2 hours, basting frequently. Serves 6-8.

Mrs. Lovett Baker (Joanne Prescott)

Cecile's Ham Loaf with Horseradish Sauce

2 pounds ground, lean, fresh pork	½ cup bread crumbs
1 pound ground ham	½ teaspoon pepper
1 teaspoon minced celery	1 cup tomato juice

Mix pork, ham, celery, bread crumbs and pepper together. Form into loaf. Make a depression in center of loaf and pour in tomato juice. Bake in 300° oven for 2 to 2-1/2 hours. Serve with Horseradish Sauce. Serves 8-10.

HORSERADISH SAUCE

1 bottle (6 oz.) prepared horseradish	½ cup mayonnaise
1 bottle (2 oz.) capers, drained	2 tablespoons Shedd's or Durkee's sauce
1 cup heavy cream	½ teaspoon cayenne
	½ teaspoon black pepper

Mix all ingredients together. Chill for several hours and serve with ham loaf.

Mrs. Harold E. Daniels (Gayle Garth)

Maharanee's Breakfast Entrée

4 slices bacon	4 tomatoes, peeled and chopped
1 small onion, finely chopped	Small pinch sweet basil (optional)
¼ cup chopped green pepper	4 slices bread

Fry bacon crisp. Pour half of the bacon drippings into another skillet. In one skillet saute onion and green pepper until tender. Add tomatoes and basil. Cook until nearly all juice has evaporated. In second skillet, fry bread slices until brown on both sides. Spread tomato mixture on each slice of toast, and crumble bacon on top. Makes 4 servings.

Mrs. Frederic B. Asche (Grace Vale)

Burgundy Ham with Green Grapes

1 tablespoon butter
2 tablespoons sugar
Dash ground ginger
1 ham slice 1½" thick

¾ cup Burgundy wine
1 tablespoon cornstarch
¼ cup cold water
1 cup seedless green grapes

Melt butter in large skillet. Sprinkle in sugar and ginger. Brown ham quickly on both sides. Remove ham from skillet and set aside. Blend wine, cornstarch and cold water; add to sugar mixture remaining in skillet. Cook and stir until mixture is boiling and thick. Return ham to sauce; cover and cook over low heat until done (about 15 minutes), turning one time. Add grapes; cover and cook 1 or 2 minutes longer. Serve grape sauce over ham. Serves 4.

Mrs. William H. Drushel, Jr. (Nancy Ferguson)

Lamb Hawaii

Boned leg or shoulder lamb
    roast (about 5 lbs.)
Juice of large lemon
Salt and pepper
6 tablespoons melted butter
1 clove garlic, crushed
1½ tablespoons grated onion
2 tablespoons chopped parsley
½ teaspoon ground ginger

1 teaspoon paprika
2 teaspoons Worcestershire
    sauce
1½ cups toasted bread crumbs
1 cup crushed pineapple
    (reserve juice)
Salt and pepper
Cayenne
1 cup pineapple juice

Sprinkle roast with lemon juice, salt and pepper. Let stand for 2 hours. To make stuffing, combine 3 tablespoons of the butter, garlic, onion, parsley, ginger, paprika, Worcestershire sauce, bread crumbs and crushed pineapple. Mix well. Fill cavity of meat with stuffing and close with skewers. Dust outside of roast with salt, pepper and cayenne. Roast at 425° for 30 minutes. Reduce heat to 350° for remainder of time, cooking about 30 minutes per pound. Baste regularly with remaining butter combined with pineapple juice. Serves 6.

Mrs. Sydney G. McGlasson (Ellen Archer)

Leg of Lamb with Mint Glaze

Leg of lamb
Salt
1¾ cups ginger ale
¼ cup vinegar

¼ cup brown sugar
½ cup mint jelly
¼ cup fresh mint leaves,
　chopped

Rub lamb with salt. Roast meat fat side up, uncovered, at 400° for 15 minutes. Reduce heat to 300° and roast meat 35-40 minutes per pound. After 1 hour, pour 1-1/2 cups of the ginger ale over roast. (Reserve 1/4 cup ginger ale for glaze.) Baste with pan drippings at 15 minute intervals, for remainder of baking time. Meanwhile make glaze by combining reserved ginger ale, vinegar, brown sugar, jelly and mint leaves in a small bowl; mix with egg beater. Pour glaze over roasted lamb and let stand for 30 minutes before carving. Serve with gravy from pan. Serves 6.

Mrs. Thomas B. Layton (Elsie Landram)

Leg of Lamb with Vegetable Gravy

Leg of lamb
½ clove garlic, slivered
Salt and pepper
1 can beef consomme
½ cup dry red wine or red
　wine vinegar

1 cup canned tomatoes
2 ribs celery, chopped
2 carrots, peeled and sliced
1 onion, chopped

Cut small slits in lamb and insert slivers of garlic. Rub with salt and pepper. Place lamb in roasting pan; add remaining ingredients, and bake in 500° oven for 30 minutes. Reduce heat to 375° and continue roasting 20 minutes per pound. Remove lamb to platter. Skim excess fat from gravy and mash vegetables. Slice lamb and serve with gravy. Serves 6.

Mrs. Paul Sherwood (Mildred Wood)

Lamb Curry

1 onion, minced
3 tablespoons butter
3 tablespoons flour
1½ cups chicken stock or water
2 cups cooked lamb (or chicken)
1 cup cooked mixed vegetables
2 tablespoons lemon juice
   or vinegar

2 or 3 tablespoons curry powder
¼ teaspoon dry mustard
1 bay leaf, crumbled
¼ teaspoon nutmeg
1 teaspoon salt
Freshly ground pepper

Saute onion in butter. Stir in flour. Add stock gradually, stirring constantly. Cook over low heat until sauce is thickened. Cut lamb (or chicken) into bite-sized pieces. Stir into sauce and add remaining ingredients; simmer 30 minutes. Serve over rice. Serve with the following condiments: raisins, chopped apples, chopped egg, crumbled bacon, chutney. Serves 4.

Mrs. David E. Park, Jr. (Virginia Lawhon)

Lamb Shishkebob

2 pounds lamb, cut into
   1½'' cubes
Juice of 2 large lemons
¼ cup olive oil
2 tablespoons grated onion
2 tablespoons ground chili
   peppers
1 teaspoon coriander
1 teaspoon ground ginger

1 clove garlic, crushed
1 teaspoon turmeric
Salt
2 tomatoes, quartered
2 onions, quartered
2 green peppers, seeded
   and quartered
8 large mushroom caps
Melted butter

Marinate meat in mixture of lemon juice, olive oil, onion, chili peppers, coriander, ginger, garlic, tumeric and salt for at least 8 hours. Thread meat on skewers alternately with tomatoes, onions, green peppers and mushrooms. Broil under a hot flame and baste with melted butter. Turn frequently until brown on all sides. Serves 4-6.

Miss Tarrant Hancock

127

Lamb Stew with Mushroom Dumplings

2½ pounds lamb stew meat
Salt, pepper and flour
2 tablespoons cooking oil or
    bacon drippings
1 tablespoon flour

2½ cups water
4 carrots, cut in quarters
6 or 8 small boiling onions
1 cup finely chopped parsley

Cut meat in 1" cubes, sprinkle with salt and pepper, and dredge with flour. Heat cooking oil in heavy pot, add meat and brown well. Stir in flour and continue browning. Add water slowly and stir until smooth. Simmer, covered, for 1 hour. Add carrots, onions and parsley. Simmer until tender. Add more water if necessary. Add dumplings 15 minutes before serving time.

MUSHROOM DUMPLINGS

1 cup flour
½ cup condensed mushroom soup
1 teaspoon salt

1 tablespoon baking powder
3 tablespoons cold water
Chopped parsley

Combine all ingredients except parsley; mix well. Drop by spoonfuls into simmering stew. Sprinkle dumplings with parsley. Cover pan tightly with glass lid or pyrex dish in order to see when the dumplings are done. (They require about 15 minutes cooking time.) Serve at once. Serves 6.

Mrs. Ralph Ellis Gunn (Esme Patterson)

Veal Grillades

2 large veal round steaks
    (about ⅓" thick)
2 tablespoons olive oil
1 large onion, finely chopped
4 green onions, minced
½ green pepper, seeded and
    finely chopped
1 clove garlic, minced

1 can (6 oz.) tomato paste
3 tablespoons flour
Salt and pepper
4 cups hot water
1 lemon, thinly sliced
3 tablespoons chopped parsley
2 ribs celery, cut in 1" pieces

Cut veal in strips, 2" wide. Saute only until grey (not brown) in hot oil in heavy skillet or Dutch oven. Remove and set aside. Lower heat and saute onion, green onions, green pepper and garlic for about 5 minutes. Add tomato paste, flour, salt and pepper; cook for about 5 more minutes, stirring constantly. Add meat, water, lemon slices, parsley and celery. Turn heat very low and simmer for 1-1/2 to 2 hours. This is often served at brunch, sometimes with hot fruit salad and always with some form of grits. Serves 6 generously.

Mrs. Wallace M. Davis, Jr. (Barbara Sterrett)

Veal Scallopini

1½ pounds baby milk-fed veal, cut into 6 thin slices across the grain	3 tablespoons butter
	1½ tablespoons olive oil
	3 tablespoons minced onion
¼ cup flour	¼ cup dry white wine
½ cup Parmesan cheese	⅔ cup beef bouillon
1 teaspoon salt	½ pound fresh mushrooms, sliced
⅛ teaspoon pepper	Parsley for garnish

Flatten each veal slice between sheets of wax paper by pounding gently with mallet until slices are about 1/4 inch thick. Pat slices thoroughly dry on paper towels. Sprinkle lightly with mixture of flour, Parmesan cheese, salt and pepper. Gently pound flour mixture into meat with edge of plate. Heat 2 tablespoons of the butter and 1 tablespoon olive oil in a large enameled or Teflon skillet (a must). Saute veal slices for 4-5 minutes on each side, until lightly browned. Remove slices to warm platter. (Add additional butter if needed.) Add onion and cook slowly for 1 minute. Pour wine and beef bouillon into skillet. Boil rapidly to reduce liquid to about 1/4 cup stirring with a wooden spoon (another must). Return veal slices to skillet and simmer for 5-10 minutes. Meanwhile saute mushrooms in remaining 1 tablespoon butter and 1/2 tablespoon olive oil; add to veal. Garnish with parsley. Serve with rice or spaghetti. Serves 6.

Mrs. Ben G. Sewell (Elizabeth Hall)

Paprika Schnitzel

4 large veal cutlets, ½" thick	Paprika
Salt	2 onions, sliced crosswise
Flour	2 cups sour cream
½ cup bacon drippings	Lemon slices
	Parsley sprigs

Season cutlets with salt and dredge with flour. Heat bacon drippings in large skillet and add enough paprika to make the drippings very red. Lightly saute onions in drippings. (Onions will separate into rings.) Remove sauteed onions and brown meat in drippings. Put onions back in skillet with browned cutlets. Add sour cream and stir. Cover and cook over very low heat until meat is completely tender. If it is necessary to thin gravy, add a little water. Garnish with lemon slices and parsley sprigs. The gravy is delicious over rice. Serves 4.

Mrs. John H. Lindsey (Sara Houstoun)

Veal Valdostana

8 slices (3" x 4") milk-fed
  veal, ⅛" thick
Lemon juice
Garlic salt
Pepper
4 tablespoons cream cheese
2 tablespoons chopped parsley
4 thin slices prosciutto (or
  boiled ham)

1 small black truffle, thinly
  sliced
Flour
¼ cup butter
¼ cup dry white wine
2 teaspoons powdered chicken
  stock base
⅓ cup hot water

Squeeze lemon juice over each veal slice. Sprinkle lightly with garlic salt and pepper. Spread each slice of veal with cream cheese and sprinkle with parsley. Place a ham slice and a little truffle on four of the veal slices. Place a second veal slice on top and seal the edges of meat by beating edges with the dull side of a knife. Sprinkle with additional garlic salt. Flour lightly and saute in butter until brown, about 10 minutes. Add wine and chicken stock base which has been dissolved in the hot water. Simmer, covered, for 15 minutes. Serve with pan juices poured over veal. I usually serve buttered green noodles sprinkled with Parmesan cheese, artichoke salad and a dry Italian wine with this meal. Serves 4.

Mrs. Richard R. McKay (Emily Ann Finch)

Baked Veal Cutlets

4 large veal cutlets
1 egg, well beaten
½ cup cream
Salt, pepper and flour
¼ cup butter

1 can condensed tomato soup
1 cup sour cream
2 green onions with tops, chopped
1 cup grated Swiss or American
  cheese

Dip cutlets in a mixture of egg and cream; dredge lightly in mixture of salt, pepper and flour. Saute in melted butter until light brown. Arrange in baking dish. Combine soup, sour cream and onions; pour over cutlets. Top with grated cheese and bake in 350° oven for 30 minutes. Serves 4.

Mrs. Ghent Graves, Jr. (Sally Sample)

Everyday Veal Cutlets

6 veal cutlets
2 tablespoons cooking oil
⅓ cup Sauterne wine
1 can (2 oz.) mushrooms, drained

1 tablespoon lemon juice
3 tablespoons water
Salt and pepper

Flour cutlets if desired. Brown cutlets on both sides in oil. Lower heat, and add remaining ingredients. Cover, and simmer slowly for 15 minutes. Serves 6.

Mrs. William Brantly Harris (Eugenia Head)

Daube and Spaghetti

Veal rump roast (5-6 lbs.)
Salt, pepper and flour
1 or 2 cloves garlic, slivered
Cooking oil for browning
1 large onion, chopped
1 green pepper, chopped

1 can (1 lb.) tomatoes
1 can (8 oz.) tomato sauce
1 cup water
2 bay leaves, crushed
6-8 sprigs parsley, minced
Spaghetti
Parmesan cheese

Sprinkle roast with salt and pepper; dredge in flour. Cut small slits in roast and insert slivers of garlic. Brown roast in oil in heavy roasting pan; remove to a platter. Add onion and green pepper to pan and saute. Add tomatoes, tomato sauce, water, bay leaves and parsley. When liquid comes to a boil, return roast to pan. Cover, and simmer over low heat for 2 hours. Remove roast, wrap in foil, and place in warm oven (170°). Continue cooking sauce for 1 hour. Cook spaghetti and add to sauce. To serve, slice roast and surround with spaghetti. Serve with Parmesan cheese. New idea for informal suppers—a real favorite with children. Serves 10.

Mrs. Edward W. Kelley, Jr. (Ellen Elizardi)

Hungarian Veal Goulash

2 pounds lean veal, cut in strips
¼ cup butter
½ cup chopped onion
¼ cup diced green pepper
2 teaspoons salt

¼ teaspoon pepper
2 tablespoons paprika
2 cans (1 lb. each)
   tomatoes
1 cup sour cream

Brown veal in butter in skillet. Add onion and green pepper; saute until lightly browned. Add salt, pepper, paprika and tomatoes. Cover, and simmer for 40 minutes. Stir in sour cream. Serve over hot noodles. Serves 6.

Mrs. Lewis A. Brown (Sidney Walsh)

POULTRY

GAME

Hints

TO ROAST CHICKEN: Do not stuff bird until ready to roast; if stuffing and bird are prepared in advance, refrigerate them separately. When ready to roast, place on rack, breast side down, in shallow roasting pan in a 325° oven. Increase the temperature to 425° for the last 15 minutes of cooking, and turn chicken breast side up for added color and a crisp skin.

TO BROIL CHICKEN: Season broiler chicken and brush with melted butter. Place chicken halves or quarters, skin side down, on lightly greased broiler rack. Place broiler pan as far away from heat as possible. Broil for 20 minutes on each side, at 350°. Brush chicken with butter after turning. Length of time under broiler depends on size of chicken. After 40 minutes, prick chicken with skewer; if juice is red, chicken needs additional cooking.

TO FRY CHICKEN: Dredge cut-up broiler-fryer with seasoned flour. (Combine 1-2 teaspoons salt and 1/4 teaspoon pepper with 1 cup flour.) Heat 1/2 inch of oil in skillet. Place chicken pieces, skin side down, in skillet over moderate heat. Brown; turn pieces and brown other side. Reduce heat and cook, uncovered, for 15-25 minutes on each side.

TO STEW CHICKEN (OR TURKEY): Place chicken or turkey in large kettle with seasonings and water to cover. Cover and simmer for 1-3 hours, or until tender. (Time depends on size and age of fowl.) If not to be used immediately, cool chicken in broth for a short time; refrigerate.

TO BARBECUE CHICKEN: Place broiler-fryer halves or quarters, skin side up, on barbecue grate 6 inches from heat. Brush with barbecue sauce. Grill slowly, turning frequently and basting with sauce. Allow 45 minutes to 1 hour, depending on size of bird.

TO BONE CHICKEN BREASTS: Turn skin side down. With fingers push against the ribs of the breast until the joints holding the breastbone break. Push the flesh away from the breastbone until it is just attached at the top. Pull out the breastbone and the piece of cartilage attached to it. With a sharp knife which has a sharp point, carefully cut the meat away from the rib bones. Continue cutting carefully until the wishbone is reached. Remove the wishbone and the remaining rib section. Fold skin over meat and stuff or cook as is.

Chicken Marengo

2 broiling chickens (or 12 thighs)	1 can (8 oz.) tomato sauce
Mixture of flour, pepper and paprika	1 bottle (3 oz.) pimiento-stuffed olives and liquid
¼ cup cooking oil	½ cup sherry
1 teaspoon salt	½ cup toasted almonds
½ teaspoon basil	¼ teaspoon monosodium glutamate
3 cloves garlic, crushed	
1 can (8 oz.) mushrooms, drained	Grated Cheddar cheese for topping

Cut chicken into serving pieces. Coat pieces lightly with flour mixture. Brown chicken pieces in oil. Add salt, basil, garlic, mushrooms and tomato sauce; cover and simmer for 15 minutes. Add olives and olive juice, sherry, almonds and monosodium glutamate. Transfer all to casserole, sprinkle with grated cheese and bake for 40 minutes in 350° oven. Serves 6.

Mrs. Arthur P. Terrell (Lorna Hume)

Chicken New Boston

3 tablespoons cooking oil	½ cup chopped onion
½ cup tarragon vinegar	¾ pound mushrooms, sliced
½ cup lemon juice	2 tablespoons butter
2 broiling chickens, (2 lbs. each) cut up as for frying	1 package frozen artichoke hearts, thawed
2 eggs, slightly beaten	1 can condensed cream of mushroom soup
1 tablespoon water	
2 cups cornflake crumbs	1¼ cups cream
½ cup butter	¼ cup sherry

Combine oil, vinegar and lemon juice; pour over the chicken. Refrigerate, covered, for 2 hours. Remove chicken from marinade; reserve marinade. Blend eggs with water. Dip chicken in egg mixture; roll in 1-1/2 cups of cornflake crumbs. Brown chicken in the 1/2 cup butter. Cook onion and mushrooms in 2 tablespoons butter until onions are golden. Pour 2 tablespoons of the reserved marinade into bottom of large shallow casserole. Add browned chicken, onion, mushrooms and artichokes. Combine soup, cream and sherry. Pour over chicken. Cover. Bake at 350° for 45 minutes. Remove cover. Sprinkle with remaining 1/2 cup cornflake crumbs. Bake, uncovered, for 15 minutes longer, or until chicken is tender. Serves 6.

Miss Janet Woods

Chicken Provincale

2 chickens (about 2½ lbs. each)	1 clove garlic, crushed
½ cup butter	1 can (28 oz.) tomatoes
1 large onion, chopped	⅓ cup flour
1 large green pepper, chopped	½ teaspoon paprika
1 pound fresh mushrooms,	Salt and pepper
chopped	¼ cup melted butter

Simmer chickens until tender. When cool, bone and cut into large pieces. Melt butter in Dutch oven; saute onion, green pepper, mushrooms and garlic until tender. Add tomatoes and simmer briefly. Mix flour, paprika, salt and pepper. Dip chicken pieces in flour mixture and brown quickly in melted butter. Return chicken to the tomato mixture and serve over rice. Serves 8.

Mrs. Lovett Baker (Joanne Prescott)

Chicken Curry

4 or 5 tablespoons minced onion	Strips of lemon peel
5 tablespoons cooking oil	1 cup cream
5 tablespoons flour	Curry powder (recipe follows)
4 cups chicken stock	2 cups cooked, diced chicken
1 cup seedless raisins	Salt
Juice of 1 lemon	

In a large skillet, saute onion in cooking oil until golden. Stir in flour. Add chicken stock and stir until slightly thickened. Add raisins, lemon juice and lemon peel. Simmer for 5 minutes. Add cream. Combine curry powder mixture (below) and a little water; add to skillet. When well blended, add chicken and salt. Simmer over low heat until mixture is reduced to desired consistency. Serve with fluffy rice and choice of condiments, such as: chutney, grated coconut, chopped pecans or almonds, crumbled bacon, green onion slices, grated egg yolks and grated egg whites. Serves 6.

CURRY POWDER

¼ teaspoon cayenne	1 bay leaf, crushed
1 teaspoon ground turmeric	½ teaspoon finely grated coconut
¼ teaspoon ground ginger	1 cardamom seed, ground, or
½ teaspoon garlic salt	½ teaspoon powdered
½ teaspoon salt	cardamom
	⅛ teaspoon cinnamon

Combine all ingredients and mix thoroughly. Use entire amount in above recipe for Chicken Curry.

Mrs. David C. Campbell (Verlyn Miller)

Hawaiian Curry

1 fresh coconut, grated (do not substitute)	1 clove garlic, crushed
4 cups milk, scalded	1 piece (1" square) fresh ginger root, finely chopped*
1 stewing chicken (4-5 lbs.)	1 tablespoon curry powder
2 tablespoons butter	1 teaspoon brown sugar
1 large onion, chopped	2 tablespoons flour

A few hints on preparing fresh coconut: Punch 2 holes in eyes of coconut with an ice pick; drain off and discard coconut milk. Then bake the whole coconut in a 400° oven for 20 minutes; let it cool. You will still need to use a hammer and lots of muscle to peel coconut.

Grate coconut meat and add to scalded milk. Let soak 2 hours. Simmer chicken in well-seasoned water. Remove bones and cut chicken into large, bite-sized pieces. Set aside. Strain coconut-milk mixture through cheese cloth into a bowl. Squeeze all possible milk from the grated coconut. Discard coconut meat (after all that!) and reserve flavored milk (you should have 2-3 cups). Melt butter; add onion, garlic and ginger root; cook until transparent. Add curry powder, brown sugar and flour. Mix well. Slowly stir in 2 cups prepared coconut-flavored milk. Bring to a boil and thin with remaining milk to desired consistency. Add chicken to sauce and season with salt to taste. Serve in a rice ring. This sauce may be frozen, but do not add salt until ready to serve, or sauce will curdle. Sauce may also be used with any seafood, lamb or with eggs. Serves 8.

*You may substitute either 1 teaspoon ground ginger, or 2 tablespoons slivered, crystalized ginger. If using crystalized ginger, wash off sugar. Do try to find fresh ginger, as it is really much better.

Mrs. Hughes Fleming (Mildred Hughes)

Chicken with Wild Rice

1 box (6 oz.) Uncle Ben's Long Grain and Wild Rice	Garlic powder
1 chicken (2½-3 lbs.)	1 can condensed onion soup
Salt and pepper	1 soup can water

Pour packet of rice and packet of seasoning into baking pan. Cut chicken into pieces and season with salt, pepper and garlic powder. Place chicken pieces, skin side up, on top of rice. Combine soup and water and pour over chicken. Bake, uncovered, in 375° oven for 1 hour. Serves 4.

Mrs. James J. Loeffler (Margo Meynier)

Chicken Raphael Weill

3 pounds frying chicken pieces
2 teaspoons salt
¼ teaspoon white pepper
¼ cup butter
1 package frozen artichoke
   hearts, thawed and drained
1 package frozen whole mushrooms,
   thawed and drained

2 teaspoons chopped onion
⅛ teaspoon thyme
1 cup heavy cream
¼ cup dry sherry
2 tablespoons water
1 tablespoon flour

Sprinkle chicken with 1-1/2 teaspoons of the salt and white pepper; brown evenly in butter in skillet over medium heat. Drain butter from pan. Add artichoke hearts, mushrooms, onion, thyme, cream and sherry. Cover and cook over low heat 25 minutes or until chicken is tender. Remove chicken and vegetables to a platter and keep warm. Combine water, flour and remaining 1/2 teaspoon salt; mix to smooth paste. Gradually add to cream mixture in skillet. Cook and stir over low heat until thickened and smooth. Continue to cook about 5 minutes, stirring occasionally. Serve sauce over chicken. Serves 4.

Mrs. Claude C. Cody, III (Muriel Fursteneau)

Chicken Caribbean

6 quarters of frying chicken
Lemon or lime juice
Salt and pepper
Flour
¼ cup butter
2 tablespoons cooking oil
1 onion, minced
3 tablespoons currants

1 teaspoon finely grated
   lemon peel
1 teaspoon brown sugar
2 tomatoes, peeled and mashed
1 ripe pineapple, peeled and
   cored; or 1 can (12 oz.)
   pineapple tidbits
1 tablespoon rum

Brush chicken quarters with lemon or lime juice; sprinkle with salt and pepper, and dust with flour. Heat butter and oil; add chicken and brown. Reduce heat and cover. Cook slowly until chicken is tender. Add onion, currants, lemon peel, brown sugar and tomatoes. Season with additional salt and pepper. Mix thoroughly and cook gently for another 10 minutes. Make sauce by crushing pineapple to a pulp with all its juice in blender. Simmer pureed pineapple until reduced to a thick sauce. Stir rum into pineapple. Pour over chicken and serve. Serves 6.

Mrs. Jane B. Pinckard (Jane Burton)

Chicken with Grapes and Oranges

2 broiling chickens, quartered
1½ teaspoons salt
1½ teaspoons monosodium
   glutamate
½ cup butter
1½ cups orange juice
2 tablespoons slivered
   orange peel
2 teaspoons instant minced onion

½ teaspoon powdered ginger
¼ teaspoon hot pepper sauce
4 teaspoons cornstarch
2 cans (11 oz. each) Mandarin
   orange segments, drained
2 cups fresh seedless green
   grapes
½ cup toasted slivered
   almonds

Sprinkle chicken with salt and monosodium glutamate; brown on both sides in butter in large skillet. Add orange juice, orange peel, onion, ginger and hot pepper sauce. Simmer, covered, 30-35 minutes, until chicken is tender. Arrange chicken on heated platter and keep warm. Blend cornstarch with a little cold water and stir into sauce in skillet. Cook, stirring constantly, until mixture thickens and comes to a boil. Add orange segments and grapes; heat gently. Add almonds. Pour a little sauce over chicken and serve remaining sauce separately. If desired, garnish with sprigs of parsley, fresh orange slices and grape clusters. Serve with rice. Serves 8.

Mrs. A. Baker Duncan (Sally Witt)

Orange-Baked Chicken Breasts

8 chicken breast halves
⅓ cup flour
1 teaspoon salt
⅛ teaspoon pepper
⅓ cup cooking oil
½ teaspoon celery seed

½ cup thinly sliced onion
¾ cup fresh orange juice or
   ¼ cup frozen orange juice
   concentrate plus ½ cup water
1 unpeeled orange, cut in
   8 wedges

Wash and dry chicken breasts. Combine flour, salt and pepper in small paper bag. Put in chicken, a few pieces at a time, and shake to coat evenly. Heat oil in heavy skillet; add chicken; sprinkle with celery seed. Brown on both sides over low heat. Remove chicken and place in a 2-quart baking dish. Cook onion in same skillet until tender. Add orange juice and bring to a boil to loosen brown particles from skillet. Pour over chicken. Arrange orange wedges over chicken in baking dish. Cover and bake in 300° oven for 1 hour. Reduce heat to 250° and bake for an additional hour, or until chicken is fork tender. Serves 4-6.

Mrs. Gleaves M. Love (Betsy Riggle)

Lemoned Chicken

2 broiling chickens, quartered	½ cup cooking oil
2 lemons	¼ cup brown sugar
⅔ cup flour	2 cups chicken broth or
1 tablespoon salt	bouillon
1 teaspoon paprika	1 teaspoon angostura bitters

Wash chickens and dry well. Cut 1 lemon in half and squeeze juice over each piece of chicken. Combine flour, salt and paprika in paper bag. Put chicken in bag and shake until pieces are coated. Brown chicken evenly and slowly in oil; arrange in baking dish. Thinly slice remaining lemon and arrange slices over chicken. Dissolve brown sugar in chicken broth; add bitters. Pour mixture over chicken. Cover and bake in 375° oven, or simmer over very low heat, until chicken is tender, about 1 hour. Serve hot with the sauce. For variation, add 1 can drained Bing cherries while chicken is baking. Serves 6-8.

Mrs. Frank C. Smith, Jr. (Sally McQueen)

Fried Chicken with Lemon Sauce

1 cup lemon juice	1 clove garlic, crushed
½ cup cooking oil	2 cut-up frying chickens, or
¼ cup grated onion	pieces of your choice
1 teaspoon thyme	Flour, salt and pepper
1 teaspoon salt	Cooking oil

Combine lemon juice, oil, onion, thyme, salt and garlic in bowl and mix well. Make sauce several hours before needed for fuller flavor. Dredge chicken in seasoned flour and fry in oil until almost done. Arrange pieces close together in baking dish and pour sauce over chicken. Bake, uncovered, in 325° oven until sauce is absorbed (about 30 minutes). Serves 6.

Buttered Crumb Chicken

1 broiling chicken, cut in half	½ clove garlic, crushed
½ cup butter	2 green onions, chopped
4 sprigs parsley, chopped	Salt and pepper
¼ pound fresh mushrooms	Bread crumbs

Place the chicken in a large skillet with butter, parsley, mushrooms, garlic, onions, salt and pepper. Cover and simmer slowly for 25 minutes, turning often. Remove chicken from skillet and roll in bread crumbs; brown under broiler until crumbs are well-browned. Serve with seasoned butter remaining in skillet poured over rice. Makes 2 generous servings.

Mrs. Pete Gardere (Nancy Penix)

Paella à la Valencia

Paella is a one-dish Spanish meal. Like chili, it is a traditional dish and, like chili, it varies greatly according to region, with each cook absolutely certain that his paella is not only superior to all others, but is actually the only genuine recipe. It should be made in a special paella pan, which resembles a very large shallow skillet; but I have also used a large shallow enamel cast iron casserole.

18 pieces frying chicken, thighs or breasts	2 teaspoons paprika
Salt, pepper and flour	1 teaspoon oregano
Olive oil	Chopped parsley
2 medium onions, chopped	12 green onions, chopped
1 green pepper, chopped	1 pound raw shrimp, shelled
2 large cloves garlic, crushed	4 peeled tomatoes, quartered
6 cups chicken stock	1 can (7½ oz.) minced clams (do not drain)
¼ to ½ teaspoon saffron, or few drops yellow food coloring	Salt and pepper
	2 cups uncooked rice
	½ pound King crabmeat

Dry chicken pieces; sprinkle with salt, pepper and flour. Quickly brown chicken in olive oil; remove chicken when brown. Saute onions and green pepper in oil. When tender, add garlic and chicken stock. Stir. Add saffron, paprika, oregano, parsley and green onions. Mix well. Add shrimp and tomatoes; heat thoroughly, stirring constantly. Add clams, clam juice, salt and pepper. Taste and correct seasonings if necessary. Allow to simmer for a few minutes. All this can be done early in the day.

One hour before serving, heat mixture and add rice. Stir well. Return chicken pieces to mixture and add crabmeat. Bake in 350° oven, uncovered, for 45 minutes or until rice is done. **Do not stir.** If paella begins to look dry, add a little **hot** water. (Cold water will ruin it.) Serves 10-12.

Mrs. Leonard V. Lombardi (Margaret Hendren)

141

Baked Curried Chicken and Peaches

1 large can (1 lb. 13 oz.)
  peach halves
¼ cup butter
1 teaspoon (or more)
  curry powder

1½ to 2 onions, chopped
2 tablespoons wine vinegar
8 chicken breast halves or
  pieces of your choice

Drain peaches, saving 1/2 cup syrup. Melt butter, add curry powder and simmer over low heat for about 5 minutes. Remove from heat and add onions, reserved syrup and vinegar. Place chicken in shallow baking dish; cover with sauce. Bake, uncovered, in 350° oven for 1 to 1-1/2 hours, basting and turning occasionally. About 15 minutes before serving, place peach halves on top of chicken, baste and bake another 10 or 15 minutes. Serve with rice. Condiments, such as chutney, pineapple, banana, peanuts, coconut and bacon can be served with the curry if desired. Serves 4.

Mrs. Frank C. Smith, Jr. (Sally McQueen)

Chicken Valencia

2 broiling chickens, quartered
  or cut up for frying
Cooking oil
1 large clove garlic, crushed
2 large onions, diced
½ cup diced green pepper
1 cup uncooked rice
4 fresh tomatoes, peeled
  and diced
Saffron to color (½ teaspoon)

3 dried red peppers, crushed,
  or Tabasco to taste
Salt and pepper
1 package frozen peas, thawed
1 package frozen green beans,
  thawed
2 jars (2 oz. each) pimientos,
  chopped
½ cup salad olives
1 can (13½ oz.) tomato juice

Brown chicken in small amount of hot oil; remove and drain. To same skillet add garlic, onions, green pepper and rice; brown in oil and transfer to large casserole. Add tomatoes, saffron, red peppers, salt and pepper; stir well. Mix in the peas, green beans, pimientos, olives and chicken pieces. Bake, covered, in 250° oven for about 3 hours. Stir once or twice. Add tomato juice, in small amounts, when liquid is needed during baking. This dish improves with age, so if time allows, make it the day before using. Can be frozen and reheated successfully. Serves 6-8.

Mrs. R. W. Tidemann (Bettie Brewster)

Chicken Piquante

2 rounded tablespoons flour
2 tablespoons shortening
2 large onions, chopped
½ cup chopped ham
1 chicken hen (6-8 lbs.), cut up
1 can (6 oz.) tomato paste
2 or 3 cloves garlic, chopped
½ cup coarsely chopped celery
¼ cup chopped parsley
¼ cup chopped green onions
12 whole pitted green olives
2 sour pickles, chopped
1 can (1 lb.) mushrooms
   with liquid
Salt
1 red pepper pod, chopped
2 cups dry red wine or water
1 jar (12 oz.) fresh oysters

In a heavy pan, brown flour in shortening. Add onions and brown. Add ham and brown. Add chicken pieces and brown well, adding more shortening if necessary. Stir in tomato paste; cover and simmer 45 minutes. Add garlic, celery, parsley and green onions; cook 45 minutes longer. Add olives and pickles and simmer a little longer. Add mushrooms and liquid; cook until chicken is tender. Add salt, red pepper, wine and oysters and simmer for 20 minutes. Serve over fluffy rice. Serves 12.

Mrs. Howard A. Tenney, Jr. (Joan Woodruff)

Senator's Chicken

2 large whole chicken breasts,
   halved and boned
2 cups port wine (or sherry)
2 tablespoons brandy
Salt and pepper
6 tablespoons butter
½ teaspoon tarragon vinegar
4 tablespoons pate de fois gras
   (or goose liver—not smoked)

Pound breasts with a plate or mallet until flat. Put them into a bowl (not metal). Pour wine and brandy over them and marinate 1 hour. Drain and reserve marinade. Sprinkle chicken on both sides with salt and pepper. Cream butter until soft; beat in vinegar. Place 1 tablespoon butter mixture on each chicken breast and top with 1 tablespoon pate. Fold breast over to enclose filling; tie with string. Brown chicken in remaining 2 tablespoons butter. Pour marinade over chicken and simmer uncovered, 30 minutes or until tender, basting occasionally with pan juices. Remove string. Place chicken on platter and spoon sauce over it. If sauce is too thin, boil down to desired consistency and then pour over chicken. Garnish with broiled mushrooms and artichoke bottoms if desired. Serves 2-4.

Mrs. J. Daviss Collett (Nancy Nixon)

Sidney's Chicken with Rice

6 chicken breast halves,
  or 1 chicken, (2½ lbs.), cut
  into serving pieces
Flour, salt and pepper
½ cup margarine
1 cup chopped onion
2 cloves garlic, crushed
½ cup diced green pepper

⅓ cup pimientos
1 cup uncooked rice
1½ cups chicken bouillon
Dash chili powder
1½ teaspoons comino seed
1 teaspoon salt
Dash pepper

Roll chicken in the seasoned flour. Brown in hot margarine and remove chicken from skillet. In the same pan, cook onion, garlic and green pepper until onion is golden brown. Add pimientos and rice; stir over low heat 2 minutes. Add bouillon, chili powder, comino seed, salt and pepper. Put rice mixture in casserole and arrange browned chicken on top. Bake, covered, 1-1/2 hours at 350°. Serves 4.

Mrs. James A. Reichert (Betsy Calhoun)

Chicken Breast L'Aiglon

4 small whole chicken breasts
4 very thin slices smoked ham
  (or proscuitto)
4 strips Swiss cheese
1 egg

1½ cups very fine cracker crumbs
Salt and pepper
½ cup butter
1 cup uncooked mixed rice (half
  white, half wild)

Remove skin and bones from whole chicken breasts and flatten with cleaver. Place in center of each breast a thin slice ham; on ham, place a 1" x 1/2" slice Swiss cheese. Fold edges of chicken over ham and cheese; secure with string or toothpicks. Dip chicken in egg which has been beaten with 1 teaspoon water; roll in cracker crumbs. Season with salt and pepper. Heat butter in skillet until foamy. Brown breasts until golden brown on both sides, reduce heat, and cook until done. Meanwhile, cook rice mixture. Make white wine sauce.

WHITE WINE SAUCE

1 can condensed cream of
  chicken soup or cream sauce
⅓ cup milk
1 tablespoon chopped pimiento

1 teaspoon instant minced onion
2 tablespoons dry white wine
  (or sherry)
1 can (3 oz.) button mushrooms,
  drained

Mix all ingredients and heat. Do not boil. Serve chicken breasts over a mound of rice and spoon wine sauce over all. Serve extra sauce as gravy. Serves 4.

Mrs. W. S. Perkins (Sue Scott)

Coq Au Vin

4 pounds chicken breasts and thighs
  (or 2 medium broilers, cut up)
¼ cup flour
Salt, pepper and paprika
8 tablespoons butter
½ pound fresh mushrooms,
  sliced
3 green onions, sliced
¼ teaspoon thyme
¼ teaspoon tarragon
1 bay leaf, crushed
1 tablespoon minced parsley
1 large clove garlic, crushed
1½ cups dry red wine
¼ cup chicken broth or stock
2 slices bacon, fried crisp and
  crumbled
1 cup pearl onions, peeled
Minced parsley

Dredge chicken in seasoned flour and brown in 6 tablespoons of the butter. After all chicken is browned, remove and add remaining 2 tablespoons butter to pan. Saute mushrooms and green onions. Add thyme, tarragon, bay leaf, parsley, garlic, wine and chicken broth; simmer 5 minutes. Place chicken in large shallow baking dish (preferably one from which chicken may be served). Spoon wine mixture over chicken. Cover tightly with foil and bake at 325° for 1 hour. Add crumbled bacon and pearl onions. Cover again and bake 1 additional hour. Sprinkle minced parsley over chicken before serving. Serve with fluffy brown-and-white rice. Sauce from chicken is good over rice. Serve 6-8.

Mrs. Richard R. McKay (Emily Ann Finch)

Chicken Breasts with Potatoes

2 large chicken breast
  halves, boned
¼ cup butter
1 onion, chopped
1-2 cloves garlic, crushed
1 tablespoon flour
½ teaspoon salt
Pepper
1 chicken bouillon cube
1 cup hot water
1 can (8 oz.) new potatoes,
  drained
¼ cup red wine

Saute chicken breasts in butter until brown on all sides. Remove chicken and set aside. Add onion and garlic to butter; cook 5 minutes. Stir in flour, salt and pepper. Dissolve bouillon cube in hot water; stir into onion mixture. Cook over low heat until thickened. Return chicken to pan. Cook slowly about 30 minutes, or until chicken is tender. Add potatoes and wine; heat thoroughly. Serves 2.

Mrs. F. Tarrant Fendley, Jr. (Mary Ann Elliott)

Laurel Chicken In Wine

1 frying chicken, cut up	4 or 5 dried laurel (bay) leaves
1 large onion, peeled and quartered	Salt and pepper
1 clove garlic, crushed	3 tablespoons olive oil or corn oil
1 or 2 ribs celery, chopped	1 cup dry white wine
2 or 3 sprigs parsley, chopped	2 tablespoons flour
	Chopped parsley

Arrange chicken in Dutch oven. Place onion, garlic, celery, parsley and laurel leaves around the edges. Sprinkle with salt and pepper. Pour oil over all. Shake pan to mix well. Cover pan and brown chicken over medium heat. (When removing cover to turn chicken, let water which has collected in the top drip into pan.) After chicken has browned, add 2/3 cup of the wine. Cover pan, turn heat low and simmer about 45 minutes or until done. When chicken is done, mix flour with remaining 1/3 cup wine and strain into chicken mixture. Let simmer a few minutes, covered, until thickened. Serve with chopped parsley sprinkled on top. Serves 4.

Mrs. Milton W. Rigney (Bernice Mee)

Chicken Under Glass

6 chicken breast halves	¼ teaspoon savory
Salt and pepper	½ cup dry sherry
¼ cup butter	¼ cup dry white wine
1 can (8 oz.) mushrooms	1 tablespoon cornstarch
½ cup mushroom liquid	1 cup heavy cream
¼ teaspoon thyme	6 slices round bread
¼ teaspoon rosemary	6 slices Canadian bacon
	1-2 tablespoons butter

Bone and skin chicken breasts; season with salt and pepper and saute in butter for 10 minutes or until brown. Drain mushrooms and set aside. Add mushroom liquid, thyme, rosemary and savory to chicken; cover and let simmer 20 minutes. Add sherry and white wine; simmer 10 more minutes. Dissolve cornstarch in cream; add to chicken. Add mushrooms and simmer for 5 minutes or until sauce has thickened. Toast bread very slowly in oven; saute Canadian bacon in a little butter. On individual serving plates, place a slice of Canadian bacon on toast, top with chicken and spoon sauce over all. Serve with heated, small glazed carrots and green peas, covering each serving with a bell glass. Serves 6.

Mrs. Robert E. Clemons (Grayson Cecil)

Carson Broiled Chicken

3 broiling chickens, quartered
½ pound melted butter
3 tablespoons Worcestershire
   sauce
3 tablespoons vinegar

2 tablespoons jalapeno pepper
   juice
½ cup lemon juice
½ cup cooking oil
Salt and pepper
Dash Tabasco

Make a sauce by combining all ingredients except the chicken. Marinate chicken quarters in sauce for at least 3 hours, turning occasionally. Remove chicken from sauce and broil quickly just to brown, 8-10 minutes on each side. Put into fairly deep baking pan, pour all the sauce over chicken and cook slowly in a 325° oven for 1 hour. Serve with sauce if desired. Makes 12 small servings.

Mrs. Garrett Stuart Livingston, Jr. (Mary Ann Ransom)

Chicken Tetrazzini

1 chicken (about 3 lbs.)
2 slices of onion
½ bay leaf
½ cup butter
¼ pound fresh mushrooms,
   thinly sliced
1 pint heavy cream
1 tablespoon sherry

2 tablespoons dry white wine
Salt and pepper
2 tablespoons flour
2 tablespoons butter
1 package (5 oz.) uncooked
   medium noodles
3 tablespoons grated
   Parmesan cheese

Simmer chicken with onion and bay leaf in salted water to cover. Remove chicken, bone and cut into bite-sized pieces. Reserve chicken broth. Melt 1/2 cup butter in skillet and saute mushrooms 2 or 3 minutes. Add chicken meat, cream, sherry, white wine, salt and pepper; heat almost to boiling. Blend flour and 2 tablespoons butter together to make a smooth paste and stir into chicken mixture, continuing to stir until smooth and somewhat thickened. Simmer 5 minutes. Meanwhile, cook noodles in chicken broth until tender, 7-10 minutes. Drain, rinse in cold water, and place in buttered shallow casserole. Gently pour chicken-mushroom mixture over noodles, sprinkle with Parmesan cheese, and brown lightly under broiler. If prepared ahead, heat in 375° oven about 20 minutes, or until top is golden brown. Serves 4.

Mrs. Roger G. Stotler (Nance Fruit)

Chicken Spaghetti

2 fryers (or 4-5 lbs. meaty
   chicken pieces)
3 ribs celery, chopped
1 green pepper, chopped
2 onions, chopped
2 cloves garlic, crushed
1 can (4 oz.) mushroom
   stems and pieces
1 package (10 oz.) spaghetti,
   broken

1 can (1 lb.) tomatoes, chopped
2 tablespoons chopped ripe olives
1 can condensed cream of
   mushroom soup
Salt and pepper
Paprika
Few dashes Worcestershire
   sauce
1 pound Velveeta cheese,
   grated

Simmer chicken until tender in well-seasoned water. Remove chicken and broth; measure 1 quart broth back into pan. Bone and dice chicken; set aside. Into broth put celery, green pepper, onions, garlic and mushrooms. Let cook a few minutes, then add spaghetti and cook until spaghetti is done. Add tomatoes, olives, soup, salt, pepper and paprika. Add Worcestershire sauce and cheese to boned chicken; then add to spaghetti mixture. This is a favorite with children and, since it uses only 1 pan, a favorite with the cook also. Serves 10-12.

Mrs. George W. Dorrance, Jr. (Margie Smith)

Chicken Spaghetti for 40

2 large chicken hens
   (5-6 lbs. each)
1 cup butter
4 onions, chopped
10 cloves garlic, crushed
3 green peppers, chopped
2 whole stalks celery,
   chopped

3 cans (1 lb. each) tomatoes
2 cans condensed mushroom
   soup
Salt and pepper
Mushrooms, if desired
3 packages (12 oz. each)
   spaghetti
1 pound sharp Cheddar
   cheese, grated

Simmer chickens; save broth. Skin, bone, chop and chill chickens. In a large heavy pot, melt butter; add onions, garlic, peppers and celery. Cook until tender. Add tomatoes, soup, salt, pepper, mushrooms and chicken meat; simmer until flavors blend. Cook spaghetti until almost tender. Put in colander, drain and rinse under cold water. Add to pot with chicken mixture. If mixture is too dry, add a little reserved broth. Thirty minutes before serving, stir in cheese and heat. The sauce can be made the day before needed and heated just before adding the spaghetti. Serves about 40.

Mrs. Suzanne S. Braden (Suzanne Schmidt)

Chicken - Green Noodle Casserole

1 large stewing chicken (about 5 lbs.)	2 teaspoons Lawry's seasoned salt
1 package (8 oz.) green spinach noodles	1 teaspoon Accent
¼ cup butter	½ teaspoon nutmeg
¼ cup flour	½ teaspoon cayenne
1 cup milk	1 teaspoon paprika
1 cup chicken stock	1 teaspoon salt
1 pint sour cream	1 teaspoon pepper
¼ to ½ cup lemon juice	1 tablespoon parsley flakes
1 can (6 oz.) mushroom pieces and juice	½ cup toasted bread crumbs
	Parmesan cheese

Cook chicken in seasoned water; remove chicken and save stock (to use in making cream sauce). Cook noodles; drain. Melt butter in a large saucepan. Stir in flour. Add milk and chicken stock. Cook over low heat, stirring constantly until sauce thickens. To the cream sauce add sour cream, lemon juice, mushrooms, seasoned salt, Accent, nutmeg, cayenne, paprika, salt, pepper and parsley flakes. Mix well. Cut chicken into large bite-sized pieces (measure 4 cups). Butter a 3-quart casserole. Place drained noodles in casserole. Add layer of chicken. Pour some sauce over chicken. Sprinkle with bread crumbs and Parmesan cheese. Repeat layers, ending with cheese on top. Heat in 350° oven until bubbly, about 25 minutes. Serves 8-10.

Mrs. John D. Staub (Alice York)

Creamy Chicken and Noodle Casserole

1 package (10 oz.) uncooked wide noodles	1 can condensed cream of chicken soup
4 cans (5 oz. each) boned chicken; or 2 cups cooked chicken	1 can (4½ oz.) chopped ripe olives
1 can condensed cream of celery soup	1 can (4 oz.) chopped pimentos
1 can condensed cream of mushroom soup	1 can (1 lb.) mushrooms, drained
	½ cup wine or sherry
	1 pound Cheddar or Longhorn cheese, grated

Cook noodles; drain. Mix other ingredients with noodles except cheese. Spoon into shallow 9" x 13" baking dish. Top with grated cheese; sprinkle with paprika. Heat in 350° oven for 10-15 minutes, or until cheese is melted. Serves 12-14.

Mrs. George W. Dorrance, Jr. (Margie Smith)

Hot Chicken or Turkey Salad

2 cups cooked, diced chicken
or turkey
1½ cups diced celery
¼ cup slivered almonds, toasted
1 tablespoon grated onion
1 tablespoon lemon juice
½ to 1 teaspoon salt

⅛ teaspoon black pepper
Few shakes Tabasco
½ cup mayonnaise
½ small can (5 oz.) water
chestnuts, sliced and
drained (optional)
½ cup grated Cheddar cheese

Toss together all ingredients, except cheese, in greased baking dish. Top with cheese. Bake at 375° for 25 minutes or until cheese bubbles. Serves 4-6.

Mrs. John M. Vetter (Virginia Tallichet)

Chicken Supreme

1 cup sour cream
2 tablespoons lemon juice
2 teaspoons celery salt
1 teaspoon paprika
1 clove garlic, crushed

1 teaspoon salt
¼ teaspoon pepper
6 chicken breast halves
1 cup bread crumbs
½ cup butter, melted

Combine sour cream, lemon juice, celery salt, paprika, garlic, salt and pepper. Coat chicken well with mixture and refrigerate overnight, uncovered. Next day, roll chicken in bread crumbs and arrange in shallow baking pan. Spoon half of the butter over chicken. Bake at 350° for 40 minutes. Spoon remaining butter over chicken and bake 15 minutes longer. Serve hot. (Leftovers may be served cold.) Serves 4-6.

Mrs. Sam E. McHard, Jr. (Lois Vincent)

Easy Baked Chicken

1 broiling chicken (2½-3 lbs.)
or equivalent in pieces of
your choice
Salt and pepper
Garlic powder
1 large onion, sliced

1 can condensed cream of
mushroom soup
⅔ cup evaporated milk
3 tablespoons dry white
wine or sherry

Cut chicken into serving pieces. Season with salt, pepper and garlic powder. Arrange chicken pieces close together, skin side up, in baking pan. Cover with onion slices. Combine soup, milk and wine; pour over onions. Bake uncovered, in 325° oven for 1 hour and 15 minutes. This is a good busy-day supper dish. Serves 3-4.

Mrs. James J. Loeffler (Margo Meynier)

Easy Chicken Divan

2 packages frozen broccoli, or
  1 bunch fresh broccoli
2 cups sliced, cooked chicken
  (about 3 large chicken
  breast halves)
2 cans condensed cream of
  chicken soup
1 cup mayonnaise

1 teaspoon lemon juice
½-1 teaspoon curry powder
½ cup grated, sharp, processed
  cheese
½ cup soft bread crumbs
1 tablespoon melted butter
Pimiento strips

Cook broccoli in boiling, salted water until tender; drain. Arrange stalks in greased 11-1/2'' x 7-1/2'' x 1-1/2'' pyrex baking dish with flowerets facing outward. Place chicken on top of broccoli. Combine soup, mayonnaise, lemon juice and curry powder; pour over chicken. Sprinkle with cheese. Combine crumbs and butter; sprinkle over all. Bake at 350° for 25-30 minutes, or until thoroughly heated. Garnish with pimiento strips. Serves 4-6.

Mrs. A. J. Hurt, Jr. (Patty Parrish)

Chicken Kiev

5 whole chicken breasts,
  halved and boned
Salt
1 heaping tablespoon chopped
  green onion
1 heaping tablespoon chopped
  parsley

1 stick butter, cut into
  10 slices
Flour
2 eggs, slightly beaten
Dry bread crumbs

Place each piece of chicken, boned side up, between two pieces of Saran wrap. Working out from center, pound to form cutlets about 1/4'' thick. Peel off Saran. Sprinkle with salt. Combine green onion and parsley; sprinkle equal amounts on each cutlet. Place slice of butter on each cutlet; roll as a jelly roll, tucking in ends of meat. Press to seal well. Dust with flour; dip in beaten eggs; roll in bread crumbs. Chill for at least 1 hour. Fry in deep, hot fat (340°) about 5 minutes or until golden brown. Sour Cream Sauce may be served with chicken. Makes 10 small servings.

SOUR CREAM SAUCE

½ cup sliced mushrooms
2 teaspoons butter

1 pint sour cream
1 tablespoon chopped chives

Saute mushrooms in butter. Add sour cream and chives. Heat thoroughly. Pour over, or serve with Chicken Kiev.

Mrs. Bruce Harrington (Anne Lawhon)

Chicken Crêpes Delores

CREPES

4 eggs, well beaten
1 ¼ cups milk

½ cup sifted flour
½ teaspoon salt

Mix all ingredients together. Make crepes one at a time in 5-inch crepe pan or electric skillet set at 380°. Stir batter before pouring each crepe. Makes 18 crepes.

CHICKEN FILLING

1 stewing chicken (3-4 lbs.)
1 ¼ pounds Swiss cheese, grated
2 (or more) jalapeno peppers,
  seeded and finely chopped

1 teaspoon salt
1 teaspoon pepper
1 pint heavy cream

Cook chicken; bone and dice. Combine chicken, all but 1 cup of the grated cheese, jalapenos, salt and pepper. Mix well. Place a large spoonful of the mixture on each crepe, then roll up. Arrange filled, rolled crepes in shallow baking dish and top with remaining cup cheese. Pour cream over all. Cook in 325° oven about 20-30 minutes, or until thoroughly heated. Freezes well. Serves 6.

Mrs. Tyler D. Todd (Bobbie Beal)

Chicken Italian - Mary Lloyd

6-7 slices bread
2 medium frying chickens (or
  equivalent in pieces of
  your choice
½ cup grated Parmesan cheese
¼ cup chopped parsley
1 clove garlic, crushed

2 teaspoons salt
1 teaspoon pepper
Dash nutmeg
Cayenne
Pinch oregano
½ pound melted butter

Heat bread in oven; grate or roll with rolling pin to make 2 cups crumbs. Mix cheese, parsley, garlic, salt, pepper, nutmeg, cayenne, oregano and crumbs. Cut chickens into serving pieces; dip each piece in melted butter, then in crumb mixture, being sure to coat well. Arrange chicken pieces in shallow roasting pan lined with foil, placing them close together. Pour remaining butter over all. Bake, uncovered, in 350° oven 1 hour, or until tender. Do not turn. Serves 10.

Mrs. Tilford Jones (Audrey Thompson)

Overnight Chicken Italiano

1 frying chicken (2½-3 lbs.)	1 teaspoon garlic salt
⅓ cup oil (half olive oil and half corn oil)	½ cup grated Romano cheese
	½ cup dry bread crumbs
¼ cup vinegar	Salt and pepper
Juice of ½ lemon	

Cut chicken into serving pieces. Marinate chicken overnight in oil, vinegar, lemon juice and garlic salt. Next day place chicken in baking pan and sprinkle lightly with cheese, bread crumbs, salt and pepper. Cover pan loosely with foil and bake at 350° for 45 minutes or until tender. Serve with cooked spaghetti seasoned only with butter and garlic. Serves 4.

Mrs. David C. Campbell (Verlyn Miller)

Yucateca Baked Chicken

3 whole frying chickens, with giblets	¼ cup butter
½ onion, chopped	1 teaspoon salt
2 cloves garlic	1 teaspoon pepper
½ cup vinegar	1 teaspoon oregano
	⅓ teaspoon nutmeg

Simmer chicken giblets in 3 cups salted water until very tender, about 1 hour. Put giblets into blender and puree with the onion, garlic, vinegar, butter, salt, pepper, oregano and nutmeg. If sauce seems too thick, thin slightly with a little of the giblet stock. Lightly salt chickens and place them breast side up in shallow roasting pan. Cover chickens with giblet sauce. Bake at 225° for 3 hours, basting four times an hour with giblet sauce. The skin becomes crispy and spicy and the meat remains tender. Serves 6.

Mrs. George H. Lane (Joan Bagby)

Chicken Livers Vin Rouge

1 pound chicken livers	¼ to ½ cup dry red wine
2 tablespoons butter	1 teaspoon dried rosemary leaves, crushed
2 medium tomatoes	Dash salt and pepper

Rinse and dry chicken livers; cut each into 2 pieces. Brown livers quickly in butter. Peel tomatoes, cut in chunks and add to livers. Add wine, rosemary, salt and pepper. Bring mixture to boil, reduce heat and simmer about 12 minutes. Serve over rice. Serves 2.

Mrs. Edgar J. Marston, III (Graeme Meyers)

Chicken Livers
Sauteed with Apples & Onion Rings

12 chicken livers
½ teaspoon salt
½ teaspoon paprika
2 tablespoons flour

3-4 tablespoons butter
½ onion, sliced in rings
4 apple rings, ½ inch thick
2 tablespoons sugar

Rinse and drain chicken livers; cut in half if very large. Season livers lightly with salt and paprika, then sprinkle with flour. Gently cook livers in 2 tablespoons butter until browned. In another small skillet cook onion rings in a little butter until soft. In a third skillet brown apple slices in remaining butter; sprinkle with sugar to glaze and flavor. Arrange livers on platter, top with onion rings and apple rings. Serves 2.

Mrs. Ford Hubbard, Jr. (Patricia Peckinpaugh)

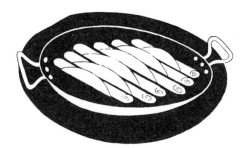

Lasagne Suisse

8 ounces lasagne noodles
1½ pounds chicken livers, diced
3 tablespoons butter
1 medium onion, sliced
1 green pepper, sliced

2 cans condensed cream of chicken soup
1 teaspoon salt
¼ teaspoon pepper
4 hard-cooked eggs, sliced
½ pound Swiss cheese, sliced

Cook noodles until tender, drain and set aside. In large skillet cook livers in butter until well done. Remove livers and set aside. Cook onion and green pepper in same skillet until tender. Combine chicken soup, salt and pepper; add to onion and green pepper; stir. In a well-greased baking dish, make alternate layers of noodles, livers, eggs, soup mixture and cheese. Start with noodles and top with strips of cheese placed lattice fashion. Bake, uncovered, for 30 minutes at 350°. Serves 4-6.

Mrs. John L. Hamilton (Ann Lowdon)

Chicken Enchilada Casserole

1 chicken (about 3½ lbs.), or
equivalent in pieces of your
choice
1 large onion, chopped
1 can (4 oz.) green chiles,
seeded and finely chopped

1 can condensed cream of
mushroom soup
1 cup grated Velveeta cheese
8 tortillas (cut each into
6 pieces)

Cook chicken, remove skin and bones, and cut into large bite-sized pieces. Saute onion in small amount of oil. Add chiles, soup and half of the grated cheese. Cook slowly until cheese melts. Line a buttered 6" x 10" casserole with tortilla pieces. Layer with half the chicken, then half the cheese sauce. Repeat layers. Top with remaining grated cheese. Bake at 325° for 45-60 minutes, until heated all the way through. Serves 4-6.

Mrs. Bass C. Wallace (Julia Picton)

Turkey Stuffing and Basting Sauce

⅓ cup butter, melted
2 tablespoons lemon juice
½ teaspoon salt
3 tablespoons cognac
2 tablespoons chopped onion
¼ cup chopped celery

1 tablespoon butter
½ cup dry white wine
1 can condensed cream of
chicken soup
¼ cup chopped parsley
1¼ packages Pepperidge Farm
herb stuffing

Melt 1/3 cup butter and add lemon juice; set aside for basting. Before stuffing turkey, dry and salt cavity. Sprinkle cavity with cognac. Saute onion and celery in 1 tablespoon butter. Add wine, soup and parsley; then add herb stuffing. Stuff turkey. Bake turkey by your favorite method, basting it with the lemon-butter sauce every 30 minutes. This is enough stuffing for a small turkey (12 pounds at most), or a large chicken hen.

Mrs. John Lock Cook (Susan Ferguson)

Extra Turkey Dressing

4 cups cooked rice
½ cup cooked, chopped
turkey giblets
12 oysters, drained and chopped

½ cup minced green onions
1 cup turkey gravy
2 eggs, beaten
Salt and pepper

Mix cooked rice, giblets, oysters, onions, gravy, eggs, salt and pepper. Spoon into greased dish and bake, uncovered, at 350° for about 30 minutes. Serve hot. Serves 6-8.

Mrs. Gordon R. West (Josephine Morrow)

Southern Cornbread Stuffing

4 cups cornbread crumbs	1½ cups (or less) boiling water
8 cups lightly-packed, day-old	½ cup butter, melted
bread crumbs	1 cup minced onion
1½ teaspoons salt	1 cup diced celery
¼ teaspoon pepper	4 eggs, beaten
Poultry seasoning (optional)	1 quart oysters, drained (optional)

Make cornbread (can be made a day ahead). Break cornbread into small pieces and mix with bread crumbs, salt, pepper and poultry seasoning. Add boiling water, melted butter, onion and celery. Mix well. Mix eggs in well. Add oysters, mixing lightly so as not to break them. Makes enough dressing to stuff 1 medium-large turkey. This is a moist stuffing.

Mrs. Thomas G. Vandivier (Bettie Ebaugh)

Turkey Bodines

2 cups diced, cooked, cold turkey	Approximately ½ cup gravy
1 cup leftover turkey stuffing	Cranberry jelly for garnish
2 eggs, well beaten	

Combine all ingredients except cranberry jelly and mold into 6 patties or pyramid shapes, flattened on top. Place bodines in shallow, well-greased baking pan. Pour Bechamel Sauce around them and bake in a 350° oven until brown. Just before serving, place a small dab of cranberry jelly on top of each bodine. A great way to use leftover turkey, stuffing and cranberry sauce. Makes 6 servings.

BECHAMEL SAUCE

2 tablespoons butter	½ cup well-seasoned chicken
2 tablespoons flour	(or turkey) stock
½ cup milk, heated	Salt
	Paprika
	1 egg yolk

Melt butter; blend in flour. Slowly add hot milk and stock, stirring constantly. Cook and stir until boiling; add salt and paprika. Beat a little of the hot mixture into egg yolk, then combine with remaining sauce. Stir over very low heat until sauce thickens slightly. Do not boil after egg has been added to the sauce. Makes 1 cup sauce.

Mrs. Gordon R. West (Josephine Morrow)

Cornish Hens

For each half bird:
Salt
Freshly ground black pepper
Paprika
2 tablespoons olive oil

¼ teaspoon thyme
¼ teaspoon poultry seasoning
1 tablespoon chopped parsley
2 teaspoons Worcestershire sauce
2 tablespoons dry red wine

Split birds in half and sprinkle each half with salt, pepper and paprika. Place each half on a square of heavy foil. Pour olive oil over birds and grease well. Place birds skin side down and fill cavity with other ingredients which have been mixed together. Fold foil squares around birds to keep in all juices. Bake in pre-heated 300° oven for 1 hour, or until birds are tender. Just before serving open foil packages, turn the birds skin side up, and raise oven heat to brown (approximately 20 minutes). Serve with pan juices.

Mrs. Ghent Graves, Jr. (Sally Sample)

Doves

12 doves
Salt and pepper
Monosodium glutamate
½ cup butter
½ cup chopped parsley

1 cup chopped green onions
1 cup beef consomme or water
¼ cup dry white wine
1 tablespoon flour (optional)

Sprinkle doves with salt, pepper and monosodium glutamate. Simmer and brown slowly in butter for almost 1 hour. Add parsley, green onions and consomme. Add wine. Cover and cook slowly until tender, about 45 minutes. Additional consomme and wine may be added, if more gravy is desired. Gravy may be thickened with flour. Serves 4.

Mrs. Lewis W. Pollok (Clemence Tacquard)

Potted Doves

Flour and salt
6 doves
¼ to ½ cup butter
¼ cup chopped onion
1 can (4 oz.) mushrooms,
   chopped (reserve juice)

1 teaspoon chopped parsley
½ to ¾ cup dry white wine
½ cup heavy cream
1 to 2 teaspoons salt

Mix flour and salt; rub into doves. Saute doves lightly in butter. Remove doves and place in greased baking dish. Saute onion, chopped mushrooms and parsley in butter remaining in skillet. Add wine and mushroom juice. Pour mixture over birds. Cook 30 minutes in 425° oven, basting frequently with pan juices. Stir in cream and season with salt. Serve thoroughly heated. May be served with wild or white rice. Serves 3.

Mrs. J. Toll Underwood (Martha Jennings)

Doves à la Peggy

12-16 doves
½ cup chopped onions
½ cup chopped celery
½ cup butter

1 package (8 oz.) cornbread
   stuffing
1 cup beef consomme
1 cup chicken broth

Remove wings from birds leaving only breasts and legs. Saute onion and celery in butter. Add cornbread stuffing and enough consomme to moisten well. Fill cavity of each dove with stuffing. Place stuffed birds breast side up in pan or baking dish. Add remaining consomme and chicken broth to the pan, partially covering birds. Cook covered on top of the stove or in a 350° oven for about 2 hours, or until birds are tender. Preparation, except for cooking, may be done the day before serving. Serves 4-6.

Mrs. Richard F. Burns (Dorothy Fields)

Tarragon Doves

15 doves
Salt, pepper and flour
2 tablespoons cooking oil
2 tablespoons butter

1 teaspoon tarragon
¼ cup sherry
½ cup water

Sprinkle the doves with salt, pepper and flour. In a large skillet brown doves slowly in oil and butter. This should take about 25 minutes. Add tarragon, sherry and water. Cover tightly and simmer slowly for 30 minutes. Serves 4-6.

Mrs. Phillip B. Sherwood (Mary Alexander)

Dove Pie

8-10 doves	1½ cups stock
Celery leaves	¼ teaspoon Kitchen Bouquet
Salt and pepper	¼ teaspoon Worcestershire sauce
⅓ cup chopped celery	Dash nutmeg
⅓ cup chopped green onions	1 can (8½ oz.) tiny green
1 tablespoon butter	peas, drained
1 tablespoon flour	Recipe for 2-crust pastry

Cook doves with celery leaves and light seasoning of salt and pepper in water to cover. (Pressure cooker may be used.) Remove meat from bones and set aside. Save stock for sauce. To make sauce, brown celery and green onions in butter. Mix in flour. Add stock, stirring until smooth. Add Kitchen Bouquet, Worcestershire sauce, nutmeg, salt and pepper. Stir thoroughly; add dove meat and peas. Line a 1-1/2-quart casserole with half the pastry; pour in sauce and dove mixture. Roll out remaining pastry and seal over top of casserole. Bake at 425° for 35-40 minutes. Serves 4 generously.

Mrs. James P. Jackson (Sarah Faulkner)

Quail or Pheasant

8-10 quail or 2-3 pheasants	1 cup chicken consomme
Salt and pepper	Poultry seasoning
¼ cup margarine	Sherry (optional)
¼ cup shortening	

Salt and pepper birds lightly. Saute in mixture of margarine and shortening until lightly browned. Remove birds to baking dish. Add consomme to the drippings and season with additional salt and pepper, and poultry seasoning. Pour gravy (it will be very thin) over birds; cover and bake in 325° oven for approximately 1 hour, or until tender. Baste birds with sherry once or twice, if desired. Serve with rice. Serves 4.

Mrs. George A. Stovall (Donna Lucas)

Pheasant à la Crème

2 pheasants (or Cornish game hens)	2 tablespoons lemon juice
Salt and pepper	2 cans (4 oz. each) sliced mushrooms with liquid
Paprika	1 medium onion, finely chopped
Flour	½ cup finely chopped celery
½ cup butter	½ cup pitted ripe olives, finely sliced
2 cups sour cream	2 tablespoons chopped pimiento

Split birds in half. Sprinkle with salt, pepper and paprika. Dredge lightly with flour. Brown in butter on top of stove until golden. Remove birds and place in roasting pan. Add remaining ingredients to butter in which birds were browned. Pour over pheasants, cover roasting pan and bake in 300° oven until tender, about 1-1/2 hours. Sauce is very good served over rice. Serves 4.

Mrs. Ghent Graves, Jr. (Sally Sample)

Wild Duck with Orange Sauce

4-6 ducks	2 oranges
Salt and pepper	Soft butter
Lemon juice	Flour
2 apples	

Have ducks at room temperature. Rub inside and out with salt, pepper and lemon juice. Stuff cavities with pieces of apple and orange. Spread ducks with butter. Wrap ducks together in foil; bake at 350° for 2-1/2 to 3 hours. To make gravy, thicken 1 cup broth from baked ducks with 1 or 2 tablespoons flour dissolved in cold water. Serve duck with gravy and Orange Sauce. Allow 1 duck per person.

ORANGE SAUCE

1 cup sugar	Juice of ½ lemon, or more to taste
½ cup butter	
½ cup orange juice concentrate	1 can (11 oz.) Mandarin orange segments, or fresh orange sections
Juice and grated rind of 1 orange	

Bring sugar, butter and orange juice concentrate to a boil. Add other ingredients. Heat and serve with duck.

Mrs. David H. Harrington (Dodie Newton)

Wild Duck Camille

24 ducks	5 soup-cans water
3 bottles dry red wine	6 ribs celery, chopped
1 lemon, sliced	3 carrots, chopped
Butter	4 cans condensed cream of
Oil	mushroom soup
Salt and pepper	3 or 4 bay leaves (optional)
3 cans beef consomme	Rosemary (optional)
	Thyme (optional)

Marinate the ducks in wine with lemon for 24 hours. Remove ducks, reserving wine. Butter and oil ducks; sprinkle with salt and pepper. Put in roasting pan in 450° oven. Turn ducks frequently until they are browned thoroughly, being careful not to puncture skin. Add consomme, water, celery and carrots. Cook, covered, for at least 1-1/2 hours in 300°-350° oven, turning occasionally until ducks are done. Remove ducks. Strain stock and discard vegetables. Pour mushroom soup into saucepan. Gradually add stock. Add bay leaves, rosemary and thyme. Bring to a boil. Add reserved wine. Return ducks with sauce to roasting pan and cook for 1 hour over direct heat. If a thicker sauce is desired, add a little flour. To serve ducks, the breast, back and rib bones may be removed, leaving each duck split in half with only wing and leg bones remaining. The ducks are so tender by this time that they can be eaten with a fork. Serve with wild rice. This recipe makes a great amount of sauce. To cook a smaller number of ducks, reduce liquids or save extra sauce for another time. Serves 24.

Mrs. Harmon Whittington (Dolores Welder)

Wild Duck Riverbend

For each duck:

1 tablespoon butter	1 tablespoon bacon drippings
1 tablespoon cooking oil	Salt and pepper

Clean each duck inside as well as out; dry. In Dutch oven melt butter, oil and bacon drippings. Salt and pepper each duck. Brown very well on all sides. Add 2 inches water; boil down over medium heat. When all water has boiled away, brown ducks a second time. Add 1 inch water; boil down again over medium heat. Brown ducks a third time. Add 2 inches water; cook down slowly over low heat until just enough liquid remains for rich gravy. Cooking time will be 1-1/2 to 2 hours in all. Serve with Sausage Rice, page 253. Allow 1 duck per person.

Mrs. James F. Hayes (Lisbeth Young)

Roast Wild Duck

2 quarts water	4-6 ducks or geese
3 ribs celery	Margarine
2 medium carrots, cut in half	Flour
1 onion, quartered	Apple quarters
1 teaspoon salt	Onion quarters

Make stock by simmering water, celery, carrots, onion and salt together for 1-2 hours. Rub each duck with mixture of softened margarine and flour. Stuff cavities of ducks with 1 or 2 quarters each of apple and onion. Bake in roasting pan, uncovered, at 450° for 30 minutes, or until browned. Reduce heat to 350° and cover pan. Cook 4 hours, basting with prepared stock every 30 minutes. To make gravy, thicken drippings with 1-2 tablespoons flour and cook until smooth. Add stock to thin gravy to desired consistency. Allow 1 duck per person. Geese also can be cooked this way, but for a longer time, about 6 hours.

Mrs. LaMar W. Lee (Mary Louise Townes)

Evelyn's Wild Duck

2 ducks	2 ribs celery
Salt and pepper	2 turnips or 5-6 Jerusalem
2 tablespoons cooking oil	artichokes, peeled
3 medium onions	1 small jar (2 oz.) pimiento
1 green pepper	2 cloves garlic, crushed
	2 slices bacon

Rub the inside of the ducks with salt and pepper. In a heavy Dutch oven, heat oil; add ducks and brown on all sides. Remove ducks and set aside. Coarsely chop onions, green pepper, celery and turnips. To remaining oil in Dutch oven add vegetables and cook until wilted. Add pimiento and garlic. Return ducks to pan. Season with salt and pepper. Pour in about 2 cups water. (Ducks should be half-covered.) Place slice of bacon on each duck. Cover pan and bake in 300° oven for 3 hours, or until ducks are tender. Serve ducks with vegetable sauce, mashing vegetables if desired. Serves 2-4.

Mrs. George N. Allen, Jr. (Bonnie Blades)

Wild Duck with Olive Sauce

3 or 4 large ducks
Flour
Salt and pepper
Bacon drippings

2½ cups water
1 cup sliced green olives
½ cup white wine

Dredge ducks in flour which has been seasoned with salt and pepper. Brown well in bacon drippings in Dutch oven. Remove ducks and set aside. Make sauce by stirring enough flour into the fat to make a thin paste; then stir in water and salt to taste. Add olives and place the ducks in the sauce. Bake, covered, in 375° oven for 2-3 hours or until tender, adding more water if necessary. To serve, remove ducks to platter, skim off excess fat, and add wine to sauce. Pour sauce over ducks to serve. Serves 6.

Mrs. Paul F. McBride, Jr. (Pattie Cunningham)

Gulf Coast Duck

2 tablespoons cayenne
1 cup flour
6 ducks
Bacon drippings
4 ribs celery, finely chopped
1 cup finely chopped green onions

⅓ cup finely chopped parsley
2 cloves garlic, crushed
3 tablespoons Worcestershire
    sauce
2 tablespoons catsup
Water

Mix cayenne with flour. Rub this mixture all over ducks. Brown the ducks slowly in bacon drippings until very brown. Remove the ducks; pour off some grease. Add celery, onions and parsley; cook over low heat until soft. Add garlic, Worcestershire sauce and catsup. Place ducks in the sauce in heavy roasting pan and add enough water to half-cover the ducks. Cook, covered, in 300° oven for 4 hours. Gravy will be very thin but good over wild rice. This recipe may be used for doves. Serves 6.

Mrs. Henry P. Luckett (Evelyn Sanford)

Venison Ham or Roast

Venison ham
Flour
Salt and pepper
Bacon drippings

1 large onion, sliced
1 cup water
1 can (4 oz.) mushrooms
½ cup white wine

Sprinkle roast with flour, salt and pepper. Brown well in drippings in heavy pot over high heat. Add onion slices and water. Cover, reduce heat, and simmer about 40 minutes per pound. One hour before roast is done, add mushrooms and white wine. Allow 1/4 to 1/2 pound per person.

Mrs. LaMar W. Lee (Mary Louise Townes)

Roast Venison with Horseradish

1 venison roast (2½ lbs.)	1 teaspoon salt
1 medium onion, sliced	6 slices bacon
1 cup cooking oil	2 tablespoons horseradish
½ cup lemon juice	6 tablespoons sherry

In a large bowl place roast and a mixture of onion, cooking oil, lemon juice and salt. Cover tightly and refrigerate for 24 hours. Remove roast from marinade and wrap it with bacon. Bake in roasting pan at 300° for 2 hours, basting frequently with marinade. When roast is done, remove to platter and skim most of the fat from the pan. Stir horseradish and sherry into remaining gravy to serve over roast. May be thickened with flour if desired. Serves 4-6.

Mrs. Claude C. Cody, III (Muriel Fursteneau)

Marinated Venison Roast

1 venison roast (6-8 lbs.)	Freshly ground pepper
Salt pork, thinly sliced	2 cups dry red wine
1 clove garlic, crushed	2 bay leaves
Salt	5 slices bacon

Make slits about 1" deep at regular intervals in the roast. Force slices of salt pork into each slit. Rub the roast with garlic, salt and pepper. Place in a roasting pan and pour wine over meat. Add bay leaves to the pan and let marinate in refrigerator 8-10 hours, turning occasionally. Arrange bacon over top of roast and bake in preheated 300° oven for 2-1/2 to 3 hours, basting occasionally. Serve hot or cold. May be served sliced thinly on biscuits with Hunters' Mustard, page 263.

Mrs. Bruce E. Barnett (Ann Poyner)

Venison Chili

1 pound ground venison	1 can (10 oz.) Rotel tomatoes
Vinegar	and green chilies
1 onion, chopped	2 tablespoons chili powder
2 tablespoons lard	Salt and pepper to taste
Beef consomme or bouillon	

Marinate meat in vinegar about 1 hour. Rinse well and drain. Brown meat, onions and garlic in lard in Dutch oven. Add enough consomme or bouillon to cover meat. Add tomatoes, chili powder, salt and pepper. Simmer, covered, at least 2 hours. Serves 4.

Mrs. James L. Bayless (Betty Lou Langston)

Peppered Venison Ham or Roast

1 venison ham or roast
(4-5 lbs.)
2-8 chili piquins (small
hot red peppers)
2 onions, chopped
1 slice bacon, cut in pieces
Salt and pepper

Flour
Bacon drippings or cooking oil
2 cups hot water or consomme
1 medium onion, chopped
1 cup catsup
2 tablespoons vinegar

Wash and dry roast well. Make about 12 thin slits in meat and insert peppers, onions and bacon pieces alternately. Rub the surface of the meat with salt, pepper and flour. Put 1/2" drippings or oil into Dutch oven. Sear until crusty. Then add hot water or consomme. Cook covered for about 4 hours in 325° oven. Remove roast and keep warm. Skim fat from pan leaving only brown drippings. Add onion and cook until limp. Stir in catsup and vinegar. Bring to a boil. Thinly slice roast and serve with sauce. (Be sure to remove hot peppers.) Serves 8.

Mrs. Seaborn Eastland, Jr. (Anne Stacy)

Hill Country Venison Stew

1 venison roast (about 2½-3 lbs.)
½ cup flour
1½ teaspoons salt
1½ teaspoons pepper
¼ teaspoon nutmeg
¼ teaspoon ground cloves
¼ teaspoon cayenne
¼ cup butter
3 large onions, sliced
1 clove garlic, crushed

2 cups peeled and quartered
tomatoes
2 tablespoons chopped parsley
1½ tablespoons Worcestershire
sauce
4 drops Tabasco
1½ cups dry red wine
1 cup sliced mushroom caps
Sour cream
Currant jelly

Cut meat into 1" cubes and roll in flour which has been seasoned with salt, pepper, nutmeg, cloves and cayenne. Melt butter in Dutch oven, add meat and sear on all sides. Add onions and garlic; saute until brown. Stir in tomatoes, parsley, Worcestershire sauce, Tabasco and wine. Cover and bake in 300° oven for 2-1/2 hours. Add additional salt and pepper if necessary. Stir well. Saute mushrooms in a little butter and add to stew. Top each serving with a spoonful of sour cream and a dollop of currant jelly. Serves 10-12.

Mrs. Frank J. Whittemore (Tay Seaman)

SEA FOOD

Hints

FISH

In selecting fish, a fresh fish has clear, bright and full eyes; bright pink gills; and firm, elastic flesh.

The flavor of fish is often improved by placing fish in a marinade of 1 part vinegar or dry white wine to 2 parts oil. If desired, add a slice of garlic to the marinade.

Frozen fish spoils very quickly after being thawed, so use immediately.

Cook fish only until tender; do not overcook.

SHELLFISH

TO BOIL SHRIMP: (Shrimp may be cleaned and deveined before or after cooking.) Drop shrimp into boiling salted water to cover, using 1 tablespoon salt per 1 quart water. (If desired, add sliced onion, parsley springs and whole peppercorns.) Simmer, covered, 2 to 5 minutes—never longer—or until shrimp are pink. Drain and refrigerate.

(Number of raw, unshelled shrimp per pound: Jumbo, 18-20; Large, 21-25; Medium, 26-35; Small, over 35.)

TO BOIL HARD-SHELL CRABS: Drop live crabs into boiling salted water to cover, using 1 tablespoon salt per 1 quart water. (If desired, add Crab Boil or additional seasonings.) Return water to boiling; lower heat. Cover and simmer about 15 minutes. Drain. Place crabs in cool water. Drain and spread on flat surface to let cool. When crabs are cool, clean and refrigerate. (If preferred, crabs may be cleaned before boiling.) 8 crabs make about 1 cup crabmeat.

OYSTERS: Oysters have one deep and one shallow shell. Use the deep shell for serving oysters raw or baking on the half-shell. (Nice shells may be washed and re-used; good to have on hand for oysters by the pint.)

Crab Superior

2 tablespoons chopped onion
2 tablespoons chopped green
　pepper
2 tablespoons butter
3 tablespoons flour
¾ cup milk
½ teaspoon salt

¼ teaspoon pepper
Dash Tabasco
1 teaspoon lemon juice
½ teaspoon tarragon vinegar
1 pound crabmeat
Buttered bread crumbs

Saute onion and green pepper in butter. Stir in flour. Add milk gradually; cook over low heat, stirring constantly until mixture thickens into a sauce. Remove from heat. Combine salt, pepper, Tabasco, lemon juice, vinegar and crabmeat; mix with sauce. Pour mixture into casserole, cover with buttered bread crumbs, and bake at 375° for 25 minutes. Serves 4.

Mrs. W. T. Hancock, Jr. (Kano Mayo)

Crabmeat Supreme

1 cup chopped onion
1 cup chopped green pepper
1 cup chopped celery
1 pound butter
2 pounds lump crabmeat
½ cup chopped parsley
4 teaspoons salt
1-2 teaspoons Tabasco
Juice of 2 lemons

4 pimientos, chopped
1 large can (1 lb.) mushrooms,
　drained
1 cup sherry
1 cup flour
1 teaspoon pepper
4 cups milk
1 cup cracker crumbs

Saute onions, green peppers and celery in half of the butter (do not brown). Remove from heat. In a large bowl, combine sauteed mixture with crabmeat, parsley, 2 teaspoons salt, Tabasco, lemon juice, pimientos, mushrooms and sherry. In large double boiler, or pan, combine flour, remaining 2 teaspoons salt and pepper. Gradually stir in milk. Cook over hot water, or low direct heat, stirring constantly until mixture is smooth. Remove from heat and add remaining half of the butter; stir until melted. Combine sauce with crab mixture. Spoon into a 4-quart casserole. Sprinkle cracker crumbs on top. Bake 20 minutes in a 325° oven; or, if casserole is cold, bake 30 minutes in a 350° oven. Serves 16.

Mrs. George N. Allen, Jr. (Bonnie Blades)

Crabmeat Jubilee

1 onion, chopped
3 tablespoons bacon drippings
2 cloves garlic, crushed
1 pound lump crabmeat
1 small box (3½ oz.) saltine
   crackers, crushed

Salt and pepper
Cayenne
1 cup cream
½ cup butter, melted

Saute onion in bacon drippings until golden. Add garlic, and continue cooking until brown. Remove from heat. Add crabmeat and half of the crushed crackers. Season with salt, pepper and cayenne. Spoon mixture into buttered casserole. Pour cream over mixture. Sprinkle remaining crackers on top. Pour melted butter over all. Bake at 350° for 20 minutes, or until brown. Serves 4.

Mrs. Joseph C. Brown (Susan Judd)

Crabmeat Lorenzo

1 cup chopped green onions
⅓ cup sliced mushrooms
1 clove garlic, crushed
¼ cup butter
2 teaspoons prepared mustard
3 teaspoons Worcestershire sauce
3 dashes Tabasco
½ cup dry white wine
3 tablespoons medium cream
   sauce, or undiluted cream of
   mushroom soup

½ teaspoon white pepper
¾ cup cracker crumbs
1 pound lump crabmeat
4 slices toast, with corners
   trimmed off
4 strips anchovy, sliced in
   half, lengthwise
8 stuffed olives, sliced in half
2 pitted ripe olives, sliced
   in half

Saute onions, mushrooms and garlic in butter. Add mustard, Worcestershire sauce, Tabasco, wine, cream sauce (or mushroom soup), white pepper, cracker crumbs and crabmeat. Mix well; warm mixture over low heat. If mixture seems too thick, add a small amount of cream. Divide into four portions and spoon on toast slices. Garnish each portion with anchovy fillets and slices of stuffed and ripe olives. Before serving, brown lightly under broiler. Serves 4.

Mrs. Gordon R. West (Josephine Morrow)

Crabmeat Imperial

1 tablespoon grated onion	1 teaspoon salt
¼ cup butter	Dash hot pepper sauce
¼ cup sifted flour	1 can (4 oz.) sliced mushrooms,
1 cup milk	drained
½ cup dry white wine	1 egg yolk, beaten
½ cup sherry	1 pound crabmeat

Saute onion in butter, blend in flour; do not brown. Gradually add milk, wine and sherry, stirring constantly until thickened. Add salt, pepper sauce and mushrooms. Remove from heat when bubbles appear; quickly stir in egg yolk and crabmeat. Serve over rice. Serves 6.

Mrs. W. Irving Phillips, Jr. (Elizabeth Brown)

Crabmeat Remick

1 pound crabmeat	Few drops Tabasco
6 strips bacon, fried crisp	1 cup chili sauce
1 scant teaspoon dry mustard	1 teaspoon tarragon vinegar
½ teaspoon paprika	⅓ cup mayonnaise
½ teaspoon celery salt	

Heap crabmeat into 6 individual, buttered shells or ramekins. Heat in oven until warm. Remove, and top each with a strip of crisp bacon. Combine mustard, paprika, celery, salt and Tabasco. Add chili sauce, tarragon vinegar and mayonnaise; mix well. Spread sauce over bacon. Heat under broiler until crabmeat is warm and sauce is glazed. Serves 6.

Mrs. Robert Mosbacher (Jane Pennybacker)

Crabmeat Quickie

1 can condensed mushroom soup	½ cup dry sherry
1½ cans condensed Cheddar	2 pounds lump crabmeat
cheese soup	Grated sharp Cheddar cheese

Combine mushroom soup, cheese soup, sherry and crabmeat. Thin with extra sherry, if desired. Spoon into 2-quart casserole. Top with grated cheese. Bake in 350° oven until all cheese is melted. Serve over wild rice. Serves 8.

Mrs. Gibbs Meador (Mary Jo Garrett)

Crab Casserole

1 cup thick cream sauce	Salt and pepper
3 tablespoons chopped celery	Paprika
1 tablespoon butter	2 tablespoons grated cheese
1 can (4 oz.) sliced mushrooms,	(Parmesan or Cheddar)
drained	1 tablespoon sherry
1 pound lump crabmeat	Bread crumbs and Parmesan
	cheese for topping

Make a thick cream sauce. Saute celery in butter until tender. Add celery, mushrooms and crabmeat to cream sauce. Stir in salt, pepper, paprika, cheese and sherry. Pour into buttered casserole or individual crab shells. Brown bread crumbs in a little melted butter; mix with Parmesan cheese and sprinkle on casserole. Bake in 400° oven for 15 minutes, or until thoroughly heated. Serves 4-6.

Mrs. J. G. Lawhon (Virginia Vinson)

Lemoned Crabmeat

1 pound lump crabmeat	¼ teaspoon salt
2 to 4 tablespoons lemon juice	½ teaspoon dry mustard
1 medium onion, minced	Dash pepper
¼ cup chopped green pepper	1 teaspoon Tabasco
¼ cup butter	1 teaspoon Worcestershire sauce
3 tablespoons flour	Buttered bread crumbs
1 cup milk	Paprika

Marinate crabmeat in lemon juice at least 1 hour. Cook onion and green pepper in butter until transparent. Stir in flour; gradually add milk. Cook over low heat, stirring constantly, until mixture is thick and bubbly. Remove from heat and add salt, mustard, pepper, Tabasco and Worcestershire sauce. Fold in crabmeat. Spoon into baking dish or individual shells. Top with buttered bread crumbs; sprinkle with paprika. Bake in 375° oven for 20-30 minutes. Serves 4-6.

Mrs. Douglas S. Craig (Alice Picton)

Crab Burger

1 pound crabmeat	1 cup grated Cheddar cheese
½ cup diced celery	1 cup mayonnaise
2 tablespoons grated onion	4 large hamburger buns

Combine crab, celery, onion, cheese and mayonnaise; refrigerate. Split buns, butter well, and heat in 325° oven for 10-15 minutes. Spread crab mixture on bun halves. Broil until hot and browned. Makes 8 open-faced crab-burgers.

Mrs. Frank J. McGurl (Mary Martin)

Crab Elegante

2 cups thick cream sauce
1 teaspoon Worcestershire sauce
Salt
White pepper
1 green pepper, minced
1 medium onion, minced
1 clove garlic, crushed

¼ cup butter
1½ cups fresh mushrooms, sliced
1 pound lump crabmeat
¼ cup chopped parsley
1 lemon, cut into 6 slices
Paprika

Make a thick cream sauce and season it with Worcestershire sauce, salt and white pepper. Saute green pepper, onion and garlic in 2 tablespoons of the butter for 5 minutes; add to the seasoned cream sauce. Saute mushrooms in remaining 2 tablespoons butter and add to cream sauce. Fold in crabmeat and parsley. Pile into 6 buttered seafood shells or ramekins; top each with a thin lemon slice. Sprinkle with paprika. Bake in 350° oven for 30 minutes, or until bubbly. This may be baked in a buttered casserole, topped with lemon slices. Serves 6.

Mrs. Jack T. Currie (Dorothy Peek)

Eggplant Stuffed with Crabmeat

4 medium eggplants
1 cup chopped green onions with tops
3 tablespoons finely chopped green pepper
1 clove garlic, crushed
1 scant tablespoon thyme
3 tablespoons finely chopped parsley

2 bay leaves, crumbled
½ pound butter
4 slices bread
2 pounds lump crabmeat
3 eggs, beaten
Salt and pepper
Bread crumbs
Paprika

Cut eggplants in half; do not peel. Parboil for 10 minutes. Let cool. Reserve liquid. Scoop out pulp and chop. Saute onions, green pepper, garlic, thyme, parsley and bay leaves in butter for 5 minutes. Soak bread in reserved liquid, then squeeze. Add bread, crabmeat and eggplant to sauteed mixture; mix well. Gradually stir in eggs. Season with salt and pepper. Cook 5 minutes, stirring constantly. Fill eggplant shells with mixture. Sprinkle with bread crumbs and paprika; dot with butter. Bake at 350° for 15 minutes, or until browned. Serves 8.

Mrs. Wallace M. Davis, Jr. (Barbara Sterrett)

Creamed Crab

5 tablespoons butter
4 or 5 large ribs celery, chopped
1 small onion, chopped
3 tablespoons flour
1½ cups milk
1 teaspoon Spice Islands
  chicken stock base

Pepper
1 pound lump crabmeat
3 tablespoons dry sherry
Cheese Ritz crackers, crumbled,
  for topping

Melt 2 tablespoons of the butter in skillet, and slowly cook celery and onion until soft, but not brown. Set aside. Melt remaining butter in double boiler. Add flour and stir until smooth; slowly add milk. Cook, stirring often, for 30 minutes. Add chicken stock base; season with pepper. Stir in crabmeat, sherry, celery and onion. Spoon into seafood shells. Sprinkle lightly with cracker crumbs. Bake in 350° oven until thoroughly heated. May be made early in day and heated just before serving. Serves 4-5.

Mrs. Edward W. Kelley, Jr. (Ellen Elizardi)

Avocado Crab Mornay

3 avocados
6 green onions, minced
1½ pounds crabmeat
⅓ cup butter

¾ cup sherry
2 cups Mornay Sauce
3 ounces grated Parmesan
  cheese

Halve avocados; remove seeds, scoop out flesh and dice. Lightly saute diced avocado, green onions and crabmeat in butter. Add sherry; stir well. Add Mornay Sauce. Pile mixture in seafood shells. Sprinkle with Parmesan cheese. Heat in 500° oven for only 5 minutes. Serves 8-10.

MORNAY SAUCE

¼ cup butter
¼ cup flour
1 cup chicken stock
1 cup cream
Dash salt

Dash cayenne
Dash nutmeg
2 tablespoons shredded
  Swiss cheese
¼ cup grated Parmesan cheese

Melt butter; stir in flour. Cook 2-3 minutes. Stir in chicken stock and cream. Cook, stirring constantly, until smooth. Add salt, cayenne, nutmeg and cheeses; stir and heat until well blended. Makes 2 cups.

Mrs. Charles B. Williams (Bobbie Ruth Richardson)

Crabmeat Au Gratin

1 cup medium cream sauce	1 tablespoon chopped pimiento
1 pound Velveeta cheese, grated	Cayenne
1 tablespoon grated green pepper	1 pound crabmeat
1 can (4 oz.) mushroom pieces, drained	Buttered bread crumbs

Prepare cream sauce. Stir in grated cheese, green pepper, mushrooms, pimientos and cayenne; mix thoroughly. Add crabmeat, stirring gently. Spoon into individual casseroles or shells; top with buttered crumbs. Bake in 300° oven until bubbly. Serves 6.

Mrs. J. Malcolm Horn (Helen Hargrove)

Crabmeat Quiche

1 unbaked 9-inch pastry shell	¼ teaspoon pepper
1½ cups crabmeat	1¼ cups heavy cream
2½ tablespoons vermouth	¼ teaspoon paprika
2½ tablespoons minced onion	⅓ cup grated Swiss cheese
¼ cup butter	4 eggs, slightly beaten
¼ teaspoon salt	

Place an 8-inch pie pan on top of 9-inch pastry shell, and bake 10 minutes in a 450° oven. Remove top pan, prick pastry with fork, and bake 3 more minutes. Marinate crabmeat in vermouth. Saute onion in butter until soft. Just before baking, combine crabmeat, sauteed onion and all remaining ingredients. Pour mixture into pastry shells and bake in upper 1/3 of 375° oven for 45 minutes. This quiche may be served as a main dish or for hors d'oeuvres.

Mrs. Frank J. McGurl (Mary Martin)

Crab on English Muffins

1 small package (3 oz.) cream cheese	Salt
	1 pound lump crabmeat
1 tablespoon minced onion	4 English muffins
2 tablespoons mayonnaise	8 thick slices tomato
2 tablespoons catsup	8 slices Old English cheese
1½ teaspoons Worcestershire sauce	

Soften cream cheese. Blend in onion, mayonnaise, catsup, Worcestershire sauce, salt and crabmeat. Split English muffins and butter each half. Place tomato slice on each half and spread with crab mixture. Top with a slice of cheese. Bake in 350° oven for 20-30 minutes. Makes 8 servings.

Mrs. George H. Lane (Joan Bagby)

Deviled Crab

½ cup butter	White pepper
¼ cup flour	2 cups milk
2 tablespoons minced parsley	2 pounds lump crabmeat
4 teaspoons lemon juice	1 cup soft bread crumbs
2 teaspoons prepared mustard	¼ cup melted butter
3 teaspoons salt	

Melt 1/2 cup butter in double boiler and stir in flour. Add parsley, lemon juice, mustard, salt, white pepper and milk. Cook, stirring, until thickened. Add crabmeat. Spoon mixture into shells or ramekins. Top with bread crumbs combined with the 1/4 cup melted butter. Bake in preheated 400° oven for 10 minutes. Makes 12 small servings.

Mrs. Thane Tyler Sponsel (Mary Jane Price)

Crab - Spaghetti Giovanni

1 package (8 oz.) thin spaghetti	1 can (1 lb.) tomatoes, drained
1 large onion, finely chopped	1 can (8 oz.) tomato sauce
1 green pepper, finely chopped	1 pound crabmeat
6-8 ounces fresh mushrooms, sliced	1 cup sour cream
Butter for sauteeing	2½ cups grated sharp cheese

Cook spaghetti; drain and set aside. Saute onion, green pepper and mushrooms in butter. Add tomatoes, tomato sauce, crabmeat, sour cream and half of the cheese; simmer for 5 minutes. Combine with spaghetti. Pour into greased casserole and top with remaining cheese. Bake 30-45 minutes in a 325° oven. May be prepared a day ahead and baked just before serving. Increase cooking time if mixture is cold. Chicken (3-4 cups) may be substituted for crab. Serves 8-10.

Mrs. Robert B. Crouch (Nancy Wencke)

Chafing Dish Crabmeat

6 tablespoons butter	2 tablespoons chopped parsley
1 pound lump crabmeat	1½ teaspoons powdered chicken
⅓ cup chopped green pepper	stock base
¼ cup chopped green onions	1 tablespoon flour
	¼ cup dry white wine

Melt butter in chafing dish or serving skillet. Saute crab, green pepper and onions in the butter over low heat about 5 minutes. Add parsley and continue cooking 2-3 minutes. Mix chicken stock base and flour with wine. Add to crabmeat mixture and cook 1 more minute. Serve immediately. Serves 4.

Mrs. Marvin V. Cluett (Lollie Lauderdale)

Bay Boil

1 onion, sliced
1 tablespoon dill seed
2 bay leaves
4 to 6 peppercorns

2 bottles beer
2 to 3 pounds large, raw
    shrimp in shells

In a deep pot, combine everything but shrimp; bring to a boil. Add shrimp; boil until just tender, about 10-15 minutes. Let cool slightly in stock. Drain and place shrimp, still in shells, on platter. Serve with melted butter seasoned with garlic powder, Worcestershire sauce, lemon juice and Tabasco. I serve this with hush puppies and sauteed cucumbers. Serves 4-6.

Mrs. Owen Finch (Betty Grey)

Shrimp with Horseradish Sauce

2 teaspoons salt
1 medium onion, chopped
2 tablespoons celery seed
2 tablespoons prepared mustard

2 tablespoons dry mustard
1 teaspoon peppercorns
3 cans beer
5 pounds raw shrimp in shells

Combine all ingredients except shrimp and simmer for about 15 minutes. Drop shrimp into boiling beer mixture and cook 15 minutes. Stir occasionally. Serve with creamy Horseradish Sauce. Serves 8-10.

CREAMY HORSERADISH SAUCE

1 package (8 oz.) cream
    cheese, softened
2 tablespoons mayonnaise
4 tablespoons horseradish,
    or less to taste

2 tablespoons Worcestershire
    sauce
2 tablespoons grated onion
1 teaspoon salt
½ cup (or more) cream

Mix all ingredients until well blended. Serve with boiled shrimp. Makes 2-1/2 cups.

Mrs. Fred T. Spangler (Zillah Mae Ford)

French Fried Shrimp

1 cup flour	2 tablespoons cooking oil
½ teaspoon salt	1 egg
½ teaspoon sugar	2 to 3 pounds raw shrimp
1 cup ice water	

Make batter by combining all ingredients except shrimp. Chill. Shell and devein shrimp; leave tails on. Dip shrimp in batter and fry in deep hot fat. Drain on paper towels and serve hot with Parsley Seafood Sauce, page 265. Serves 4-6.

Mrs. Ghent Graves, Jr. (Sally Sample)

Barbecued Shrimp

2 pounds raw shrimp	1 teaspoon dry mustard
1 cup salad oil	2 tablespoons chopped parsley
2 cloves garlic, crushed	1 teaspoon salt
2 tablespoons chili sauce	Juice of 2 lemons
2 tablespoons Worcestershire sauce	1 jalapeno pepper, seeded and chopped
1 teaspoon prepared mustard	

Shell and devein shrimp. Combine all other ingredients to make sauce. Marinate shrimp in sauce for 2 hours. Broil, 5 to 10 minutes on each side, basting several times with sauce. Serves 4 as a main course or 8-10 as hors d'oeuvres. *Mrs. James Howard Park, III (Bette Naylor)*

Shrimp Fricassee

2 pounds raw shrimp	1 teaspoon salt
⅓ to ½ pound salt pork	Cayenne
½ cup flour	Parsley
1 large onion, chopped	

Shell and devein shrimp. Cut salt pork in very small cubes and fry slowly in heavy pan until brown and crisp. Remove pork and set aside. Add flour to drippings; cook and stir over low heat until dark brown in color. Add onion and cook until tender. Add about 1/2 cup boiling water and stir until gravy is thick; add shrimp, salt, several dashes cayenne, cooked salt pork and a little chopped parsley. Cover and simmer about 15-20 minutes, stirring occasionally. Gravy will thin as shrimp cooks. (More hot water may be added, cautiously, if needed for desired consistency.) Serve over rice. Serves 4-6.

Mrs. Douglas S. Craig (Alice Picton)

Shrimp Florentine

3 packages frozen chopped spinach
2 tablespoons grated onion
Juice of 1 large lemon
Salt and pepper
Cayenne
6 tablespoons butter
¼ cup flour
2 cups cream

2 cloves garlic, crushed
1 teaspoon Worcestershire sauce
3 drops Tabasco
¼ teaspoon paprika
1 tablespoon sherry
2 pounds cooked, shelled shrimp
Grated Parmesan cheese

Cook spinach. Drain and mash as dry as possible. Season with grated onion, lemon juice, salt, pepper and cayenne. Make a cream sauce of butter, flour and cream. Blend in garlic, Worcestershire sauce, Tabasco, paprika and sherry. In a shallow casserole alternately layer the shrimp, spinach and cream sauce. Sprinkle grated Parmesan cheese on top. Heat in 325° oven for about 30 minutes. Serves 8-10.

Mrs. Patrick Reardon (Agnes Butz)

Shrimp and Wild Rice

12 ounces uncooked wild rice
    or long grain and wild
    rice mixture
3 pounds raw shrimp
1 onion, chopped

1 green pepper, chopped
2 tablespoons butter
1½ cups cream
½ cup sherry
2 cups chili sauce

Cook rice; set aside. Cook shrimp in highly seasoned water. When done drain off liquid and allow shrimp to cool. Shell and devein shrimp. Saute onion and green pepper in butter until tender. Add cream, sherry and chili sauce. Add rice and shrimp to sauce and mix well; pour into buttered 3-quart casserole. Bake, covered, in 350° oven for one hour. Serves 12-14.

Mrs. Dudley C. Sharp (Tina Cleveland)

Creamed Shrimp

1 pound cooked, shelled shrimp
2 cans condensed cream of
    mushroom soup
2 cans (4 oz. each) mushroom
    stems and pieces, drained

10 ounces Cheddar cheese,
    grated
1 soup can milk
1 teaspoon salt
Cayenne
2 tablespoons sherry (optional)

Combine shrimp with mushroom soup, mushrooms, grated cheese and milk. Simmer until mixture is smooth. Season with salt and cayenne. Blend in sherry if desired. Serve over buttered rice. Serves 4-6.

Mrs. Robert W. Davis (Betty Faulkner)

Shrimp Stew à la Panama

2 pounds large, raw shrimp
¼ teaspoon crushed bay leaves
Salt and pepper
2 peeled potatoes, diced
2 peeled carrots, diced
1 medium onion, minced

¼ cup olive or vegetable oil
1 can (6 oz.) tomato paste
¼ teaspoon oregano
1 cup shredded cabbage
2 hard-cooked eggs, thinly
  sliced

Drop shrimp into boiling water seasoned with bay leaves, salt and pepper. Boil 5 minutes. Remove shrimp, reserving stock. Shell, devein, and dice shrimp. Boil potatoes and carrots in 3 cups of the stock, until just tender. Set aside; do not drain. Saute onion and shrimp in oil until onion is soft. Add tomato paste and oregano. Add potatoes, carrots and stock in which they were cooked. Add remaining stock as needed. Add cabbage and hard-cooked eggs. Heat thoroughly, taste, and correct seasoning. Serves 4-6.

Mrs. Merrick W. Phelps (Marie Lee)

Shrimp - Cheese Strata

4 to 5 slices buttered bread
2 cans (7 oz. each) shrimp, drained
2 cups grated American or Old
  English cheese
3 eggs, well beaten

1½ cups milk
1 teaspoon dry mustard
½ teaspoon salt
1 can condensed cream of
  mushroom soup (optional)

Arrange bread slices in greased 9" x 12" baking dish, completely covering bottom of dish. Rinse shrimp in cold water and drain well. Arrange shrimp on bread. Sprinkle cheese over shrimp. Mix eggs, milk, mustard and salt together. Pour mixture over casserole. Bake in 350° oven for 45-50 minutes. Cut into squares to serve. May be served with diluted mushroom soup or well-seasoned cream sauce on top of each square. Serves 6.

Mrs. Ralph Bowen, Jr. (Sheila Smith)

Shrimp Delight

1 small green pepper, minced
1 medium onion, chopped
3 tablespoons cooking oil
3 tablespoons flour
1 cup milk
1 small can (2 oz.) mushrooms

1 small jar (2 oz.) pimiento
½ teaspoon salt
1 egg, beaten
2 cups cooked, shelled shrimp
Dash Tabasco

Continued on next page

Saute green pepper and onion in oil until transparent. Add flour, milk, mushrooms and pimiento. Cook until thickened, stirring constantly. Add salt; stir in the beaten egg. Add shrimp and season with Tabasco. Serve over Holland Rusk or rice. Serves 4.

Mrs. John L. Hamilton (Ann Lowdon)

Shrimp and Eggplant

1 eggplant, peeled and diced	1 green pepper, chopped
1 pound raw shrimp	Parsley, finely chopped
1 onion, chopped	½ cup butter
1 bunch green onions, chopped	¾ cup bread crumbs
3-4 ribs celery, chopped	Heavy cream

Cook eggplant in small amount of salted water and drain well. Shell, devein and finely chop shrimp. Saute other vegetables in butter until tender. Add eggplant, shrimp and 1/2 cup of the bread crumbs. Stir in a generous amount of cream. Pour into a buttered 1-1/2 quart baking dish. Top with remaining bread crumbs and dot with extra butter. Bake in 350° oven for 45-60 minutes. Serves 4.

Mrs. George A. Hill, III (Gloria Lester)

Shrimp Homestead

2 pounds raw, jumbo shrimp	2 sprigs parsley, finely chopped
¼ cup shortening	1 cup peeled and chopped,
¼ cup flour	fresh tomatoes
2 tablespoons chopped onion	¾ cup dry white wine
2 tablespoons chopped	2 cups bottled clam broth
green pepper	Salt and pepper
1 tablespoon chopped celery	1 sprig thyme, or ¼ teaspoon
Butter	powdered thyme
½ teaspoon crushed garlic	2 bay leaves

Shell and devein shrimp. Make a roux with shortening and flour. Saute onion, green pepper, celery in small amount of butter; add to roux. Add garlic, parsley, tomatoes, shrimp, wine, clam broth, salt, pepper, thyme and bay leaves. Simmer 20 minutes. Correct seasonings. Serve over rice. Serves 6.

Mrs. W. Brantly Harris (Eugenia Head)

Shrimp Istanbul

1½ pounds small cooked,
    shelled shrimp
Butter (½ cup or more)
2-3 onions, finely sliced
¼ pound fresh mushrooms, sliced

¼ cup dry sherry
¼ cup finely sliced green pepper
1 can (6 oz.) tomato paste
1 cup sour cream
Salt

Toss shrimp in foaming butter in skillet for about 2 minutes. Remove. Saute onions in butter. Remove. Add more butter if needed. Saute mushrooms. Add sherry and green pepper. Cook for a few minutes. Add tomato paste, sour cream and salt. Return shrimp and onions to pan. Simmer for about 15 minutes. Serve over rice pilaf. Serves 6-8.

Mrs. Robert B. Crouch (Nancy Wencke)

Shrimp Creole

1 cup chopped onion
1 cup chopped celery
1 green pepper, chopped
3 tablespoons bacon drippings
1½ teaspoons salt
1 tablespoon flour

2 teaspoons chili powder
½ teaspoon Tabasco
1 can (1 lb.) green peas
Liquid from green peas
1 can (1 lb.) tomatoes, chopped
2 cups cooked, shelled shrimp

Over low heat, lightly brown onion, celery and green pepper in bacon drippings. Add salt, flour, chili powder and Tabasco. Add liquid from peas plus enough water to make 1 cup. Simmer, uncovered, for 10 minutes, stirring until thickened. Blend in peas and tomatoes; simmer 10 minutes longer. Add shrimp; heat thoroughly. Serve over rice. This can be cooked ahead of time and can be frozen successfully. Serves 6.

Mrs. Robert L. Easton (Elizabeth Szilagyi)

Curried Shrimp

1 small onion, chopped
1 garlic clove, crushed
½ cup butter
½ cup flour
2-4 teaspoons curry powder

2 cups chicken bouillon
1 cup cream
2 tart apples, peeled, cored
    and chopped
1-1½ pounds cooked, shelled
    shrimp

Saute onion and garlic in butter. Add flour and curry powder; blend. Slowly add bouillon and cream; stir until thickened. Add apples and heat. Add shrimp. Serve on rice with toasted coconut, golden raisins, chutney and toasted almonds. Serves 4-6.

Mrs. Nelson Robinson (Mary Washington)

Shrimp Orleans

3 to 4 tablespoons cooking oil
1 large onion, chopped
½ green pepper, chopped
2 or 3 ribs celery, chopped
1 small clove garlic, crushed
2 tablespoons flour

1 can (1 lb.) tomatoes
1 can (8 oz.) tomato sauce
Salt and pepper
Several sprigs parsley,
    finely chopped
2 or 3 bay leaves, crushed
1½ pounds raw shrimp

In a heavy skillet, heat oil; add onion, green pepper, celery and garlic and brown slowly. Add flour and continue cooking until brown. Add tomatoes, tomato sauce, salt, pepper, parsley and bay leaves. Cook slowly, covered, for 2-1/2 hours, stirring occasionally. (A little water, 1/2 cup or less, may be needed during cooking.) Meanwhile, shell and devein shrimp. Add shrimp to sauce after about 2 hours; continue cooking for 30 minutes. Serve over rice. Serves 4.

Mrs. Edward W. Kelley, Jr. (Ellen Elizardi)

Party Shrimp

1 pound cooked, shelled shrimp
1 can (1 lb.) whole artichoke
    hearts, well drained
¼ pound fresh mushrooms, or
    1 can (4 oz.) button
    mushrooms
¼ cup butter
5 tablespoons flour

1 teaspoon salt
½ teaspoon pepper
1 cup milk
1 cup cream
2 teaspoons Worcestershire sauce
½ cup (or less) dry sherry
¼ cup Parmesan cheese
Paprika

Arrange shrimp, artichoke hearts and mushrooms in a casserole. Melt butter in saucepan over low heat. Stir in flour, salt and pepper. Gradually add milk and cream, stirring constantly. Add Worcestershire sauce and sherry. Pour sauce over shrimp mixture in casserole. Sprinkle Parmesan cheese and paprika on top. Bake in 375° oven for 30 minutes. May be served over rice. This may be prepared in advance and baked before serving. Freezes well, but sauce will need to be thinned after being frozen. Serves 4-6.

Mrs. Tyler D. Todd (Barbara Beal)

Shrimp Tempura with Vegetables

3 pounds raw, medium shrimp
Flour to coat shrimp
1 cup flour
½ teaspoon salt
2 eggs, beaten
¾ cup milk
Cooking oil for frying
1 cup sliced, fresh mushrooms
6 small green onions with tops,
  sliced
2 tablespoons butter
1 tablespoon cornstarch

2 cups chicken broth
4 or 5 ribs celery, sliced
  diagonally
1 can (5 oz.) bamboo shoots
1 small head Chinese cabbage,
  sliced (do not use coarse
  stems)
2 small cans (5 oz. each) water
  chestnuts, drained and sliced
¼ pound snow peas, or 1 package
  frozen
Soy sauce

Shell and devein shrimp. Make a thin batter of flour, salt, eggs and milk. (Add a little more milk if batter seems too thick.) Dip shrimp lightly in flour, then in batter; brown in hot fat about 5 minutes. Drain and keep warm. Saute mushrooms and green onions in butter in large skillet. Mix cornstarch with a little chicken broth and set aside. Add celery, bamboo shoots, cabbage, water chestnuts and snow peas to mushrooms and onions; pour in chicken broth and bring to a rapid boil. Cover, and cook **no longer** than 5 minutes. Thicken with cornstarch mixture; add soy sauce and shrimp. Serve immediately, over rice. Large bite-sized pieces of raw chicken may be substituted for shrimp, if desired. Serves 6-8.

Mrs. H. Edward Maddox, III (Donna Gray)

Sherried Seafood Supper

1 can frozen shrimp soup,
  undiluted
2 cups cooked, shelled shrimp
  or 2 cups canned Alaskan king crab

2 tablespoons sherry
Toasted English muffins

Put frozen soup in double boiler. When warm add shrimp or crab. Heat, then add sherry and remove from heat. Serve over toasted English muffins. Serves 4-6.

Mrs. David H. Harrington (Doris Newton)

Crab and Shrimp Casserole

1 pound lump crabmeat
1½ pounds cooked, shelled shrimp
1 package Pepperidge Farm
herb stuffing
1½ cups mayonnaise
1 large onion, chopped

1 cup finely chopped celery
1 green pepper, chopped
1 can (4 oz.) pimiento, sliced
1 tablespoon Worcestershire
sauce
Dash cayenne

Mix all ingredients together; spoon mixture into buttered baking dish. Bake at 220° for 1 hour. Raise heat to 350° and brown for 5-10 minutes. This recipe can also be used as dressing to go with turkey or chicken. Serves 8.

Mrs. Jack Trotter (Betty Wheless)

Lobster Newburg

¼ cup butter
1 tablespoon cornstarch
1½ cups cream
3 egg yolks, beaten
1 teaspoon salt
¼ teaspoon cayenne

¼ cup (or less) sherry
3 cups cooked, diced
lobster meat
Paprika
Chopped parsley

Melt butter over low heat. Stir in cornstarch. Add cream and cook until thickened, stirring constantly. Add egg yolks, salt, cayenne and sherry; cook and stir 2 minutes. Stir in lobster. Before serving, sprinkle with paprika and chopped parsley. Serve over hot, buttered toast. Serves 6.

Mrs. Robert F. Flagg (Nancy White)

Seafood Medley

1 box (9 oz.) frozen lobster tails
1 pound lump crabmeat
1 pound cooked, shelled shrimp
1 cup mayonnaise
1 cup finely chopped celery

½ cup finely chopped green onion
¼ cup finely chopped green
pepper
½ teaspoon salt
1 package (6 oz.) onion-garlic
potato chips

Cook lobster tails; remove meat and chop. Mix with crabmeat, shrimp, mayonnaise, celery, onions, green pepper and salt. Add a little cream or extra mayonnaise if mixture seems too dry. Spoon into buttered casserole. Crush the potato chips into very fine crumbs with a rolling pin (while the potato chips are still in the bag). Sprinkle crumbs over top of casserole. Bake at 350° for 30 minutes. Serves 6.

Mrs. George H. Lane (Joan Bagby)

Seafood Casserole

1 small onion, chopped	Pepper
1 can (4 oz.) mushrooms, drained	Dash Tabasco
¼ green pepper, finely chopped	½ cup sliced ripe olives
3 tablespoons butter	1 can (6½ oz.) solid pack tuna
1 can condensed cream of chicken or mushroom soup	1 can (5 oz.) shrimp, drained
	½ cup cream
1 tablespoon Worcestershire sauce	¼ cup grated sharp Cheddar cheese
Garlic powder	Slivered almonds

Brown onion, mushrooms and green pepper in butter. Add soup. Season with Worcestershire sauce, garlic powder, pepper and Tabasco. Simmer 3 minutes. Add olives, tuna, shrimp, cream and cheese. Mix gently. Spoon mixture into casserole and sprinkle with almonds. Cover and cook until thoroughly heated. Serve over Chinese noodles. Serves 4-6.

Mrs. J. Malcolm Horn (Helen Hargrove)

Oysters Gourmet

1 quart oysters, drained	1 small clove garlic, crushed
Salt and pepper	1 cup catsup
Lemon juice	2 teaspoons Worcestershire sauce
½ cup butter	1½ cups soft rye bread crumbs
1 cup finely chopped celery	12 large oyster shells

Cut oysters in half; season with salt, pepper and lemon juice. Melt butter in heavy skillet and add celery, garlic, catsup and Worcestershire sauce. Add seasoned oysters. Simmer on very low heat for about 20 minutes. Pile mixture into oyster shells. Saute rye crumbs in additional butter until toasted; sprinkle over oyster mixture, and dot with more butter. Bake in hot oven, or under broiler, just until browned. Do not overcook. Makes 12 filled shells.

Mrs. John Thad Scott, Jr. (Sadie Ruth Aldridge)

Scalloped Oysters

2 large boxes (1 lb. each) Ritz crackers, finely rolled	Freshly ground pepper
	Worcestershire sauce
1 gallon oysters (do not drain)	1½ cups butter
Salt	

In 2 well-greased, shallow baking dishes (9" x 14") alternately layer cracker crumbs, oysters, salt, pepper, Worcestershire sauce and pieces of butter. Repeat layers, ending with cracker crumbs. Bake in 450° oven for 30 minutes. Serves 24.

Mrs. J. Bryan Grubbs, Jr. (Neat Eddleman)

Baked Oysters

1 tablespoon minced onion	2 tablespoons cream
2 tablespoons minced celery	6 tablespoons oyster liquor
½ cup butter, melted	1 pint oysters
⅔ cup toasted bread crumbs	Salt and pepper
¾ cup crushed saltine crackers	½ cup slivered almonds
2 teaspoons minced parsley	
1 tablespoon chopped green onions	

Saute minced onion and celery in small amount of the butter. Mix bread crumbs and cracker crumbs together and stir in remaining butter, celery and onion. Add parsley and green onions. Combine cream and oyster liquor. In a buttered casserole, make layers of crumb mixture, oysters, salt, pepper, and cream mixture. Repeat layers, ending with crumbs. Sprinkle with almonds. Bake in 400° oven for 30 minutes. Serves 4.

Mrs. Richard R. McKay (Emily Ann Finch)

Marshall's Oyster Casserole

¼ cup butter	1 pint oysters, drained
1 small onion, finely chopped	2 tablespoons flour
½ clove garlic, crushed	¾ cup milk
12 saltine crackers, crumbled	1 tablespoon very sharp grated
2 hard-cooked eggs, sliced	cheese (optional)
½ teaspoon salt	1 can (3 oz.) chopped mushrooms,
¼ teaspoon pepper	with liquid
Dash thyme	1 small hot red pepper, finely
	chopped (optional)

Melt butter in casserole. Add onion, garlic and cracker crumbs. Place in hot oven briefly until crackers are golden and have absorbed butter. Combine eggs, salt, pepper and thyme. Add drained oysters; sprinkle with flour, and mix together well. Add milk, cheese, mushrooms, mushroom liquid and red pepper. Mix thoroughly; pour onto browned crumbs in casserole. Sprinkle with extra cracker crumbs, if desired. Bake at 350° for 30 minutes. Serves 4-6.

Mrs. Ralph Ellis Gunn (Esme Patterson)

Baked Oysters Grand Isle

4 dozen oysters (approximately)
1 medium onion, grated
2 ribs celery, finely chopped
1 clove garlic, crushed
½ cup butter
1 tablespoon flour
1 can (8 oz.) tomato sauce

1 teaspoon chopped parsley
Salt
Cayenne
3 tablespoons Worcestershire sauce
1 small can (4 oz.) mushrooms, drained
Cracker crumbs

Cook oysters slightly to evaporate some of the liquid; drain. Saute onion, celery and garlic in butter until tender. Add flour, stirring until smooth. Add tomato sauce, parsley, salt, cayenne, Worcestershire sauce, mushrooms and oysters. Spoon into buttered baking dish; sprinkle with cracker crumbs and dot with additional butter. Bake at 350° for about 15 minutes, or until bubbly and slightly browned. Serves 6.

Mrs. Douglas S. Craig (Alice Picton)

Rockefeller Casserole

2 packages frozen chopped spinach
1 quart oysters, drained
6 tablespoons melted butter
1 cup fine, dry bread crumbs
1 tablespoon anisette liqueur

½ onion, grated
1 clove garlic, crushed
2 tablespoons anchovy paste
Salt and pepper
Tabasco
Parmesan cheese

Cook spinach slightly; drain well. Cut oysters into pieces and combine with spinach. Add melted butter, bread crumbs, anisette, onion, garlic, anchovy paste, salt, pepper and Tabasco. Mix well and spoon into casserole. Sprinkle with cheese and bake, covered, at 350° for 20 minutes. Remove cover and bake 10 minutes longer. Serves 8-10.

Mrs. George A. Hill, III (Gloria Lester)

Oyster - Corn Bake

1 can (1 lb.) creamed corn, drained	½ cup cream
1 cup crushed Ritz crackers	¼ teaspoon black pepper
1 egg, beaten	1 teaspoon sugar
½ teaspoon salt	¼ cup melted butter
	1 jar (12 oz.) oysters, drained

Combine ingredients in order listed. Pour mixture into buttered casserole and bake at 375° for 25 minutes. Do not overbake. If casserole is prepared in advance and refrigerated, bake for 35 minutes. Serves 4.

Mrs. John H. Meyers (Alice Baker Jones)

Artichoke - Oyster Casserole

8 large artichokes	Oyster liquor
3 tablespoons flour	1 can (7 oz.) mushroom pieces
½-¾ cup butter, melted	with liquid
3 tablespoons minced green onion	Salt and pepper
	Bread crumbs
2½ dozen oysters, cut in half	Butter

Place artichokes in large pan with about 1'' boiling water. Cover and cook 45 minutes, or until tender. Drain and cool. Scrape meat from leaves and cut hearts in half. Discard leaves and choke portion. Stir flour into melted butter; add onion and cook about 5 minutes. Mix in scrapings from artichoke leaves, oysters, oyster liquor, mushrooms with liquid, salt and pepper. Simmer 10 minutes. Arrange halved artichoke hearts in shallow casserole; add oyster mixture. Top with bread crumbs and dot with butter. Bake at 350° for 15 minutes, or until crumbs are brown. Serves 6-8.

Mrs. James W. O'Keefe (Helen Ann Garrett)

Trout Amandine

6 trout fillets	⅓ cup butter
1 cup milk	½ cup slivered almonds
½ cup flour	Finely chopped parsley
Salt and pepper	Lemon wedges

Dip fillets in milk; roll in flour which has been seasoned with salt and pepper. Brown fish on both sides in butter. Arrange fish on serving platter; keep warm. Saute almonds in butter and pour browned butter and almonds over fish. Garnish with parsley and lemon wedges. Serves 4.

Mrs. F. Fox Benton (Ann Temple)

Sole or Flounder Meunière

2½ to 3 pounds fish fillets
(10 small fillets)
Salt
White pepper
Cream
Flour

2 tablespoons cooking oil
4 tablespoons butter
2 tablespoons finely chopped
parsley
¼ cup lemon juice

Season fish with salt and white pepper. Dip in cream and dredge lightly in flour. Heat oil and half of the butter in skillet; lightly brown fish fillets 2-3 minutes on each side. Remove to serving platter; keep warm. Heat remaining 2 tablespoons butter, in clean skillet. Sprinkle fish with parsley and lemon juice. Pour hot butter over all. Serves 5.

Mrs. Walter Browne Baker (Adelaide Lovett)

Trout Meunière

1 pound trout fillets
Salt and pepper
Milk
Flour
½ cup olive oil

½ cup butter
½ cup chopped parsley
1 or 2 cloves garlic, crushed
1 tablespoon lemon juice

Season fillets with salt and pepper. Dip in milk, then in flour. Brown on each side in olive oil. While trout is cooking, brown butter in small saucepan. Add parsley, garlic and lemon juice. Serve hot sauce over browned trout. Serves 2-3.

Mrs. Charles B. Moore (Mary Alice Bone)

Baked Fish Italienne

¼ cup butter
2½ to 3 pounds trout or
red snapper

¼ cup lemon juice
¼ cup Worcestershire sauce
Progresso seasoned bread crumbs

Lightly brown butter in large baking dish in 450° oven. Fillet fish and season with salt. Dip in browned butter to coat well. Arrange, skin side down, in pan. Mix lemon juice and Worcestershire sauce; pour over fish. Bake in 450° oven for about 15 minutes or until just done, basting once or twice with pan juices. Remove from oven, top with seasoned bread crumbs, and baste well again. Return to oven for 5 minutes. Serves 2-4.

Mrs. Jack T. Currie (Dorothy Peek)

Fried Fish Fillets

Fish fillets, ¾" thick
(trout, mackerel, redfish
or red snapper)
Fine cracker crumbs

Flour
Salt and pepper
Cooking oil, margarine, or
bacon drippings

Cut fillets into serving-sized pieces. Roll in mixture of half cracker crumbs and half flour, seasoned with salt and pepper. Pour oil 1/4" deep in heavy frying pan; heat until hot but not smoking. Saute fillets in uncovered pan for exactly 3 minutes. Remove pan from heat and cover immediately with tight-fitting lid. After exactly 2 minutes, return to heat and remove lid. Turn fillets over and saute, uncovered, for exactly 3 minutes. Fish should be removed from pan and served immediately. If using thicker fillets, increase cooking times accordingly. This method of frying assures moist, but not overcooked, fish.

Mrs. Nelson Robinson (Mary Washington)

Redfish with Creole Sauce

½ cup chopped onion
½ cup chopped celery
1 clove garlic, crushed
½ cup cooking oil
2½ cups canned tomatoes
2 cans (8 oz. each) tomato sauce
1 cup cold water

1 redfish (about 5 lbs.)
Salt
Freshly ground pepper
Cayenne
Chopped green onion tops
Chopped parsley
1 lemon, thinly sliced

In heavy pot saute onion, celery and garlic in oil for 10 minutes. Add tomatoes and tomato sauce. Cook, uncovered, over medium heat for 40 minutes, stirring occasionally. Add water. Cook for 20 additional minutes. Meanwhile, fillet fish and season with salt, pepper and a few grains cayenne. Arrange fish in baking dish. Pour tomato mixture over fish. Bake in 325° oven for 30 minutes, basting often. Garnish with onion tops, parsley and lemon slices. Serves 6.

Mrs. P. G. Bell, Jr. (Sue Ledbetter)

Buttered Fish Fillets

2 pounds redfish or red
snapper fillets
½ pound melted butter

1 medium onion, very thinly
sliced
1 tablespoon dried lemon peel or
equivalent in fresh lemon slices

Roll fillets in about half the melted butter and place, close together, in shallow baking pan. Arrange onion slices over fish and sprinkle with lemon peel (or cover with thin lemon slices). Pour remaining melted butter over all. Bake in 450° oven for about 10 minutes. This fish can also be cooked over hot charcoal fire on covered grill. Serves 4-6.

Mrs. Baxter Adams (Carol Nash)

Fish Paprika

2 or 3 medium onions, sliced
1-3 teaspoons paprika
¼ cup butter
1 fish (about 3 lbs.)
1 lemon

Salt and pepper
⅛ teaspoon rosemary
¼ cup (or more) sherry
½ cup sour cream
Minced parsley

Saute onions with 1/2 teaspoon (or more) paprika in half the butter until onions are golden. Remove skin from fish and rinse in lemon water. (Squeeze 1 lemon into 1 quart water.) Place in well-buttered baking dish. Dot with remaining butter; sprinkle with salt, pepper, rosemary, 1/2 teaspoon paprika and sherry. Arrange onions over fish. Spread sour cream over all. Bake at 375° for 30 minutes, basting occasionally with pan juices. When fish flakes easily, place under broiler to brown. Sprinkle with parsley and paprika. Serves 4-6.

Mrs. John H. Meyers (Alice Baker Jones)

Fancy Fish Fillets

1 pound butter
2-3 tablespoons sherry
Juice of ½ lemon
½ teaspoon salt

¼-½ teaspoon pepper
1 teaspoon basil
6 small, or 4 large, fish fillets
(sole, flounder or trout)

Put butter in baking dish large enough to hold all fish fillets. Heat butter in 375° oven until it is light brown (about 15 minutes). Stir in sherry, lemon juice, salt, pepper and basil. Arrange fish in butter sauce and bake in 450° oven for 15-20 minutes, basting every 5 minutes. Serves 4.

Mrs. Donald A. Moffitt (Bonner Baker)

Fish Bahamian

1¼ pounds fish fillets
Salt and pepper
⅓ cup lime juice
1 can (1 lb.) tomatoes, drained
    (reserve liquid)

Butter
2 onions, sliced in rings
2 tablespoons shortening
1 teaspoon monosodium
    glutamate
½ teaspoon thyme

Arrange fish fillets in baking dish. Season with salt and pepper. Pour lime juice and tomato liquid over fish. Let marinate at room temperature for 4-5 hours. Drain off marinade, dot with butter, and bake at 350° until done, about 15-20 minutes. Meanwhile, saute onions in shortening. Add tomatoes, monosodium glutamate and thyme. Simmer a few minutes. Remove fish to serving platter and cover with sauce. Makes 2 generous servings.

Mrs. Allen W. Hamill, Jr. (Peggy Golding)

Royal Red Snapper

¾ cup chopped celery
½ cup chopped onion
¼ cup butter
1 quart toasted bread cubes
½ cup sour cream
¼ cup chopped lemon sections
2 tablespoons grated lemon rind

1 teaspoon salt
1 teaspoon paprika
2 or 3 whole red snappers, or
    redfish (3-4 lbs. dressed fish)
Salt
3 tablespoons melted butter
¼ cup dry white wine

To prepare stuffing, saute celery and onion in butter until tender; combine with bread cubes in large bowl. Add sour cream, lemon sections, lemon rind, salt and paprika; mix thoroughly. Spread stuffing in well-greased baking dish. Sprinkle fish inside and out with salt. Cut into individual sized portions and arrange over stuffing. Bake in 350° oven for 40-60 minutes, or until fish flakes easily. Make basting sauce by combining melted butter and wine. Baste fish occasionally while cooking. Serves 6.

Mrs. Rotan McGown (Charlotte Rotan)

Red Snapper Hollandaise

4 teaspoons salt
2 bay leaves
1 lemon, sliced
1 onion, sliced
Dash cayenne
2 quarts water

4 pounds red snapper
2 cups Hollandaise sauce
2-3 tablespoons chopped
parsley
Lemon wedges for garnish

Add salt, bay leaves, lemon slices, onion and cayenne to the water. Cut fish into fillets and poach in seasoned water for about 15 minutes. Remove fish from stock, drain well, and arrange on serving platter. Cover fish with Hollandaise sauce and sprinkle with chopped parsley. Garnish with lemon wedges. Serves 4.

Mrs. John H. Meyers (Alice Baker Jones)

Charcoal Broiled Flounder

4 small, whole flounders
1 cup butter
Juice of 1 large lemon

Salt
Paprika

Remove heads from fish and put flounders in freezer until they are completely frozen (scaling is unnecessary). About 2 hours before cooking, remove fish from freezer. Run tap water over fish briefly enough to thaw skin, but not meat. With a pair of pliers, remove skin from fish. Place each fish in a "sizzling" plate. Melt butter and mix with lemon juice. Pour over each frozen fish. Butter should completely cover fish and will congeal. Cook in plates on charcoal over red hot coals, with lid of cooker closed. Cook until juice is milky, approximately 10-15 minutes. Season with salt and paprika and serve, sizzling, on the cooking plates. Serves 4.

Mrs. Baxter Adams (Carol Nash)

Charcoaled Kingfish or Ling

6 fish steaks
½ cup butter, melted
2 tablespoons Worcestershire
sauce

1 teaspoon pepper
Juice of 1 large lemon
½ teaspoon garlic powder
1 teaspoon soy sauce

Skin fish and cut crosswise into steaks, about 1" to 1-1/4" thick. Make basting sauce by combining butter, Worcestershire sauce, pepper, lemon juice, garlic powder and soy sauce. Broil slowly over low charcoal fire, brushing frequently with sauce. (Any fish may be cooked this way.) Serves 6.

Mrs. Carroll E. Church (Jean-Marie Ormondroyd)

Baked Scallops

2 pounds scallops
¼ cup butter
¼ cup chopped onion
2 cups fresh mushrooms,
    chopped
¼ cup flour

1 teaspoon salt
Cayenne
Pepper
2 cups cream
Buttered bread crumbs

If scallops are large cut them in half. Cook in boiling water 5 minutes. Melt butter; add onion and mushrooms and cook 5 minutes, stirring constantly. Add flour, salt, cayenne and pepper. Slowly stir in cream. Cook over low heat until thick, stirring constantly. Add scallops, mix well. Pour into a greased baking dish. Cover with buttered bread crumbs and bake in 350° oven until brown, 15-20 minutes. Serves 6.

Mrs. Langdon Dearborn (Elizabeth Goodridge)

Scallops in Wine Sauce

3 pounds scallops
2 envelopes instant chicken
    broth mix
1¼ cups hot water
½ cup chopped onion
½ cup chopped green pepper
¼ cup butter
¼ cup flour

1 pint cream
2 cans (3 oz. each) mushrooms,
    drained
¼ cup dry white wine
Salt and pepper
8 slices crisp bacon, crumbled
½ cup chopped parsley

Cook scallops in salted water for 10 minutes; drain and cut into small pieces. Dissolve chicken broth mix in hot water; set aside. Saute onion and green pepper in butter. Stir in flour. Slowly add cream and chicken broth; cook over medium heat, stirring constantly, until thickened. Add scallops, mushrooms, wine, salt and pepper. Serve in individual shells, topped with bacon and parsley. Makes 12 small servings.

Mrs. Reagan Cartwright (Jean Bates)

MEXICAN FOOD

Hints

Mexican food encompasses a wide variety of foods, and is not necessarily hot or overspiced. Mexican food reflects its history and is an interesting blend of Aztec, Spanish and European cooking.

This section includes favorite versions of Texas-type Mexican food as well as less typical dishes not found in most Mexican restaurants. Mexican dishes may be served with American dishes and add a source of interest to any meal.

EXPLANATION OF WORDS USED OFTEN IN MEXICAN COOKING:

Masa—corn kernels soaked in lime water then ground to a meal. Masa is Mexican flour.

Mole—a sauce, prepared in powder or liquid form, made of a wide range of chiles and spices and flavored with chocolate. It is used in small quantities to season Mexican dishes.

Jack Cheese—a creamy, white, bland cheese which complements Mexican food. If not available, substitute a mild Cheddar.

Oregano—wild marjoram. Oregano is a widely used herb, and is almost as common as chili powder in Mexican foods.

Chili powder—a powder compounded of dried peppers and herbs. It varies in strength according to brand. Also, the fresher the chili powder, the more intense the flavor.

Cominos—derived from cumin seed. Gives the true Mexican flavor to authentic Mexican dishes.

Tortillas—thin corn cakes, made from masa. The bread of Mexico.

Tostadas—tortillas, often cut into quarters or eighths, fried or toasted until crisp.

Jalapeno—thick skinned, hot green pepper.

Whole green chiles (canned)—these are usually peeled and have most of the seeds removed, making them much less hot than chopped green chiles.

Chopped green chiles (canned)—these are chopped with their seeds, making them very, very hot.

Ceviche

1½ pounds fish fillets
10-12 fresh limes
3 large, or 5 small, fresh
    tomatoes
¼ cup chopped parsley
2 tablespoons olive oil
Dash Tabasco

1 small onion, finely chopped
¼ teaspoon ground cloves
1 teaspoon oregano
1 tablespoon salt
Small jar (2½ oz.) pitted green
    olives, chopped

Cut fish into 1/4" cubes. Place in glass dish and cover with freshly squeezed lime juice. Let stand for at least 6 hours at room temperature, or overnight in refrigerator. (The fish is cooked by acid in lime juice.) Meanwhile, prepare sauce by peeling, chopping and mashing tomatoes in large bowl. (Do not use blender.) Add parsley, olive oil, Tabasco, onion, cloves, oregano, salt and olives. When fish is "cooked," drain in sieve and rinse very quickly in cold water. Add fish to sauce and chill for at least 1 hour, preferably longer, in refrigerator. Served as soup or cocktail, Ceviche is very popular in all the ports of Mexico. Serves 8-10.

Mrs. H. L. Simpson (Betty Feagin)

Scallops Ceviche

½ pound scallops
1 large fresh tomato
2 small green chiles
1 onion, finely chopped

Juice from 4 lemons or 5 limes
¼ cup olive oil
1 teaspoon oregano
Salt and pepper

Cut scallops in bite-sized pieces. Peel tomatoes and dice. Remove seeds, and chop green chiles into very small pieces. Combine all ingredients, mix well, and let stand at least 12 hours, stirring occasionally. (Lemon juice "cooks" the scallops.) This is a classic Mexican favorite. Serve in seafood cocktail glasses. Serves 5.

Mrs. Paul Sherwood (Mildred Wood)

Sopa Seca

1 package (10 oz.) twisted vermicelli	1 can (1 lb.) tomatoes
4 tablespoons cooking oil	Half of a 10-ounce can Rotel tomatoes and green chilies
2 large onions, chopped	1 teaspoon ground cumin
1 large clove garlic, crushed	2 teaspoons chili powder
1 green pepper, chopped	Salt and pepper
2 pounds ground round steak	4 cups beef stock

In 12" skillet, brown vermicelli "nests" (only) in 3 tablespoons oil. Remove, drain, and set aside. Add remaining 1 tablespoon oil to skillet and saute onions, garlic, green pepper and ground meat. Add tomatoes, Rotel tomatoes, cumin, chili powder, salt and pepper. Simmer 10 minutes. Arrange vermicelli in 3-quart casserole; cover with meat sauce. Pour stock over all. Bake, uncovered, at 350° for 1 hour. Remove from oven and mix well before serving. Much better if made at least 1 day before serving. When re-heating, add more stock if necessary. Freezes well. Serves 8-10.

Mrs. George Sealy (Ann McSween)

Chili Posole

2½-3 pounds lean pork roast, boned	1 clove garlic, chopped
2 or 3 large cans (15 oz. each) white hominy	Salt
	½ teaspoon (or more) oregano
1-2 cans (4½ oz. each) Whitson's moist chili seasoning	½ pound Longhorn or Cheddar cheese, shredded

Cut roast into small cubes; brown in large pan. When meat is browned, add hominy, chili seasoning, garlic, salt and oregano. Cover, and simmer until meat is very tender and chili has cooked into hominy, about 2 hours. It will probably be necessary to add water as it simmers; however, the final consistency should be moist but not soupy. (The right amount of moisture makes a difference and, by trial, error and practice, you can figure out how you like it best.) When Posole is done, transfer to Mexican casserole, top with cheese, and place in 350° oven until cheese bubbles. Posole improves with freezing, which makes it a convenient dish to prepare in advance for a party. Freeze before cheese is added. Thaw, top with cheese, and heat in oven. Serves 6 generously.

Mrs. James Noel (Virginia Grubbs)

Posole a la de León

1 chicken hen (4½-5 lbs.)	3 cans (15 oz. each) hominy,
6 quarts water	drained
1 teaspoon basil	3 tablespoons margarine
2 onions, sliced	3 tablespoons onion flakes
1 teaspoon poultry seasoning	¾ teaspoon seasoned salt
4 ribs celery, chopped; or 4	¾ teaspoon seasoned pepper
tablespoons celery flakes	½ teaspoon monosodium
4 tablespoons parsley flakes	glutamate
8 teaspoons seasoned salt	Lime wedges
8 small bay leaves	Chili piquins, crushed
1 bunch cilantro, Chinese parsley	Oregano
or fresh coriander (optional)	1 onion, very finely chopped

Simmer chicken until tender in the 6 quarts water, combined with basil, sliced onions, poultry seasoning, celery, parsley flakes, 8 teaspoons seasoned salt, bay leaves and cilantro. Remove chicken and bay leaves from stock. Bone chicken and cut meat into bite-sized pieces. Skim fat from stock. Return chicken meat to the stock. Saute hominy in margarine. Add onion flakes, 3/4 teaspoon seasoned salt, seasoned pepper and monosodium glutamate. Add to chicken and stock. Add salt if needed. When served, accompany with small bowls of lime wedges, chili piquins, oregano and finely chopped onion. (Use chili piquins sparingly; they are very hot.) This is a hearty, main-dish soup. Makes about 6 quarts. Serves 16.

Mrs. Jack C. Payne (Mary Hoehn)

Chili Con Carne

10 pounds lean chili meat, lean	2 soup-cans water
ground beef, or 5 pounds	2 cloves garlic, chopped
each venison and beef	2 or 3 bay leaves
5 envelopes (1 oz. each)	6 ribs celery, minced
Williams Chili seasoning	1 teaspoon comino seed
5 medium onions, chopped	1 fresh hot red pepper, chopped
2 cans condensed tomato soup	Salt

Put meat **alone** in roaster on low, 200°. Cook until meat is done, about 3 hours, turning meat often and removing grease as it appears. When meat is done, add all ingredients except salt. Cook slowly for several more hours. Add salt to taste before serving. Makes approximately 6 quarts.

Mrs. Richard R. Nelson (Marjorie Shepherd)

Texas Jailhouse Chili

½ pound beef suet
2½ pounds coarsely ground
  beef chuck
3 cloves garlic, minced
1½ tablespoons paprika
1 tablespoon ground cumin
1 tablespoon salt

1 tablespoon white pepper
1½ tablespoons diced green
  pepper
1 teaspoon coriander
3 cups water
3 tablespoons chili molido (chili
  powder with no additives; if
  unobtainable, use Spice
  Islands)

Melt suet in Dutch oven; add meat and brown. Add all other ingredients and cook, covered, for 4 hours. (If a less "hot" chili is desired, increase paprika to 2-1/2 tablespoons and decrease chili powder to 2 tablespoons.) Add more water while cooking, if necessary. If desired, pink oval chili beans may be added. Serves 6.

Mrs. James H. Weyland (Alta Jean McConathy)

Chili with Beans

1½ pounds chili-ground beef
2 tablespoons bacon drippings
  or beef suet
1½ large onions, coarsely
  chopped
2 tablespoons flour
1 teaspoon sugar

1½ teaspoons salt
1 teaspoon ground cumin
3-4 tablespoons chili con carne
  seasoning powder
1 can (1 lb.) tomatoes
1 can (1 lb.) kidney beans

Sear meat in fat, over high heat, until very dry, brown, and crisp. (Stir meat often to keep it from burning.) Add onions and cook on low heat until soft. Tilt pan after browning onions and remove excess fat (amount will depend on leanness of meat). Add flour, sugar, salt, cumin and chili powder; cook and stir until meat is well coated, about 5 minutes. Remove from heat and add tomatoes, stirring well. Add 1 cup water, return to heat, and bring to a boil, stirring constantly. (Mixture will be thick.) Boil 1 minute, then thin to desired consistency with a little more water. Cover and simmer slowly for 30 minutes. Allow to stand until cool enough for fat to rise to top; skim off fat. Pour excess juice from beans; add beans to chili. Simmer 30 more minutes, then correct seasoning if necessary. Serves 4-6.

Mrs. H. Edward Maddox, III (Donna Gray)

Chili Puerto Vallarta

½ pound dried pinto beans	½ cup butter
5 cups canned tomatoes	2½ pounds ground beef chuck
3 large green peppers, chopped	1 pound ground lean pork
1½ tablespoons cooking oil	1 cup chili powder
8 medium onions, chopped	2 tablespoons salt
2 cloves garlic, crushed	1½ teaspoons pepper
½ cup chopped parsley	1½ teaspoons cumin

Wash beans and soak overnight in water to cover. Simmer in same water until tender, adding more water if necessary. Add tomatoes and simmer 5 more minutes. Remove from heat. Saute green peppers in oil for 5 minutes. Add onions and cook until tender. Add garlic and parsley. Remove from heat. Melt butter in large skillet and saute beef and pork for 15 minutes. Combine meat and onion mixtures. Stir in chili powder, and cook 20 minutes. Combine chili mixture and beans; add salt, pepper and cumin. Simmer, covered, for 1 hour. Skim off fat. Freezes well. Makes 4 quarts.

Mrs. George A. Hill, III (Gloria Lester)

Favorite Mexican Enchiladas

2 cups finely chopped onions	2 tablespoons (or more)
¾ cup cooking oil	chili powder
2 cloves garlic, minced	1 teaspoon comino seed
2 tablespoons flour	1 tablespoon salt
2½ cups canned tomatoes, or	12 tortillas
2½ cups tomato juice	2 pounds American cheese,
2 cups water	grated

Saute 1/4 cup of the onions in 1/4 cup of the oil until soft but not brown. Add garlic and flour; blend well. Combine tomatoes (or tomato juice) and water; add to skillet. Add chili powder, comino seed and salt. Simmer for about 1 hour. (If sauce gets too thick, add a little water. It should be the consistency of cream.) Heat remaining 1/2 cup cooking oil. Dip tortillas, one at a time, in hot oil, then dip in hot enchilada sauce. Spread dipped tortilla with about 2 teaspoons grated cheese and 1 teaspoon chopped, raw onion. Roll, and fasten with toothpick. Place enchiladas side by side in shallow baking or enchilada dish. Sprinkle with remaining onion and cheese; pour remaining sauce over all. Heat in 400° oven for 10 minutes, or until cheese is melted. Makes 12 enchiladas.

Mrs. Hughes Fleming (Mildred Hughes)

Cheese Enchiladas

2 cans (10 oz. each) enchilada
   sauce (preferably Ashley's)
1 cup corn oil
1 dozen tortillas

1 pound processed American
   cheese (do not substitute)
1 onion, chopped

Heat enchilada sauce slightly; do not dilute. Heat corn oil; dip tortillas, one at a time, into hot oil just long enough to soften. Put about 1 tablespoon enchilada sauce, some grated cheese and some onion on each tortilla. Roll, and place side by side in shallow baking dish. Spoon about 3 tablespoons sauce over each enchilada and sprinkle with remaining onions and cheese. Heat in 350° oven until hot and bubbly. These can be frozen after tortillas are rolled, before adding remaining cheese and onion. Serves 4.

Mrs. Edward D. Pressler (Maxine Blalack)

Chicken Enchiladas
with Green Tomato Sauce

4 cans (8½ oz. each) Tomatitos
   Verdes, drained (small green
   tomatoes in salt water)
1 clove garlic, minced
1 large onion, chopped
½ teaspoon (heaping) coriander
1 teaspoon salt

1 pint sour cream
2 dozen tortillas
2 cups cooking oil, heated
1 pound American cheese,
   grated
2 cups cooked, diced
   chicken

To make sauce, put tomatoes, garlic, onion, coriander and salt into blender; puree. Pour into saucepan, and simmer for 30-40 minutes. Remove from heat, stir in sour cream. Dip each tortilla in **very hot** oil, then in sauce, then roll up with 1 tablespoon cheese and 1-1/2 tablespoons chicken inside. (Toothpick may be needed to secure enchilada.) Place in shallow, rectangular casserole dish, side by side. (This much may be completed several hours before meal, if desired.) Pour remaining sauce over enchiladas, sprinkle with remaining cheese. Bake at 325° for 20-30 minutes. Makes 24 enchiladas.

Mrs. Richard Gray (Betsy Bonnet)

Green Enchiladas Mavis

ENCHILADAS

2 dozen tortillas
1 cup cooking oil

Grated cheese(Monterey Jack,
Cheddar, or any that will melt
smoothly)
Chopped onions

Dip each tortilla in very hot oil, just long enough to soften. Generously spread each tortilla with cheese and onion; roll up. (Toothpicks are sometimes necessary for holding.) Place in shallow baking dish, side by side. Cover with Green Sauce.

GREEN SAUCE

1 package frozen spinach
2 cans condensed cream of
chicken soup
3 or 4 green onions, minced

2 cans (4 oz. each) Ortega whole
green chiles, drained and
chopped
¼ teaspoon salt
1 pint sour cream
1½ cups grated cheese

Cook spinach in about 1-1/2 cups water. Add soup, green onions, chiles and salt. Put through blender. (Do not taste, as sauce will be awfully hot.) Add sour cream and mix well. Pour over enchiladas. Sprinkle with grated cheese, cover, and bake at 350° for about 30 minutes. (Any extra sauce makes a zesty salad dressing for tossed greens.) Makes 24 enchiladas.

Mrs. Richard G. Rorschach (Justa Helm)

Green Enchiladas Caliente

1 dozen tortillas
Oil for frying
1 cup chopped onion
1 cup (or more) grated
American cheese
1 can (14 oz.) evaporated milk

1 can condensed cream of
mushroom soup
½-1 can (4 oz.) Ortega diced
chiles
1 teaspoon salt
½ teaspoon pepper

Fry tortillas in hot (smoking) oil, turning quickly so that they are still soft. Lay 6 tortillas flat on cookie sheet which has 1/2" sides. Sprinkle with half the onion and cheese. Combine milk, soup, chiles, salt and pepper, blending well. (If entire can of diced chiles is used, these are **really** hot. If you would rather not cry while eating, use only half a can.) Pour sauce over tortillas. Repeat layer of tortillas, sprinkle with remaining onion, and top with remaining cheese. Bake at 325° until bubbly, about 20-30 minutes. (Do not overcook.) Serves 6.

Mrs. Jack C. Payne (Mary Hoehn)

Stacked Enchiladas

2 tablespoons cooking oil or
   bacon drippings
1½ pounds ground meat
1 can (10 oz.) Ashley's
   enchilada sauce
½ sauce-can water

1½ pounds Cheddar cheese
2 onions
½ head lettuce
Oil for frying tortillas
1 dozen tortillas

Heat oil in large, heavy skillet. Brown meat, separating and stirring with fork. When meat is crumbly and browned, pour in enchilada sauce and water. Simmer for 30-45 minutes. Grate cheese, chop onions and shred lettuce (do not mix); set aside. To make each serving, soften tortilla in 1" hot cooking oil; dip in meat sauce. Place tortilla on warm plate, spoon some sauce on top, and sprinkle liberally with onion and cheese. Repeat process to make a stack of 3 layers. When final tortilla (covered with sauce, onion and cheese) is placed on stack, spoon 2 or 3 additional tablespoons sauce over top. Keep stacks warm, in oven, until all servings are completed. Before serving, sprinkle handful of lettuce on top of each stack. Makes 4 servings.

Mrs. Jack L. Maxwell (Nancy Nelms)

Mexican Chicken Casserole

1 chicken hen (about 4 lbs.) or
   3 whole chicken breasts
2 teaspoons salt
1 teaspoon pepper
1 bay leaf
1 can condensed cream of
   chicken soup
1 can condensed cream of
   mushroom soup

1 can (10½ oz.) Rotel tomatoes
   with green chilies
½ cup chicken stock
Additional salt and pepper
12 tortillas, torn in small pieces
2 onions, finely chopped
3 cups grated sharp cheese
   (about ¾ lb.)

Cook chicken in water to which has been added 2 teaspoons salt, 1 teaspoon pepper and bay leaf. Remove cooked chicken; reserve 1/2 cup of the chicken stock. Cut chicken into large, bite-sized pieces; set aside. Combine soups, tomatoes, chicken stock, salt and pepper to taste. Mix well. In a 3-quart casserole, make 3 layers in the following order: torn tortillas, chicken, tomato mixture, chopped onions and grated cheese. Use all ingredients in the 3 layers, being sure that cheese is on top. Bake at 350° for about 45 minutes. Serves 6-8.

Mrs. Jay W. Colvin, Jr. (Elaine Lester)

Tamale Pie

¼ pound salt pork, or ¼ cup
  bacon drippings
1 cup chopped onion
¾ cup chopped green pepper
2 cloves garlic, crushed
2 pounds lean ground beef
3 tablespoons chili powder
1 teaspoon salt
1 can (8 oz.) tomato sauce
1 can (1 lb., 12 oz.) tomatoes,
  drained

1 cup sliced ripe olives
1 can (1 lb.) whole kernel
  corn, drained
1¼ cups milk
1½ cups yellow corn meal
2 eggs
1 tablespoon cooking oil
1 tablespoon butter
Grated sharp cheese

Dice salt pork and fry in large skillet or Dutch oven. Add onion, green pepper and garlic; saute. Add meat and lightly brown. Add chili powder, salt, tomato sauce, tomatoes, ripe olives and corn. Remove from heat. Scald milk; mix with corn meal to make mush. Add unbeaten eggs, one at a time. Stir oil and butter into mush. Combine corn meal and meat mixtures. Pour into large baking dish; liberally sprinkle cheese over top. Bake slowly in a 325° oven for 1 hour. Serves 10-12.

Mrs. Richard R. McKay (Emily Ann Finch)

Tamale Casserole

½ pound pork sausage
1 cup minced onion
¾ cup diced green pepper
½ pound ground beef
1 can (12 oz.) whole kernel corn
⅓ cup sliced ripe olives
  (reserve liquid)

1½ cups tomato sauce
1-1½ teaspoons salt
1 teaspoon chili powder
½ teaspoon garlic salt
2 cans (15 oz. each) tamales
⅓ cup tamale liquid
1½ cups grated Cheddar cheese

In large skillet, brown sausage. Remove sausage and drain. Spoon out all but 3 tablespoons drippings from skillet. Add onion and green pepper; saute until tender. Stir in ground beef and cook until browned. Drain corn; reserve liquid. Add corn, 1 teaspoon corn liquid, ripe olives, 1 teaspoon ripe olive liquid, and sausage to skillet. Mix in tomato sauce, salt, chili powder and garlic salt. Simmer gently for 15 minutes. Meanwhile, drain tamales; add 1/3 cup tamale liquid to meat mixture. Remove wrappings from tamales, slice tamales in half, lengthwise. Spoon meat mixture into large, shallow casserole and arrange tamales on top. Bake, uncovered, in 350° oven for 15 minutes. Sprinkle with cheese and return to oven until cheese is melted, about 20 more minutes. Serves 6.

Mrs. Roland M. Howard (Joan Lander)

Chicken Tamale Pie

1 chicken hen (about 5 lbs.) or
4 cups cooked chicken
2 cans (15 oz. each) tamales
2 cans (12 oz. each) whole
kernel corn, drained

2 cans (1 lb. 3 oz. each) chili
without beans
2 cans (1 lb. each) tomatoes,
(do not drain)
Grated cheese

Cook chickens and cut into slices. In a 5-quart casserole, make 2 layers of chicken, tamales, corn, chili, tomatoes and cheese. Sprinkle salt and pepper over the corn and tomato layers. Cover with grated cheese. Bake at 350° for about 2 hours. Cooked turkey may be substituted for chicken. Serves 12-14.

Mrs. Robert E. Clemons (Grayson Cecil)

Fiesta Casserole

1 pound ground beef
1 large onion, chopped
1 teaspoon salt
¼ teaspoon pepper
2 cans (4 oz. each) whole
green chiles

1½ cups shredded sharp
Cheddar cheese
1½ cups milk
¼ cup flour
½ teaspoon salt
¼ teaspoon pepper sauce
4 eggs, beaten

Lightly brown meat and onion; drain off excess fat. Sprinkle with salt and pepper; remove from heat. Cut chiles crosswise and remove seeds. Place half the chiles in bottom of greased 6" x 10" x 2" casserole. Sprinkle evenly with cheese. Arrange meat on top of cheese, then place remaining chiles over meat. Combine milk, flour, salt, pepper sauce and eggs. Pour over chiles. Place casserole in pan of hot water. Bake at 350° for about 50 minutes, or until set. Cool 5 minutes before cutting in squares to serve. Serves 6.

Mrs. Raymond Thornton (Dee Ann Minnis)

Mexican Masa Muffins

1 cup masa (Mexican flour)
2 teaspoons baking powder
½ teaspoon soda
½ teaspoon salt

1 cup buttermilk
1 egg, beaten
2 tablespoons corn oil

Sift dry ingredients together. Add buttermilk, egg and oil. Stir just until all ingredients are mixed. Fill greased muffin tins half full. Bake at 450° for 15-20 minutes. Makes 12 small, or 6 large, muffins.

Mrs. Paul Sherwood (Mildred Wood)

Chalupas

6 tortillas	1½ cups refritos (refried beans)
1 cup cooking oil	2 cups grated cheese
½ pound ground beef	Salt and pepper
1 tablespoon bacon drippings	6 teaspoons finely chopped
½ teaspoon cumin	onion
¼ teaspoon chili powder	¾ cup chopped fresh tomatoes
1 teaspoon salt	3 cups finely chopped lettuce

Fry tortillas in cooking oil until crisp; drain and set aside. Saute ground meat in bacon drippings; mix in cumin, chili powder and salt. Remove from heat. Spread each tortilla with 1/4 cup refritos; layer about 2 tablespoons meat mixture on top of refritos, and sprinkle about 1/3 cup grated cheese over meat. Place on cookie sheet and bake at 350° until thoroughly heated, about 10 minutes. While piping hot, place on 6 individual plates; sprinkle each chalupa with salt and pepper, 1 teaspoon chopped onion, 2 tablespoons chopped tomato, and 1/2 cup chopped lettuce. Serve immediately. (Chalupas are not very successful when done ahead of time.) Serves 6.

Mrs. William G. Guerriero (Margaret Ann White)

Mac's Meat Tacos

1 pound ground lean beef	1½ teaspoons salt
1 tablespoon (or more) chili	1 or 2 chili piquins, crushed; or
powder	⅛ teaspoon cayenne plus
1 clove garlic, crushed	3 dashes Tabasco
2 tablespoons finely choped onion	12 taco shells
2½ cups canned tomatoes; or	Mexican hot sauce
2¼ cups peeled, diced	Shredded lettuce
fresh tomatoes	

Brown meat in slightly greased skillet or Dutch oven, over medium heat. Cook about 30 minutes. Add chili powder, garlic, onion, tomatoes, salt and chili piquins. Simmer over low heat for 2 hours, adding a little water from time to time to keep mixture juicy. Place about 3 tablespoons meat mixture into each taco shell, dribble a little hot sauce over meat, and fill remainder of shell with shredded lettuce. Or, occasionally, serve "do-it-yourself" style. Makes 12 tacos.

Mrs. Hughes Fleming (Mildred Hughes)

Hamburger Olé

2 pounds ground beef
1 green pepper, chopped
1 large onion, chopped
1 large fresh tomato, peeled
    and diced

1 can (15 oz.) Ranch Style beans
1 can (1 lb. 3 oz.) chili
    without beans
Salt and pepper

Brown meat, in very little oil, in large heavy skillet or Dutch oven. When meat is browned, add green pepper and onion, and cook for 5 minutes. Add tomatoes, beans and chili; heat thoroughly. Serve as filling for tacos (makes at least 25); or over rice (serves 8-10).

Mrs. Joseph H. Russell, Jr. (Ruth Arbuckle)

Chiles Rellenos de Cuernavaca

4 or 5 cans (4 oz. each) Ortega
    whole green chiles (18 peppers)
3 large onions, chopped
6 large tomatoes, peeled and
    chopped
¾ cup cooking oil
Salt and pepper
2 cups cooked, shredded chicken
1 cup cooked, cubed ham

12 stuffed olives, chopped
½ cup raisins
½ cup slivered almonds
6 eggs
3 additional egg whites
Flour
Cooking oil for deep fat frying
1½ pints cream, slightly
    warmed

Carefully split and seed chile peppers; place on cookie sheet and set aside. Make sauce by sauteeing onions and tomatoes in oil. Season with salt and pepper, cover, and simmer gently for 30 minutes. Let cool and puree in blender. Set aside. Meanwhile, make stuffing by combining chicken, ham, olives, raisins, almonds and 6 tablespoons of the tomato puree. Fill each pepper with about 2 tablespoons stuffing, wrapping pepper around stuffing, and securing with toothpicks. (Pepper skins are fragile and difficult to work with, but persevere. Stuffing does **not** fall out, as suspected, when peppers are fried.) Beat the 9 egg whites until stiff; fold in the 6 slightly beaten yolks. Roll stuffed peppers in flour, dip in beaten eggs, and fry in deep fat. Drain. Place fried peppers, side by side, in large, shallow baking dish (or Mexican earthenware dish). Cover with remaining tomato puree. Bake in 350° oven for about 20 minutes, or until thoroughly heated. Remove from oven and pour slightly warmed cream over peppers. Serve immediately. Makes 18 chiles rellenos. Allow 2-3 per person.

Mrs. Jack C. Payne (Mary Hoehn)

Chili Con Queso

1 large onion, finely chopped	1 can (4 oz.) whole green chiles
1 tablespoon bacon drippings	1 teaspoon salt
1 can (1 lb.) tomatoes	Several dashes pepper
Juice from tomatoes	1 pound processed American cheese, grated

Saute onion in bacon drippings until soft but not brown. Drain tomatoes, reserving juice. Coarsely chop tomatoes and chiles; add to onion. Add salt and pepper. Simmer slowly about 15 minutes. Add cheese and stir over low heat until melted. Thin to desired consistency by adding reserved tomato juice, a tablespoon at a time. Serve over hot, crisp tortillas as a side dish with Mexican food; or, serve from chafing dish as a dip with Doritos or corn chips. Freezes well. Makes about 1 quart.

Mrs. H. Edward Maddox, III (Donna Gray)

Pinto Beans

1 pound dried pinto beans	1 tablespoon chili powder
4 slices bacon, cut in thin strips	2 teaspoons cumin
	1 teaspoon thyme
1 large onion, chopped	Salt

Wash beans thoroughly. Set aside. In Dutch oven, fry bacon until crisp; add onions and saute until soft. Add beans, chili powder, cumin, thyme and salt. Cover with water (about 3-1/2 to 4 cups). Cook slowly for 5-6 hours, or until beans are tender. To thicken gravy, spoon out about 1/2 cup beans, mash with fork, and return to pot. Serve hot. These beans freeze very well and are great to have on hand for refritos, chalupas or nachos. Makes about 4 cups cooked beans.

Mrs. William G. Guerriero (Margaret Ann White)

Re-Refritos

2 cans (1 lb. each) Rosarita refried beans
½ cup butter
Salt and pepper

Saute beans in butter until brown. Season with salt and pepper. Serves 6.

Mrs. Denman Moody (Ted Lewis)

Refried Mexican Beans

½ pound dried pinto beans	Salt
4 quarts water	Additional bacon drippings
1 onion, chopped	Finely chopped onion
2 tablespoons bacon drippings	Grated cheese

Soak beans in 4 quarts cold water for 8 hours, or overnight. Do not drain. Add enough fresh water to cover, and bring to a boil. Add onion. Simmer slowly in a covered pot, preferably earthenware. When skins begin to wrinkle, add bacon drippings. As liquid is absorbed, add more water, always hot. Cook about 3-1/2 hours; add salt, and cook another 30 minutes, or until beans are soft. Separate beans from broth by adding beans to frying pan, a little at a time, with additional bacon drippings. Mash beans with spoon and add broth, a little at a time. When all beans have been mashed, saute the whole mixture until it thickens into a heavy paste that can be rolled up. (Do not let it get too dry.) Serve hot, with chopped onions and grated cheese on top. Serves 3-4.

Mrs. Garrett S. Livingston, Jr. (Mary Ann Ransom)

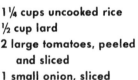

Rice Mexicali

1 ¼ cups uncooked rice	1 clove garlic, sliced
½ cup lard	1 cup cold water
2 large tomatoes, peeled and sliced	2 teaspoons salt
1 small onion, sliced	2 cups beef broth
	Avocado slices for garnish

Soak rice for 15 minutes in hot water to cover. Rinse in cold water; drain thoroughly. Melt lard; fry rice until golden brown. Combine tomatoes, onion and garlic in blender; blend until pureed. (If fresh tomatoes are not available, substitute 6 tablespoons tomato paste, 1/2 teaspoon onion juice and 1 crushed garlic clove for the fresh tomato puree.) Add tomato puree to browned rice and simmer until dry. Add 1 cup cold water and salt; cook until water is absorbed. Heat broth until boiling; add to rice. Cover, and simmer until rice is dry and every grain separate. Garnish with slices of avocado. Serves 6-8.

Mrs. Garrett S. Livingston, Jr. (Mary Ann Ransom)

Mexican Rice

2 tablespoons shortening	1 cup canned tomatoes or
1 cup uncooked rice	tomato juice; or 1 large, fresh
3 tablespoons finely chopped	tomato, peeled and chopped
onion	2 teaspoons salt
1 clove garlic, minced (optional)	3 cups water

Put shortening in heavy frying pan or Dutch oven; heat, and add rice. Cook over medium heat, stirring frequently, until rice turns brown and begins to soften. Add onion, garlic, tomatoes, salt and water. Cover, and reduce heat. Allow to simmer about 30 minutes, or until rice is tender. Remove cover and let rice dry out. If rice becomes too dry, add a little water. (Some like this rice slightly moist; others prefer it quite dry.) Do not stir rice any more than is necessary to keep it from sticking to pan. Serves 6-8.

Mrs. Hughes Fleming (Mildred Hughes)

Mexican Scrambled Eggs

¼ cup finely chopped onion	Salt and pepper
¼ cup finely chopped green pepper	1 tomato, peeled, chopped
2 tablespoons bacon drippings	and drained
4 eggs, beaten	Hot Mexican sauce, optional

Saute onion and pepper in bacon drippings, until tender. Pour off most of the grease. (Do not add milk or cream to eggs.) Add eggs, salt and pepper to the skillet, and cook, stirring, until eggs begin to set. Add tomato, and cook a little more, until eggs are firm. If desired, top with few dashes hot Mexican sauce. Serves 2.

Mrs. J. R. Goodearle (Mary Bertron)

Sopaipillas

3 cups flour	1 tablespoon shortening
2 teaspoons baking powder	1 cup (or more) water
1 teaspoon salt	

Mix together flour, baking powder and salt; cut in shortening. Add enough water to make a stiff dough. Roll out very thin and cut into 2" squares. Fry in **very hot, deep** fat until brown. These will puff up like pillows. Makes approximately 32.

Mrs. Lyon L. Brinsmade (Susannah Tucker)

Flan Café

3 eggs, slightly beaten	1 teaspoon vanilla
6 tablespoons sugar	2¼ cups milk, scalded
¼ teaspoon salt	6 tablespoons Kahlua liqueur
3 tablespoons powdered instant coffee	Whipped cream

Combine eggs, sugar, salt, coffee and vanilla. Mix thoroughly. Gradually add milk, stirring vigorously. Pour into custard cups. Place in pan of hot water, and bake at 375° for 25 minutes, or until firm. Chill thoroughly. Serve in baking dishes, or unmold. Top each serving with a tablespoon of Kahlua and whipped cream. Serves 6.

Mrs. Rotan McGown (Charlotte Rotan)

Almendrado

9 egg whites	Pinch salt
2 envelopes unflavored gelatin	3 drops almond extract
1 cup cold water	Red and green food coloring
1¾ cups sugar	¼ cup blanched almonds, ground

Be sure egg whites are at room temperature. Soften gelatin in cold water. Place over hot water to dissolve; cool. (If too hot, gelatin will thin egg whites too much.) Beat egg whites until stiff but not dry. Gradually fold in sugar, salt, gelatin and almond extract. Divide mixture into 3 bowls. Color one part red, one part green, and, to remaining white part add the ground almonds. Spoon in layers (red, white and green), into Pyrex loaf pans. Chill until firm. Cut in slices and serve with Custard Sauce. This snow pudding, in the national colors of Mexico, is a perfect ending to a Mexican meal. Makes 18 servings.

CUSTARD SAUCE

6 egg yolks	2 cups milk, scalded
¼ cup sugar	¼ teaspoon almond extract
⅛ teaspoon salt	

In top of double boiler, beat egg yolks slightly. Add sugar and salt. Add milk gradually, stirring constantly. Continue stirring while mixture cooks over hot, not boiling, water until custard coats spoon (about 7 minutes). Add almond extract. Chill. Serve with Almendrado.

Mrs. John H. Meyers (Alice Baker Jones)

VEGETABLES

Hints

TO CUT ONIONS: Refrigerate before cutting to avoid tears. After cutting onions, rub hands with salt and vinegar, then rinse in cold water.

TO PEEL TOMATOES: Dip tomatoes, one at a time, in boiling water. Peel off skin and refrigerate promptly.

COOKING VEGETABLES

TO COOK FLUFFY RICE: Put 2 cups water and 1 teaspoon salt in large pot with tight-fitting lid. Bring to a boil. Add 1 cup rice, stir slightly; let return to a hard boil. Put lid on tight, turn heat to simmer, and leave, without stirring or peeking, for 14 minutes. (Rice increases three times or more in cooking.)

TO KEEP COOKED RICE WARM: Place rice in colander over simmering water, and cover with cloth or paper towels.

TO REHEAT RICE: Steam rice in colander; or, add very little water to rice in saucepan and warm over direct heat.

TO BAKE POTATOES: Scrub skin, dry thoroughly; prick skin with fork to let steam escape during cooking. Place in 425° oven and bake 50-60 minutes. (Potatoes are done when they are easily pierced with a fork or feel soft when squeezed slightly.) If crisp skins are not desired, oil potatoes before placing in oven. As soon as potatoes are baked, slash tops and gently squeeze, so that steam escapes and potatoes fluff up.

MASHED POTATOES: Add a pinch of baking powder or soda, as well as milk and butter, to make mashed potatoes light and fluffy.

SPAGHETTI, MACARONI AND NOODLES: Place a teaspoon of butter or vegetable oil in cooking water to keep it from boiling over.

CAULIFLOWER, CABBAGE AND BROCCOLI: Add a little vinegar to cooking water to absorb odors.

SPINACH AND FRESH GREENS: Add 1/4 cup olive oil to cooking water to enhance flavor.

ARTICHOKES: Soak in cold, salted water for 30 minutes before cooking.

Artichokes au Gratin

2 packages frozen artichoke hearts	⅓ cup flour
1 tablespoon lemon juice	½ cup artichoke liquid
¼ cup butter	1½ cups milk, heated
Dash white pepper	1 egg, slightly beaten
¾ teaspoon salt	½ cup grated Swiss cheese
1 teaspoon onion salt	2 tablespoons dry bread crumbs
¼ teaspoon dry mustard	Paprika

Heat oven to 450°. Cook artichoke hearts according to package directions, adding lemon juice to water. Drain, reserving 1/2 cup liquid. Place artichoke hearts in single layer in a 9-inch square shallow casserole. Melt butter in saucepan. Add pepper, salt, onion salt, mustard and flour. Stir until smooth. Gradually add artichoke liquid and hot milk; cook, stirring constantly, until thickened. Remove from heat; add egg and half the cheese. Stir until blended. Pour over artichokes. Sprinkle with remaining cheese, bread crumbs and paprika. Bake at 450° for 15 minutes. Serves 4-6.

Mrs. Ben A. Brollier (Marilyn Oden)

Artichoke Hearts Supreme

1 cup milk	Salt and pepper
1 cup cream	Paprika
3 tablespoons instant flour	3 cans (1 lb. each) small artichoke hearts
3-4 ounces Blue cheese	

Slowly heat milk and cream; add flour and stir until thickened. Add cheese, salt, pepper and paprika and continue stirring over low heat until well blended. Drain artichoke hearts; rinse thoroughly to remove brine. Add to cheese sauce. Stir gently to avoid breaking hearts. Simmer. (The longer the artichokes are simmered in the sauce the more subtle the flavor.) This may be prepared in advance and reheated before serving. (Never put over high heat.) This is a delicate side dish with game birds, steak or seafood. Serves 6.

Mrs. Nelson Robinson (Mary Washington)

Artichoke Bottoms with Spinach

1 package frozen chopped spinach	6 artichoke bottoms
1 tablespoon chopped onion	2 tablespoons melted butter
¼ cup sour cream	Cracked pepper

Cook and drain spinach; whip in blender with onion. Combine with sour cream and salt to taste. Mound spinach on each artichoke bottom. Drizzle melted butter over each and sprinkle with cracked pepper. Heat in oven until just hot. Serve as a vegetable or garnish for meat. Serves 6.

Mrs. John H. Meyers (Alice Baker Jones)

Artichokes and Peas

2 cans (1 lb. each) artichoke hearts, drained	1 can (1 lb.) tiny green peas, drained
2 tablespoons (or more) butter	¼ cup (or less) sherry

Saute artichoke hearts in butter until hot. Add peas and warm. Add sherry and simmer for 10 minutes. Serve immediately. Serves 4.

Mrs. David E. Park, Jr. (Virginia Lawhon)

Asparagus with Blue Cheese

1 package (10 oz.) Pepperidge Farm patty shells	1 can condensed cream of asparagus soup
½ pound small fresh mushrooms or 1 can (4 oz.) button mushrooms, drained	2 tablespoons sherry
	3 cups crumbled Danish Blue cheese
2 tablespoons minced onion	1 large can (19 oz.) green asparagus spears
¼ cup butter	

Let patty shells thaw. Knead patty shells into one ball and roll out, on a cookie sheet, to 1/2" thickness. Bake pastry at 400° for 25 minutes. Cut into 8 pieces and place on large bake-and-serve platter. Simmer mushrooms and onion in butter, just slightly. Blend in soup and sherry. Simmer until heated. Add cheese and stir until melted. Heat asparagus in separate pan; drain. Place asparagus on pastry and cover with sauce. Broil 3-5 minutes at least 4" below heat. Garnish with extra sauteed mushrooms, if desired. Serves 6-8.

Mrs. Lorenzo B. Taylor (Marilyn Dubach)

Party Green Beans

3 cans (1 lb. each) Blue Lake
   green beans
1 can condensed mushroom
   soup
½ cup milk

½ cup finely chopped onion
2 cups grated cheese
   (Velveeta, preferably)
Salt and pepper
1 can (3½ oz.) fried onion rings

Combine green beans, mushroom soup, milk, onion and cheese. Mix gently; season with salt and pepper. Pour into greased casserole. Top with onion rings. Bake at 350° for 30 minutes. Serves 8-10.

Mrs. James L. Bayless (Betty Lou Langston)

Creole Green Beans

3 slices bacon
1 package frozen French-cut
   green beans
1 medium onion, chopped

1 tablespoon flour
1 can (1 lb.) tomatoes
Salt and pepper
Dash Tabasco

Cook bacon until crisp; then drain. Cook green beans in boiling water for 10 minutes, adding 1 tablespoon bacon grease while cooking. Saute onion until golden; stir in flour. Add tomatoes, cutting up large pieces. Stir until heated. Drain beans and add to tomato mixture. Season with salt, pepper and Tabasco. Cook until thickened. Serve with bacon crumbled on top. Serves 4.

Mrs. Thomas B. Wilkinson, III (Mildred Edwards)

Green Beans Canton

2 packages frozen French-cut
   green beans, thawed and
   slightly cooked
1 cup water chestnuts, sliced
1 can (1 lb.) bean sprouts,
   drained
½ pound fresh mushrooms,
   sliced

1 medium onion, chopped
2 cups medium cream sauce
Salt
1½ cups grated American
   cheese
1 can (3½ oz.) French-fried
   onion rings, crumbled

In a 2-quart casserole, make two layers alternating half the beans, water chestnuts, bean sprouts, mushrooms and onion. Cover each layer with half the cream sauce and sprinkle with salt and cheese. Bake at 400° about 30 minutes or until heated through and bubbly, topping with onions the last 10 minutes of baking. Serves 8-10.

Mrs. Ben A. Brollier (Marilyn Oden)

Green Bean Casserole

1 can (1 lb.) French-cut green beans	2 tablespoons finely chopped onion
1 can condensed cream of mushroom soup	About ½ cup of packaged herb stuffing crumbs
	1 tablespoon melted butter

Drain beans well and mix with soup and onion. Put in 1-1/2-quart casserole. Toss crumbs with melted butter and sprinkle over top. Bake at 350° for about 30 minutes. Serves 4.

Mrs. A. J. Hurt, Jr. (Patty Parrish)

String Bean Casserole

2 packages frozen French-cut green beans	½ pint sour cream
2 tablespoons butter	1 onion, grated
2 tablespoons flour	Dash garlic salt
1 teaspoon salt	½ pound Swiss cheese, grated
¼ teaspoon pepper	1 cup grated Cheddar cheese
1 tablespoon sugar	3 cups corn flakes, crushed
	2 tablespoons butter, melted

Cook and drain beans. Combine butter, flour, salt, pepper, sugar, sour cream, grated onion and garlic salt in saucepan. Cook until thickened. Mix sauce with beans and pour into buttered casserole dish. Cover with mixture of grated cheeses. Top with crushed cornflakes. Drizzle melted butter on top. Bake at 400° for 20 minutes, or until bubbly. Serves 8.

Mrs. James Howard Park, III (Bette Naylor)

Broccoli-Rice Whiz

⅓ cup uncooked rice	1 package frozen chopped broccoli, cooked
½ cup chopped onion	1 can condensed cream of mushroom soup
½ cup chopped celery	1 small jar (8 oz.) Cheez Whiz
2 tablespoons butter	Pepper

Cook rice until tender. Saute onion and celery in butter. Stir in rice and well-drained broccoli; then add soup and Cheez Whiz. Season with pepper. Spoon into greased baking dish and bake at 350° for 20-30 minutes, or until thoroughly heated. Serves 4-6.

Mrs. E. Dale Shepherd, Jr. (Marjorie Ilfrey)

Broccoli Casserole

¼ cup finely chopped onion
6 tablespoons butter
2 tablespoons flour
½ cup water
1 jar (8 oz.) processed
    American cheese spread

2 packages frozen chopped
    broccoli, thawed and well
    drained
3 eggs, well beaten
½ cup soda cracker crumbs

Saute onion in 4 tablespoons of the butter until soft. Stir in flour. Add water. Cook over low heat, stirring, until mixture thickens and comes to a boil. Blend in cheese. Combine sauce and broccoli. Add eggs; mix gently until blended. Turn into greased 1-1/2-quart casserole. Cover with cracker crumbs. Dot with remaining butter. Bake at 325° for 30 minutes. Serves 6-8.

Mrs. Charles T. Niblack (Eleanor Allen)

Maria's Cabbage

¼ pound highly-seasoned
    smoked link sausage
1 medium onion, chopped
2 or 3 tomatoes, peeled and
    chopped

1 medium head cabbage,
    coarsely shredded
Salt and pepper

Remove casing from sausage and crumble meat; saute with onion. Pour off any grease. Add tomatoes, cabbage, salt and pepper. Cover pan tightly and simmer over low heat until cabbage is tender, about 10 minutes. Serves 6.

Mrs. John B. Abercrombie (Virginia Townsend)

Cabbage Casserole

1 medium head cabbage
2 tablespoons butter
2 tablespoons flour
1 cup milk
1 teaspoon salt

½ teaspoon pepper
3 drops Tabasco
2 hard-cooked eggs, sliced
1 cup grated sharp cheese
½ cup bread crumbs

Shred cabbage (makes about 4 cups) and steam for 5 minutes; drain. Make cream sauce of butter, flour and milk. Season cream sauce with salt, pepper and Tabasco. Remove from heat. In 2-quart casserole, place a layer of cabbage, sliced egg and grated cheese. Repeat layers. Cover with cream sauce and top with bread crumbs. Bake in 350° oven for 20 minutes. Serves 6-8.

Mrs. C. Harcourt Wooten (Evelyn Wilkey)

Cabbage in Sour Cream

1 small head cabbage, cored
  and finely chopped
1 egg, slightly beaten
¼ cup cider vinegar
1 tablespoon butter
1 teaspoon sugar

1 teaspoon salt
¼ teaspoon pepper
½ cup sour cream
1 tablespoon finely chopped
  green pepper
Dash paprika

Cook cabbage in boiling salted water until tender but still crisp, about 5 minutes. (Or steam 8-10 mintues.) Drain well; place in bowl. In top of double boiler, blend together egg, vinegar, butter, sugar, salt and pepper. Cook over boiling water, stirring until thick, 2-3 minutes. Cool slightly. Stir in sour cream and green pepper. Pour over drained cabbage. Toss to coat well. Serve warm or chilled, sprinkled with paprika. Serves 6.

Mrs. Lewis A. Brown (Sidney Walsh)

Carrot Ring

6 to 8 carrots
3 tablespoons butter
Celery salt
Monosodium glutamate
Salt and pepper

1 tablespoon grated onion
½ cup bread crumbs
3 eggs, separated
Chopped parsley

Cook peeled, sliced carrots until tender; reserve cooking water. Mash carrots and measure 1-1/2 cups. Season with 1 tablespoon of the butter, celery salt, monosodium glutamate, salt, pepper and onion. Stir in 1/2 cup water, bread crumbs and the well-beaten egg yolks. Fold in stiffly-beaten egg whites and bake in buttered ring mold in 325° oven for 25-30 minutes. Melt remaining butter; pour it over ring after unmolding, before serving. Sprinkle with chopped parsley. Creamed peas may be served in center. Serves 4-6.

Mrs. Richard R. McKay (Emily Ann Finch)

Fried Cauliflower

1 package frozen cauliflower	5 tablespoons flour
3 eggs, separated	Salt and pepper

Cook cauliflower 5-10 minutes. Pour off water. Separate cauliflower into bite-sized flowerets; place on absorbent paper. Beat egg whites until stiff but not dry. Add egg yolks one at a time; beat until blended. Add 2 tablespoons of the flour; add salt and pepper. Dredge cauliflower in remaining 3 tablespoons flour. Dip into egg mixture. Fry in deep fat until lightly brown. Serve immediately with Ranchero Sauce. Serves 4.

RANCHERO SAUCE

2 tablespoons bacon drippings	2 tomatoes, peeled and
1 medium onion, finely	finely chopped
chopped	1 green chile pepper,
1 clove garlic, minced	finely chopped
	Salt

In bacon drippings, saute onion and garlic until clear. Add tomatoes, chile pepper and salt. Cover; simmer about 10 minutes. Stir and mash sauce. Serve warm over fried cauliflower. Sauce can also be served on eggs or any meat. Makes about 1-1/2 cups sauce.

Mrs. Harry H. Hudson (Carolyn Brock)

Cauliflower with Shrimp Sauce

1 medium cauliflower, broken	Salt and pepper
into flowerets	¼ cup slivered toasted almonds
1 can frozen cream of	(optional)
shrimp soup	Chopped parsley for garnish
½ cup sour cream	

Cook cauliflower in small amount of salted water until tender. Drain. Warm soup over low heat, stirring frequently. Add sour cream, heat, and season with salt and pepper. Add almonds. Pour sauce over the hot cauliflower and garnish with parsley. Serves 4-6.

Mrs. Charles W. Pyle (Ida McFaddin)

Baked Celery

2 whole stalks celery
2 cans condensed beef bouillon
2 envelopes French's Brown
   Gravy Mix

¼ cup butter
2 cups shredded Mozzarella
   cheese

Cut celery into 3-inch pieces. Boil for 15 minutes in beef bouillon. Prepare brown gravy mix as directed, adding butter to it. Drain celery; arrange in shallow casserole. Pour gravy over celery. Cover with cheese. Bake at 325° for 45 minutes. Serves 6-8.

Mrs. Gentry Kidd (Winifred Crawford)

Party Celery

1 whole stalk celery, cut in
   2'' lengths
1 can condensed cream of celery
   or cream of mushroom soup

1 can (5 oz.) water chestnuts,
   sliced
¼ cup chopped pimientos
Toasted sliced almonds
Browned bread crumbs

Cook celery in salted water for 5 minutes; drain. Combine celery, soup, water chestnuts and pimientos. Spoon into casserole. Sprinkle almonds, then crumbs over mixture. Bake at 350° for 30 minutes. This dish may be prepared early, then baked just before serving. Serves 6-8.

Mrs. William C. French, Jr. (Frances Griggs)

Festive Corn Casserole

¼ cup butter
¼ cup flour
2 teaspoons salt
1 tablespoon sugar
1¾ cups milk

3 cups fresh corn kernels,
   or 1½ packages
   frozen white corn
3 eggs, beaten until frothy
⅓ cup chopped green onions

Melt butter in saucepan; stir in flour, salt and sugar. Cook until bubbly; add milk and cook, stirring constantly, until thick. Stir in corn. Remove from heat. With table knife, scrape cob to squeeze out any remaining juice and add to mixture. Stir in eggs and onions. Pour into well-buttered casserole and bake at 325° about 45 minutes, or until slightly brown. Frozen white corn may be substituted for the fresh, but the fresh corn makes it even better. Serve 6-8.

Mrs. Anne E. Neff (Anne Eastham)

Madeline's Corn Pudding

3 tablespoons butter	3 eggs, beaten
12 ears fresh white corn	3 tablespoons sugar
2 cups milk	Salt and pepper

Place butter in 2-quart casserole to melt. Slit corn kernels and scrape off the cobs. Combine corn with remaining ingredients and pour into casserole. Place casserole in pan of hot water. Bake in 325° oven for 30-45 minutes, or until firm. Serves 8.

Mrs. Otis Meredith (Mary Wilkins)

Poached Cucumbers

6 medium cucumbers	½ teaspoon sugar
2 teaspoons lemon juice	¼ cup water
1 teaspoon salt	¼ cup butter

Pare cucumbers. Slice into thin rounds. Add lemon juice, salt, sugar and water. Bring to a boil; cook 1 minute. Remove from heat; let stand 5 minutes. Drain and toss lightly with butter. Serves 8.

Mrs. Raleigh W. Johnson, Jr. (Marjorie Bintliff)

Sauteéd Cucumbers

1½ large cucumbers per person	Salt and pepper
Butter	Monosodium glutamate

Peel and slice cucumbers; saute in butter until just tender. Season with salt, pepper and monosodium glutamate. These cucumbers are like zucchini and go well with seafood.

Mrs. Owen Finch (Betty Grey)

Eggplant Casserole

1 small eggplant (1½ cups mashed)	1 cup canned tomatoes
1 tablespoon bacon drippings	1 cup mild grated cheese
1 large onion, chopped	⅓ cup bread crumbs
1 green pepper, chopped	2 eggs, beaten
2 or 3 ribs celery, chopped	Salt and pepper
1 small jar (2 oz.) pimiento, chopped	1 cup buttered bread crumbs

Peel eggplant, cut in pieces, and cook in salted water until tender. Drain well and mash. Put bacon drippings in heavy skillet. Add onion, green pepper, celery and pimiento. Saute until done, but not brown. Add mashed eggplant, tomatoes, cheese and 1/3 cup bread crumbs. Bring mixture to a boil; remove from heat and add eggs, salt and pepper. Stir until eggs are set. Spoon into 1-1/2-quart baking dish and cover with buttered crumbs. Bake at 350° for 30 minutes. Serves 6.

Mrs. Thomas E. Berry (Joan Jester)

Fluffy Eggplant

1 large or 2 small eggplants	1½ teaspoons lemon juice
1 onion, minced	½ teaspoon dry mustard
2 eggs	Salt and pepper
⅓ cup milk	1 cup bread crumbs
¼ cup butter, melted	½ cup grated Cheddar cheese

Peel and cube eggplant; cook until tender. Drain well and mash. Add onion. Beat eggs and milk together and stir into eggplant. Add butter, lemon juice, mustard, salt and pepper. Stir in 1/2 cup, or more, of the bread crumbs. Combine remaining bread crumbs with grated cheese for topping. Bake in a buttered 1-1/2-quart casserole in 325° oven for 30-40 minutes. Great for those who love eggplant; greater for those who don't. Serves 6.

Mrs. Arthur H. Jones (Patricia Forbes)

Mother's Eggplant Soufflé

1 medium eggplant, peeled
and diced
2 tablespoons butter
2 tablespoons flour
1 cup milk
½ cup grated sharp cheese

¾ cup soft bread crumbs
2 teaspoons finely grated
onion
1 tablespoon catsup
1 teaspoon salt
2 eggs, separated

Cook eggplant until tender; drain and mash very fine. Melt butter and stir in flour. When blended, add milk and cook until thick and smooth, stirring constantly. Add eggplant, cheese, bread crumbs, onion, catsup, salt and slightly beaten egg yolks. Mix well. Fold in stiffly-beaten egg whites. Turn into greased, 2-quart casserole and bake at 375° for 45 minutes. Serves 6.

Mrs. James A. Walsh (Harriet Brady)

Eggplant Manicotti

1 pound Ricotta cheese
(or creamed cottage cheese)
2½ ounces Romano cheese,
grated
2 eggs, slightly beaten

Salt and pepper
1 medium eggplant
Vegetable oil (or use
½ olive oil)
1 small can (8 oz.) tomato sauce

Mix cheeses together, beat in eggs, season with salt and pepper. Peel eggplant and slice **very** thin (not paper thin, but as thin as can be managed.) Saute slices in shallow oil until soft, turning once. Spread 1-1/2 to 2 tablespoons cheese mixture on each slice and roll up. Pour thick layer of tomato sauce in shallow baking dish, (approximately 9" x 12"). Arrange eggplant rolls close together on top of sauce. Bake at 400° for 15 minutes or until sauce is bubbly. Allow 2-3 rolls per person. Serves 6-8. For an easier version of this dish slice eggplant thicker (1/8"-1/4"). Saute as before, but slices will be too thick to roll. Instead, spread filling on half of slice and fold over as a turnover. Arrange on sauce and bake as directed above. (The amount of cheese filling given will prepare two small eggplants if the thicker slices are used, as each slice holds less filling than the eggplant rolls.) This dish may be prepared ahead of time and refrigerated until ready to bake.

Mrs. W. Browne Baker, Jr. (Anne Watts)

Stuffed Eggplant

1 medium eggplant
1 hard-cooked egg, finely
   chopped
1 small onion, minced
2 tablespoons finely diced celery
1 tablespoon melted butter

Few drops Worcestershire
   sauce
1 egg, beaten
½-¾ cup toasted buttered
   bread crumbs
Salt and pepper

Cut eggplant in half lengthwise; scoop out the pulp. Sprinkle inside of each shell with a little salt and set aside. Dice eggplant pulp and cook in salted water until tender. Drain and mash. Add hard-cooked egg, onion, celery, melted butter, Worcestershire sauce, beaten egg, bread crumbs, salt and pepper. Mix well. Spoon into eggplant shells. Sprinkle top generously with additional toasted bread crumbs, dot with butter, and bake in a moderate oven (325°-350°) for 30 minutes. Brown under broiler if desired. Serves 4.

Mrs. Gordon R. West (Josephine Morrow)

Maybelle's Eggplant with Shrimp

2 medium eggplants
Salt and pepper
Pinch of sugar
2 tablespoons finely chopped
   celery
¼ cup finely chopped
   green pepper
4 green onions with tops,
   chopped

1 medium onion, chopped
2 tablespoons finely chopped
   parsley
2 or 3 cloves garlic, crushed
3 tablespoons butter
1 pound raw shrimp, or ½ pound
   shelled, frozen shrimp
Ritz cracker crumbs

Peel and slice eggplant; cook until tender in small amount of salted water. Drain well and mash; season with salt, pepper and sugar. Saute all chopped vegetables and garlic in 2 tablespoons of the butter until tender, but not browned. Shell, chop, and saute shrimp in remaining tablespoon of butter. Combine shrimp, eggplant and sauteed vegetables. (If mixture seems too thin, add cracker crumbs until of desired consistency.) Place in a greased 2-quart baking dish and cover with cracker crumbs. Bake at 350° for 40 minutes. Freezes successfully. Serves 4-6.

Mrs. James A. Baker, Jr. (Bonner Means)

Lima Beans with Celery

1 package frozen baby lima beans	2 tablespoons cream cheese
2 tablespoons unsalted whipped butter	1-2 teaspoons sugar
Salt and pepper	2 ribs celery, chopped very finely

Cook lima beans in lightly salted water. Drain, leaving a little juice in pan. Add butter, salt, pepper, cream cheese, sugar and celery. Stir until cheese is melted and celery is thoroughly heated. Serves 4.

Mrs. John H. Meyers (Alice Baker Jones)

Lima Beans and Mushrooms

2 packages frozen baby lima beans	2 tablespoons flour
1 onion, minced	½ teaspoon nutmeg
5 ribs celery, diced	Salt and pepper
½ cup butter	1 cup cream
1 pound fresh mushrooms, coarsely chopped	2 tablespoons sherry (optional)

Cook lima beans; drain. Saute onion and celery in butter until golden; then add mushrooms and cook until tender. Sprinkle flour, nutmeg, salt and pepper over mushrooms and toss until well blended. Stir in lima beans. Reduce heat and stir in cream. Add sherry if desired. Serves 10-12.

Mrs. Lorenzo B. Taylor (Marilyn Dubach)

Mushroom Casserole

1 teaspoon minced parsley	Grated nutmeg (optional)
1 teaspoon minced chives	Pinch dried tarragon (optional)
1 teaspoon minced onion	⅓ cup butter, softened
1 teaspoon onion juice	1 cup heavy cream
1 teaspoon salt	18 large fresh mushrooms,
¼ teaspoon cayenne	washed and stemmed

Cream butter with parsley, chives, onion, onion juice and seasonings. Butter a 9-inch shallow baking dish. Arrange mushroom caps in dish, open side up. Fill each mushroom cap with butter mixture. Pour cream over all. Bake in very hot oven (450°) for 10 minutes or until the cream bubbles. Serves 6.

Mrs. Joe B. Ehresman (Kay Weeks)

Mushrooms Polonaise

½ cup butter
1½ pounds fresh mushrooms,
   sliced
1 onion, minced
2 tablespoons flour
1 cup sour cream

¼ cup heavy cream
Salt and pepper
¼ teaspoon nutmeg (optional)
2 tablespoons chopped parsley
¼ cup buttered bread crumbs

Melt butter in heavy skillet; add sliced mushrooms. Saute over medium heat until mushrooms begin to brown slightly and liquid has evaporated. Add onion and continue to saute until onion is soft but not brown. Stir in flour; cook for 5 minutes over very low heat. Blend in sour cream and heavy cream; season with salt, pepper and nutmeg. Cook until mixture thickens. Stir in parsley. Pour into buttered shallow baking dish. Sprinkle top with buttered bread crumbs. Bake at 325° for 35 minutes or until mixture has set and crumbs have lightly browned. Serves 6.

Mrs. James Howard Park, III (Bette Naylor)

Herbed Mushrooms

1½ pounds large, fresh
   mushrooms
⅓ cup grated Parmesan cheese
½ cup dry bread crumbs
¼ cup grated onion
1 or 2 cloves garlic, crushed

2 tablespoons minced parsley
½ teaspoon salt
¼ teaspoon freshly ground
   black pepper
½ teaspoon oregano
⅔ cup olive oil

Wash mushrooms in water with a little lemon juice. Do not peel; dry. Remove stems and chop; mix stem pieces with cheese, bread crumbs, onion, garlic, parsley, salt, pepper and oregano. Stuff mushroom caps with this mixture. Pour a little olive oil into baking pan; arrange mushrooms in pan. Pour remaining oil over them, being sure to get a little oil in each mushroom. Bake at 350° for 25 minutes. Serves 6-8.

Mrs. Ben A. Brollier (Marilyn Oden)

Stuffed Mushroom Caps

18 large, fresh mushrooms
¼ cup butter

6 green onions, minced
1 package frozen spinach
souffle, thawed

Wash and stem mushrooms. Slightly saute mushroom caps in butter, just enough to heat through. Remove caps and drain on absorbent paper. In same butter, saute onions; add thawed spinach and stir a few minutes over low heat. Remove from heat. Stuff caps with spinach mixture (mixture will seem thin), and arrange in a shallow pan. When ready to serve, run under broiler just enough to heat. Stuffed caps may be stored in refrigerator until ready to broil; they may also be sprinkled with Parmesan cheese before broiling, if desired. These are a nice accompaniment for steaks, or garnish for meat platter. Allow 2 per person.

Mrs. R. Henry Lake (Fredrica Lanford)

Onion Quiche

1 cup salted cracker crumbs
4 tablespoons melted butter
4 cups thinly sliced onions
1½ cups milk

4 eggs, slightly beaten
1½ teaspoons salt
Pepper
½ cup grated Cheddar cheese

Toss cracker crumbs with 2 tablespoons of the melted butter. Press against bottom and sides of 10-inch pie plate. Cook onions over low heat in remaining 2 tablespoons butter, until tender. Spread over crumb crust. Add milk to eggs and pour slowly over onions. Sprinkle salt and pepper over all. Sprinkle grated cheese over top. Bake at 350° for 25 minutes or until firm. This quiche may be prepared in advance and baked later. Serves 6-8.

Mrs. E. H. Thornton, Jr. (Ramona Meyers)

Sherried Onions

5 white onions, peeled and sliced
⅓ cup butter
1 teaspoon monosodium glutamate
½ teaspoon sugar

½ teaspoon salt
Freshly ground pepper
½ cup sherry
2 tablespoons Parmesan cheese

Saute onions in butter. Stir to separate rings. Season with monosodium glutamate, sugar, salt and pepper. Cook until tender. Add sherry and sprinkle with Parmesan cheese. Serves 4.

Mrs. Paul S. Ache (Betsy Evans)

Dilled Onions in Tomato Juice

6 medium onions	2 tablespoons brown sugar
2 tablespoons melted butter	1 teaspoon salt
¼ cup tomato juice	¼ teaspoon paprika
	Dried Dill

Peel onions and cut in halves, crosswise. Place in greased casserole. Mix melted butter, tomato juice, brown sugar, salt and paprika together. Pour over onions, spinkle lightly with dill. Bake, covered, at 350°, for about 1 hour. Serves 6.

Mrs. James A. Baker, Jr. (Bonner Means)

Potluck Blackeyed Peas

¼ pound bacon, diced	2 cans (1 lb. each)
2 cups chopped celery	tomatoes
2 cups chopped green pepper	2 cans (1 lb. each)
2 cups chopped onion	blackeyed peas

Saute bacon with celery, green pepper and onion. Add tomatoes and peas; simmer 30-40 minutes. Serve in soup bowls. Accompany with jalapeno cornbread. Serves 6-8.

Mrs. George A. Hill, III (Gloria Lester)

Snow Peas

1 can (5 oz.) water chestnuts	1 teaspoon sugar
2 tablespoons peanut or cooking oil	1 teaspoon monosodium glutamate
¼ cup chopped green onions, including tops	½ cup chicken broth
2 cups (½ lb.) fresh snow peas or 1 package frozen snow peas	2 teaspoons cornstarch
	Salt
	White pepper

Drain water chestnuts; slice very thin and set aside. Heat oil in skillet. Add onions; cook and stir until tender, but not brown. Add water chestnuts, snow peas, sugar, monosodium glutamate and 6 tablespoons of the chicken broth. Bring to a boil, separate pods with a fork; cover and let cook 2 minutes. Blend remaining 2 tablespoons broth and cornstarch; stir into peas. When clear and thickened, season with salt and white pepper. Serve hot. Serves 4-5.

Mrs. John M. Hopper (Tany Pollard)

Peppers à la Grecque

4 large green peppers	¼ cup olive oil
3 tablespoons capers	2 tablespoons fine bread crumbs
10 black olives, pitted	½ teaspoon salt
and cut into pieces	½ teaspoon pepper

Roast peppers in 450° oven for 10-15 minutes, or until skin is easily removed. (Peppers look scorched, but it is skin deep and peels right off.) Peel, remove seeds and cut into wide slices. Place in oiled baking dish, dot with capers and olives; sprinkle with oil, bread crumbs, salt and pepper. Bake at 375° for 20 minutes. Serve either hot or cold. Serves 4.

Mrs. Latane Temple (Josephine Bond)

Baked Spinach

4 packages frozen chopped spinach	Dash Worcestershire sauce
1 large package (8 oz.)	Salt and cracked pepper
cream cheese	1 can (3½ oz.) fried onion
1 can condensed cream of	rings, crushed
mushroom soup	

Cook spinach in double boiler until just done. Add cream cheese, soup, Worcestershire sauce, salt and pepper. Stir until cheese is melted; spoon into casserole. Top with crushed onion rings. Bake at 350° for 45 minutes. Serves 10-12.

Mrs. Henry T. Hilliard (Lydia Caffery)

Spinach-Tomato Bake

10-12 ounces fresh spinach	3 fresh tomatoes, peeled
2 tablespoons lemon juice	and thinly sliced
4 tablespoons sour cream	Salt and pepper
1 can (3 oz.) broiled-in-butter	Parmesan cheese
mushrooms	

Chop spinach in blender or with scissors. Mix with lemon juice, sour cream and mushrooms. Season with salt and pepper. Place in buttered casserole and cover with tomato slices. Dust with salt and pepper and a thick layer of Parmesan cheese. Bake at 300° until brown and bubbly, about 15 minutes. Serves 4-6.

Mrs. Roger G. Stotler (Nance Fruit)

Spinach Quiche

8-inch pie shell, partially baked
1 ¼ cups fresh chopped spinach;
  or 1 package frozen chopped
  spinach
2 tablespoons chopped onion or
  shallots
3 tablespoons butter
½ teaspoon salt

⅛ teaspoon freshly ground
  pepper
Generous pinch nutmeg
3 eggs
1 ½ cups heavy cream
⅛ teaspoon pepper
¼ cup grated cheese
  (preferably Gruyere or Swiss)

Cook spinach until barely tender; drain. Saute onion in 2 tablespoons butter until tender. Add spinach and stir over moderate heat for several minutes. Stir in salt, ground pepper and nutmeg. Combine eggs, cream and pepper in large bowl; blend well. Add spinach and cheese. Add additional salt and pepper if necessary. Pour mixture into pie shell, dot with remaining tablespoon butter. Bake in the upper third of preheated 375° oven for 25-30 minutes. Serves 6.

Mrs. John Roger Kelsey, Jr. (Mary Margaret Wier)

Spinach Ring

2 pounds fresh spinach, chopped;
  or 3 packages frozen chopped
  spinach, thawed
1 green pepper, chopped
1 onion, chopped
1 cup toasted bread crumbs
3 eggs, well beaten
3 tablespoons melted butter

2 teaspoons salt
½ teaspoon pepper
¼ cup butter
2 tablespoons Worcestershire
  sauce
1 tablespoon lemon juice
Salt
2 hard-cooked eggs, for garnish

Combine spinach, green pepper and onion. Stir in bread crumbs, eggs, melted butter, salt and pepper. Pour into greased 1-1/2-quart ring mold. Place mold in pan containing 1" hot water; steam in 350° oven for 1 hour or until set. To make sauce, combine the 1/4 cup butter, Worcestershire sauce and lemon juice. Heat; season with salt. Unmold spinach ring onto serving plate; spoon sauce over ring (or serve sauce separately). Garnish with hard-cooked eggs which have been put through a ricer. Serves 6-8.

Mrs. Daly Williams (Betty Blalock)

Spinach Casserole

2 packages frozen chopped
   spinach
½ pint sour cream

1 envelope Lipton's
   Onion Soup Mix

Cook spinach and drain well, pressing all possible water from spinach. Add sour cream and soup mix. Spoon into buttered casserole and heat at 350° for 20-25 minutes. This casserole may be made ahead, or frozen, if desired. Serves 6-8.

Mrs. R. Henry Lake (Fredrica Lanford)

Baked Acorn Squash

3 acorn squash
Salt and pepper
¼ cup melted butter

1 can (1 lb.) lima beans, drained
½ cup sour cream
Chives

Cut unpeeled squash in halves. Arrange halves in baking dish, cut side down. Pour in boiling water to 1/4" depth. Bake at 400° for 25 minutes. Remove from oven and turn squash right side up. Sprinkle salt and pepper on squash; brush with melted butter. Season lima beans; mix with sour cream and chives. Fill squash halves with bean mixture. Place in 350° oven to heat thoroughly. Serves 6.

Mrs. Bruce E. Barnett (Ann Poyner)

Squash Casserole

4 pounds yellow squash
   (approximately 16)
2 pounds zucchini
   (approximately 8)
1 onion
2 teaspoons sugar
1 teaspoon salt
¼ cup butter

Salt and pepper
1 cup grated Cheddar cheese
1 cup grated Velveeta cheese
½ cup milk
½ cup cream
Additional grated cheese
   for topping (optional)

Cook sliced squash, zucchini and onion in small amount of water, with sugar and salt, until tender. Drain. Add butter and mash well. Season with salt and pepper. In a deep 2-quart casserole, make 4 layers of vegetables and mixed cheeses ending with cheese layer. Combine milk and cream and pour over all. Sprinkle more cheese on top, if desired. Bake at 300° for 15 minutes or until bubbly. Serves 12-14.

Mrs. Thomas R. Reckling, III (Isla Cowan)

Squash Surprise

2 pounds yellow squash	1 cup heavy cream
½ teaspoon salt	¼ cup soft bread crumbs
Pepper	1 cup salted peanuts, crushed
2 tablespoons butter	8 strips bacon, fried crisp
1 small onion, grated	and crumbled

Cook squash in small amount of salted water until tender. Drain and mash squash. Add salt, pepper, butter, onion and cream. Mix well. Grease baking dish and cover bottom and sides with bread crumbs. Spoon squash into crumbed baking dish and bake at 350° for 50 minutes. Before serving, sprinkle top with peanuts and bacon. Serves 6.

Mrs. Ralph Ellis Gunn (Esme Patterson)

Creamy Baked Squash

2½ pounds yellow or	¾ cup butter
white squash	¼ cup cream
1 onion, chopped	Salt and pepper
3 hard-cooked eggs, chopped	24 small salted crackers

Slice squash and cook with onion in boiling salted water until tender. Drain well. Cream squash, onion, eggs, 1/4 cup of the butter and cream together. Season with salt and pepper; spoon into buttered baking dish. Combine remaining 1/2 cup of butter (softened) with cracker crumbs and sprinkle over squash. Bake in 350° oven 30-45 minutes. Serves 8.

Mrs. Jean Mills Worsham (Roberta Murfee)

Squash San Luis Potosi

1 small onion, chopped	½ to 1 teaspoon cumin powder
2 tablespoons bacon drippings	½ clove garlic, crushed
3 pounds Mexican squash, zucchini	Salt and pepper
or yellow squash	½ to ¾ cup grated mild
2 fresh tomatoes, peeled and	cheese
chopped	

Saute onion in bacon drippings. Add sliced squash and saute. Add tomatoes, cumin powder, garlic, salt and pepper. Cover tightly and cook until tender. When ready to serve add grated cheese. Serves 8.

Mrs. John B. Abercrombie (Virginia Townsend)

East Indian Summer Squash

2½ pounds yellow squash
¼ cup chopped onion
2 or 3 tablespoons bacon
   drippings
1 teaspoon curry powder

¼ cup sour cream
Cracker crumbs
Butter
Paprika
Grated Parmesan cheese
   (optional)

Slice squash and cook in salted water until just tender. Drain well and mash. Saute onion in bacon drippings until soft but not brown. Stir into squash. Add curry powder and sour cream, mixing well. Pour into baking dish and cover with crumbs. Dot with butter, paprika and a little Parmesan cheese. Bake at 350° for about 30 minutes until crumbs are golden brown. Serves 6.

Mrs. Theodore D. Whiteford (Betsy Letzerich)

Stuffed Squash

2 pounds yellow or white squash
2 onions, chopped (reserve
   1 tablespoon)
1 clove garlic, crushed
¾ to 1 cup toasted bread crumbs,
   rolled fine

6 slices bacon, fried crisp and
   crumbled
1 teaspoon sugar
Salt and pepper
Dash cayenne
1 teaspoon Worcestershire sauce

Cook whole squash with onions and garlic until tender. Drain squash; cut tops from squash, scoop out pulp and arrange squash shells in baking dish. Mash squash pulp and mix with bread crumbs, bacon, seasonings and re-served onion. (Mixture should be dry.) Fill squash shells, top each with a dab of butter and bake at 350° for 15 minutes. Allow 2 squash per person.

Mrs. Huey C. Keeney (Lucile Vennard)

Broiled Tomatoes Brookhollow

4 large, juicy ripe tomatoes
Italian salad dressing
1 jar (6 oz.) marinated
   artichoke hearts

Basil
Bread or cracker crumbs
Parmesan cheese
Butter

Peel and slice tomatoes in half, early in the morning. Pour some Italian dressing over tomato halves in a pyrex dish. Refrigerate. About 1 hour be-fore serving, slice artichoke hearts and place on tomato halves. Sprinkle with basil, bread crumbs and Parmesan cheese. Place a dab of butter on top of each tomato half. Bake at 350° for 20 minutes. Serves 8.

Mrs. William G. Guerriero (Margaret Ann White)

Tomatoes Stuffed with Broccoli

1 package frozen chopped broccoli	3 tablespoons flour
	1 cup milk
6 small, or 4 medium, tomatoes	Salt and pepper
3 tablespoons butter	Buttered bread crumbs

Cook broccoli until barely tender; drain well. Complely hollow out and drain tomatoes. Make a cream sauce of the butter, flour, milk, salt and pepper. Combine cream sauce and broccoli; stuff tomatoes with this mixture. Place stuffed tomatoes in shallow pan containing small amount of water. Sprinkle tomatoes with buttered bread crumbs. Bake at 350° for approximately 15 minutes. If made ahead of time and refrigerated, bake at 350° for approximately 30 minutes. Serves 4-6.

Mrs. William S. Clarke (Carolyn Monteith)

Tomatoes
Stuffed with Mushrooms

8 firm tomatoes	¼ teaspoon Spice Islands fines herbes
½ cup butter	
1¼ pounds fresh mushrooms, sliced	1 teaspoon chopped parsley
	1 or 2 tablespoons sherry
1 cup sour cream	Salt and pepper
4 teaspoons flour	Blanched almonds, chopped
2 or 3 ounces Roquefort cheese, softened	(optional)

Cut tops off tomatoes; scoop out pulp and reserve tomato cases. In large skillet melt butter and saute mushrooms until liquid has evaporated. Mix sour cream with flour and blend into mushrooms, stirring until thickened. Blend Roquefort cheese into mixture. Add fines herbes, parsley, sherry, salt and pepper. Let cool. Fill tomato cases; top with almonds. Bake at 375° for 15 minutes. (Do not overcook.) Serves 8.

Mrs. John E. Chapoton (Sally Eastham)

Stuffed Tomatoes Florentine

6 large, ripe, firm tomatoes
1 package frozen chopped spinach
1 tablespoon instant minced onion
1 teaspoon garlic salt

1 teaspoon oregano
Dash nutmeg
1½ cups grated Velveeta cheese
  (reserve enough for topping)

Hollow out tomatoes, saving pulp from 4 of the 6. Chop pulp and drain it well. Heat spinach, without water, over low heat in tightly covered sauce pan until barely thawed. Drain well. Combine spinach and tomato pulp; add remaining ingredients and mix well. Fill tomato cases. Sprinkle with reserved cheese. Bake at 350° for 20-30 minutes. (Baking time will depend on firmness of tomatoes. Do not overcook.) Serves 6.

Mrs. Jack T. Currie (Dorothy Peek)

Turnip Fluff

2 pounds turnips, pared and cubed
¼ cup cream
1 egg, beaten
2 tablespoons butter

2 tablespoons light brown sugar
2 tablespoons uncooked cream
  of wheat
Salt and pepper

Cook turnips in 1" of boiling, salted water until tender. Drain thoroughly and mash. Add other ingredients and blend well. Pile lightly into greased, 1-quart casserole. Bake at 350° for 40 minutes. Serves 6.

Mrs. George A. Hill, III (Gloria Lester)

Zucchini with Sour Cream

3 medium zucchini
½ cup sour cream
2 tablespoons butter
2 tablespoons grated cheese
Salt and pepper

Paprika
1 tablespoon chopped chives
Bread crumbs for topping
Additional grated cheese for
  topping

Slice zucchini into thin rounds; do not peel. Simmer zucchini in small amount of water for 6-8 minutes. Shake pan frequently. Drain. Combine sour cream, butter, cheese, salt, pepper and paprika. Stir over low heat to melt cheese. Remove from heat and mix in chives. Add zucchini, tossing lightly to coat with sour cream mixture. Place in greased 1-quart baking dish. Top with crumbs and dot with additional butter. Sprinkle with more grated cheese. Brown in 375° oven for about 10 minutes. If prepared in advance and refrigerated, increase baking time to 30 minutes. Serves 4.

Mrs. Nelson Robinson (Mary Washington)

Zucchini-Vermicelli Casserole

1 large rib celery, chopped	Pepper
3 green onions, chopped	Seasoned salt
1 small green pepper, diced	Garlic powder
¼ cup olive oil	½ teaspoon oregano
3 medium tomatoes, peeled and diced, or 1 can (1 lb.) tomatoes	½ teaspoon basil
4 medium zucchini, sliced into ⅛" rounds	5 ounces vermicelli
	¼ cup Parmesan cheese

Saute celery, onions and green pepper in olive oil. Add tomatoes and zucchini. Season with pepper, seasoned salt, garlic powder, oregano and basil. Cover and cook until limp, stirring occasionally. Meanwhile, break vermicelli into small pieces and boil until barely tender; drain. Combine with squash mixture and pour into a 2-quart casserole. Stir in Parmesan cheese. Bake at 325° for 30 minutes, or until bubbly. Additional grated cheese may be added as a topping. Serves 6-8.

Mrs. James B. Thompson (Sandra Settegast)

Stuffed Zucchini

4 medium unpeeled zucchini	2 tablespoons minced parsley
¼ cup olive oil	2 tablespoons choppped capers (optional)
¾ cup chopped onion	½ teaspoon salt
1 clove garlic, crushed	½ teaspoon freshly ground black pepper
¾ cup peeled, chopped fresh tomatoes	¼ teaspoon basil
½ cup chopped mushrooms	
½ cup fine dry bread crumbs	

Cover zucchini with water, bring to boil, and cook over low heat 3 minutes. Drain, cool, and cut in half, lengthwise. Scoop out pulp and reserve shells. Heat olive oil in skillet; saute onion 5 minutes. Dice zucchini pulp and add with garlic to skillet; saute 3 minutes. Mix in tomatoes and mushrooms; cook 5 minutes. Remove from heat and mix in bread crumbs, parsley, capers, salt, pepper and basil. Stuff the shells and arrange in an oiled baking dish. Sprinkle with extra olive oil if desired. Bake in 350° oven 30 minutes. Serve hot or cold. Makes 8 servings.

Mrs. Ben A. Brollier (Marilyn Oden)

Zucchini-Tomato Bake

1 onion, chopped	Celery salt
¼ cup butter	2 large tomatoes,
4 unpeeled zucchini, finely sliced	peeled and chopped
Salt and pepper	Parmesan cheese

Brown onion in butter. Add zucchini and cook only until soft, adding more butter if needed. Season with salt, pepper and celery salt. Add tomatoes and bring to boil. Pour into a 1-quart casserole. Sprinkle generously with Parmesan cheese. Bake in 350° oven for 1 hour. Serves 4.

Mrs. Holcombe Crosswell (Emily Attwell)

Vegetable Casserole

3 cups thinly sliced onions	5 tomatoes, peeled and thinly
½ cup olive oil	sliced
4 green peppers, sliced	3 cloves garlic, crushed
1 eggplant, peeled and thinly	2 teaspoons salt
sliced	¾ teaspoon freshly ground
4 zucchini, thinly sliced	black pepper

Saute onions in 2 tablespoons of the oil for 5 minutes. Remove onions. Add 2 more tablespoons oil and saute green peppers for 5 minutes. Remove peppers. Add 2 more tablespoons oil and saute eggplant on each side for 2 minutes. Remove eggplant. Add remaining 2 tablespoons oil and saute zucchini for 3 minutes. Arrange alternate layers of the sauteed vegetables and tomatoes in a casserole. Sprinkle each layer with garlic, salt and pepper. Cover and bake in a 325° oven for 45 minutes. Remove cover and bake 5 minutes longer. Serve hot or cold. Serves 6-8.

Mrs. James A. Baker, Jr. (Bonner Means)

California Vegetable Bowl

¼ cup butter	½ cup chopped onion
4 cups sliced, unpeeled zucchini (about 1 lb.)	⅓ cup chopped green pepper
	½ teaspoon salt
1½ cups fresh, frozen, or canned whole kernel corn	1 tablespoon fresh, snipped dill (or about 1 teaspoon dried dill)

Melt butter in skillet; add zucchini, corn, onion and green pepper. Sprinkle with salt. Cover and cook, stirring occasionally, 10-12 minutes, or until vegetables are done. Sprinkle with dill. Serves 4-6.

Mrs. Raleigh W. Johnson, Jr. (Marjorie Bintliff)

Green Vegetable Medley

1 package frozen French-cut green beans	1 green pepper, julienne-cut
	Salt and pepper
1 package frozen baby lima beans or corn	1 cup heavy cream, whipped
	1 cup mayonnaise
1 package frozen English peas	Grated Parmesan cheese

Cook frozen vegetables separately. Parboil green peppers. Drain all vegetables; combine, and season with salt and pepper. Arrange in buttered casserole. Mix whipped cream and mayonnaise together; spoon over vegetables. Top with Parmesan cheese. Bake at 300° until brown on top about 30-40 minutes. This casserole can be made a day ahead and baked just before serving. Serves 8-10.

Mrs. King W. Bridges, Jr. (Kathleen Cearnal)

Baked Beans

½ cup minced onion	3 cans (28 oz. each) pork and beans
2 tablespoons bacon drippings	
½ cup chopped celery	½ cup dark molasses
1 can (10 oz.) Rotel tomatoes and green chilies	Salt and pepper
	3 slices bacon

Saute onion in bacon drippings. Mix celery, tomatoes, pork and beans, molasses, salt and pepper. Add onion. Pour in large, greased baking dish. Top with bacon slices. Bake for about 2 hours in 350° oven. Serves 10-15.

Mrs. George H. Black, Jr. (Carolyn Cave)

Bunk House Beans

1 pound dried pinto beans	1 teaspoon salt
3 whole green onions, or 1 small onion, quartered	1 tablespoon honey
	2 teaspoons paprika
¼ pound salt pork	5-6 hot chili piquins,
2 tablespoons sugar	crushed

In large heavy pot, soak pinto beans overnight in water to cover. When ready to cook, add enough fresh water to the pot to cover the beans. Add onions and salt pork, and bring beans to a slow boil. Add hot water as needed while cooking. When beans have softened, add sugar, salt, honey, paprika and chili piquins. Simmer for at least 8 hours, stirring occasionally. Add hot water as it is absorbed. Beans should be very soft. Serves 12.

Mrs. W. Carter Grinstead (Linda Rowe)

First Prize Beans

2 pounds dried navy beans	1 pound smoked ham or ham hocks
10 whole cloves	
1 onion, peeled	3 onions, chopped
1 bay leaf	3 cloves garlic, crushed
1 tablespoon salt	1 tablespoon dry mustard
1 pound lean salt pork	½ cup Jamaican rum

Cover beans with water and soak overnight. Drain. Put beans in a large pot and add fresh water to a depth of 3" above the beans. Stick cloves into peeled onion and add to bean pot with bay leaf and salt; bring to a boil Boil rapidly 5 minutes; skim foam from top of beans. Reduce heat and simmer until beans are tender but not mushy. Drain and reserve liquid.

Simmer salt pork in water for 25 minutes. Remove pork and cut into small pieces. Cut ham into strips. Combine chopped onion and garlic. Blend dry mustard with enough water to dissolve mustard. Pour a layer of beans in large baking dish or casserole. Add a layer of salt pork, ham, and onion-garlic mixture. Repeat layers ending with beans. Pour dissolved mustard over all and add enough bean liquid to cover. Bake in 350° oven. Add more bean liquid if needed during baking. At the end of 1-1/2 hours, pour rum over beans and bake 45 minutes longer (2 hours, 15 minutes in all). Serves 16.

Mrs. Walter L. Parsley (Sarah Bertron)

Deviled Bean Bake

6 slices bacon	3 tablespoons black molasses
4 medium onions, thinly sliced	1 small jar (3 oz.) Smithfield
4 large fresh tomatoes	deviled ham
1 jar (1 lb., 6 oz.) Boston	1 teaspoon Worcestershire
baked beans	sauce
1 heaping tablespoon Creole or	1 teaspoon minced parsley
Dijon mustard	Salt and pepper

Fry bacon until crisp, then crumble. Saute onions in bacon drippings until golden brown. Peel tomatoes and cut into thin slices. In a casserole make layers of half the onions and half the tomato slices. Mix beans with mustard, molasses, ham, Worcestershire sauce and parsley. Taste before seasoning with salt and pepper. Pour bean-ham mixture into casserole. Top with another layer of onions and tomatoes. Sprinkle crumbled bacon over top and bake in 350° oven for 35 minutes. Serves 4-6.

Mrs. Victor F. Grima (Chlotille Cole)

Creamy Grits Casserole

1 cup uncooked grits	1 cup condensed cream of
½ pound Cheddar cheese,	chicken soup
grated	Cayenne, to taste
	Paprika

Cook grits. Add cheese, soup and cayenne. Mix well. Pour into greased casserole, sprinkle with paprika, and bake in 350° oven until crusty and brown, about 1 hour. This can be frozen. Serves 10.

Mrs. Kline McGee (Adrian Rose)

Grits Casserole

1 cup uncooked grits	½ pound sharp cheese,
½ cup butter, melted	grated
6 tablespoons milk	3 eggs, beaten

Cook grits. Remove from heat; let cool for 10 minutes. Add butter, milk and cheese. Stir in eggs, one at a time. Bake in greased casserole for 1 hour in 400° oven. Serves 6.

Mrs. Charles W. Moody (Patti Hunter)

Garlic Cheese Grits

2 cups uncooked grits
1 roll (6 oz.) garlic cheese
½ pound sharp Cheddar
  cheese, grated

½ cup butter
2 eggs, beaten
1 teaspoon Tabasco
¼ teaspoon Worcestershire sauce
Paprika

Cook grits. Add other ingredients, except paprika, and mix well. Pour into large, shallow casserole. Sprinkle with paprika. Bake in 350° oven about 30 minutes. May be made early in the day and heated at serving time. Serves 12.

Mrs. Edward H. Patton, Jr. (Anne Berry)

Fire Hot Grits

2 cups uncooked grits
½ pound sharp cheese, grated
½ cup margarine
2 teaspoons Tabasco
Salt

1 or 2 cloves garlic, crushed
3 eggs, well beaten
1 can (4 oz.) green chilies,
  chopped
2 jalapeno peppers, seeded
  and chopped

Cook grits. Mix in other ingredients. Bake in a large, greased casserole, at 350° for 45 minutes. Serves 12-14.

Mrs. C. Harcourt Wooten (Evelyn Wilkey)

Hominy Mahon

1 can (1 lb., 14 oz.) hominy,
  drained
1 can condensed cream of
  mushroom soup
½ cup cream
¼ teaspoon red pepper

½ teaspoon black pepper
1 teaspoon salt
1 teaspoon Worcestershire sauce
1 teaspoon celery seed
½ cup slivered almonds, toasted
Buttered bread crumbs

Pour hominy into well-buttered, 2-quart baking dish. Mix soup, cream and seasonings in saucepan; simmer and stir until well blended. Add almonds. Pour over hominy and top with buttered bread crumbs. Bake in 350° oven for 30 minutes. Serves 4-6.

Mrs. Herman P. Pressler (Elsie Townes)

Linguine in Egg Sauce

1 pound uncooked linguine or
noodles

8 slices bacon, diced

3 eggs at room temperature,
slightly beaten

1 cup grated Romano or
Parmesan cheese

Freshly ground pepper

¼ cup butter

Cook liguine in boiling salted water 8-10 minutes. Drain, season with salt, and return to pan to keep warm. Fry bacon until crisp, drain, and keep hot. Reserve bacon drippings and keep hot. Add eggs, cheese, pepper, hot bacon pieces and hot bacon drippings to linguine. Mix well. If eggs are not entirely set, mixture may be heated slightly. Place in heated serving dish and top with slices of butter. If all ingredients are mixed while very hot, the eggs will be set and the linguine ready to serve when the slices of butter have melted. Serves 4-6.

Mrs. Frank Wozencraft (Shirley Cooper)

Noodles and Spinach Romanoff

1 small package (5¾ oz.) Noodles
Romanoff

1 package frozen chopped
spinach

Butter

2 tablespoons chopped onion

1 cup sour cream

Parmesan cheese (optional)

Cook noodles and spinach separately. Drain each, mix together and season with butter and onion. Mix sauce from envelope in Noodles Romanoff package with sour cream. Add sauce to spinach-noodle mixture. Pour into buttered baking dish. Dot with additional butter. Top with Parmesan cheese, if desired. Bake in 350° oven for 30 minutes. Serves 6.

Mrs. Edgar W. Monteith (Mary Frances Dorrance)

Macaroni and Cheese

7 ounces (1¾ cups) uncooked
macaroni

1 pound sharp cheese, grated

2 cups milk

¼ cup butter

1 egg, beaten

1 teaspoon salt

Pepper

Paprika

Cook macaroni until tender, place in a strainer, and rinse with cold water. In a 2-quart casserole, alternate layers of macaroni and cheese, ending with cheese. Bring milk to a boil. Stir in butter, egg, salt and pepper. Pour over the macaroni and cheese. Sprinkle paprika on top. Bake in 350° oven for 45 minutes. Serves 8-10.

Mrs. Thomas E. Berry (Joan Jester)

Nettie's Macaroni

4 ounces (1 cup) uncooked
  macaroni
2 tablespoons butter
1 tablespoon flour
½ cup milk

Salt and pepper
Lawry's seasoned salt
1½-2 tablespoons minced
  green onion tops
Parmesan cheese
Paprika

Cook macaroni until tender. Make cream sauce with butter, flour and milk. Season with salt, pepper and Lawry's salt. Add onion tops and macaroni. Pour mixture into greased casserole dish. Top with generous sprinkling of Parmesan cheese and paprika. Bake in 300°-325° oven for 45 minutes, or until bubbly. Serves 2-3.

Mrs. John H. Meyers (Alice Baker Jones)

Roni Ring

½ cup uncooked macaroni
1½ cups milk
1 cup soft bread crumbs
¼ cup melted butter
2 tablespoons chopped green
  pepper

2 tablespoons chopped pimiento
2 tablespoons chopped onion
½ pound Velveeta cheese, grated
Salt and pepper
Dash paprika
3 eggs, well beaten

Cook, rinse, and drain macaroni. Scald milk and pour over bread crumbs. Add melted butter, green pepper, pimiento, onion, cheese, salt, pepper and paprika. Stir in eggs. Spoon macaroni into buttered 6-cup ring mold. Pour egg mixture over macaroni. Bake in a slow 300° oven until firm, about 50 minutes. The center of ring may be filled with creamed peas and mushrooms. Serves 6.

Mrs. Lorenzo B. Taylor (Marilyn Dubach)

Breakfast Potatoes

1 can (1 lb.) whole Irish
  potatoes
Salt and pepper

2 tablespoons butter, diced
½ pound Velveeta cheese, diced
Paprika

Drain potatoes and grate into 1-quart buttered casserole. Season with salt and pepper. Mix in chunks of butter and cheese. Sprinkle with paprika. Bake at 350° for 20 minutes. Serves 4.

Mrs. John L. Hamilton (Ann Lowdon)

Chantilly Potatoes

2 cups mashed hot potatoes
¼ cup milk, heated
2 tablespoons butter
Salt and pepper
Paprika

¼ cup chopped, cooked ham
½ cup heavy cream
1 cup shredded sharp cheese
Chopped parsley

Thoroughly mix potatoes, milk, butter and seasonings. Spoon in 2-1/2-quart baking dish and sprinkle with chopped ham. Whip the cream and fold in cheese. Spread mixture over ham and potatoes. Bake in 450° oven for 10-15 minutes. Sprinkle with chopped parsley. Serves 6.

Mrs. Robert F. Flagg (Nancy White)

Country Potatoes

6 medium potatoes
½ cup butter
1 cup sour cream

¾ cup chopped green onion tops
Salt and pepper
1½ cups grated sharp Cheddar cheese

Cook peeled and sliced potatoes in salted water; drain and mash, leaving them a little lumpy. Add butter, sour cream, green onions, salt and pepper. Place in buttered casserole and top with cheese. Bake in 325° oven until potatoes are heated thoroughly and cheese is melted, about 20-30 minutes. Serves 6-8.

Mrs. David J. Braden (Jane White)

Scalloped Potatoes

6 medium potatoes, peeled,
    cooked and sliced
¼ cup diced onion
¼ cup celery leaves
2 sprigs parsley
3 tablespoons flour
¼ cup butter

1½ teaspoons salt
¼ teaspoon pepper
1½ cups milk
1-2 cups grated sharp
    Cheddar cheese
Paprika

Blend onion, celery leaves, parsley, flour, butter, salt, pepper, and milk in blender, mixing thoroughly (may be done the day before). Arrange potato slices in a buttered, 2-quart baking dish. Pour mixture over potatoes; sprinkle with grated cheese and paprika. Bake in 350° oven about 50 minutes, until bubbling and brown. This potato dish holds up very well. Serves 8.

Mrs. Roger G. Stotler (Nance Fruit)

Cheesy New Potatoes

12 medium new potatoes
Salt and pepper
2 cups grated Old English
  cheese

16 slices bacon, fried crisp and
  crumbled
½ cup butter, melted
¼ cup chopped parsley, for
  garnish

Wash and cube potatoes (do not peel), and cook in boiling water until just barely tender. Remove from heat, drain, and season to taste with salt and pepper. In a large casserole, place layer of potatoes, half the bacon, half the butter, and half the cheese. Repeat the layers. Heat in a 350° oven for 20-30 minutes, or until cheese is bubbly. Remove from oven and garnish with parsley. Serves 6-8.

Mrs. John H. Lindsey (Sara Houstoun)

Scott Sweet Potatoes Supreme

2 cups mashed sweet potatoes
2 tablespoons cream
2 tablespoons melted butter
Scant teaspoon salt
¼ teaspoon paprika

½ cup brown sugar, packed
½ cup butter
Pecan halves to cover casserole
  (approximately 1 cup)

Thoroughly mix potatoes, cream, melted butter, salt and paprika. Spread in greased casserole. Make the topping by heating brown sugar and butter over low heat, stirring constantly, until butter is barely melted. (It is important not to cook after the butter is melted, or the topping will harden when casserole is heated.) Spread topping over potatoes and cover with pecan halves. Refrigerate until ready to heat. This casserole may be warmed in an oven of any temperature, but should be bubbling hot before serving. Serves 4.

Mrs. John Thad Scott, Jr. (Sadie Ruth Aldridge)

Sweet Potato Croquettes

6 small sweet potatoes, peeled
2 tablespoons butter
½ cup sugar
½ teaspoon cinnamon

1 teaspoon salt
Marshmallows
Cornflake crumbs
Fat for deep frying

Boil sweet potatoes until tender; drain and mash. Season with butter, sugar, cinnamon and salt. Form into balls, placing a marshmallow in center of each ball. Chill well for several hours. Roll croquettes in cornflake crumbs and fry in deep fat. Drain and serve immediately. Serves 4.

Mrs. Hughes Fleming (Mildred Hughes)

Sweet Potato and Orange Casserole

2 pounds fresh sweet potatoes
⅓ cup sugar
3 tablespoons butter
1 teaspoon salt

1 teaspoon grated orange rind
½ teaspoon grated lemon rind
  (optional)
½ cup fresh orange juice

Cook unpeeled potatoes until tender. Peel and mash potatoes while hot; measure 4 cups. Add sugar, butter, salt, orange rind, lemon rind and orange juice to potatoes. Beat with rotary beater, or mixer, until fluffy. Spoon into buttered, 1-1/2-quart casserole. Bake, uncovered, at 350° for 30 minutes, or until lightly browned. Serves 8.

Mrs. Gleaves M. Love (Betsy Riggle)

Sweet Potatoes in Orange Cups

3 small sweet potatoes
1½ teaspoons cinnamon
1 egg, beaten
2 tablespoons butter

2 tablespoons fresh orange juice
Pinch salt
2 oranges
4 maraschino cherries

Cook, peel, and mash sweet potatoes. Add cinnamon, egg, butter, orange juice and salt. Cut oranges in half; remove pulp from orange halves to make shells. Fill orange shells with potato mixture, top with cherry, and bake about 15 minutes in a 400° oven. Serves 4.

Mrs. James C. Boone (Frances Sara Gieseke)

Almond Rice

1½ cups uncooked rice
¼ cup butter
1 onion, finely chopped
Pepper
3 cups beef consomme

3 cans (3 oz. each) mushrooms,
  drained
½ cup almonds, chopped
2 tablespoons poppy seeds
Salt

In heavy pan, brown rice in butter. Add onion and pepper. Cook until onion is tender. Spoon into buttered casserole. Add consomme, mushrooms, almonds, poppy seeds and salt if needed. Mix well. Bake, uncovered, for 1 hour in 375° oven. Serves 6-8.

Mrs. Daniels Hanson (Dee Daniels)

Mushroom Rice

½ cup uncooked rice
2 tablespoons butter
1 can (4 oz.) sliced mushrooms,
with liquid

1 can condensed
onion soup
Pepper

Brown rice in butter. Drain mushrooms (reserve liquid); saute with rice. Add enough water to mushroom liquid to make 1 cup. Add onion soup and mushroom liquid to rice. Season with pepper. Simmer, covered, for 30 minutes. Serves 3-4.

Mrs. Marvin V. Cluett (Lollie Lauderdale)

Red Rice

1 cup uncooked rice
3 tablespoons butter
1 small onion, grated
1 can beef bouillon

1 soup-can tomato juice
3 tablespoons minced parsley
Salt, if needed

Saute rice in butter for 2-3 minutes, or until golden brown. Stir in onion, bouillon and tomato juice. Bake in large casserole with tight cover in 375° oven for 30 minutes. Stir lightly with fork, uncover, and cook 30 minutes more or until rice is dry and tender. Stir in parsley, and add salt if needed. Rice will keep well in a slow oven if dinner is delayed. Serves 4-6.

Mrs. Thomas B. Eaton, Jr. (Margot Teague)

Santa Maria Rice

2 cups uncooked rice
⅓ cup cooking oil
2 cloves garlic, crushed
¼ cup grated onion

3¾ cups boiling water
3 teaspoons powdered
chicken stock base
Salt

Soak rice in warm water for 10 minutes; drain well. Heat oil in skillet or heat-proof casserole. Add rice and cook until hard and golden yellow. Add garlic and onion. Mix well. Add boiling water, chicken stock base and salt. Cover skillet and cook rice slowly over low heat until water is evaporated and rice is dry (about 20 minutes). Serves 10.

Mrs. Richard Gray (Betsy Bonnet)

Dirty Rice

1½ cups uncooked rice
1 pound ground beef
1 pound chicken livers, chopped
½ pound butter
1 cup chopped onion
½ cup chopped green pepper
1 clove garlic, crushed
½ cup chopped celery

6-8 green onions with tops,
  chopped
Salt and pepper
Tabasco
Pinch thyme
Pinch basil
1 tablespoon chopped parsley
Chicken stock

Cook rice. Saute beef and livers in half of the butter. In another skillet, saute onion, green pepper, garlic, celery, and green onions in remaining half of the butter. Combine rice and both sauteed mixtures. Add seasonings and parsley. Add chicken stock, if needed, until moisture content seems correct. Serve with game. May also be used as dressing for turkey. Serves 12-14.

Mrs. James Howard Park, III (Bette Naylor)

Louisiana Dirty Rice

Neck and giblets of turkey
2½ cups turkey stock
1 cup uncooked rice
2 tablespoons cooking oil
2 tablespoons flour

1 onion, chopped
2 cloves garlic, crushed
2 ribs celery, chopped
Several green onions, finely
  chopped
Salt and pepper

Simmer neck and giblets in salted water until tender. Remove meat and reserve stock. Finely chop meat. Cook rice until tender in boiling salted water. Make roux of oil and flour. Add onion to roux and cook until onion is soft. Add stock and meat. Add garlic, celery and green onions. Allow to simmer about 1 hour. Add stock mixture to rice, taste and season with salt and pepper if necessary. Keep warm until serving time. Serves 4-6.

Mrs. James A. Moore (Margaret Landry)

Snappy Green Rice

2 cups uncooked rice
½ pint sour cream
½ cup salad oil
1 clove garlic, crushed
1 cup chopped parsley

1 can (4 oz.) green chilies,
  chopped
1 pound sharp cheese, grated
2 fresh jalapenos, seeded and
  chopped (optional)

Cook rice. When rice is tender, add all other ingredients. Mix well. Pour into large casserole and bake in 275° oven for 1 hour. Serves 12.

Mrs. Joseph C. Brown (Susan Judd)

Green Rice

1 cup uncooked rice	1½ teaspoons salt
3 tablespoons finely chopped	Dash garlic powder
onion	¾ cup minced parsley
6 tablespoons butter	¾ cup minced green onion
3 eggs	1½ cups grated sharp cheese,
1¾ cups milk	or Parmesan cheese

Cook rice. Saute onion in butter until limp. Slightly beat eggs in large bowl; add milk and salt; mix well. Add sauteed onion-butter mixture, garlic powder, parsley, green onion, cheese and rice. Pour mixture into greased 1-1/2 quart casserole; set in pan of hot water. Bake in 325° oven for 1 hour, or until set. Serves 6-8.

Mrs. Charles W. Dabney, Jr. (Julia Vinson)

Sausage Rice

1 cup uncooked rice	½ cup chopped green
½ pound bulk sausage	pepper
½ cup chopped celery	½ cup chopped onion

Cook rice in salted water until tender. Fry sausage meat in skillet until crumbly and brown. Remove meat from skillet. In sausage drippings saute celery, green pepper and onion until tender. Return sausage to pan and stir rice into mixture, a little at a time, until all rice is mixed in well. Serve with game. Also may be used as dressing for turkey. Serves 4-6.

Mrs. James F. Hayes (Lisbeth Young)

Monterey Rice

1 cup uncooked rice	12 ounces Monterey Jack
1½ pint sour cream	cheese, thinly sliced
1 can (4 oz.) Ortega whole	
green chilies	

Cook rice until tender. Mix with sour cream. In a baking dish (about 6-1/2" x 8-1/2"), place a layer of rice mixture and top with cheese. Remove seeds from peppers and arrange in thin layer on rice. Top with more thin slices of cheese. Repeat layers. Bake in preheated oven at 350° for 30 minutes. A can (9-1/4 oz.) of tuna may be added to the rice mixture if desired for a main course. Serves 6.

Mrs. James A. Walsh (Harriet Brady)

Risotto Wild Rice

1½ cups uncooked wild rice	3-4 chicken livers
3 cups bouillon	1 cup fresh mushrooms,
1 cup water	chopped
½ cup chopped onion	1 cup heavy cream
½ cup chopped green pepper	Parmesan cheese
½ cup soft butter	

Boil rice gently in bouillon and water until liquid is almost absorbed and rice is tender. Saute onion and green pepper in a little of the butter until tender. Saute chicken livers in small amount of the butter, and chop. Saute mushrooms lightly in additional butter (mushrooms will retain light color if sprinkled with lemon juice before sauteeing). Spoon rice into casserole and add onion and green pepper, livers, mushrooms, cream, and remaining butter. Mix well. Top with Parmesan cheese and run under broiler to brown. This rice may be prepared in advance, heated in 350° oven, then placed under broiler for a few minutes. Serves 6.

Mrs. Nelson Robinson (Mary Washington)

Barley Bake

1 cup finely chopped onion	½ cup finely chopped chives
½ cup butter	4 cups beef bouillon
1 cup uncooked barley	1 teaspoon salt
1 cup finely chopped parsley	Freshly ground black pepper

Saute onion in butter; add barley and brown lightly. Add parsley, chives, bouillon, salt and pepper. Spoon into casserole. Bake, uncovered, in 350° oven for 1 hour and 20 minutes, stirring once after 30 minutes. Serves 6.

Mrs. James A. Baker, III (Mary Stuart McHenry)

Wheat Pilaf

1 cup uncooked cracked	1 can beef consomme
wheat	1 soup can water
¼ cup butter	Salt and pepper

Saute wheat in butter for a minute or two. Add consomme and water; bring to a boil. Pour into casserole. Bake in 325° oven for 35-45 minutes, or until wheat seems dry and fluffy. Serves 6.

Mrs. Paul Sherwood (Mildred Wood)

SAUCES
RELISHES
PRESERVES

Hints

TO MAKE BASIC WHITE SAUCE (MEDIUM):

2 tablespoons butter	1/8 teaspoon pepper
2 tablespoons flour	1 cup milk
1/4 teaspoon salt	

In saucepan, slowly heat butter just until melted. Add flour, salt and pepper; stir over low heat until smooth, 1 or 2 minutes. Remove from heat and add milk, a small amount at a time, stirring after each addition. Return to heat. Over medium heat, bring to a boil, stirring constantly. Reduce heat; simmer for 1 minute. Makes 1 cup sauce.

> THIN WHITE SAUCE: Reduce butter and flour to 1 tablespoon each. Proceed as above. Use for soups.

> THICK WHITE SAUCE: Increase butter and flour to 3 tablespoons each. Proceed as above. Use as a binder in croquettes, or as a base for souffles.

PICKLING AND PRESERVING

TO STERILIZE JARS: Wash jars and lids thoroughly, and place in deep kettle; cover with water. Boil, covered, for 5-10 minutes. Keep hot.

TO FILL JARS: Remove jars from hot water with tongs, and set on wet cloth. To prevent cracking, place sterilized spoon in jar. Immediately fill jars. (Fill jellies 1/4 inch from top; pickles 1/8 inch from top, being sure liquid covers top pickle.) Wipe sealing edges of jars free of food or liquid with paper towels or damp cloth before sealing with paraffin or lid.

TO SEAL JARS: Pickles and relishes must be sealed with lids, airtight, while still boiling hot. To seal jellies and jams, pour a thin layer of melted paraffin over jelly soon after it has been ladeled into jar. On the second day, cover the jelly again with a thin layer of paraffin, tilting the glass to permit the paraffin to cover entire surface. Protect the paraffin with a cover of metal or foil.

TO MELT PARAFFIN: Always use fresh paraffin; old paraffin often causes spoilage. Melt paraffin in a small pot over hot water, over low heat. (Over direct heat, paraffin may smoke or spatter and if it gets too hot, it may flavor jelly objectionably.)

TO STORE JARS: Store pickles and preserves in a cool, dry, dark place.

Versatile Spaghetti Sauce

1 pound bacon
Olive oil for cooking vegetables
4 large cloves garlic, crushed
2 whole stalks celery with
   leaves, chopped
10 large onions, chopped
1 eggplant, peeled and cut
   into 1" cubes
12 cans (6 oz. each) tomato paste
2 cans (1 lb. each) tomatoes
1 bottle (14 oz.) catsup

1 quart green olive pieces
   and juice
1 teaspoon dry mustard
3 heaping tablespoons sugar
2 bay leaves, crushed
2 cans (8 oz. each) mushroom
   stems and pieces
3 quarts (or more) water
1 tablespoon black peppercorns
1 teaspoon oregano
Tabasco
Salt

Fry bacon until crisp, drain and crumble. Put olive oil in 2 large iron skillets or Dutch ovens; saute garlic, celery and onions until onions are transparent. Transfer to huge preserving kettle and add all remaining ingredients. Simmer over low heat for 4 hours, (stir often—it sticks). Cooked meat, shrimp, chicken or crab may be added to sauce before serving. Serve over spaghetti. Sauce alone can be served over eggs. Keep sauce on hand in freezer. Makes approximately 2 gallons.

Mrs. George A. Hill, III (Gloria Lester)

Easy Creole Sauce

1 cup sliced onions
2 green peppers, sliced
⅓ cup butter
1 can (1 lb.) tomatoes
12 stuffed green olives, sliced
1 can (8 oz.) mushrooms

1 tablespoon minced parsley
½ teaspoon thyme
2 whole cloves
1 bay leaf
½ clove garlic, crushed
Salt and pepper

Saute onions and peppers in butter, stirring constantly, for 5 minutes. Cover and simmer 5 minutes more. Add all other ingredients; simmer, covered, for about 25 minutes. Remove cloves and bay leaf. Serve over shrimp, fish or any left-over meat. Makes approximately 5 cups.

For creole chicken, add 1 cup dry white wine to sauce and pour over 8 browned chicken breast halves. Cover and bake at 350° for 1 hour, or until chicken is tender. Serve over rice. Serves 6.

Mrs. George McNeille Brooks (Lisbeth Gibson)

Tangy Thyme Sauce

½ cup mayonnaise
1 tablespoon lemon juice

½ teaspoon onion salt
¼ teaspoon powdered thyme

Mix all ingredients together. Taste. Add more thyme if desired. Warm sauce over low heat (will curdle if placed over high heat). Serve over any green vegetable. Sauce can also be chilled and served as salad dressing. Makes 1/2 cup sauce.

Mrs. Kline McGee (Adrian Rose)

Easy Sauce for Vegetables

½ cup sour cream

½ cup mayonnaise

Heat sour cream and mayonnaise together. Do not boil. Serve over broccoli or cauliflower; or over asparagus or broccoli souffle.

Mrs. William G. Guerriero (Margaret Ann White)

Mornay Sauce

1 onion, finely chopped
10 tablespoons butter
10 tablespoons flour
3 cups milk
3 cups cream

2 cups grated sharp cheese
1 teaspoon dry mustard
1½ teaspoons Worcestershire
   sauce
Salt and white pepper

Slowly simmer onions in butter until they are transparent. Gradually add flour; stir to make a smooth paste. Using wire whisk, stir in 2 cups of the milk and 2 cups of the cream. Add cheese, mustard, Worcestershire sauce, salt and white pepper. Cook until thick, stirring constantly. Add the remaining 1 cup milk and 1 cup cream. Heat thoroughly, stirring constantly. A great way to glamourize leftover chicken, turkey or vegetables. This sauce reheats well. Makes 7 cups, or about 12 servings.

Mrs. John B. Carter (Sue Browne)

Blender Bearnaise Sauce

2 tablespoons white wine
1 teaspoon dried tarragon or
   1 tablespoon chopped fresh
   tarragon

2 teaspoons chopped green
   onions
¼ teaspoon freshly ground
   pepper
1 cup hollandaise sauce

In small skillet, combine white wine, tarragon, green onions and pepper. Boil rapidly until there is only about 1 tablespoon liquid left. Strain into hollandaise and blend at high speed for 4 seconds. Serve on steak or eggs. Makes about 1 cup.

Mrs. Pete Gardere (Nancy Penix)

Hollandaise Sauce

2 egg yolks
½ teaspoon salt
Dash cayenne

½ cup butter, melted
1 tablespoon lemon juice

Beat yolks at high speed until thick. Add salt and cayenne. Add 3 tablespoons of the hot melted butter, a little at a time, beating constantly. Beat in remaining butter alternately with lemon juice. Keep warm over hot water. Makes about 3/4 cup sauce.

Mrs. James E. McAshan (Elizabeth Sanford)

Never - Fail Blender Hollandaise

1 cup butter
4 egg yolks
¼ teaspoon salt
¼ teaspoon sugar

¼ teaspoon Tabasco
¼ teaspoon dry mustard
2 tablespoons lemon juice

Heat butter until bubbling. Combine all other ingredients in blender. With blender turned on, pour butter into yolk mixture in slow stream until all is added. Turn blender off. Keeps well in refrigerator for several days. When reheating, heat over hot, not boiling, water in double boiler. Makes about 1-1/4 cups sauce.

Mrs. James Howard Park, III (Bette Naylor)

Freezer Hollandaise Sauce

6 egg yolks	1 tablespoon garlic vinegar
8 tablespoons boiling water	1 teaspoon dry mustard
3 tablespoons strained lemon juice	¼ teaspoon salt
	Dash pepper
½ pound butter, melted	Dash cayenne

Put egg yolks in a small round-bottomed (not metal) bowl that will fit over saucepan. Put hot, not boiling, water in saucepan over very low heat. Fit bowl on top of saucepan being certain that water does not touch bottom of bowl. Beat yolks with a wire whisk as you **very slowly** add boiling water, 1 tablespoon at a time, beating constantly, until you have added 8 tablespoons in all. (If water is beaten into yolks too fast, the sauce will be too thin.) Remove bowl from over water and continue to beat as you slowly add lemon juice, butter and vinegar. Stir in mustard, salt, pepper and cayenne. This sauce can be frozen for future use or can be refrigerated in a covered jar up to 10 days. Never re-heat this sauce on direct heat; the container of sauce should be placed over hot water (off the stove) until sauce is warm. Makes about 2 cups.

Mrs. Frank J. McGurl (Mary Martin)

Steak Butter

1 pint sour cream	1 large clove garlic, crushed
1 carton (8 oz.) whipped butter	2 tablespoons chopped chives
2-3 tablespoons minced parsley	Salt and pepper

Mix all ingredients thoroughly and refrigerate. Remove from refrigerator at least 1 hour before using. This butter can be frozen and re-frozen successfully. If frozen, let thaw, and whip before using. Dab one (or more) tablespoons of butter on steaks while they are hot, so it will melt over meat. Can also be used as a dressing for baked potatoes. Makes 3 cups.

Mrs. John H. Lindsey (Sara Houstoun)

Barbecue Sauce

1 tablespoon Worcestershire sauce	½ teaspoon Tabasco
1 tablespoon dry mustard	1 cup catsup
1½ tablespoons cooking oil	Salt and pepper

Thoroughly mix Worcestershire sauce and mustard. Add remaining ingredients; stir. Use to baste broiled chicken or spareribs. Makes approximately 1 cup.

Mrs. Cullom E. Connely (Margaret Deuel)

Barbecue Sauce for Chicken

½ cup cooking oil	3 tablespoons liquid smoke
½ cup butter	3 tablespoons Worcestershire
2 onions, chopped	sauce
2 cloves garlic, crushed	2 tablespoons vinegar
2 hot peppers (or bell peppers	2 tablespoons prepared mustard
with seeds), chopped	½ cup sugar
3 cans (8 oz. each) tomato sauce	2 tablespoons salt
2 cups water	2 tablespoons pepper
1 can (1 lb.) tomatoes	3 bay leaves, crushed
¾ cup chili sauce	4 slices lemon

Combine all ingredients and simmer for 4 hours. Soak chickens in salted water for 1 hour before cooking. Baste chickens often with sauce while they broil. Freezes well. Makes 2-1/2 quarts, enough sauce for 4-5 chickens.

Mrs. George F. Neff (Anne Lummis)

Bee's Barbecue Sauce

1 small onion, finely	1 clove garlic, crushed
chopped	½ cup Worcestershire sauce
½ cup butter	¼ cup sugar
1 bottle (14 oz.) catsup	½ cup vinegar

Saute onion in butter. Add remaining ingredients and cook over medium heat about 5 minutes. Especially good for basting spareribs or short ribs. Makes approximately 2-1/2 cups sauce.

Mrs. Lewis A. Brown (Sidney Walsh)

Buck Miller's Sauce for Fish or Game

¾ cup butter	1 tablespoon (or more)
Juice of 1 lemon	Durkee's sauce
6 dashes Tabasco	3 tablespoons dry white wine
3 dashes celery salt	or sherry
1 tablespoon Worcestershire	½ teaspoon liquid smoke
sauce	(optional)

Mix all ingredients and simmer over low heat until well-blended. Use for basting fish, game or chicken while broiling. Makes 1 cup.

Mrs. Phillip B. Sherwood (Mary Alexander)

Wine Barbecue Sauce

1 cup rose wine
1½ tablespoons lemon juice
2 teaspoons sugar

1½ teaspoons salt
6-10 drops Angostura bitters
¼ cup chili sauce

Combine all ingredients and simmer 10-15 minutes. Makes 1-1/4 cups.

Mrs. William Brantly Harris (Eugenia Head)

Glamourburger Sauce

1 bouillon cube
¼ cup water
1 teaspoon butter
1 tablespoon flour
½ clove garlic, chopped
1 can (4 oz.) mushrooms,
    with liquid

1 tablespoon Worcestershire
    sauce
3 tablespoons red wine
¼ teaspoon salt
Dash pepper

Dissolve bouillon cube in water. Combine all ingredients in saucepan. Cook until thickened, stirring constantly. Serve sauce over broiled or fried hamburger patties. Makes approximately 3/4 cup.

Mrs. James Howard Park, III (Bette Naylor)

Ida's Meat Sauce

1 rib celery, finely chopped
1 onion, chopped
1 clove garlic, crushed
1 tablespoon bacon drippings
1 can (1 lb.) tomatoes, chopped

1 can (10 oz.) Rotel tomatoes
    and green chilies
1 can (8 oz.) tomato sauce
Half of a can (6 oz.) tomato paste
Salt and pepper, to taste

Saute celery, onion and garlic in bacon drippings. Add remaining ingredients. Cook slowly for about 45 minutes, stirring often. Goes well with meat loaf. Makes about 4 cups.

Mrs. Tilford Jones (Audrey Thompson)

Ham Sauce

1 can (8½ oz.) crushed
  pineapple
1 can (8 oz.) tomato sauce
½ cup raisins

¼ cup brown sugar
⅓ cup currant jelly
3 tablespoons prepared mustard
½ cup tarragon vinegar

Mix all ingredients in saucepan and simmer for 15 minutes. Serve with baked ham. Makes about 3-1/2 cups sauce.

Mrs. Herman P. Pressler (Elsie Townes)

Mustard Sauce for Ham

½ cup brown sugar
½ cup vinegar
¼ cup dry mustard

½ cup butter
3 egg yolks

Put all ingredients in double boiler and cook, stirring constantly, until mixture is consistency of custard. If sauce tends to curdle, beat it smooth again. Chill, and serve with ham. Keeps well in refrigerator. Makes 1-1/2 cups.

Mrs. R. Henry Lake (Fredrica Lanford)

Hunter's Mustard

1 cup prepared mustard
1 cup vinegar
⅔ cup sugar

2 eggs
1 teaspoon white pepper

Mix mustard, vinegar and sugar. Let stand overnight. Beat eggs well and add to mustard mixture. Stir well and add white pepper. Cook in double boiler until thick. Serve with venison and biscuits. Also good with Canadian bacon or ham. Makes 2 cups.

Mrs. Bruce E. Barnett (Ann Poyner)

Hot Mustard

½ cup vinegar
1 cup Coleman's dry mustard

1 egg
1 cup sugar

Combine vinegar and mustard; soak overnight. Beat egg slightly, add sugar and stir in mustard mixture. Cook in double boiler until thick. Cool before serving. Keeps indefinitely in refrigerator. Serve with Chinese food or any cold, sliced meat. Makes about 1 pint.

Mrs. Harry H. Hudson (Carolyn Brock)

Remoulade Sauce

1 cup mayonnaise
3 green onions with tops,
  finely chopped
3 hard-cooked eggs, finely
  chopped
1 tablespoon prepared Creole
  mustard
¼ cup strained lemon juice
1 clove garlic, crushed

½ teaspoon salt
½ teaspoon coarsely ground
  pepper
1 tablespoon finely chopped
  parsley
4 ounces cream cheese (half of
  a large package)
1 teaspoon capers

Mix together all ingredients. Chill and serve with shrimp, crab, lobster or tomatoes. (This sauce may serve as a dip if thickened with an additional 4 ounces cream cheese.) Makes about 1 pint.

Mrs. Hughes Fleming (Mildred Hughes)

Cajun Remoulade Sauce

¼ cup horseradish mustard
½ cup tarragon vinegar
2 tablespoons catsup
1 tablespoon paprika
½ teaspoon cayenne
1 teaspoon salt

1 cup salad oil
½ cup finely minced green
  onions with tops
½ cup finely minced celery
1 clove garlic, crushed

Mix together mustard, vinegar, catsup, paprika, cayenne and salt. Slowly add oil, beating constantly. Stir in onions, celery and garlic. Chill. Serve over shrimp. Makes about 1 pint.

Mrs. Paul F. McBride, Jr. (Pattie Cunningham)

Spicy Remoulade Sauce

2 cups mayonnaise
1 jar (5¾ oz.) Zatarain's mustard
  (or other creole mustard)
3 grated hard-cooked eggs
2 medium cloves garlic, crushed
¼ of a large onion, grated
2 tablespoons Worcestershire
  sauce

1½ tablespoons lemon juice
1 tablespoon wine vinegar
2 tablespoons anchovy paste
1 tablespoon prepared
  horseradish (optional)
1 tablespoon sherry
2 teaspoons celery seed

Combine all ingredients and mix until well blended. Make at least one day before needed. Serve with crabmeat or shrimp or as a dip for vegetables. Makes about 1 quart.

Mrs. Richard R. McKay (Emily Ann Finch)

Red Cocktail Sauce

¼-½ cup prepared horseradish
Juice of 2 lemons
2 teaspoons Worcestershire sauce
1 cup chili sauce

1 cup catsup
Salt and pepper
Pinch of sugar
1 teaspoon olive oil

Mix all ingredients together. Chill at least 30 minutes before serving. Serve with cold boiled shrimp. Makes about 2-1/2 cups.

Mrs. Howard A. Tenney, Jr. (Joan Woodruff)

Parsley Sauce for Seafood

1 cup mayonnaise
½ cup finely chopped parsley
Scant cup catsup
½ cup finely chopped onion
2 tablespoons chopped ripe olives
2 tablespoons chopped dill pickles

Salt
Dash Worcestershire sauce
Dash Tabasco
1 small package (3 oz.) cream
   cheese, softened (optional)

Combine all ingredients. Serve as sauce for fried shrimp, page 178. May also be used on other fried seafood. Makes about 3 cups.

Mrs. Ghent Graves, Jr. (Sally Sample)

Glendorn Sauce

1 bottle (12 oz.) Monarch shrimp
   cocktail sauce
2 bottles (14 oz. each) catsup

2 tablespoons Worcestershire
   sauce
1 pound butter
4 tablespoons prepared
   horseradish

Cook all ingredients slowly, stirring constantly for about 15 minutes. Serve hot in individual bowls with boiled lobster, steamed clams or boiled shrimp. Makes enough sauce for 12-16 servings.

Mrs. David F. Dorn (Julie Leary)

Fresh Tomato Sauce

½ cup mayonnaise
½ cup peeled, chopped and
   drained fresh tomatoes
¼ cup finely chopped onions

1 tablespoon finely chopped
   green pepper
1 teaspoon mashed jalapeno
   peppers or coarsely ground
   black pepper
Salt to taste

Combine all ingredients. Chill and serve with cold boiled shrimp. Makes about 1-1/4 cups.

Mrs. John H. Meyers (Alice Baker Jones)

Salsa Fria

1 cup finely chopped onion
1 clove garlic, crushed
1 tablespoon olive oil
1 pound tomatoes, peeled and
   chopped
1 teaspoon sugar

2 or 3 large, canned, green
   chiles or jalapenos, finely
   chopped
Chili powder, to taste
½ teaspoon oregano
Dash garlic salt

Saute onion and garlic in oil until tender, but not brown. Add remaining ingredients. Bring to a boil and simmer gently about 15 minutes, stirring frequently. Serve hot or cold. This sauce can be incorporated in many dishes; is also tasty served on top of eggs. Makes approximately 2 cups.

Mrs. James Howard Park, III (Bette Naylor)

Henry Bain's Meat Sauce

1 bottle (12 oz.) chili sauce
1 bottle (14 oz.) catsup
1 bottle (10 oz.) Worcestershire
   sauce

1 bottle (18 oz.) Major Grey's
   chutney, finely chopped
Evangeline hot sauce or Tabasco
Chopped watercress (optional)

Mix all ingredients, except watercress, and blend thoroughly. Replace sauce in original bottles. This sauce keeps indefinitely, unrefrigerated, and goes with all meats. Finely chopped watercress gives additional flavor and may be added just before serving. Makes 6-3/4 cups.

Mrs. James Howard Park, III (Bette Naylor)

Chili Sauce

12 large, ripe tomatoes	2 teaspoons cinnamon
4 large onions, finely chopped	1 tablespoon dry mustard
1 scant cup sugar	1 teaspoon salt
3½ cups vinegar	6 chili piquins, or 2 small hot
2 teaspoons ground cloves	fresh peppers, or cayenne
	to taste

Dip tomatoes in boiling water. Peel and finely chop. Place all ingredients in large, heavy pot. Simmer over low heat for about 2 hours, or until desired consistency is reached. Stir often. Spoon into hot, sterilized jars. Seal immediately with paraffin (to keep from discoloring), then with lid. Makes about 9 half-pints.

Mrs. Tilford Jones (Audrey Thompson)

Artichoke Relish

3 quarts coarsely chopped Jerusalem artichokes (about 7 lbs.)	6 cups sugar
	10 cups white vinegar
1 quart coarsely chopped onions (about 2 lbs.)	3 tablespoons mustard seed
	1 tablespoon pepper
3 pounds cabbage, chopped	1 tablespoon turmeric
6 green bell peppers, chopped	¾ cup sifted flour
1 head cauliflower, chopped	1 small jar (6 oz.)
2 cups salt	prepared mustard

Combine artichokes, onions, cabbage, green peppers and cauliflower. Add salt and 1 gallon water. Mix well. Let stand at least 4 hours, or overnight. Drain by squeezing vegetables with hands, and put into large pot (roaster is ideal). Add sugar, 9 cups of the vinegar, mustard seed, pepper and the turmeric. Cook for 10 minutes, stirring with wooden spoon. Do not allow to boil. Mix flour, prepared mustard and remaining 1 cup vinegar to make a smooth paste; stir into relish. Turn heat to low and simmer until it thickens, 5-10 minutes. Do not overcook. Ladle into hot, sterilized jars, seal with paraffin (to keep from discoloring), then with lid. Makes 24 half-pints.

Mrs. Thomas B. Eaton, Jr. (Margot Teague)

Corn Relish

2 cans (1 lb. each) whole
  kernel corn, well drained
1 clove garlic, minced
½ cup chopped celery
½ cup chopped onion
½ cup chopped cucumber pickles
¼ cup chopped pimiento
¼ cup chopped green bell pepper

½ cup salad oil
¼ cup vinegar
1 teaspoon sugar
Juice of 1 lemon
1 teaspoon cornstarch
1 teaspoon dry mustard
Salt

Combine corn, garlic, celery, onion, pickle, pimiento and green pepper. Set aside. Combine salad oil, vinegar, sugar and lemon juice; cook until mixture begins to boil. Stir in cornstarch and dry mustard, which have been mixed with a small amount of water. Combine with corn mixture; mix well. Season with salt. Chill before serving. Makes 6 cups relish.

Mrs. W. K. King (Rosalie Meek)

Corn Relish Piquante

3 cans (12 oz. each) whole
  kernel corn
¼ cup liquid from corn
1 cup chopped onion
1 cup thinly sliced celery
½ cup chopped green bell
  pepper
1 can (4 oz.) pimiento,
  drained and diced
1 cup sugar
1 tablespoon salt

1 teaspoon crushed, dried, sweet
  red pepper (optional)
1 large garlic clove, minced
  (optional)
1 tablespoon celery seed
1 tablespoon mustard seed
½ teaspoon ground ginger
3 cups white vinegar
1½ tablespoons dry mustard
1 teaspoon turmeric
¼ cup flour

Drain corn thoroughly, reserving 1/4 cup liquid. Combine onion, celery, green pepper, pimiento, sugar, salt, red pepper, garlic, celery seed, mustard seed, ginger and 2-1/2 cups of the vinegar. Boil 5 minutes. Blend dry mustard, turmeric and flour with reserved corn liquid until smooth. Thin with remaining 1/2 cup vinegar. Add to hot mixture. Cook 5-6 minutes, or until liquid thickens to consistency of cream. Add corn. Boil 5 minutes. Pour boiling-hot relish to within 1/4" of top of sterilized fruit jars and seal immediately. Makes about 8 half-pints.

Mrs. Charles B. Williams (Bobbie Ruth Richardson)

Dilled Sauerkraut

Cabbage
Salt
Fresh Dill

Shred cabbage. Take handful of cabbage, 1/2 teaspoon salt and sizeable pinch of fresh dill; knead together in crock. Repeat process until desired amount of cabbage is in crock. Put heavy plate on top of cabbage to weight it down. Cover top of crock with Saran wrap. Put in cool place for 2 to 3 weeks. (A mold will form on top.) After 2 weeks, pick through mold and taste. Continue testing every day or so until kraut is ready. Scrape off mold; spoon kraut into sterilized jars. Chill before serving.

Mrs. Maria W. Maclay (Maria Winterbotham)

Green Tomato Relish

10 pounds green tomatoes	2 teaspoons dry mustard
7 medium onions	2 teaspoons cinnamon
⅔ cup salt	½ teaspoon (rounded) cayenne
5 cups cider vinegar	½ teaspoon (rounded) allspice
2½ cups sugar	½ teaspoon (rounded) ground
3½ teaspoons mustard seed	cloves
1¼ teaspoons celery seed	3 cloves garlic, peeled and
	thinly sliced

Peel tomatoes and onions; slice very thin. Place in crock, sprinkle with salt, and mix slightly. Let stand overnight. Wash in clear water; drain thoroughly. Place in large preserving kettle. Combine all remaining ingredients; stir until spices are dissolved. Pour over tomatoes and onions. Cook slowly for 1 hour, stirring frequently, or until tomatoes are transparent. Ladle into hot, sterilized jars; seal immediately. Makes 9 pints.

Mrs. John H. Lindsey (Sara Houstoun)

Pear Chutney

5 cups peeled, cored and
    chopped hard pears
2 ripe tomatoes, peeled and
    chopped
3 apples, peeled, cored
    and chopped
3 peaches, peeled, seeded
    and chopped
2 lemons, seeded and chopped

1 lime, seeded and chopped
1½ cups raisins
4 tablespoons crushed, dried
    red peppers
1 large clove garlic, minced
2½ cups brown sugar
2 cups vinegar
2 tablespoons powdered ginger
1 tablespoon salt

Combine all ingredients in large preserving kettle. Simmer 2 hours. Spoon into hot, sterilized jars and seal immediately. Makes about 6 pints.

Mrs. R. B. Bowen (Emma Smith)

Pear Relish

12 pounds hard pears (about 40),
    peeled, cored and quartered
2 pounds onions, peeled and
    quartered
4 green bell peppers, seeded
    and quartered

5 cups white vinegar
4 cups sugar
2½ tablespoons salt
2 tablespoons pickling spice
2 tablespoons turmeric

Put pears, onions and peppers through food grinder. Drain off all liquid. Combine vinegar, sugar, salt, pickling spices and turmeric. Boil 10 minutes. Add pears, onions and peppers. Boil 15 minutes. Spoon into hot, sterilized jars and seal immediately. Makes 8-9 pints.

Miss Tarrant Hancock

Pickled Pickles

1 gallon "bought" sour pickles
1½ teaspoons alum
1 box (1¼ oz.) pickling spice,
    or less

5 cups sugar
1 clove garlic, peeled
½ cup tarragon vinegar

Drain pickles; slice into crock or other large container. Add other ingredients; mix well. Let stand overnight, then refrigerate for about 7 days. Skim off spices, remove garlic clove, and spoon pickles with juice into jars. These pickles must be kept in refrigerator, but will keep indefinitely. Makes about 4 quarts.

Mrs. Robert B. Crouch (Nancy Wencke)

Crisp Bread and Butter Pickles

18 medium cucumbers
8 small white onions, thinly sliced
1 green bell pepper, cut in
   narrow strips
1 red bell pepper, cut in
   narrow strips
½ cup coarse salt

Cracked (or crushed) ice
5 cups sugar
5 cups white vinegar
1½ teaspoons turmeric
½ teaspoon ground cloves
2 tablespoons mustard seed
2 teaspoons celery seed

Slice unpeeled cucumbers into rounds not quite 1/4" thick; place in enameled cooking pot. Add onions, green and red peppers and salt. Cover with crushed ice; mix thoroughly. Let stand, undisturbed, for 3 hours. Drain off liquid, leaving cucumber mixture in pot. Combine sugar, vinegar, turmeric, cloves, mustard seed and celery seed. Pour over cucumber mixture. Bring to a boil, stirring occasionally. As soon as boiling point is reached, remove from heat. Ladle pickles with juice into hot, sterilized jars and seal immediately. Makes 8 pints. (1/2 bushel of cucumbers will make 32 pints of pickles. To pickle 1/2 bushel of cucumbers, quadruple all the above amounts.)

Mrs. John H. Lindsey (Sara Houstoun)

Dill Pickles

¾ peck (about 30-40) 3"
   cucumbers
12 sprigs fresh dill
6 dried chili peppers
6 whole cloves garlic, peeled

Alum
3 quarts water
1 quart pickling or white
   vinegar
1 cup coarse salt

Scrub cucumbers well and dry thoroughly. Sterilize 6 quart jars. Into each jar put 1 dill sprig, 1 chili pepper, 1 clove garlic and 1 pinch alum. Pack cucumbers tightly in jars. Place an additional dill sprig on top. Combine water, vinegar and salt; bring to a boil. Fill each jar with boiling vinegar mixture; seal immediately. Allow pickles to ripen for at least 2 weeks before using. Makes 6 quarts.

Mrs. John E. Bailey (Eleanor Bering)

Dilled Okra

3 pounds okra
16 or 24 fresh hot peppers
16 heads fresh dill
8 teaspoons mustard seed

8 cloves garlic, peeled (optional)
3 cups vinegar
3 cups water
6 tablespoons salt

Wash okra; pack neatly into 8 sterilized pint jars. To each jar add: 2 or 3 hot peppers, 2 heads dill, 1 teaspoon mustard seed, and 1 clove garlic if desired. Bring vinegar, water and salt to a rolling boil. Fill jars with boiling mixture. Seal immediately. Makes 8 pints.

Mrs. Paul S. Ache, Jr. (Betsy Evans)

Dilled Green Beans

4 pounds tender, stringless
    green beans
8 large heads fresh dill
8 cloves garlic, peeled
8 fresh, thin, hot green peppers

8 fresh, thin, hot red peppers
4 cups white vinegar
4 cups water
½ cup salt

Thoroughly wash beans, do not stem. Pack beans upright in hot, sterilized jars. Add to each jar: 1 head dill, 1 clove garlic, 1 hot green pepper and 1 hot red pepper. Boil vinegar, water and salt together. Pour boiling mixture over beans; seal immediately. Allow to stand for 2 weeks before using. Chill before serving. Makes 8 pints.

Mrs. John H. Lindsey (Sara Houstoun)

Pickled Onions

12 pounds small pearl onions
2 cups salt
8 scant teaspoons salt
8 scant teaspoons celery seed

8 scant teaspoons mustard seed
16 hot red peppers
3 quarts white vinegar
4 cups sugar

Cover onions with boiling water for about 3 minutes; drain and slip off skins. Cover onions with brine made of 4 quarts boiling water and 2 cups salt. Let stand for 24 hours. Pour off brine, reheat it, and pour back on onions. Repeat this procedure once a day for 3 days. At the end of third day, wash onions in clear water and drain. In each of 8 hot, sterilized pint jars, put 1 scant teaspoon salt, 1 scant teaspoon celery seed, 1 scant teaspoon mustard seed and 2 hot peppers. Pack onions in jars. Boil vinegar and sugar until sugar is dissolved. Pour boiling mixture over onions and seal immediately. Chill before serving. Makes 8 pints.

Mrs. W. Meade Wheless, Jr. (Nancy Park)

Famous Pickled Onions

12 pounds tiny, silver-skin onions	4 teaspoons celery seed
2 cups salt	1½ quarts white vinegar
16 long, slender, hot peppers	6 cups sugar
4 teaspoons mustard seed	1 tablespoon celery salt

Pour boiling water over onions to cover. After 3 minutes, drain, and slip skins off. Put peeled onions in large crock. Put salt in 1 gallon boiling water, and pour over onions. Cover, and let stand overnight. Drain off water, boil it, and pour back on onions. Next day, drain onions, and rinse in clear, cold water. Pack onions in hot, sterilized pint jars, placing two peppers in each jar. To each jar, add 1/2 teaspoon mustard seed and 1/2 teaspoon celery seed. Combine vinegar, sugar and celery salt; bring to a boil. Pour over onions and seal immediately. Chill well before serving. Makes 8 pints.

Mrs. H. M. Croswell, Jr. (Elizabeth Holcombe)

Marinated Onion Rings

1 cup water	1 teaspoon salt
½ cup white vinegar	1 teaspoon pepper
¼ cup salad oil	2 to 3 purple or Bermuda
2 tablespoons sugar	onions, sliced

Shake all ingredients, except onions, in a quart jar. Add enough onion slices to fill jar. Refrigerate for at least 2 hours before serving. Serve as a pickle or use in salads or sandwiches. Makes 1 quart.

Mrs. Otis Meredith (Mary Wilkins)

Pickled Mushrooms

1 can (8 oz.) large mushroom caps	1 teaspoon finely chopped
1 tablespoon garlic vinegar	parsley
1 tablespoon olive oil	1 teaspoon finely chopped green
1 teaspoon oregano	onions

Drain mushrooms and place in small bowl. Combine vinegar, olive oil, oregano, parsley and green onions; pour over mushrooms, cover and refrigerate for at least 2 hours before serving. Stir once or twice. Serves 2 as salad or 4 as relish.

Mrs. John H. Meyers (Alice Baker Jones)

Jalapeño Jelly

¾ cup ground green bell pepper
¼ cup ground fresh jalapeno
   peppers
1 cup cider vinegar

5 cups sugar
1 bottle (6 oz.) liquid fruit
   pectin
Green food coloring

Combine green pepper, jalapeno peppers, vinegar and sugar in large saucepan; bring to a boil. Boil 4 minutes. Remove from heat and let cool 1 minute. Add pectin and a few drops green food coloring. Pour into hot, sterilized jelly glasses and seal. (Be sure to use Saran or rubber gloves when grinding jalapenos as they burn your hands.) Makes about 5 (6 oz.) glasses of jelly.

Mrs. Leslie Coleman (Eloise Steele)

Tabasco Jelly

1 cup water
⅓ cup lemon juice
2 teaspoons Tabasco

3 cups sugar
6 tablespoons liquid fruit pectin
Red or green food coloring

In large saucepan, combine water, lemon juice, Tabasco and sugar. Bring to a boil, stirring constantly. Add pectin and few drops of food coloring. Stir until mixture comes to full, rolling boil. Boil hard for about 30 seconds. Remove from heat and skim off foam. Pour into hot, sterilized jelly glasses. Seal with 1/8" melted paraffin. This jelly is very spicy and is especially good with cold turkey, roast beef or game. Fills about 4 (6 oz.) jelly glasses.

Mrs. Ralph Ellis Gunn (Esme Patterson)

Port Wine Jelly

2 cups port wine
3 cups sugar

½ teaspoon rosemary
6 tablespoons liquid fruit pectin

Combine port, sugar and rosemary in top of double boiler. Place over boiling water and stir until sugar dissolves, about 2 minutes. Remove from heat. Strain through several layers of cheese cloth; then stir in pectin. Ladle into hot, sterilized jelly glasses. For best flavor, this jelly should be made 2-3 months before serving. Especially good with duck or game. Fills about 5 (6 oz.) jelly glasses.

Mrs. R. W. Tidemann (Bettie Brewster)

Bourbon Jelly

1½ cups sour mash bourbon
½ cup water

3 cups sugar
6 tablespoons liquid fruit pectin

Combine bourbon, water and sugar in top of double boiler. Place over boiling water; stir until sugar is dissolved. Remove from heat, stir in pectin and pour into hot, sterilized jelly glasses. Seal immediately with paraffin. Fills about 5 (6 oz.) jelly glasses.

Mrs. John H. Meyers (Alice Baker Jones)

Brandied Cranberries

1 pound fresh cranberries
2 cups sugar
¼ cup (or more) peach brandy

Wash and pick over cranberries, discarding soft or green ones. Spread in single layer in shallow baking pan. Sprinkle sugar over berries. Cover **tightly** with foil, and bake in 350° oven for 1 hour. Let cool. Stir in brandy. Taste and add more sugar, if desired. (Any brandy or cognac may be substituted for the peach brandy.) Do not double recipe. Makes approximately 1-1/2 cups.

Mrs. Robert B. Crouch (Nancy Wencke)

Jellied Cranberry Sauce

2 pounds fresh cranberries
4 cups boiling water
4 cups sugar

Wash cranberries, discarding any that are not firm. Put into large pan with boiling water. As soon as water comes to a boil again, lower heat and cover, tipping lid so steam can escape. Cook very slowly for 20 minutes, stirring occasionally. Put juice and berries through food mill, or mash through strainer. Add sugar to strained berries and juice. Bring mixture to a boil as quickly as possible; boil 4 or 5 minutes. Rinse a 6-cup mold (or several smaller molds) in cold water and fill with jelly. Chill. Unmold to serve. Do not make a larger quantity than this at one time. Makes 3 pints.

Mrs. Ben M. Anderson (Mary Greenwood)

Wild Grape Jelly

3 quarts wild green grapes
2 cups sugar

Wash and stem at least 3 quarts wild green grapes. (Grapes should be about to turn purple; for sweeter jelly, use riper grapes.) Put grapes in preserving kettle and cover with water. Bring to a boil and simmer for 10 minutes. Pour grapes with juice into jelly bag, or cheese cloth bag, and allow juice to drip through (do not squeeze). Measure 3 cups strained juice into deep heavy pot. If grapes yield more than 3 cups juice, extra grape juice may be stored in refrigerator for making jelly later. Boil rapidly for 5 minutes. Add 2 cups sugar; boil rapidly on **high** heat (mixture will bubble high) until jelly sheets from a metal spoon (220° on candy thermometer). Skim off foam as if forms while jelly is cooking. Pour into hot, sterilized jars and seal with paraffin. Fills 3 (6 oz.) jelly glasses.

Mrs. Phillip B. Sherwood (Mary Alexander)

Wild Plum Jelly

4 pounds fully ripe wild plums   **Food coloring (optional)**
1 cup water   **6 tablespoons liquid fruit**
6½ cups sugar   **pectin**

Crush plums; do not peel or pit. Add water, bring to a boil, and simmer, covered, 10 minutes. Place in large jelly or cheese cloth bag and allow juice to drip through. Measure exactly 4 cups plum juice into **very large** preserving kettle. Add sugar; mix well. (Yellow plums will make a gold-colored jelly. If a rosy-red jelly is desired, add 30 drops red food coloring, 3 drops yellow food coloring and 2 drops blue food coloring. The coloring in no way affects the flavor, and makes a beautiful jelly.) Place kettle over high heat and bring to a boil, stirring constantly. As soon as boiling point is reached, immediately stir in pectin. Then bring to a full, rolling boil and boil hard for 1 minute, stirring constantly. Remove from heat; skim off foam with metal spoon. Pour quickly into hot, sterilized jelly glasses. Cover at once with 1/8" hot paraffin. Makes approximately 5 pints jelly, or fills 10 (6 oz.) jelly glasses.

Mrs. John H. Lindsey (Sara Houstoun)

Texas Fig Preserves

1 pound figs
1 cup sugar
½ lemon, thinly sliced

(If unpeeled figs are used, wash them in solution of 1 quart water and 1 tablespoon baking soda. Remove and let stand about 15 minutes; rub off fuzz.) Place figs and sugar in a large preserving kettle; let stand overnight. Remove figs from syrup and set aside. Add lemon slices to syrup and bring to a boil. Lower heat and cook slowly until syrup is reduced by about 1/4 (about 50 minutes). Add figs and simmer for 30 minutes. Skim off foam. Spoon into hot, sterilized jars; seal immediately. Makes about 1 pint.

Mrs. Thomas G. Vandivier (Bettie Ebaugh)

Pear Conserve

8 pounds (about 25) hard pears
2 lemons, seeded
1 orange, seeded
1 cup water

12 cups sugar
1 can (8 oz.) crushed pineapple
½ pound candied or preserved ginger

Peel, core and chop pears. Finely grind lemons and orange. Combine with pears. Add water and sugar. Cook about 2 hours. Stir often; do not let burn or stick. Add pineapple and ginger; cook 30 minutes longer. Spoon into hot, sterilized jars. Seal immediately. Makes about 12 pints.

Mrs. Thomas E. Kelly (Jane Moore)

Hot Curried Fruit

2 cans (1 lb. each) fruit-for-salad, (or equivalent in assorted canned fruits)

2 bananas, sliced
½ cup butter, melted
¾ cup brown sugar
1½ teaspoons curry powder

Drain canned fruit and let stand in colander, overnight, in refrigerator. Next day, make a sauce of butter, brown sugar and curry powder. Arrange drained fruit and bananas in shallow casserole (7" x 12"), spoon sauce over fruit, and bake 1 hour at 300°. Serves 6-8.

Mrs. William C. Braden, Jr. (Dorothy Jane Reed)

Gandy's Blue Cheese Butter

½ cup butter
4 ounces Blue cheese

Soften butter and cheese; blend together. Cut 6 hard rolls (or 2 small loaves French bread) in half, lengthwise. Spread with cheese butter; brown under broiler.

Mrs. George F. Neff (Anne Lummis)

Herb Butter

½ cup butter
1 tablespoon finely chopped
  watercress
1 tablespoon finely chopped
  parsley

1 tablespoon finely chopped
  chives
¼ teaspoon salt

Cream butter. Gradually blend in remaining ingredients; chill. Spread on rye bread or broiled steaks; or top individual servings of soup with dollop of mixture. Makes about 3/4 cup.

Mrs. Henry G. Safford, Jr. (Georgia Howard)

Orange Butter

¼ cup frozen orange juice concentrate
⅔ cup butter
1 box (1 lb.) powdered sugar

Cream all ingredients together. Use as a spread for hot rolls. Can be stored indefinitely in refrigerator. Makes 2 cups.

Mrs. Raleigh W. Johnson, Jr. (Marjorie Bintliff)

B R E A D S

Hints

DISSOLVING YEAST: Sprinkle dry yeast, or crumble compressed yeast, into warm water. (Hot water will kill yeast and prevent dough from rising.)

KNEADING: Turn out dough onto lightly floured board or pastry cloth. With floured hands, pick up dough. Fold dough over toward you, then push it down and away from you, with heel of hand. Give dough a quarter turn; repeat kneading, developing a rocking rhythm. Knead until dough is satiny and elastic. (The longer you knead, the finer textured the bread will be.)

TESTING FOR "DOUBLED IN BULK": To determine when rising dough is doubled in bulk, press the tips of two fingers into dough. If the dent stays, dough is doubled in bulk.

SHAPING LOAVES: Be sure that dough does not fill more than 2/3 of pan. (If a highly-glazed crust is desired, brush loaf with mixture of 1 egg yolk beaten with 1 tablespoon water, before baking.)

COOLING LOAVES: Remove baked bread from pans; let cool on wire racks or across the top edges of baking pans, so air can circulate.

CUTTING BREAD: To cut very fresh bread, use a heated knife. (Dip knife in very hot water; dry quickly. Keep knife hot and dry.)

QUICK BREADS

BISCUITS AND ROLLS: Place biscuits or rolls one inch apart on baking sheet if you like them crusty on all sides; place them touching each other if you prefer them soft.

MUFFINS: If muffins get done a little before the rest of the meal, loosen them, and tip slightly in the pans. Otherwise, they may steam and get soggy on the bottom.

PANCAKES: If pancake batter must stand a long time, add extra baking powder.

Banana Muffins

½ cup shortening	1½ cups sifted flour
1 cup sugar	1 teaspoon nutmeg
2 eggs	1 teaspoon soda
1 cup mashed ripe bananas	2 teaspoons hot water
(2 or 3 bananas)	1 teaspoon vanilla

Cream shortening and sugar. Add eggs and bananas; mix well. Stir in flour and nutmeg. Dissolve soda in hot water; add to banana mixture. Stir in vanilla. Fill greased muffin pans, or paper baking cups, about half full. Bake in 350° oven for about 20 minutes, or until golden brown. These are a favorite for children's school lunches, and stay moist and fresh quite a long time. Makes 24 medium muffins.

Mrs. Bruce E. Barnett (Ann Poyner)

Blueberry Muffins

⅔ cup shortening	1 teaspoon salt
1 cup sugar	1 cup milk
3 eggs	1 can (1 lb.) blueberries,
3 cups sifted flour	well drained
2 heaping teaspoons double-acting baking powder	

Cream shortening and sugar. Add eggs, one at a time, beating well after each addition. Sift flour, baking powder and salt together; add alternately with milk. Fold in blueberries. Fill greased muffin cups 2/3 full. Bake at 375° for 25-30 minutes. Batter will keep in refrigerator for 2 or 3 weeks. Makes about 24 medium muffins.

Mrs. Raleigh W. Johnson, Jr. (Marjorie Bintliff)

Scotch Oatmeal Muffins

1 cup quick-cooking oats	½ teaspoon soda
1 cup buttermilk	1 egg, slightly beaten
1 cup flour	⅓ cup brown sugar
1 teaspoon baking powder	⅓ cup cooking oil
½ teaspoon salt	

Soak oats in buttermilk for 15 minutes or longer. Sift together flour, baking powder, salt and soda; stir into oat mixture. Add egg, brown sugar and oil; stir until just blended. Fill greased muffin pans 2/3 full. Bake at 400° for 20-25 minutes. Makes 12 large muffins.

Mrs. Rotan McGown (Charlotte Rotan)

Buttermilk Biscuits

2 cups flour	3 tablespoons shortening
6 rounded teaspoons tartrate baking powder	½ teaspoon soda
1 teaspoon salt	1 cup buttermilk

Combine flour, baking powder and salt. Cut in shortening until consistency of coarse meal. Add soda to buttermilk; stir into flour mixture. Mix well. Roll dough on floured board and cut into rounds. Bake at 450° on ungreased baking sheet for 10-12 minutes, or until browned. Makes 12-15 large biscuits.

Mrs. Lyon L. Brinsmade (Susannah Tucker)

Refrigerator Rolls

(DINNER OR CINNAMON)

1 package dry yeast, or 1 yeast cake	⅔ cup shortening
2 cups lukewarm water	1 teaspoon salt
2 eggs, unbeaten	7 cups flour
½ cup sugar	Melted butter

Add yeast to lukewarm water, mixing with hand until yeast is dissolved. Add eggs, sugar, shortening and salt. Stir well. Sift in 4 cups of the flour. Stir well. Sift in 2 more cups flour and stir well. Add remaining 1 cup flour and mix with hands. Cover dough with wet dish towel that has been folded 4 times. Place in refrigerator overnight. When ready to use, remove desired amount from refrigerator and allow to rise at least 4 hours. Do not work with more than half of the dough at a time. Knead to get air out.

For dinner rolls, roll out 1/4-1/2" thick. Cut in rounds with small cheese glass, or similar-sized cutter. Dip both sides of each roll in melted butter and fold over. Place in greased pan. Let rise until double in size, about 40 minutes. Bake at 400° for 15-20 minutes, or until brown. Makes at least 5 dozen small rolls.

For cinnamon rolls, roll dough as thin as possible. Spread dough with melted butter, cinnamon and sugar. Sprinkle with raisins and pecans, if desired. Roll up. Cut in slices, about 1/2" thick. Place slices in greased pan or in muffin pans. Let rise until double in size. Bake as directed above.

Mrs. Thane Tyler Sponsel (Mary Jane Price)

Butter Horn Rolls

2 tablespoons sugar	1 cup lukewarm water
2 tablespoons warm water	½ cup melted shortening
2 yeast cakes	½ teaspoon salt
3 eggs	5 cups flour
½ cup sugar	Melted butter

Combine sugar, 2 tablespoons warm water and yeast; stir. Let stand for 5-10 minutes, until dissolved. Beat eggs in another, larger bowl; add 1/2 cup sugar, 1 cup lukewarm water, shortening, yeast mixture, salt and flour. Knead until dough is very elastic. Dough will be very soft and difficult to work with. (It will get all over your hands, but do not despair.) Divide dough into 3 equal parts. Flour a pastry cloth and rolling pin. Working with one part at a time, roll dough into a circle, 1/4" thick. Brush melted butter over the round of dough. Cut into 4 pie-shaped wedges, and cut each wedge into 3 smaller wedges. Roll up each wedge, starting with wide edge. Place on cookie sheet with pointed end on bottom. Let rise until double in size (about 1-1/2 to 2 hours). Bake at 350° for 10-12 minutes, or until golden brown. These may be frozen after they are shaped (before rising). If frozen, allow approximately 3 hours to rise. Makes 3 dozen.

Mrs. Phillip B. Sherwood (Mary Alexander)

Fanny's Potato Icebox Rolls

1 yeast cake	⅔ cup sugar
½ cup lukewarm water	1 teaspoon salt
1 cup milk, scalded	2 eggs, well beaten
1 cup mashed potatoes	7 cups flour
⅔ cup cooking oil	

Dissolve yeast in water; set aside. Combine scalded milk and mashed potatoes. Add oil, sugar and salt; mix thoroughly. When potato mixture is lukewarm, add yeast, and mix well. Stir in eggs. Mix in flour, and turn out onto floured board. Knead thoroughly. Place in very large greased bowl. Brush top of dough with oil. Cover, and place in refrigerator overnight. When ready to bake, pinch off only amount desired and punch down remaining dough. Brush again with oil, cover, and return to refrigerator. Form dough into rolls of desired shape on floured board. Place in greased pan, and brush with melted butter. Let rise until double in size. Bake at 400° for 15-20 minutes. Makes approximately 4 dozen medium-sized rolls.

Mrs. Harold E. Daniels (Gayle Garth)

All Bran Icebox Rolls

1 yeast cake
1 cup lukewarm water
1 cup All-Bran cereal
½ cup sugar
1½ teaspoons salt

½ cup shortening
1 cup boiling water
2 eggs, well beaten
6 cups sifted flour

Dissolve yeast in lukewarm water. Combine All-Bran, sugar, salt, shortening and boiling water. Stir until shortening is melted. Cool to lukewarm. Add yeast mixture. Stir in eggs. Gradually sift in flour, mixing thoroughly. Cover and place in large bowl; refrigerate overnight. When ready to use, shape as desired. Brush with melted butter, and let rise in warm place until double in size. Bake at 400° for 20 minutes. Makes 2-1/2 dozen large rolls.

Mrs. Baxter Adams (Carol Nash)

Sour Cream Coffee Cake

½ pound butter
2 cups sugar
2 eggs
1 cup sour cream
1 teaspoon vanilla
2 cups sifted flour

¼-½ teaspoon salt
1 teaspoon baking powder
2 teaspoons cinnamon
4-5 tablespoons brown sugar
¾ cup chopped pecans

Grease and flour large bundt pan. Using electric mixer, cream butter and sugar. Add eggs, one at a time. Mix sour cream and vanilla together. Sift flour, salt and baking powder together. Add flour mixture to butter alternately with sour cream. Pour 1/3 to 1/2 of batter into prepared pan. Combine cinnamon, brown sugar and nuts; sprinkle over cake batter. Spoon remaining batter into cake pan. Bake at 350° for 60-65 minutes. Cake will rise; then fall slightly. Cool for at least 10 minutes before removing from pan. Sift powdered sugar over top of warm cake if desired.

Mrs. A. M. Tomforde, Jr. (Jo Alice Wynne)

Party Coffee Cake

½ cup butter	1 teaspoon soda
¾ cup sugar	1 cup sour cream
1 teaspoon vanilla	1 cup light brown sugar
3 eggs	2 teaspoons cinnamon
2 cups sifted flour	1 cup chopped nuts
1 teaspoon baking powder	6 tablespoons butter, melted

Cream butter, sugar and vanilla. Add eggs, one at a time, beating well after each addition. Sift together flour, baking powder and soda. Add to creamed mixture alternately with sour cream, beginning and ending with dry ingredients. Spread half of batter in greased 10'' tube pan. Add brown sugar, cinnamon and nuts to melted butter; mix well. Sprinkle half of the cinnamon-nut mixture on batter in pan. Cover with remaining batter. Sprinkle remaining cinnamon-nut mixture on top. Bake at 350° for 50 minutes. Cool slightly in pan; turn out onto serving plate. Serve plain or with Butter Frosting.

BUTTER FROSTING

¼ cup melted butter	1 teaspoon vanilla
2 cups powdered sugar	3 tablespoons cream

Combine all ingredients and blend until creamy. Spoon over top of cooled cake.

Mrs. Holcombe Crosswell (Emily Attwell)

Brown Sugar Coffee Cake

2 cups brown sugar, lightly packed	1 teaspoon nutmeg
	1 teaspoon soda
2 cups flour	1 cup sour cream
½ cup butter, softened	½ teaspoon cinnamon
1 egg, beaten	½ cup chopped nuts

Thoroughly mix together brown sugar, flour and butter. Spread half of mixture into 9'' square pan. To remaining brown sugar mixture, add egg and nutmeg. Mix soda into sour cream and add, stirring well. Spread batter over first mixture in pan. Sprinkle cinnamon and nuts over batter. Bake at 350° for 40 minutes. Serve as coffee cake, or top with whipped cream and serve as dessert. Serves 6-8.

Mrs. R. Henry Lake (Fredrica Lanford)

Fresh Apple Coffee Cake

3 medium tart apples	¼ teaspoon salt
1 cup sugar	½ teaspoon allspice
1 egg	½ teaspoon nutmeg
½ cup cooking oil	½ teaspoon cinnamon
1½ cups flour	1 cup nuts, chopped (optional)
1 teaspoon soda	

Peel, core and dice apples. Add sugar; mix and let stand 20 minutes. Beat egg; add oil. Sift together flour, soda, salt, allspice, nutmeg and cinnamon; add to egg mixture. Stir in apples and nuts. Bake in greased 9'' cake pan at 350° for 45 minutes. Dust with powdered sugar. Serve warm. May be frozen successfully.

Mrs. Phillip B. Sherwood (Mary Alexander)

Dusty's Apricot Horns

½ pound butter, softened	1 package (8-10 oz.) dried
½ pint (1 cup) creamed	apricots
cottage cheese	1½ cups sugar
2 cups flour	¼ teaspoon mace
	Powdered sugar

Blend butter and cottage cheese. Work in flour, a little at a time, until all is absorbed. Chill. (Refrigerated dough will keep a month.) Cover apricots with water and simmer until tender. Drain and mash well. Add sugar and mace. Cook slowly until very thick. Chill. Pinch off only enough dough to make into 6 balls, about 1-1/2'' in diameter. Keep remaining dough chilled. Roll each ball very thin into a 4'' circle. Spread 1 teaspoon chilled apricot mixture at one edge of each circle. Roll circles into horn shapes. Bake at 350° for about 12 minutes, or until lightly browned. Dust with powdered sugar. May be successfully frozen after baking. Makes approximately 36 apricot horns.

Mrs. William F. Yeoman (A. J. Vance)

Party Cinnamon Toast

1 loaf unsliced white bread	2 teaspoons cinnamon
½ pound butter, softened	1 cup powdered sugar

Trim crusts from bread and slice 1-1/2'' thick; then cut each slice into thirds. Spread bread on all sides with butter. Combine cinnamon and sugar; roll bread in mixture. Place on cookie sheet, and bake at 350° about 20 minutes, turning once, until golden brown. Serve hot. Makes about 24 squares.

Mrs. Carroll E. Church (Jean-Marie Ormondroyd)

Hot Cheese Squares

½ pound Old English cheese, grated	3 eggs, well beaten
½ pound American cheese, grated	1 teaspoon Worcestershire sauce
½ cup butter, softened	2 loaves unsliced bread
	Paprika
	Red pepper

Cream grated cheeses and butter. Add eggs and Worcestershire sauce. Trim crust from bread. Slice bread 1-1/2'' thick. Cut each slice into four squares. Spread cheese mixture on all sides of bread squares; sprinkle with paprika and red pepper. Refrigerate overnight. Bake in 350° oven, about 10 minutes. Serve hot. Makes 32 squares.

Mrs. Francis Brown (Martha Anne Francis)

Blender Popovers

1 cup flour	1 teaspoon sugar
¼ teaspoon salt	⅞ cup milk
1 tablespoon butter, melted	2 eggs

Preheat oven to 450°. Butter, and heat popover pan, deep muffin pans or Pyrex custard cups, until sizzling. Put all ingredients in blender and blend well. Fill heated cups 2/3 full. Bake at 450° for 12 minutes. Reduce temperature to 350°, and bake for 10 more minutes. Unlike most popovers, these, which are made in blender, do not fall. Makes 10-12 popovers.

Mrs. Pete Gardere (Nancy Penix)

Versatile Pancake – Waffle Batter

2 eggs, separated	2 cups milk
2 cups sifted flour	½ cup margarine, melted
1 tablespoon sugar	1 tablespoon baking powder
1 teaspoon salt	

Beat egg yolks. Sift together flour, sugar and salt. Add flour mixture and milk alternately to egg yolks. Stir in margarine. Beat egg whites until stiff; fold into batter. Add baking powder last. This batter will keep for several days in refrigerator. If it gets too thick, thin with milk.

When making pancakes, drop by spoonfuls onto heated, ungreased, griddle or iron skillet. Makes approximately 30 pancakes.

When making waffles, spoon batter into heated waffle iron. Makes 6-8 waffles.

Mrs. Lewis A. Brown (Sidney Walsh)

Favorite Pancakes

3 eggs, separated
1⅔ cups buttermilk
1 teaspoon soda
1¼ cups white flour
¼ cup whole wheat (or white) flour

1 tablespoon sugar
2 teaspoons baking powder
½ teaspoon salt
3 tablespoons butter, melted

Beat egg yolks well. Add buttermilk and beat thoroughly. Sift dry ingredients together and stir into buttermilk mixture. Add butter. Fold in stiffly beaten egg whites. Let stand 5 or 10 minutes before cooking. Makes about 16 pancakes, 4'' in diameter.

Mrs. Richard R. McKay (Emily Ann Finch)

Sour Dough Pancakes

1 package dry yeast
1 cup water
1¾ cups flour
¼ teaspoon soda

¾ teaspoon salt
3½ tablespoons sugar
2 eggs

Put yeast in moderately large, dry bowl; add water and stir. Add flour to make very stiff mixture. Cover with wet cloth and let stand, overnight, in warm place. The next morning, before making pancakes, remove and refrigerate about 3 tablespoons yeast mixture. (This will be a "starter" to keep on hand in refrigerator.) To make the pancakes, add to remaining yeast mixture, the soda, salt, sugar and eggs; batter will be very thin. Brush griddle with bacon grease and cook pancakes. When bubbles rise and burst, turn cakes over. Cook only once on each side. Makes 12 pancakes, about 5'' in diameter.

Any night before pancakes are desired, add 1 cup water and 1-3/4 cups flour to refrigerated "starter." Cover with wet cloth and let stand, overnight, in warm place. Next day, reserve another "starter," then proceed as before to make pancakes. Process may be repeated indefinitely.

Mrs. H. E. Hunt (Elinor Pierce)

Corn Griddle Cakes

1 cup cornmeal	1 egg
1 teaspoon baking powder	1 cup milk
¼ teaspoon salt	1 tablespoon bacon drippings

Combine all ingredients and mix well. If necessary, add more milk to thin batter. Cook on hot, greased griddle. Serve with syrup. Makes approximately 12 pancakes, 4'' in diameter.

Mrs. Lyon L. Brinsmade (Susannah Tucker)

Banana Bread

2 teaspoons baking powder	⅔ cup sugar
¼ teaspoon soda	2 eggs
1 teaspoon salt	3 ripe bananas, mashed
2 cups flour	1 teaspoon vanilla
⅓ cup shortening	

Sift baking powder, soda, salt and flour together; set aside. Cream shortening and sugar. Add eggs, one at a time, beating thoroughly after each addition. Stir in bananas and vanilla. Add flour mixture in several parts, beating after each addition. Spread batter into greased, 8'' x 4'', loaf pan. Bake at 350° for 50 minutes. Do not slice until cool. This bread slices well, and can be spread with cream cheese for tea sandwiches.

Mrs. Robert M. Davant (Diana Risien)

Banana Nut Bread

2 cups sifted flour	1 cup sugar
1 tablespoon baking powder	2 eggs
½ teaspoon salt	1 cup mashed ripe bananas
1 cup chopped nuts	(2 or 3 bananas)
½ cup shortening	1 teaspoon lemon juice

Sift flour, baking powder and salt together. Add nuts. Cream shortening and sugar. Beat eggs until light and add to creamed mixture. Add bananas and lemon juice. Add flour mixture, stirring only until flour is moistened. Bake in greased, 8'' x 4'', loaf pan at 350° for 1 hour. Let cool thoroughly before slicing. This is a rich, cake-like bread.

Mrs. W. S. Perkins (Sue Scott)

Hawaiian Banana Bread

1 cup shortening	2 teaspoons soda
2 cups sugar	1 teaspoon cinnamon
6 ripe bananas	1 teaspoon allspice
4 eggs	½ teaspoon ground cloves
2¼ cups flour	½ teaspoon nutmeg
1 teaspoon salt	1 cup chopped pecans (optional)

Cream shortening and sugar. Thoroughly mash bananas and add to the creamed mixture. Add eggs, one at a time, beating after each addition. Sift together, 3 times, the flour, salt, soda, cinnamon, allspice, cloves and nutmeg. Add banana mixture, blending thoroughly. Add pecans if desired. Spread into 2 greased 8'' x 4'' loaf pans, or several smaller pans. Bake at 350° for 45-50 minutes.

Mrs. Thomas E. Kelly (Jane Moore)

Orange Nut Bread

Rind of 4 large, thick-skinned oranges	4 teaspoons baking powder
1½ cups water	½ teaspoon salt
1 teaspoon soda	1 cup chopped pecans
2 cups sugar	2 eggs, well beaten
3½ cups flour	⅔ cup milk
	3 tablespoons butter, melted

Boil orange rind in 1 cup of the water with soda 4 minutes. Drain and rinse 3 times with fresh water. Cut or chop rind in very small pieces, using scissors or knife. Combine rind, remaining 1/2 cup water and 1 cup of the sugar; boil for 3 minutes. Set aside to cool. Sift remaining 1 cup sugar, flour, baking powder and salt together; add pecans. To the cooled orange mixture, add well-beaten eggs, milk and melted butter. Combine both mixtures, stirring well. Bake in 3 small well-greased loaf pans (7"x3"), at 325°, for 45-55 minutes. Orange peel may be prepared, chopped, and stored in refrigerator ahead of time if desired. This bread is also good toasted or buttered and warmed in 400° oven. Makes 3 small loaves.

Mrs. Richard R. McKay (Emily Ann Finch)

Orange Marmalade Bread

2 tablespoons butter
1 cup sugar
3 eggs
4 cups flour
3½ teaspoons baking powder
½ teaspoon salt

⅞ cup milk
2 tablespoons orange juice
1 cup chopped pecans
1 cup orange marmalade
1 tablespoon grated orange rind

Cream butter and sugar together. Add eggs, one at a time, beating well after each addition. Sift flour, baking powder and salt together; add alternately with milk and orange juice. Add pecans, marmalade and orange rind. Stir well. Spoon into 3 well-greased 3" x 7" loaf pans. Bake at 350° for 50 minutes, or until done. Makes 3 small loaves.

Mrs. Fred G. Yost (Jody Stedman)

Cranberry Nut Bread

2 cups flour
1 cup sugar
1½ teaspoons baking powder
½ teaspoon soda
1 teaspoon salt
¼ cup butter

½ cup chopped pecans
1 cup cranberries, coarsely
   chopped
¾ cup orange juice
1 tablespoon grated orange rind
1 egg, well beaten

Sift together flour, sugar, baking powder, soda and salt. Cut in butter. Add pecans and cranberries. Combine orange juice, orange rind and egg. Pour, all at once, into cranberry mixture. Stir just until blended. Pour into large (9" x 5" x 3"), well-greased, loaf pan; or into 3 small pans. Spread batter in corners and sides of pan slightly higher than center. Bake at 350° for 1 hour, or until golden brown. (When baking in smaller pans, reduce baking time slightly.) Remove from pan, cool, and wrap in foil. Store overnight before serving. Pineapple-flavored cream cheese may be spread on thin slices for tea sandwiches. Makes 1 large or 3 small loaves.

Mrs. Raymond Thornton (Dee Anne Minnis)

Quick Molasses Brown Bread

1 cup flour	1 egg
1¼ teaspoons soda	1 cup buttermilk
¾ teaspoon salt	½ cup molasses
¾ cup fine dry bread crumbs	½ cup raisins
3 tablespoons soft butter	

Sift flour, soda and salt together. Add bread crumbs and mix well. Cut in butter. Beat egg and combine with buttermilk, molasses and raisins. Add to dry mixture; stir until just blended. Pour into well-greased 2-quart ring mold or 8" tube pan. Bake at 400° for about 30-35 minutes, or until toothpick comes out clean. This is a heavy, non-sweet bread, similar to steamed Boston bread, only much easier and quicker. Serve warm with baked beans. Serves 6-8.

Mrs. H. Edward Maddox, III (Donna Gray)

Homemade Bread

2 cups milk, heated	2 yeast cakes
¼ cup sugar	2 cups lukewarm water
4 teaspoons salt	12 cups sifted flour
5 tablespoons shortening	

Combine milk, sugar, salt and shortening; let cool. Dissolve yeast in lukewarm water. When milk mixture is lukewarm, combine with yeast mixture. Add 6 cups of the flour, all at once, and stir well. Add remaining flour, one cup at a time. Dough will be hard to handle. Knead by hand until smooth and elastic. Put into greased bowl, cover, and set in warm place. Let rise until double in size (about 1 hour). Punch down, and divide into 4 parts. Shape each part into loaf and put into greased bread pan. Brush tops of loaves with melted butter, and let rise again until double in size (about 1 hour). Bake at 425° for 25-30 minutes. Makes 4 loaves.

Mrs. Richard R. Nelson, Jr. (Marjorie Shepherd)

Old Fashioned White Bread

1 yeast cake, or 1 package	½ cup sugar
dry yeast	1 tablespoon salt
⅓ cup warm water	2 cups lukewarm water
¼ cup melted shortening	6 cups flour

Dissolve yeast in 1/3 cup warm water. In separate bowl, combine shortening, sugar, salt and 2 cups lukewarm water. Add yeast. Stir in flour and mix well. Turn onto floured board and knead until smooth. Put dough in greased bowl and let rise until double in size (1-2 hours). Punch down, and shape into 2 large loaves. Put into well-greased bread pans and let rise until double in size, about 30-40 minutes. Bake at 350° for 40-45 minutes. Makes 2 loaves.

Mrs. Baxter Adams (Carol Nash)

Twelve Hour Icebox Bread

½ cup butter	1 teaspoon salt
2 cups hot water	6 to 6½ cups flour
1 package dry yeast	2 eggs
⅓ cup sugar	

Melt butter in hot water. Cool to lukewarm. Add yeast, sugar and salt; blend until well mixed. Mix in 3 cups of the flour. Add eggs, one at a time, blending well. Stir in remaining flour and beat until smooth. Form large ball and knead until dough is no longer sticky. Add more flour if necessary. Cover, and place in refrigerator for 12 hours, or more. When ready to bake, knead dough until all bubbles are gone. Divide dough in half. Shape into 2 loaves; place in well-greased bread pans. Let rise in warm place until double in size, about 1 hour. Bake at 350° for 45 minutes. Makes 2 loaves.

Mrs. Sanford E. McCormick (Balene Cross)

Whole Wheat Bread

1 yeast cake, or 1 package dry yeast	3½ cups white flour ½ cup hot water
2 cups lukewarm water	3 tablespoons shortening
2 tablespoons sugar	½ cup brown sugar
2 teaspoons salt	3 cups whole wheat flour

Dissolve yeast in 1/4 cup of the lukewarm water. Combine the remaining 1-3/4 cups lukewarm water, sugar, salt and white flour. Add yeast and beat with mixer until smooth. Let rise until light and bubbly (about 2 hours). Combine hot water, shortening and brown sugar. Cool to lukewarm; add to dough. Beat in whole wheat flour by hand. Knead on floured board; place in greased bowl, cover and let rise until double in size (about 2 hours). Divide into 2 loaves and let rest on board for 15 minutes. Shape each loaf in a greased pan, and let rise 1 to 1-1/2 hours. Bake at 325° for 45 minutes. Makes 2 loaves.

Mrs. Robert F. Flagg (Nancy White)

Onion Bread

1 package dry yeast	1 teaspoon dill seed or caraway seed
¼ cup warm water	
1 cup creamed cottage cheese	1 teaspoon salt
2 tablespoons sugar	¼ teaspoon soda
1 tablespoon dried, minced onion	1 egg
1 tablespoon butter	2¼ to 2½ cups flour

Dissolve yeast in water. Heat cottage cheese to lukewarm. Combine sugar, onion, butter, dill seed, salt, soda, egg and cottage cheese in mixing bowl. Stir in yeast. Add flour slowly, mixing with electric mixer at low speed. Cover, and let rise in warm place for about 50-60 minutes, or until double in size. Punch down dough, and shape into 1 large loaf or 2 small loaves. Put in greased bread pan, and let rise in warm place for 30-40 minutes. Bake at 350° for 40 minutes. When done, brush top with soft butter and sprinkle with salt. Makes 1 large loaf, or 2 small loaves.

Miss Janet Woods

Kneadless Oatmeal Bread

1 cup quick cooking oats	2 tablespoons butter
½ cup sorghum molasses	1 yeast cake
2 cups boiling water	¼ cup warm water
1 ½ teaspoons salt	5 cups flour

Combine oats, molasses, boiling water, salt and butter; let cool. Dissolve yeast in warm water, add to molasses mixture. Stir in flour until well blended. Cover dough with a towel and let rise in warm place until double in size (1-2 hours). Punch down dough. Divide dough into 2 equal parts and place in greased bread pans. Cover and let rise again (30-60 minutes). Bake at 400° for 30 minutes, or until bread leaves side of pan. Makes 2 loaves.

Mrs. Elbridge H. Gerry (Barbara Eisner)

Moncrief Monkey Bread

1 cup milk, scalded	1 yeast cake
1 cup mashed potatoes	½ cup lukewarm water
⅔ cup shortening	2 eggs, well beaten
1 teaspoon salt	5 to 6 cups flour
⅔ cup sugar	Melted butter

Combine milk, potatoes, shortening, salt and sugar in large bowl. Let stand until lukewarm. Dissolve yeast in water; add to potato mixture. Stir in eggs. Add 1-1/2 cups of the flour; beat well. Continue to add flour until dough is stiff. Turn out on floured board and knead thoroughly. Place in greased bowl. Brush oil over top of dough, and cover loosely. Let rise 2 hours. Put in refrigerator to chill. About 1-1/2 hours before serving time, roll out dough to about 1/2" thick. Cut into 2" diamonds. Pull diamonds at opposite ends to elongate. Dip in melted butter. Arrange layer of diamonds in 2 well-buttered, 2-quart ring molds. Arrange a second layer of diamonds on top of first layer, staggering diamonds so they are not on top of each other. Continue layering dough evenly in both ring molds, until all is used. Let rise until double in size, at least 1 hour. Bake at 400° for 20-25 minutes. Makes 2 rings.

Mrs. John H. Meyers (Alice Baker Jones)

Fluffy Spoon Bread

2 cups milk	¼ teaspoon salt
½ cup cornmeal	3 eggs, separated
2 tablespoons butter	

Place well-greased, deep, baking dish in 350° oven to heat. Bring milk to a boil. Slowly stir in cornmeal. Simmer gently for 5 minutes. (Make certain there are no lumps.) Add butter and salt. Remove from heat; let stand for 5 minutes. Stir in well-beaten egg yolks. Fold in stiffly-beaten egg whites. Turn into heated baking dish; bake at 350° for about 25 minutes, or until set and golden brown. Serves 4-6.

Mrs. Dean Emerson, Jr. (Martha Vinson)

Country Corn Bread

1 cup yellow cornmeal	1 cup buttermilk
½ cup flour	½ cup sweet milk
1 teaspoon salt	1 egg
½ teaspoon soda	½ cup cooking oil
1 tablespoon baking powder	

Preheat oven to 450°. Grease 8'' x 8'' pan and place in oven to heat until piping hot. Combine cornmeal, flour, salt, soda and baking powder; mix thoroughly. Add buttermilk, sweet milk, egg and oil to dry ingredients, and stir well. Pour corn bread batter into hot pan and bake at 450° about 20 minutes, or until golden brown. (Omit cooking oil if making corn bread for stuffing.) Makes 16 two-inch squares.

Mrs. Clarence A. Thomas (Gene Hunt)

Snappy Corn Bread

1 can (4 oz.) jalapeno peppers	1½ cups grated Cheddar cheese
3 cups yellow corn bread mix	1 large onion, grated
(Pioneer brand preferred)	2 cups milk
¼ cup corn oil	3 eggs
2 cups creamed corn	

Drain and chop jalapeno peppers. Mix all ingredients together to make thin batter. Pour into well-greased, 9'' x 13'', baking pan. Bake at 425° for 30-45 minutes. Serves 12.

Mrs. George A. Hill, III (Gloria Lester)

Mexican Corn Bread

2 eggs
⅔ cup cooking oil
1 cup sour cream
1 cup yellow cornmeal
1 cup yellow creamed corn

1 tablespoon baking powder
1½ teaspoons salt
4 jalapeno peppers, seeded
  and finely chopped
1 cup grated sharp cheese

Combine eggs, oil, sour cream, cornmeal, corn, baking powder and salt. Add chopped peppers and half of the cheese. Spread in well-greased baking pan (12" x 8" x 2") and cover with remaining cheese. Bake in 425° oven for 20-25 minutes. Serves 8-10.

Mrs. Henry Oliver (Catherine Bowman)

Jalapeño Corn Sticks

½ cup flour
1 tablespoon baking powder
½ teaspoon salt
1½ cups yellow cornmeal
2 eggs

1 cup sour cream
1 cup grated cheese
1 can (8 oz.) creamed corn
½ cup seeded and chopped
  jalapeno peppers
½ cup shortening

Sift flour, baking powder and salt together. Add remaining ingredients and mix well. Bake in greased corn bread stick pans, at 450° for 15-20 minutes. Makes about 24 corn sticks (or muffins).

Mrs. Mavis P. Kelsey (Mary Wilson)

Mock Monkey Bread

2 cans (12 rolls each) Pillsbury butterflake rolls
¾ cup butter, melted

Separate rolls into thin sections; dip each section in melted butter. Stand sections upright, side-by-side, in buttered, 1-1/2 quart ring mold. Continue dipping and stacking sections until pan is filled. Pour any remaining butter over rolls. For variety, grated onion, powdered herbs, poppy seeds, or garlic powder may be added to the butter. Bake at 375° for about 12 minutes, or until brown. Invert onto serving plate. Serves 8.

Mrs. James R. Kennicott (Julie Dossett)

Herbed Bread

1 loaf French bread
½ cup butter, softened
1 teaspoon parsley flakes
¼ teaspoon oregano

¼ teaspoon dill seed
1 clove garlic, crushed
Parmesan cheese
Additional parsley flakes

Cut bread in half, lengthwise. Cut each half into 4 pieces. Blend butter, parsley, oregano, dill seed and garlic. Spread on bread. Sprinkle liberally with cheese and additional parsley flakes. Place in 375° oven, until hot. Serves 8.

Mrs. Charles B. Williams (Bobbie Ruth Richardson)

Cheese Stuffed Rolls

1 cup ripe olives, chopped
4 slices crisp bacon, crumbled
1 cup grated cheese
1 green onion, chopped

¼ cup mayonnaise
Dash Worcestershire sauce
12 brown-and-serve
    butterflake rolls

Combine all ingredients, except rolls. Pull rolls apart slightly and stuff generously with mixture. Bake in muffin tins, in 375° oven, for 15-20 minutes.

Mrs. James L. Whitcomb (Mary Hill Brown)

CANDIES

COOKIES

Hints

COOKIES

Always preheat oven before baking cookies.

Cookie sheets should never touch walls of oven while cookies are baking.

WHEN ROLLING AND CUTTING COOKIES, flour all utensils before each use.

TO INSURE UNIFORM BAKING, make all cookies the same size.

TO COOL COOKIES, place on wire racks or on sheets of brown paper. Never stack warm cookies.

CANDY

Always cook candy in a very large pot.

A candy thermometer is a real aid in making candy. When using one, the bulb must be completely covered with boiling candy yet must not rest on bottom of pot. Watch candy carefully, especially during last few minutes of cooking, for temperature rises quickly.

TO PREVENT CANDY FROM BOILING OVER, butter the inside top rim of pot.

TO HASTEN COOLING OF CANDY, immerse pot in 2 or 3 inches of cool water.

TO INSURE SMOOTHNESS OF CANDY, allow candy to cool to lukewarm before beating.

IF CANDY WILL NOT HARDEN, add a tablespoon of corn syrup and cook a little longer. Cool to lukewarm, and beat again.

Sugar Cookies

1 cup butter	2 cups flour
1 cup sugar	½ teaspoon soda
1 egg	½ teaspoon cream of tartar
2 teaspoons vanilla	

Cream butter and sugar. Add egg and vanilla. Sift together flour, soda and cream of tartar; blend into butter mixture. Form into small balls and place (far apart) on ungreased cookie sheets. Dip bottom of a drinking glass in sugar and use it to flatten dough into thin, round cookies. Dip glass in sugar before flattening each cookie. Bake at 375° for 10-12 minutes. Remove from cookie sheets while hot and allow cookies to cool on brown paper. Makes about 5-1/2 dozen cookies.

Mrs. William Buck Arnold (Lucy Gray)

Old-Fashioned Drop Sugar Cookies

½ cup butter	½ teaspoon vanilla
1 cup sugar	½ teaspoon salt
1 egg	2 teaspoons baking powder
2 tablespoons cream	1⅓ cups flour

Cream butter; beat in sugar, egg, cream and vanilla. Sift salt, baking powder and flour together; add to creamed mixture. Mix well and chill dough. Drop from tip of spoon onto ungreased cookie sheets. Bake at 375° for 8-10 minutes or until golden brown. Makes 50-60 cookies.

Mrs. John H. Meyers (Alice Baker Jones)

Cut-out Sugar Cookies

½ cup butter	2 cups sifted flour
¾ cup sugar	½ teaspoon soda
¾ teaspoon vanilla	Pinch salt
1 egg	

Cream butter and sugar. Add vanilla and egg. Sift flour, soda and salt together; mix into butter mixture. (Dough will be stiff.) Working with a small amount of dough at a time, roll out very thin between sheets of floured wax paper. Cut into desired shapes and place on greased cookie sheets. Sprinkle with sugar and bake in 375° oven for 10-12 minutes. Makes approximately 6 dozen cookies.

Mrs. George V. Kane, Jr. (Alafair Benbow)

Grandma's Pecan Cakes

1 cup butter	Grated rind of 1 orange
1 cup plus 2 tablespoons sugar	4 cups flour
4 eggs, separated	4 teaspoons baking powder
½ teaspoon cinnamon	1¼ cups powdered sugar
	3 cups pecans, chopped

Cream butter and sugar; add egg yolks, cinnamon and orange rind. Blend in flour and baking powder. On lightly-floured surface, roll out dough 1/4" thick. Cut out with a 2-inch round cookie cutter. Place on lightly-greased cookie sheet; set aside. To make meringue topping beat egg whites until stiff; add powdered sugar and pecans. Put about 1/2 teaspoon topping on each cookie and bake at 325° about 10 minutes, until light brown. Makes 6 dozen cookies.

Mrs. William James Wooten (Lou Ellen Bryan)

Cream Cheese Cookies

½ cup butter, softened	1 cup flour
1 small package (3 oz.) cream	1 cup sugar
cheese, softened	½ cup chopped walnuts or pecans

Blend butter with cream cheese. Mix in flour and sugar. Add nuts. Drop from teaspoon onto ungreased cookie sheets. Bake in 350° oven for 10-12 minutes. Makes 4 dozen small chewy cookies.

Mrs. George A. Hill, III (Gloria Lester)

Pressed Sour Cream Cookies

2 cups flour	1 cup sugar
½ teaspoon baking powder	1 egg, beaten
¼ teaspoon soda	½ teaspoon lemon extract
¼ teaspoon nutmeg	⅓ cup sour cream
½ cup margarine	

Sift together flour, baking powder, soda and nutmeg; set aside. Cream margarine and sugar. Add egg, lemon extract and sour cream. Gradually blend in sifted dry ingredients. Press from cookie press (or drop from teaspoon) onto ungreased cookie sheets. Bake at 375° for 10-15 minutes, or until brown around edges. Makes about 4 dozen cookies.

Mrs. Sydney G. McGlasson (Ellen Archer)

Mame's Meringues

2 egg whites
½ cup sugar

1 cup chopped pecans
1 teaspoon vanilla

Beat egg whites until stiff. Add 2/3 of the sugar. Beat until smooth. Fold in pecans, vanilla and remaining sugar; mix well. Drop on very well-greased cookie sheet. Bake in 300° oven for 45-50 minutes, until slightly crisp. Makes about 30 cookies.

Mrs. Ben A. Calhoun (Katharine Seymour)

Forget Me Cookies

2 egg whites
¾ cup sugar
½ teaspoon vanilla

1 small package (6 oz.) semi-
sweet chocolate chips
1 cup pecans, chopped

Preheat oven to 350°. Beat egg whites until stiff. Add sugar gradually. Beat at high speed for about 5 minutes. Fold in vanilla, chocolate chips and pecans. Drop from teaspoon onto foil-lined cookie sheets. Put in oven and turn off heat. Leave overnight (or at least 8 hours). Makes about 3 dozen meringue-like cookies.

Mrs. George N. Allen, Jr. (Bonnie Blades)

Cooper's Chewy Cookies

1 cup soft bread crumbs
1 cup finely chopped pecans
1 cup sugar

2 eggs
¼ teaspoon salt
2 tablespoons salad oil
1 teaspoon lemon extract

(To make bread crumbs, put fresh or day-old bread through fine blade of grinder, or chop in blender.) Combine all ingredients and mix thoroughly. Drop from teaspoon onto **very** well-greased cookie sheets. Bake at 350° for about 15 minutes. Remove from cookie sheets as quickly as possible and let cool on wire racks. (If cookies "harden" onto cookie sheet before you can remove them all, hold cookie sheet over low heat until cookies become pliable.) Makes approximately 5 dozen cookies.

Mrs. John H. Lindsey (Sara Houstoun)

Sesame Seed Cookies

1½ cups sugar
3 eggs, separated
1 teaspoon salt
1½ teaspoons vanilla

1½ cups shortening
3 cups flour
Sesame seeds

Combine sugar and egg yolks; mix thoroughly. Add salt, vanilla and shortening. Beat a few minutes. Add flour and mix well. Pinch off small bits of dough and roll into balls. Dip in unbeaten egg whites, then in sesame seeds. Bake at 300° for 15-20 minutes, or until light brown. Makes about 6 dozen cookies.

Mrs. James A. Reichert (Betsy Calhoun)

Pecan Puffs

½ cup butter, softened
2 tablespoons sugar
1 cup flour

1 cup pecans, finely chopped
1 teaspoon vanilla
Pinch salt
Powdered sugar

Blend all ingredients together, except powdered sugar. Roll into small balls and place on ungreased cookie sheets. Bake 20-25 minutes in 350° oven. Roll in powdered sugar while hot. Makes about 2 dozen cookies.

Mrs. William C. Braden, Jr. (Dorothy J. Reed)

Sand Tarts

1 cup butter
⅓ cup sugar
2½ teaspoons vanilla
2 teaspoons water

2 cups flour
1 cup chopped pecans
Sifted powdered sugar

Cream butter and sugar; mix in vanilla and water. Add flour and pecans; blend well. Chill until firm (1-2 hours). Shape into crescents and place on ungreased cookie sheet. Bake at 325° about 20 minutes, or until edges are pale brown. Cool slightly, but roll in powdered sugar while still warm. Makes 4-5 dozen cookies.

Mrs. John L. Hamilton (Ann Lowdon)

Jelly-Filled Sand Tarts

1 cup butter, softened
1 cup ground pecans
2 cups flour

3 tablespoons powdered sugar
Tart jelly
Pecan halves

Combine butter, pecans, flour and powdered sugar; mix well. Mold into small cookies. Make small depression in each cookie and fill with tart jelly; place a pecan half on jelly. Bake on ungreased cookie sheet at 350° for 20-25 minutes. Makes about 5 dozen cookies.

Mrs. Otis Meredith (Mary Wilkins)

Four O'Clock Cookies

1 cup butter
2 cups sifted cake flour
¼ cup powdered sugar

2 teaspoons vanilla
1 teaspoon cold water
1 cup pecans, finely chopped
Additional powdered sugar

Cream butter; combine with flour, powdered sugar, vanilla and water. Blend thoroughly. Add pecans. Form dough into long roll about 1-1/2" in diameter; wrap in wax paper and refrigerate. When ready to bake, slice about 1/8" thick and bake in 400° oven for about 8 minutes. Do not let the cookies get brown. Remove from oven and sift additional powdered sugar over cookies. Makes about 4 dozen cookies.

Mrs. Lorenzo B. Taylor (Marilyn Dubach)

Dainty Lemon Bars

1 cup flour
½ cup butter, softened
¼ cup powdered sugar
2 eggs, beaten

1 cup sugar
2 tablespoons lemon juice
1 teaspoon lemon rind

Combine flour, butter and powdered sugar; mix thoroughly. Spread in a 9-inch square pan. Bake at 350° for 15 minutes. Meanwhile, mix together eggs, sugar, lemon juice and lemon rind; spread over first layer in pan. Return to oven for 25 minutes. When cool, frost with Lemon Glaze. Cut into 1" x 1-1/2" bars. Makes 3 dozen bars.

LEMON GLAZE

½ cup powdered sugar
1 teaspoon lemon juice
1 teaspoon water

Mix powdered sugar, lemon juice and water together and spread thinly over Dainty Lemon Bars.

Mrs. James Howard Park, III (Bette Naylor)

Dream Bars

½ cup butter, softened
1½ cups brown sugar
1 cup flour
2 eggs
1 teaspoon vanilla

½ teaspoon baking powder
½ teaspoon salt
1½ cups shredded coconut
1 cup chopped nuts

Cream butter and 1/2 cup of the brown sugar; add flour and mix well. Spread in 9" x 13" pan. Bake at 350° for 10 minutes. Mix together remaining cup of brown sugar, eggs, vanilla, baking powder and salt. Stir in coconut and nuts. Spread over baked layer in pan. Bake 20 additional minutes at 350°. Cut into bars about 1" x 2-1/2". Makes 42 bars.

Mrs. Clifford G. Campbell (Lynne Tyrrell)

Hello Dolly Cookies

6 tablespoons margarine
1 cup crushed vanilla wafers
1 package (6 oz.) semi-sweet
    chocolate chips

1 can (4 oz.) Angel Flake coconut
1 cup chopped pecans
1 can (15 oz.) Eagle Brand
    sweetened condensed milk

Melt margarine in 9" x 13" Pyrex pan. Add vanilla wafer crumbs and press into very thin layer. Over crumbs, sprinkle chocolate chips, then coconut, then pecans. Drizzle sweetened condensed milk over all. Bake at 325° for approximately 30 minutes. Cool for several hours before cutting into small (1" x 2") bars. Makes 54 cookies.

Mrs. William A. Bramley (Kay Borden)

Lunch Box Cookies

½ cup shortening, melted
½ cup butter, melted
1 cup white sugar
1 cup brown sugar
2 eggs
2 cups sifted flour
1 teaspoon baking powder

2 teaspoons soda
¼ teaspoon salt
2 teaspoons vanilla
4 cups puffed corn flakes
1 package (12 oz.) semi-sweet
    chocolate chips
1 cup shredded coconut
1 cup chopped pecans

Combine ingredients in order listed; mix well. Drop from teaspoon onto greased cookie sheets. Bake at 350° for 8-10 minutes. Makes about 8 dozen cookies.

Mrs. Sydney G. McGlasson (Ellen Archer)

Francis' Corn Flake Cookies

3 egg whites	1 cup shredded coconut
1 cup sugar	1 cup chopped pecans
1 teaspoon vanilla	2 cups corn flakes

Beat egg whites until stiff; fold in sugar and vanilla. Gently stir in coconut, pecans and corn flakes. Drop on well-greased cookie sheets. Bake in 325° oven for 25-30 minutes. Makes approximately 5 dozen cookies.

Mrs. Harold E. Daniels (Gayle Garth)

Gingerbread Boys

½ cup shortening	¼ teaspoon salt
⅔ cup sugar	1 teaspoon ginger
⅔ cup molasses	1 teaspoon cinnamon
1 egg	½ teaspoon ground cloves
3½ cups flour	Currants or raisins (optional)
1 teaspoon soda	

Cream shortening and sugar; blend in molasses and egg. Combine flour, soda, salt, ginger, cinnamon and cloves; sift into molasses mixture. Mix dough until smooth. (Dough will be stiff.) Chill dough before rolling. Roll out dough 1/8" to 1/4" thick on lightly floured board. Cut with floured gingerbread boy cutter. Carefully place cut-out boys on lightly greased baking sheet. If desired, press currants or raisins into dough to make face and buttons. Bake at 350° for about 10 minutes. Cool on wire rack. Makes 30 small boys.

Mrs. John H. Lindsey (Sara Houstoun)

Glendorn Ginger Snaps

¾ cup shortening	2 teaspoons soda
1 cup sugar	½ teaspoon salt
¼ cup molasses	1 teaspoon cinnamon
1 egg	1 teaspoon ground cloves
2 cups flour	1 teaspoon ginger

Cream shortening and sugar together. Add molasses, then egg. Sift together flour, soda, salt, cinnamon, cloves and ginger. Add to sugar mixture and blend well. Chill. Form dough into small balls and roll in additional sugar. Place on cookie sheets about 1" apart. Flatten balls of dough with a glass tumbler. Bake at 350° to 375° for 15 minutes, or until crisp. Remove cookies to wire racks and let cool. Makes about 5 dozen cookies.

Mrs. David F. Dorn (Julie Leary)

Oatmeal Spice Cookies

¾ cup butter
2 cups sugar
2 eggs, beaten
2 cups flour
2 cups oats
1 cup chopped pecans

1½ cups raisins
1 teaspoon vanilla
1 tablespoon cinnamon
1 tablespoon ground cloves
1 tablespoon nutmeg
2 tablespoons water
½ teaspoon soda

Cream butter and sugar; add eggs and mix well. Then add in the following order, mixing thoroughly after each addition: flour, oats, pecans, raisins, vanilla, cinnamon, cloves and nutmeg. Combine water and soda; mix into dough. Drop from a spoon onto greased cookie sheets and bake in 350° oven for 15-20 minutes, or until brown. Makes 8-10 dozen cookies.

Mrs. James P. Jackson (Sarah Faulkner)

Oatmeal Lace Cookies

½ cup margarine
½ cup butter
1 cup white sugar
1 cup brown sugar
2 eggs

2½ cups quick-cooking oats
1 teaspoon baking powder
1 teaspoon vanilla
1 cup finely chopped pecans

Cream margarine and butter. Add white sugar and brown sugar; cream well. Mix in eggs, oats and baking powder. Then add vanilla and pecans. Line cookie sheets with wax paper. Drop dough from a teaspoon onto wax paper allowing at least 4" between cookies, as they spread. Bake at 350° for about 8 minutes. Remove cookie sheet from oven. Allow cookies to cool slightly before removing from wax paper to wire rack. (If cookies are removed while too warm they will lose their shape; if allowed to cool too much, cookies will stick to wax paper.) Store in an air-tight container. Makes 5 dozen cookies.

Mrs. James E. McAshan (Elizabeth Sanford)

Oatmeal Icebox Cookies

1 cup shortening
1 cup brown sugar
1 cup white sugar
2 eggs, well beaten
1 teaspoon vanilla

1½ cups flour
1 teaspoon salt
1 teaspoon soda
3 cups quick-cooking oats
½ cup chopped pecans

Cream shortening, brown sugar and white sugar. Add eggs and vanilla; beat well. Sift flour, salt and soda together; add to creamed mixture and blend well. Stir in oats and pecans. Shape into rolls and wrap in wax paper. Chill several hours or overnight. Slice 1/4" thick. Bake on ungreased cookie sheets in 350° oven for 10 minutes. Makes 5 dozen cookies.

Mrs. Clarence A. Thomas (Gene Hunt)

Vanilla Icebox Cookies

½ cup butter
1 cup sugar
1 egg, beaten
1 teaspoon vanilla

1½ cups sifted flour
¼ teaspoon salt
1½ teaspoons baking powder
½ cup (or more) chopped nuts

Cream butter and sugar; beat in egg and vanilla. Resift flour with salt and baking powder; add gradually to butter mixture. Add nuts, mix well. Form into two rolls; wrap in wax paper and refrigerate until firm. Cut into 1/8" slices; place on lightly-greased cookie sheets. Bake at 400° for 8-10 minutes, or until cookies are light brown around the edges. Makes approximately 70 small cookies.

Mrs. Will H. Thanheiser (Mary Ellen Ford)

Chocolate Mint Icebox Cookies

1 package (20 oz.) devil's food
  cake mix
1 egg
3 tablespoons water

1 package (6 oz.) semi-sweet
  chocolate chips
½ cup chopped pecans
1 teaspoon peppermint extract

Mix all ingredients together. Form into two rolls and chill for several hours. Slice chilled cookie dough 1/4" thick and place on greased cookie sheets. Bake at 350° for about 12 minutes. Makes approximately 6 dozen cookies.

Mrs. John H. Lindsey (Sara Houstoun)

Starlight Mint Surprise Cookies

1 cup butter
1 cup white sugar
½ cup firmly packed brown sugar
2 eggs
1 tablespoon water

1 teaspoon vanilla
3 cups sifted flour
Rockwood Chocolate Mint
   Candy Wafers (about 5 dozen)
Pecan or walnut halves

Cream butter; gradually add white sugar and brown sugar, beating until thoroughly blended. Add eggs, water and vanilla. Add flour and mix well. If dough is too soft to handle, chill in refrigerator until it becomes workable. Wrap a chocolate mint wafer in about 1 tablespoon of dough. (Completely cover wafer.) Place on ungreased baking sheet, 2 inches apart. Top with pecan or walnut half. Bake in 375° oven for 10-12 minutes. Makes about 5 dozen cookies.

Mrs. James Howard Park, III (Bette Naylor)

Chocolate Cookies with Chocolate Icing

½ cup butter, softened
1 cup brown sugar
1 egg
1½ cups flour
Scant ½ teaspoon soda

½ cup milk
2 ounces unsweetened
   chocolate, melted
½ cup chopped nuts

Cream butter and brown sugar. Mix in egg. Sift flour with soda and add to creamed mixture alternately with milk. Stir in chocolate and nuts. Drop from teaspoon onto lightly-greased cookie sheets. Bake in 375° oven for 8-10 minutes. Spread cooled cookies with chocolate icing. Makes about 5 dozen cookies.

CHOCOLATE ICING

1 egg, well beaten
2 ounces unsweetened
   chocolate, melted

2 rounded cups powdered
   sugar
3 tablespoons cream

Combine egg, chocolate and sugar; add cream until icing is of desired consistency. Spread on cooled cookies.

Mrs. Joseph T. Painter (Ann Hill)

Chuck's Chocolate Cookies

¼ cup butter	1 cup flour
2½ ounces semi-sweet chocolate	2 teaspoons baking powder
	1 teaspoon vanilla
1 cup sugar	1 cup broken pecans
2 eggs	Powdered sugar

Melt butter and chocolate in top of double boiler over hot water. Combine sugar and eggs. Sift flour and baking powder together; add to egg mixture. Stir in chocolate mixture, vanilla and pecans. Blend well. Refrigerate for 1 hour. Pinch off small amounts of dough; form into 1" balls and roll in powdered sugar. Place on lightly-greased cookie sheets, allowing space for cookies to spread. Bake at 350° for 10 minutes. Makes 6-8 dozen cookies.

Mrs. Herbert E. Smith, Jr. (Barbara Hartung)

Chocolate Brownies

2 ounces unsweetened chocolate	Dash salt
½ cup butter	1 teaspoon vanilla
2 eggs	½ cup (or more) chopped pecans
1 cup sugar	2 tablespoons molasses
½ cup flour	(optional)

Melt chocolate and butter in double boiler; cool slightly. Beat eggs and add sugar gradually. Add cooled chocolate mixture. Sift flour and salt together; stir in. Add vanilla and pecans; mix well. (If a very chewy brownie is desired, stir in molasses.) Pour into well-greased, 9-inch square pan. Bake at 375° for about 20 minutes. Cut into 1-1/2" squares and remove from pan while hot. Makes 36 brownies.

Mrs. William Buck Arnold (Lucy Gray)

Muy's Marvelous Brownies

⅔ cup butter	¼ teaspoon salt
2 cups sugar	2 ounces unsweetened chocolate, melted
3 eggs	
1 cup flour	1 teaspoon vanilla
	1 cup chopped pecans

Cream butter and sugar. Beat in eggs just until blended. Sift flour and salt; stir gradually into egg mixture. Blend in melted chocolate and vanilla; add pecans. Spread in well-greased 9" x 12" pan and bake at 350° for about 25 minutes. Cut into 1-1/2" squares when cool. Makes 48 brownies.

Mrs. John L. Hamilton (Ann Lowdon)

Congo Squares

⅔ cup shortening	2½ teaspoons baking powder
1 box (1 lb.) brown sugar	½ teaspoon salt
3 eggs	1 cup chopped nuts
1 teaspoon vanilla	1 package (6 oz.) semi-sweet
2¾ cups flour	chocolate chips

Cream shortening and brown sugar. Add eggs, one at a time, beating after each addition. Add vanilla. Sift together flour, baking powder and salt; add to creamed mixture. Stir in nuts and chocolate chips. Bake in greased, 9" x 13" pan at 350° for 40 minutes. Makes 4 dozen 1-1/2" squares.

Mrs. Dean Emerson, Jr. (Martha Vinson)

Marbled Brownies

1 package (4 oz.) German's	½ cup plus 1 tablespoon flour
sweet chocolate	1½ teaspoons vanilla
5 tablespoons butter	½ teaspoon baking powder
1 small package (3 oz.)	¼ teaspoon salt
cream cheese	½ cup coarsely chopped nuts
1 cup sugar	¼ teaspoon almond extract
3 eggs	

Melt chocolate and 3 tablespoons of the butter in a small saucepan over very low heat, stirring constantly. Let cool. Cream remaining 2 tablespoons butter with cream cheese. Gradually add 1/4 cup of the sugar, creaming until light and fluffy. Blend in 1 egg, 1 tablespoon of the flour and 1/4 teaspoon of the vanilla. Set aside. In a large bowl, beat remaining 2 eggs until thick and light in color. Gradually add remaining 3/4 cup sugar, beating until thickened. Add baking powder, salt and remaining 1/2 cup flour. Blend in cooled chocolate mixture, remaining 1 teaspoon vanilla, nuts and almond extract. Spread about half of the chocolate batter in a greased, 9-inch, square pan. Then spread cream cheese batter evenly over the chocolate layer. Spoon remaining chocolate batter gently over cream cheese layer. Zigzag a spatula through batter one time in each direction to marble. Bake at 350° for 30 minutes, or until top springs back when lightly pressed in center. Let cool and cut into squares. Makes about 20 brownies.

Mrs. Claude C. Cody, III (Muriel Fursteneau)

Bob Jones' Butterscotch Brownies

¼ cup butter	½ teaspoon baking powder
1 cup dark brown sugar	½ teaspoon salt
1 egg	1 cup chopped pecans
1 teaspoon vanilla	½ cup butterscotch chips
½ cup flour	1 tablespoon milk

Melt butter in saucepan. Stir in brown sugar; let cool. Beat in egg and vanilla. Sift together flour, baking powder and salt; add to brown sugar mixture. Add pecans and mix well. Pour batter into greased 8-inch square pan.
Bake at 350° for 30 minutes. Frost with butterscotch frosting. To make
frosting, melt butterscotch chips in milk over hot water. Drizzle icing over
brownies while they are still warm and in the pan. Let cool and cut into 1"
x 2" bars. Makes 32 brownies.

Mrs. Frank Lawson (Virginia Cronin)

Deleese Cookies

4 eggs, beaten	1 cup chopped pecans
1 box (1 lb.) light brown sugar	2 cups Bisquick

Mix all ingredients together. Bake in greased pan (9" x 13") at 300° for
1 hour. Cut into squares or bars. Makes about 4 dozen cookies.

Mrs. Ralph Ellis Gunn (Esme Patterson)

Persimmon Cookies

1 cup persimmon pulp (3 or 4 ripe persimmons)	½ teaspoon cinnamon
½ cup shortening	½ teaspoon ground cloves
1½ cups sugar	½ teaspoon nutmeg
2 cups sifted flour	1 cup chopped nuts
Pinch salt	1 cup raisins
½ teaspoon soda	1 egg, beaten
	1 teaspoon vanilla

Put persimmons through a food mill or strainer and measure 1 cup pulp.
Set aside. Cream shortening and sugar. Combine flour, salt, soda, cinnamon, cloves and nutmeg; mix with nuts and raisins. Add to creamed mixture. Stir in persimmon pulp, egg and vanilla. Drop from teaspoon onto
greased cookie sheets. Bake at 375° for 13-15 minutes. Makes about 5
dozen cookies.

Mrs. Edward A. Blackburn, Jr. (Sadie Gwin Allen)

COOKIES

Pecan Bars

1 cup butter	3 tablespoons cinnamon
1 cup sugar	1 cup flour
1 egg, separated	1 cup finely chopped nuts

Cream butter and sugar. Beat egg yolk and add. Mix in cinnamon and flour. Spread on lightly-buttered, 10" x 15", baking pan with 1/2" sides. Batter should cover pan. Brush slightly-beaten egg white over top of batter. Sprinkle with chopped nuts and pat lightly. Bake in 325° oven for 30 minutes. While still warm, cut into bars, about 1" x 2-1/2", but do not remove from pan until cool. Makes 4 dozen bars.

Mrs. F. Fox Benton (Ann Temple)

Date Nut Bars

2 eggs, separated	½ cup water
1 cup sugar	1 pound dates, pitted and
1 cup flour	chopped
2 teaspoons baking powder	¾ cup raisins
Pinch salt	1 cup chopped pecans

Beat egg yolks and add sugar. Sift flour with baking powder and salt; add to sugar mixture alternately with water. Fold in stiffly-beaten egg whites, dates, raisins and pecans. Spread in greased, 8-inch square pan. Bake at 350° for 25-30 minutes, or until done. Cut into 1" x 2" bars while warm and roll in powdered sugar. Makes 32 bars.

Mrs. Elbridge H. Gerry (Barbara Eisner)

Rum or Bourbon Balls

2¼ cups vanilla wafer crumbs	1 cup powdered sugar
1 cup pecans, finely chopped	3 tablespoons cocoa
½ cup rum or bourbon	2 tablespoons white corn syrup
	Additional powdered sugar

Combine vanilla wafer crumbs and pecans. In another bowl combine rum or bourbon, powdered sugar, cocoa and corn syrup; beat well. Add to crumb mixture and blend thoroughly. Form into 1" balls and roll in additional powdered sugar. Pack in tins lined with wax paper. Makes about 4 dozen rum balls.

Mrs. C. Cage Mooney (Catherine Cage)

Christmas Lizzies

¼ cup butter
1 cup brown sugar, packed
2 eggs
½ pound candied cherries,
    chopped
½ pound candied pineapple,
    cut into small pieces
½ pound white raisins

1 pound pecans, chopped
1½ cups flour
¼ teaspoon ground cloves
½ teaspoon nutmeg
½ teaspoon cinnamon
2 tablespoons buttermilk
1½ teaspoons soda
⅓ cup bourbon (or orange juice)

Cream butter and brown sugar. Add eggs, one at a time, mixing well after each addition. Combine cherries, pineapple, raisins and pecans. Sift flour, cloves, nutmeg and cinnamon over fruit and mix well. Combine buttermilk and soda; add alternately with bourbon to the floured fruit. Stir in creamed mixture. Line cookie sheets with wax paper. Drop dough from teaspoon onto wax paper and bake at 300° for 20-25 minutes. Remove from paper and let cool on wire racks. Pack in cookie tins and sprinkle with additional bourbon. This is a favorite Christmas cookie—simple enough for the children to help, but well-liked by adults (even non-fruitcake lovers). Makes 8-9 dozen cookies.

Mrs. John L. Hamilton (Ann Lowdon)

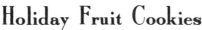

Holiday Fruit Cookies

1 cup pecans, chopped
1 cup candied cherries,
    coarsely chopped
1 cup pitted dates,
    coarsely chopped
¼ cup flour
½ cup shortening

1 cup brown sugar
1 egg
1½ cups flour
½ teaspoon salt
½ teaspoon soda
¼ cup sour milk

Combine pecans, cherries, dates and 1/4 cup flour; mix lightly and set aside. Cream shortening and brown sugar; add egg and mix well. Sift together 1-1/2 cups flour, salt and soda; add to creamed mixture alternately with sour milk; blend well. Stir in fruit-nut mixture. Drop from teaspoon onto greased cookie sheets. Bake at 375° for 10-12 minutes. Makes 3-4 dozen cookies.

Mrs. Jack T. Currie (Dorothy Peek)

Frosted Fruit Bars

½ cup butter, softened
1 cup sugar
1 egg
1 tablespoon grated orange
rind
½ cup fresh orange juice
2½ cups sifted flour
1 teaspoon soda
½ teaspoon salt

½ teaspoon cinnamon
½ teaspoon nutmeg
1 cup raisins
1 cup chopped mixed candied
fruit
½ cup chopped nuts
Powdered sugar for icing
Additional candied fruit for
decoration

Cream butter and sugar; mix in egg and orange rind. Stir in orange juice. Sift together flour, soda, salt, cinnamon and nutmeg; stir into creamed mixture. Mix in raisins, candied fruit and nuts with hands. Divide dough in half. Roll each half on lightly-floured board (or between sheets of wax paper) into a 7'' x 12'' rectangle. Bake on lightly-greased baking sheet at 400° for 10-12 minutes. While still warm, spread with powdered sugar icing. (Make icing by adding small amount of water to powdered sugar; do not cook.) Decorate with additional candied fruit. Cut into bars, about 1-1/2'' x 2''. Makes about 5 dozen bars.

Mrs. Gordon R. West (Josephine Morrow)

Almond Toffee

1 pound butter
2 cups sugar
6 tablespoons water
2 tablespoons white corn syrup
Pinch salt

1 teaspoon vanilla
2 packages (4 oz. each) German's
sweet chocolate
1 cup almonds, coarsely
ground

Combine butter, sugar, water, corn syrup, salt and vanilla in large heavy pot. Cook, stirring constantly, until candy thermometer registers 290°. Pour onto 2 large buttered baking sheets with 1/2'' sides. Let cool. Melt chocolate over hot, not boiling, water and spread over cool, hardened candy. Sprinkle immediately with ground almonds. (Sometimes, to harden chocolate, candy must be placed in refrigerator for a little while.) When topping has hardened, break candy into pieces. Makes about 2 pounds toffee.

Mrs. Robert E. Clemons (Grayson Cecil)

Chocolate Treasures

1 package (8 oz.) semi-sweet
   chocolate squares
1 tablespoon butter
2 eggs
1 cup powdered sugar

12 large marshmallows, cut
   into small pieces
1 cup chopped pecans
1 teaspoon vanilla

Melt chocolate in double boiler over hot, not boiling, water. Add butter, stir, remove from heat and set aside. Beat eggs, add sugar and beat well. Stir chocolate mixture into egg mixture. Add marshmallows, pecans and vanilla; mix well. Drop candy by small teaspoonfuls onto wax paper. Let harden before eating or storing. Makes 3-4 dozen candies.

Mrs. John L. Hamilton (Ann Lowdon)

Mrs. Cottingham's Caramels

2 cups sugar
2 cups cream
1¾ cups white corn syrup

½ cup butter (do not substitute)
1 tablespoon vanilla
1 pound broken pecan pieces

Put sugar, 1 cup of the cream, corn syrup and butter in large saucepan. Bring to a boil and, stirring constantly, let mixture boil for exactly 10 minutes. Then slowly stir in remaining cup cream, being careful not to let boiling cease. Continue boiling until, when tested in cold water, mixture forms a firm (not hard) ball. Remove from heat. Stir in vanilla and pecans. Pour into buttered pan. When cool, remove from pan onto cutting board and cut with scissors into bite-sized pieces. Wrap each candy, individually, in wax paper. These caramels, made from this old and treasured family recipe, will keep for a month in closed tins; no need to refrigerate. Makes 90-100 caramels.

Mrs. J. C. LaRoche (Katherine Cottingham)

Patience

4 cups sugar
1 cup milk
⅓ cup white corn syrup

½ cup margarine
1 teaspoon vanilla
2 cups broken pecans

Slowly heat one cup of the sugar in heavy skillet, stirring constantly until sugar is melted and browned (caramelized). In a large saucepan, combine remaining 3 cups sugar, milk and corn syrup; bring to a boil. Stir in caramelized sugar and cook over low heat to soft ball stage (238° on candy thermometer). Remove from heat and stir in margarine. Let cool. Add vanilla and pecans; beat until creamy and thick. Pour into greased 11" x 15" pan. When completely cool, cut into squares.

Mrs. George M. O'Leary (Joan Davis)

Friendship Divinity

Dry weather
3 cups sugar
¾ cup white corn syrup
1 cup water

3 egg whites, stiffly beaten
1 teaspoon vanilla
1 cup chopped pecans

Boil sugar, corn syrup and water until it forms a firm ball when tested in cold water. Gradually pour syrup into stiffly beaten egg whites, beating vigorously as you pour. Beat until mixture loses its gloss. Add vanilla and pecans. Spread candy in buttered pan, or drop from teaspoon onto buttered wax paper. If drop candies are made, omit chopped pecans and place a pecan half on top of each piece of candy. If candy is too soft to hold its shape, put back into mixing bowl, place over hot water, and heat "until you can write your name on top of candy with spoon-drippings." If candy hardens in pan before all candy can be dropped, add a small amount of water and stir vigorously. Do not double recipe. Makes about 2 pounds candy.

Mrs. Dick H. Gregg (Katharine Red Parker)

Mother's
Creamy New Orleans Pralines

1 cup white sugar
2 cups dark brown sugar
1 cup whipping cream
2 cups pecans

¼ cup butter
1 tablespoon vanilla
Pinch salt

Combine white sugar, brown sugar and cream in large saucepan. Cook slowly, stirring constantly, for at least 15 minutes, until a soft ball forms in a cup of cold water. Add pecans and cook a little longer, stirring constantly. Remove from heat. Add butter, vanilla and salt; beat until mixture looks sugary around edges of pan. (To speed the process, put saucepan in cold water.) Place wax paper on wooden or metal surface. Drop candy from spoon onto wax paper. If pralines "run" when dropped on paper and do not set, they have not been cooked long enough. Scoop up candy, cook a little longer, beat, and try again. Let cool before removing from wax paper. Makes 3 dozen pralines.

Mrs. Edward W. Kelley, Jr. (Ellen Elizardi)

Pralines

2 cups light brown sugar, firmly packed	1 cup white sugar
1 cup cream	1 cup water
	2 cups pecans (halves, preferred)

Combine brown sugar and cream in one pan; boil gently, stirring frequently. In another pan combine white sugar and water; boil gently. When both mixtures reach the softball stage, combine the two sugar mixtures and beat until creamy. Add pecans; drop from large spoon onto buttered surface. If candy hardens in pan, add a little hot water to make it right consistency to drop. (This can be done several times if necessary.) Makes 60-70 pralines.

Mrs. Douglas S. Craig (Alice Picton)

Octavia's Pralines

1 cup light brown sugar	2 tablespoons butter
2 cups white sugar	1 teaspoon vanilla
1 cup water	2 cups pecans
¼ teaspoon salt	

Combine brown sugar, white sugar and water in large saucepan. Boil until syrup forms a soft ball when tested in cold water. Remove from heat and add salt, butter and vanilla. Beat until creamy; stir in pecans. Drop from spoon onto a buttered surface. If candy hardens in pan, stir in a few drops of water. Makes 18-36 pralines, depending on size.

Mrs. James A. Darby (Charlotte Williams)

Orange Candy

2 cups sugar	2 tablespoons butter
½ cup white corn syrup	Grated peel of 1 orange
½ cup evaporated milk	1 cup chopped nuts

Combine sugar, corn syrup, milk, butter and orange peel in large saucepan. Cook, stirring constantly, until mixture reaches soft ball stage when tested in cool water (238° on candy thermometer). Remove from heat, stir in nuts and beat vigorously until mixture is creamy. Drop from a tablespoon onto wax paper. Makes 3-4 dozen candies.

Mrs. William A. Bramley (Kay Borden)

Apricot Sticks

1 pound dried apricots	¾ cup chopped pecans
1 orange, quartered and seeded	Additional sugar (powdered
1½ cups sugar	or granulated)

Grind apricots and orange (including peel) in food grinder. Moisten sugar with just a little water. Add ground apricots and orange to sugar and boil 10 minutes, stirring constantly. Remove from heat and add pecans. Drop from teaspoon into sugar and roll into sticks. Let stand on wax paper for several hours. Store in tins with wax paper between layers. Will keep for several weeks. Makes at least 50 apricot sticks.

Mrs. Fred T. Spangler (Zillah Mae Ford)

Peanut Brittle

1 can (6¾ oz.) salted peanuts	½ teaspoon salt
1⅓ cups sugar	3 tablespoons butter
1 teaspoon soda	

Put peanuts in oven to warm while preparing candy. In a heavy skillet lightly caramelize sugar. When sugar is light brown and completely dissolved, remove from heat. Add soda, salt and butter; stir well. Stir in peanuts. Immediately pour into buttered 9" square pan. Break into pieces when cool. Makes 1/2 pound candy.

Mrs. Richard R. McKay (Emily Ann Finch)

Sugared Pecans

1 heaping cup pecan halves	½ cup cream (not milk)
½ teaspoon vanilla	½ teaspoon butter
1 cup sugar	Pinch salt

Sprinkle pecans with vanilla. Set aside. Combine sugar, cream, butter and salt in large saucepan. Boil, stirring frequently to prevent scorching, until mixture forms a soft ball when tested in cold water. Remove from heat and beat until creamy. Stir in pecans. Drop from teaspoon onto wax paper. Store in tightly covered container. If candy hardens in pan, add a little hot water. Makes 70-80 candies.

Mrs. Gordon R. West (Josephine Morrow)

CAKES

PIES

Hints

CAKES

MIXING CAKES:

When making cakes, all ingredients should be at room temperature.

Butter and sugar should be creamed until sugar has dissolved. Insufficient creaming will cause a coarse-textured cake.

Do not overbeat cakes; excessive beating makes them fall. Dry ingredients should be beaten into batter only until flour disappears, unless recipe states otherwise.

BAKING CAKES:

To measure pans, measure from one inside edge to the other. (Mark dimensions on bottom of pans with nail polish.)

If there are any doubts about the size of cake pans, it is always a safe rule to fill them only half full with batter. (Bake any extra batter in cupcake papers.)

Most cakes are done when they shrink from the sides of pan. Or, they will spring back if touched lightly with the finger.

FROSTING CAKES:

If boiled frosting will not stiffen, beat powdered sugar into it until it reaches the right consistency. If a boiled frosting hardens while being spread, add a few drops of hot water to soften it.

PIES

TO MAKE MERINGUE FOR PIE TOPPING (9-inch): Using electric mixer and medium bowl, beat 3 egg whites and 1/4 teaspoon cream of tartar until soft peaks form. Gradually beat in 6 tablespoons sugar. Continue to beat until stiff peaks form. Spread meringue over filling, sealing to edge of crust. Bake at 400° for 7-10 minutes, or until peaks of meringue are golden.

Pastry for a 2-crust, 9-inch pie will make 8-10 individual tart shells, in 3-4 inch tart pans.

Pie dough will keep for days in the refrigerator if wrapped tightly.

Cocoa Cake with Heavenly Hash Icing

4 eggs	¼ cup cocoa
2 cups sugar	1 cup butter, melted and cooled
1½ cups self-rising flour	2 teaspoons vanilla

Heat oven to 350°. Grease and flour a 9" x 12" pan. Beat eggs until light. Add sugar, flour, cocoa, butter and vanilla. Mix until well blended. Pour into prepared pan. Bake in preheated oven for 40-45 minutes. Leave cake in pan; frost with Heavenly Hash Icing while cake is still hot.

HEAVENLY HASH ICING

1 package (6¼ oz.) miniature marshmallows	¼ cup cocoa
	¼ cup butter, melted and cooled
1 box (1 lb.) powdered sugar	6 tablespoons milk

Place marshmallows over top of cake while it is still hot. Sift sugar and cocoa together; blend in butter and milk. Spread on top of marshmallows. Let cool. Cut into generous squares. Makes enough icing to frost a 9" x 12" cake.

Mrs. W. Carter Grinstead, Jr. (Linda Ruth Rowe)

Luci's Chocolate Layer Cake

2 ounces unsweetened chocolate	2 eggs
½ cup margarine	2 cups flour
2 cups sugar	Pinch salt
1 cup boiling water	½ cup buttermilk
1 teaspoon soda	1 tablespoon vanilla

Heat oven to 325°. Grease and flour two 8-inch cake pans. Melt chocolate in top of double boiler. Cream margarine and sugar; set aside. Add 1/2 cup boiling water to melted chocolate. In another small pan, put remaining 1/2 cup boiling water and soda; bring to a boil and add to the melted chocolate. Place over direct heat at low temperature and let mixture bubble high for 30 seconds. Remove from heat and allow to cool slightly. Add eggs to creamed mixture, one at a time, beating well after each addition. Mix in flour and salt alternately with buttermilk. Blend in slightly cooled chocolate mixture and vanilla. Pour into prepared pans and bake for 35-40 minutes in pre-heated oven. Invert onto wire racks, remove pans, and let cool. When cool, frost with favorite icing or dust with powdered sugar.

Mrs. Tyler D. Todd (Bobbie Beal)

Mocha Mellow Layer Cake

4 ounces unsweetened chocolate	1½ teaspoons soda
or 1 cup cocoa	1 teaspoon baking powder
½ cup butter	1 teaspoon salt
1 cup hot water	½ cup sour cream
2 cups sugar	2 eggs, well beaten
2 cups flour	½ teaspoon vanilla

Heat oven to 350°. Grease and flour two 9-inch cake pans. In top of double boiler, combine chocolate, butter and hot water. When melted, remove from heat and beat until thickened. Stir in sugar. Sift flour, soda, baking powder and salt together. Add to chocolate mixture alternately with sour cream. Stir in eggs and vanilla. Pour into prepared pans and bake in preheated oven for 25-30 minutes. Invert onto wire rack, remove pans, and let cool. When cool, frost with Coffee Icing. This cake is dark and moist, and keeps well.

COFFEE ICING

1 small package (3 oz.)	¼ cup fresh coffee
cream cheese	Pinch salt
1 box (1 lb.) powdered sugar	1 teaspoon vanilla

Cream cheese thoroughly. Add sugar and enough coffee to make the right consistency to spread. Stir in salt and vanilla. Makes enough icing to frost a 9-inch, 2-layer cake.

Mrs. R. Henry Lake (Fredrica Lanford)

20-Minute Chocolate Cake

½ cup margarine	½ cup buttermilk
¼ cup cocoa	2 eggs
1 cup water	1 teaspoon soda
2 cups flour	½ teaspoon salt
2 cups sugar	1 teaspoon cinnamon
	1 teaspoon vanilla

Heat oven to 400°. Grease and flour 15" x 10" sheet pan. Combine margarine, cocoa and water in saucepan. Bring to a boil; remove from heat. Sift flour and sugar into large mixer bowl. Add chocolate mixture and beat at medium speed until blended. Continue beating while adding buttermilk, eggs, soda, salt, cinnamon and vanilla. Pour into prepared pan and bake in preheated oven for only 20 minutes. (Cake may not appear to be done,

Continued on next page

but it is.) Remove from oven, let cake remain in pan and frost with Cocoa Icing while cake is still hot. Allow cake to cool thoroughly before cutting.

COCOA ICING

1 box (1 lb.) powdered sugar, sifted
½ cup margarine, melted
¼ cup cocoa

6 tablespoons milk
1 teaspoon vanilla
1 cup chopped pecans (optional)

Combine sifted powdered sugar, margarine, cocoa and milk; mix well. Stir in vanilla and pecans. Spread on cake WHILE HOT. Makes enough icing to frost 15" x 10" sheet cake.

Mrs. James A. Reichert (Betsy Calhoun)

Chocolate Syrup Cake

½ cup margarine
1 cup sugar
4 eggs
1¼ cups sifted flour

¾ teaspoon soda
1 cup plus 2 tablespoons
    Hershey's chocolate syrup
1 teaspoon vanilla

Heat oven to 350°. Grease and flour a 9" x 13" pan. Cream margarine and sugar. Add eggs, one at a time, beating after each addition. Combine flour and soda, add to egg mixture alternately with chocolate syrup. Mix in vanilla. Pour into prepared pan and bake in preheated oven for approximately 35-40 minutes. Remove cake from oven; let cool in pan. While cake is still warm, frost with Chocolate Frosting.

CHOCOLATE FROSTING

⅔ cup evaporated milk
2 cups sugar

½ cup margarine
1 cup semi-sweet chocolate chips

Combine milk, sugar and margarine in saucepan; cook for 2 minutes after mixture begins to bubble, stirring constantly. Remove from heat and stir in chocolate chips. Beat until chocolate is melted and frosting is of spreading consistency. Makes enough frosting for top of 9" x 13" cake.

Mrs. John H. Lindsey (Sara Houstoun)

Fabulous Fudge Frosting

2 cups sugar	2 ounces unsweetened
¼ cup white corn syrup	chocolate, grated
½ cup milk	¼ teaspoon salt
½ cup butter	1 teaspoon vanilla

Mix all ingredients, except vanilla, in saucepan. Stir over low heat until chocolate and butter are melted. Bring to a rolling boil, stirring constantly. Boil 1 minute. Remove from heat. Place pan in a bowl of cold water. Beat until lukewarm. Stir in vanilla. Continue beating until of spreading consistency. Makes enough frosting to fill and ice an 8-inch, 2-layer cake.

Mrs. Norman De Graaf Adams, Jr. (Ann Shannon)

German's Sweet Chocolate Cake

1 package (4 oz.) German's	1 teaspoon vanilla
Sweet Chocolate	2½ cups sifted cake flour
½ cup boiling water	1 teaspoon soda
1 cup butter	½ teaspoon salt
2 cups sugar	1 cup buttermilk
4 eggs, separated	

Heat oven to 350°. Line bottom of 3 deep, 8-inch, cake pans with brown or wax paper. Melt chocolate in boiling water. Cool. Cream butter and sugar until light and fluffy. Add egg yolks, one at a time, beating after each addition. Add vanilla and melted chocolate and mix until well blended. Sift flour with soda and salt; add to chocolate mixture alternately with buttermilk, beating after each addition. Beat until smooth. Beat egg whites until they form stiff peaks; fold into batter. Pour batter into prepared pans. Bake in preheated oven for 35-40 minutes, or until cake springs back when lightly pressed in center. Cool cake in pans for 15 minutes; then invert onto wire racks, remove pans, and let cool. Spread Coconut-Pecan Frosting between layers and over top of cake.

COCONUT-PECAN FROSTING

1 cup evaporated milk	1 teaspoon vanilla
1 cup sugar	1⅓ cups Angel Flake Coconut
3 egg yolks, slightly beaten	1 cup chopped pecans
½ cup butter	

Combine milk, sugar, egg yolks, butter and vanilla in saucepan. Cook over medium heat, stirring constantly until mixture thickens, about 12 minutes. Remove from heat. Add coconut and pecans. Beat until mixture is thick enough to spread. Makes 2-1/2 cups, or enough frosting to cover tops of three 8-inch layers.

Mrs. Claude C. Cody, III (Muriel Fursteneau)

Devil's Food Layer Cake

⅔ cup butter
1½ cups sugar
3 eggs, separated
⅔ cup cocoa
½ cup hot water

½ teaspoon soda
1 cup buttermilk
2 cups sifted cake flour
2 teaspoons baking powder
1 teaspoon vanilla

Heat oven to 350°. Grease and flour three 9" cake pans. Cream butter and sugar. Stir in well-beaten egg yolks. Blend cocoa and hot water; dissolve soda in buttermilk. Sift together flour and baking powder. Add flour to creamed mixture alternately with chocolate and buttermilk. Add vanilla. Fold in stiffly beaten egg whites. Divide batter evenly into prepared cake pans. Bake in preheated oven 30-35 minutes, or until cake is springy to the touch. When cake is cool, fill and frost as desired.

Mrs. H. M. Crosswell, Jr. (Elizabeth Holcombe)

Teachers' Favorite Cupcakes

4 ounces unsweetened
    chocolate
½ cup margarine
1 cup water
2 teaspoons soda

1 cup buttermilk
2 eggs, beaten
1 teaspoon vanilla
2 cups flour
2 cups sugar

Heat oven to 350°. Combine chocolate, margarine and water in saucepan; bring to a boil. Remove from heat and let cool. In large bowl, mix soda with buttermilk. Blend in eggs and vanilla. Sift in flour and sugar. Add cooled chocolate mixture. (Batter will be thin.) Spoon batter into paper baking cups which have been placed in muffin pans. Bake in preheated oven for 25 minutes. When cool, frost with Chocolate Icing. These cupcakes are ideal for small children because they don't crumble. Makes at least 30 cupcakes.

CHOCOLATE ICING

2 ounces unsweetened chocolate
6 tablespoons margarine
1 box (1 lb.) powdered sugar, sifted

⅓ cup evaporated milk
1 teaspoon vanilla

Melt chocolate and margarine in double boiler. Add sugar and milk alternately, mixing well. Stir in vanilla. Makes enough icing to generously frost at least 30 cupcakes.

Mrs. Michael B. Raine (Mary Jane Inglish)

Lemon Layer Cake

½ cup butter
½ cup shortening
2 cups sugar
4 eggs, separated

3 cups sifted flour
2 heaping teaspoons baking powder
1 scant cup milk
Juice and grated rind of 1 lemon

Heat oven to 350°. Grease and flour three 9-inch cake pans. Cream butter, shortening and sugar. Beat egg yolks thoroughly, and add to creamed mixture. Sift flour and baking powder together; add to creamed mixture alternately with milk. Add lemon juice and rind. Fold in stiffly beaten egg whites. Divide batter evenly into 3 cake pans. Bake in preheated oven for 30-35 minutes, or until cake tests done. Remove from oven, invert onto wire racks, remove pans, and let cool. Frost with Lemon Glaze Icing.

LEMON GLAZE ICING

1 egg, beaten
Juice and grated rind of 1 lemon

1 cup sugar
3 tablespoons water

Combine all ingredients and boil to jelly-like consistency. Let cool slightly. Beat well. (Recipe may be doubled if thicker glaze is desired.) Makes enough icing for layers and top of 3-layer cake.

Mrs. C. Pharr Duson, Jr. (Betty Tomforde)

Carey's White Layer Cake

1 cup butter
2 cups sugar
8 egg whites, beaten stiff, not dry

3 cups sifted flour
1 scant cup milk
1 teaspoon vanilla
1 tablespoon baking powder

Heat oven to 325°. Grease, but do not flour, three 9-inch cake pans. Cream butter and sugar. Add a scant cup of the beaten egg whites. Slowly add flour alternately with milk. Beat thoroughly. Stir in vanilla. Fold in remaining beaten egg whites and baking powder. Pour into prepared cake pans. Bake in preheated oven for 25-30 minutes, or until cake is springy to the touch. Invert onto wire rack, remove pans, and let cool. Frost with Carey's Chocolate Icing.

Continued on next page

CAREY'S CHOCOLATE ICING

4 ounces unsweetened chocolate	2 teaspoons light corn syrup (optional)
½ pint cream	2 tablespoons butter
2 cups sugar	1½ teaspoons vanilla

Combine chocolate and cream. Heat slowly over low heat until chocolate is melted, stirring frequently. Gradually stir in sugar and corn syrup. Allow to boil gently, without stirring, until icing reaches the soft ball stage when tested in cold water. Add butter. Remove from heat and add vanilla. Let cool. Beat until icing is of spreading consistency. Makes enough icing to fill and frost three 9-inch layers.

Mrs. C. Cage Mooney (Catherine Cage)

Pound Cake

3 cups sifted flour	3 cups sugar
¼ teaspoon soda	4 large eggs
Pinch salt	1 teaspoon vanilla
1 cup butter	1 cup buttermilk

Heat oven to 350°. Grease and flour large Bundt or tube pan. Sift flour, soda and salt together; set aside. Cream butter and sugar. Add eggs, one at a time, beating well after each addition. Add vanilla. Add sifted dry ingredients alternately with buttermilk, beginning and ending with dry ingredients. Beat only until combined. Pour batter into prepared pan. Bake in preheated oven for 50-70 minutes, or until cake tests done. (Baking time will depend on size of pan.) Let cake stand in pan 15 minutes before inverting onto wire rack to cool.

Mrs. Preston Moore, Jr. (Betty Kyle Walker)

Rum Glaze

1 cup butter	1 cup sugar	¼ cup rum

Melt butter with sugar over low heat while stirring constantly. Remove from heat and stir in rum. Pour over warm pound cake while it is still in pan. Let stand in pan approximately 2 hours before serving. Makes enough glaze for a large tube or Bundt cake.

Mrs. Thomas G. Vandivier (Bettie Ebaugh)

Blue Ribbon Pound Cake

Butter and sugar to prepare pan
1 cup butter
1¾ cups sugar
2 cups sifted cake flour

5 eggs
1 teaspoon vanilla
1 teaspoon lemon extract

Heat oven to 350°. Grease Bundt pan with butter; sprinkle generously with sugar. Cream 1 cup butter and 1-3/4 cups sugar, using electric mixer. Continue to beat, adding flour and eggs alternately. Mix in vanilla and lemon extract. Pour into prepared pan and bake in preheated oven for 1 hour. This airy cake needs no glaze as the butter-sugar coating gives it a glossy crunch.

Mrs. W. Meade Wheless, Jr. (Nancy Park)

Feathery Pound Cake

4 cups (slightly heaping) cake flour
½ teaspoon baking powder
Dash salt
1 cup butter
½ cup shortening

3 cups sugar
6 eggs
1 tablespoon lemon juice
1 teaspoon vanilla
1 scant cup milk

Do not preheat oven. Grease and flour 10-inch tube pan. Sift flour, baking powder and salt together; set aside. In large bowl, using electric mixer, combine butter, shortening and sugar. Beat at medium speed until light. Add eggs, one at a time, beating after each addition. Mix in lemon juice and vanilla. At low speed, beat in flour mixture alternately with milk. Pour into prepared pan; place in cold oven. Turn oven to 325° and bake for 1 hour and 20 minutes, or until done. Remove from oven, leave upright in pan for 15 minutes; then invert onto wire rack, remove pan and let cool.

Mrs. Charles B. Moore (Mary Alice Bone)

Annie Betty's Chocolate Pound Cake

3 cups flour	5 eggs
½ teaspoon salt	2 teaspoons vanilla
1 teaspoon baking powder	½ cup cocoa
1 cup margarine	1 cup milk
½ cup shortening	Powdered sugar (optional)
3 cups sugar	

Heat oven to 325°. Grease and flour Bundt pan. Sift flour, salt and baking powder together; set aside. Cream margarine, shortening and sugar until fluffy. Add eggs, vanilla and cocoa; beat until smooth. Add sifted dry ingredients alternately with milk, beginning and ending with dry ingredients. Mix well. Remove 2 cups batter, and make cupcakes. (Bake the cupcakes while cake is baking but bake them only 30-45 minutes.) Pour remainder of batter into prepared Bundt pan. Bake in preheated oven at least 1 hour, or until done. Let cake stand in pan for about 30 minutes; then invert onto wire rack. Powdered sugar may be sifted on top just before serving. (Sugar turns brown if put on in advance.) This cake is even better 1 or 2 days after it is made, as it becomes more moist. Freezes well.

Mrs. Tyler D. Todd (Bobbie Beal)

Regal Almond Cake

2 tablespoons butter	1 teaspoon grated lemon peel
¾ cup thinly sliced almonds	3 eggs, separated
1 tablespoon sugar	2½ cups sifted cake flour
¾ cup butter	3 teaspoons baking powder
1½ cups sugar	1 teaspoon salt
1 teaspoon vanilla	1 cup milk
¾ teaspoon almond extract	

Heat oven to 325°. With the 2 tablespoons butter, generously grease bottom and sides of a 10-inch tube pan; press almond slices into butter on both bottom and sides; sprinkle with the 1 tablespoon sugar. Set aside. Thoroughly cream the 3/4 cup butter with the 1-1/2 cups sugar. Add vanilla, almond extract and lemon peel. Beat in egg yolks until light and fluffy. Sift together flour, baking powder and salt. Add to creamed mixture alternately with milk, beating after each addition. Beat egg whites until stiff but not dry. Gently fold egg whites into batter. Carefully turn batter into prepared pan. Bake in preheated oven about 1 hour and 10 minutes. Let cake stand upright in pan for about 10 minutes; then invert cake onto wire rack to cool.

Mrs. John H. Lindsey (Sara Houstoun)

Nell's Rum Cake

3 cups flour	4 eggs
½ teaspoon soda	1 teaspoon vanilla
½ teaspoon baking powder	1 teaspoon lemon extract
1 teaspoon salt	(optional)
1 cup butter	1 teaspoon rum extract
2 cups sugar	1 cup buttermilk

Heat oven to 350°. Grease large tube pan. Sift together flour, soda, baking powder and salt; set aside. Cream butter and sugar; add eggs, vanilla, lemon extract and rum extract. Beat with electric mixer for approximately 3 minutes. Add dry ingredients alternately with buttermilk, beginning and ending with dry ingredients. Bake in prepared pan in preheated oven for 60-70 minutes. While cake is baking, prepare Rum Syrup and let cool. When cake is done, immediately pour cooled Rum Syrup over it. Do not remove from pan until cake is completely cooled.

RUM SYRUP

1 cup sugar	¼ cup dark rum or
½ cup water	2 teaspoons rum extract

Bring sugar and water to a boil; add rum. Let cool before pouring over Rum Cake.

Mrs. Robert B. Crouch (Nancy Wencke)

Lemon Bundt Cake

1 box (1 lb., 2½ oz.) Duncan	½ cup sugar
Hines Lemon Supreme cake mix	4 eggs
1 cup apricot nectar	⅔ cup salad oil

Heat oven to 350°. Grease and flour a 10-inch tube pan or Bundt pan. Combine all ingredients in large mixer bowl. Beat at medium speed for 2 minutes. Pour batter into prepared pan. Bake in preheated oven for 45-55 minutes, or until center springs back. Let cake stand upright in pan for 15 minutes; then invert onto serving plate and pour glaze over cake while still warm.

GLAZE

1 cup sifted powdered sugar
2 tablespoons lemon juice

Mix powdered sugar and lemon juice together and spoon over cake while warm.

Mrs. Bruce E. Barnett (Ann Poyner)

Lemon Cake Supreme

1 box (1 lb., 2½ oz.) Duncan Hines
Lemon Supreme cake mix
1 large package (5½ oz.) Jello
Instant Lemon Pudding mix (or
1½ small packages)

½ cup salad oil
4 eggs
1 cup water

Heat oven to 350°. Butter and flour Bundt pan (even if Teflon-lined). Combine all ingredients in large mixer bowl and beat at high speed for 4 minutes. Pour into prepared pan and bake in preheated oven for 50 minutes, or until done. Let cake stand upright in pan for 15 minutes; then invert onto serving plate and drizzle Lemon Glaze over cake while cake is still warm.

LEMON GLAZE

1 cup sifted powdered sugar
Grated rind of 1 lemon

1½ tablespoons lemon juice

Combine all ingredients, mix thoroughly, and drizzle over warm cake.

Mrs. Charles W. Dabney, Jr. (Julia Vinson)

Orange Cake with Orange Rum Glaze

2½ cups sifted flour
2 teaspoons baking powder
1 teaspoon soda
½ teaspoon salt
1 cup butter
1 cup sugar

Grated rind of 2 large oranges
Grated rind of 1 lemon
2 eggs
1 cup buttermilk
1 cup finely chopped walnuts

Heat oven to 350°. Grease and flour Bundt pan. Sift together flour, baking powder, soda and salt. Set aside. Cream butter; gradually add sugar and beat until light. Stir in orange rind and lemon rind. Add eggs, one at a time, beating well after each addition. Add flour mixture alternately with buttermilk, beating well after each addition. Fold in walnuts. Pour batter into prepared pan and bake in preheated oven for 40-60 minutes, or until done. Make Orange Rum Glaze while cake is baking, and pour over cake as soon as it is removed from oven.

ORANGE RUM GLAZE

Juice of 2 large oranges
Juice of 1 lemon

2 tablespoons rum (light or dark)
1 cup sugar

Strain juices into saucepan and add sugar and rum. Bring to a boil. Remove from heat. As soon as cake is removed from oven, and while still in pan, pour glaze over cake. Turn cake out onto plate. If all the glaze has not been absorbed, pour it over cake, or reserve to drizzle over cake when serving.

Mrs. John L. Hamilton (Ann Lowdon)

Surprise Cake

1 cup margarine	2 teaspoons cinnamon
2 cups sugar	1½ teaspoons ground cloves
4 eggs	¼ cup milk
1 cup cold, unseasoned,	¼ cup maraschino cherry juice
mashed potatoes	1 teaspoon vanilla
2 cups flour	1 cup pecans, chopped
2 teaspoons baking powder	¾ cup maraschino cherries,
½ cup cocoa	halved

Heat oven to 300°. Grease 10-inch tube pan or 2 loaf pans. Cream margarine and sugar; beat in eggs and add potatoes. Sift together flour, baking powder, cocoa, cinnamon and cloves; add to potato mixture alternately with milk and cherry juice. Add vanilla. Gently fold in pecans and cherries. Pour into prepared pan. Bake in preheated oven for 1-1/2 hours. (Baking time will be slightly shorter if using loaf pans.) Remove cake from pan and cool on wire rack.

Mrs. Raymond Thornton (Dee Anne Minnis)

Strawberry Jam Cake

¾ cup butter	2¼ cups sifted cake flour
1¾ cups brown sugar	1½ teaspoons vanilla
3 eggs, separated	½ teaspoon maple flavoring
1 teaspoon soda	¾ cup strawberry jam
¾ cup buttermilk	

Heat oven to 350°. Grease three 8-inch cake pans. Cream butter and brown sugar. Beat in egg yolks. Dissolve soda in buttermilk. Add flour to creamed mixture alternately with buttermilk, mixing well. Stir in vanilla and maple flavoring. Fold in strawberry jam. Gently fold in stiffly beaten egg whites. Pour into prepared pans. Bake in preheated oven for 30 minutes, or until done. Invert onto wire racks, remove pans and let cool. Frost with Brown Sugar Icing.

BROWN SUGAR ICING

1½ cups brown sugar	1 cup cream
1 cup white sugar	¾ cup chopped pecans
3 tablespoons butter	1½ teaspoons vanilla

In a saucepan, combine brown sugar, white sugar, butter and cream and cook to soft ball stage. Remove from heat and allow to cool for 6 minutes. (Cook a little longer if not stiff enough to spread. Add more cream if too thick to spread.) Stir in pecans and vanilla. Makes enough icing to fill and frost three 8-inch layers.

Mrs. Edgar A. Christy (Gloria Parker)

Blackberry Jam Cake

½ cup butter
1 cup sugar
2 cups cake flour
1 teaspoon cinnamon
1 teaspoon nutmeg
1 teaspoon allspice

1 teaspoon ground cloves
1 teaspoon soda
½ cup sour cream
3 eggs, separated
1¼ cups blackberry jam

Heat oven to 350°. Grease and flour two 9-inch layer pans. Cream butter; add sugar gradually. Combine flour, cinnamon, nutmeg, allspice and cloves. Dissolve soda in sour cream. Sift flour mixture into batter mixture alternately with sour cream, mixing well. Add beaten egg yolks and jam; fold in stiffly beaten egg whites. Pour into prepared pans and bake in preheated oven for 35-40 minutes. Remove from oven, invert onto wire racks, remove pans and let cool. Frost with your favorite white icing.

Mrs. Douglas S. Craig (Alice Picton)

Fresh Apple Cake

¼ cup shortening
1 egg, well beaten
1 cup sugar
3 medium apples, peeled
   and cored

1 cup flour
1 teaspoon soda
¼ teaspoon salt
½ teaspoon cinnamon
¼ cup chopped walnuts

Heat oven to 350°. Grease 8-inch square pan. Cream shortening; stir in egg and sugar. Grate apples finely and add to creamed mixture. Sift together flour, soda, salt and cinnamon; add to apple mixture, stirring well. Mix in walnuts. Pour batter into prepared pan and bake in preheated oven for 45 minutes. Serve warm with Vanilla Sauce.

VANILLA SAUCE

½ cup butter
½ cup cream

1 cup sugar
1½ teaspoons vanilla

Put all ingredients in top of double boiler and cook over hot water for approximately 10 minutes, stirring occasionally. Sauce will be thin. Spoon hot sauce over each serving of warm Apple Cake. Makes 2 cups sauce.

Mrs. Charles B. Williams (Bobbie Ruth Richardson)

Apple Nut Cake

1½ cups salad oil
2 cups sugar
2 eggs
3 cups flour
1 teaspoon soda

1 teaspoon cinnamon
½ teaspoon salt
2 teaspoons vanilla
3 cups unpeeled, cored, chopped
   Winesap apples
1 cup chopped pecans

Heat oven to 350°. Grease and flour a large tube pan, or 9″ x 15″ sheet pan. Combine oil and sugar; mix well. Add eggs, one at a time, beating well after each addition. Sift flour, soda, cinnamon and salt together and add to egg mixture. Add vanilla; mix well. Fold in apples and pecans. Bake in preheated oven for 60-70 minutes if baking in tube pan, or 45 minutes of baking in sheet pan.

Mrs. Charles W. Moody, Jr. (Patti Hunter)

Peach Spice Cake

1 package (12 oz.) dried
   peaches
1 cup butter
2 cups sugar
4 eggs
2 teaspoons soda
1 cup buttermilk

2 cups (heaping) flour
½ teaspoon cinnamon
½ teaspoon ground cloves
½ teaspoon nutmeg
½ teaspoon allspice
1 cup pecans, chopped
1 cup raisins

Cook peaches and sweeten with 1/4 cup sugar. (Drain off any liquid.) Mash and cool. Grease and flour 10-inch tube pan. Set aside. Cream butter and sugar. Add eggs, one at a time, beating thoroughly after each addition. In large bowl, dissolve soda in buttermilk. Sift flour and spices together and add to creamed mixture alternately with buttermilk. Stir in peaches, pecans and raisins. Pour batter into prepared pan. Bake in preheated 325° oven for 1 hour and 15 minutes. Let cool in pan for a few minutes before turning onto a cake rack. This rich, moist cake needs no icing and is a good Christmas cake.

Mrs. Sam E. McHard, Jr. (Lois Vincent)

Fresh Pear Cake

4 cups peeled, cored and
   chopped pears
2 cups sugar
1 cup chopped pecans
3 cups flour
½ teaspoon cinnamon

½ teaspoon nutmeg
½ teaspoon salt
2 teaspoons soda
2 eggs
1 cup salad oil
1 teaspoon vanilla

Grease and flour large tube pan. Combine pears with sugar and pecans. Let stand 1 hour, stirring often. Sift flour, cinnamon, nutmeg, salt and soda together and add to pears. Beat eggs well; add oil and vanilla and stir into pear mixture. Pour batter into prepared pan. Bake at 350° for 1 hour and 15 minutes. This cake is moist and keeps well. (Apples may be substituted for pears.)

Mrs. George A. Hill, III (Gloria Lester)

Prune Cake

2 cups sugar
3 eggs
2 cups flour
1 teaspoon soda
1 teaspoon cinnamon
1 teaspoon nutmeg

1 teaspoon allspice
1 teaspoon ground cloves
1 cup buttermilk
1 cup salad oil
1 cup cooked prunes, seeded
   and finely chopped
1 cup chopped pecans

Heat oven to 250°. Grease and flour a 10-inch tube pan. Combine sugar and eggs; beat well. Sift together flour, soda, cinnamon, nutmeg, allspice and cloves. Add to sugar mixture alternately with buttermilk and salad oil. Stir in prunes and pecans. Pour into prepared pan and bake in preheated oven for 1 to 1-1/2 hours. (Top will spring back when done.) Remove cake from pan while still warm. Let cool on wire rack. Frost with Buttermilk Glaze Icing. This is a rich, moist cake and keeps very well.

BUTTERMILK GLAZE ICING

½ cup sugar
¼ cup buttermilk

¼ cup butter

Combine sugar, buttermilk and butter in saucepan. Cook for 6 or 7 minutes, stirring often. Pour or spread over cooled cake.

Mrs. Robert S. Cutherell (Suzanne Sailer)

Holiday Lemon Nut Cake

1 pound butter	2 tablespoons lemon extract
2 cups sugar	Grated rind of 1 lemon
6 eggs, separated	4 cups pecans, chopped
2¼ cups flour	1 pound raisins
1 teaspoon baking powder	

Heat oven to 275°. Grease and flour 10-inch tube pan or loaf pans. Cream butter and sugar; add egg yolks. Beat well. Sift together flour and baking powder; add to creamed mixture. Add lemon extract, lemon rind, pecans and raisins. Fold in stiffly beaten egg whites. Bake in preheated oven for 2 hours. During second hour of baking, place a pan of water on lower rack in oven. This is a very moist cake, especially good during holidays.

Mrs. A. M. Singer (Cynthia Russ)

Pineapple Carrot Layer Cake

2 cups flour	2 cups sugar
2 teaspoons baking powder	4 eggs
1½ teaspoons soda	2 cups grated raw carrots
2 teaspoons cinnamon	1 small can (8½ oz.)
1 teaspoon salt	crushed pineapple
1½ cups salad oil	½ cup chopped pecans (optional)

Heat oven to 350°. Grease and flour three 9-inch cake pans. Sift together flour, baking powder, soda, cinnamon and salt. Set aside. Combine oil and sugar in large bowl; add eggs, one at a time, beating after each addition. Add sifted dry ingredients; mix well. Stir in carrots, pineapple and pecans. Pour batter into prepared pans; bake in preheated oven for 35-40 minutes. Do not overbake. Frost with Pineapple Icing. This cake is rich and moist. Freezes well.

PINEAPPLE ICING

¼ cup butter, softened	1 teaspoon vanilla
1 large package (8 oz.)	1 small can (8½ oz.) crushed
cream cheese, softened	pineapple, drained
1 box (1 lb.) powdered sugar	1 cup pecans, finely chopped
	(optional)

Combine all ingredients and mix well. Makes enough icing to fill and frost top and sides of 9-inch, 3-layer cake.

Mrs. William Yeoman (Alma J. Vance)

Carrot Cake

2 cups flour	1⅓ cups salad oil
2 cups sugar	4 eggs
1 tablespoon cinnamon	2 cups grated carrots
2 teaspoons soda	1 cup chopped pecans

Heat oven to 350°. Grease a large tube pan. Sift flour, sugar, cinnamon and soda into large bowl. Stir in oil. Add eggs, one at a time, beating after each addition. Stir in carrots and pecans. Pour batter into prepared pan. Bake in preheated oven for 1 hour and 20 minutes. When cool, frost with Cream Cheese Frosting.

CREAM CHEESE FROSTING

1 large package (8 oz.) cream cheese, softened	¼ cup butter
	1 teaspoon vanilla
1 small package (3 oz.) cream cheese, softened	2½ cups powdered sugar, sifted

Combine cream cheese and butter; mix well. Add vanilla. Stir in powdered sugar and beat until smooth. Makes enough frosting for 1 large tube cake.

Mrs. Roland M. Howard (Joan Lander)

Fruit Cake

2 pounds raisins	3¼ cups sugar
2 pounds currants	12 eggs
1 pound citron	2 tablespoons cinnamon
1 pound almonds	2 tablespoons ground cloves
1 pound pecans	2 tablespoons mace
½ pound orange peel	2 tablespoons ground allspice
½ pound lemon peel	1 cup molasses
6 cups flour	1 teaspoon soda
1½ pounds butter	1 cup brandy

Heat oven to 325°. Grease and flour 5 medium-large loaf pans. Chop all fruits and nuts. Combine with 1-1/2 cups of the flour; set aside. Cream butter and sugar. Add eggs and mix well. Sift remaining 4-1/2 cups flour and spices together. Combine molasses and soda. Add flour alternately with molasses. Stir in fruits and nuts. Mix well. Divide batter evenly into prepared pans. Bake in preheated oven in a water bath for 2 hours. (Or, steam for 2-1/2 hours; then bake in 325° oven an additional 40 minutes.) Pour brandy over warm cakes before removing from pans. Remove cakes from pans and wrap in cheese cloth. Seal in airtight containers. Sprinkle occasionally with brandy to keep moist.

Mrs. Hughes Fleming (Mildred Hughes)

Dark Fruit Cake

2 cups dark raisins	1 cup halved candied cherries
1 cup white raisins	1 cup sliced almonds or
1 cup mashed, canned	chopped pecans
cling peaches	2½ cups sifted flour
1 cup shortening	1 teaspoon baking powder
1 cup firmly packed brown sugar	1½ teaspoons salt
½ cup sherry or brandy	1 teaspoon cinnamon
1 cup (or more) sliced dates	1 teaspoon nutmeg
1 cup diced candied orange peel	½ teaspoon ground cloves
1 cup diced candied citron	4 large eggs, well beaten
(optional)	

Heat oven to 300°. Grease and flour 4 or 5 loaf pans. In a large saucepan combine raisins, white raisins, peaches, shortening, brown sugar and sherry. Bring to a boil; remove from heat. Add dates, orange peel, citron, cherries and nuts; mix lightly. Sift flour, baking powder, salt, cinnamon, nutmeg and cloves together; stir into fruit mixture. Add eggs and mix well. Spread batter in prepared pans. Bake in preheated oven for 1-1/2 to 2 hours, depending on size of pans. Sprinkle cake with additional sherry or brandy and store in tightly covered container. This cake ages well, or may be cut the very next day. Makes about 5 pounds fruit cake.

Mrs. Robert L. Grainger (Ida Jo Butler)

Cheesecake Royale

CRUST

1⅔ cups graham cracker crumbs	1½ teaspoons cinnamon
2 tablespoons sugar	6 tablespoons butter, melted

Mix crumbs, sugar, cinnamon and butter. Press evenly onto bottom and sides of 10-inch spring-form pan. Do not bake.

FILLING

3 large packages (8 oz. each)	1 cup sugar
cream cheese, softened	½ teaspoon vanilla
3 eggs, well beaten	

Beat cheese well in electric mixer. Add eggs, sugar and vanilla; continue beating until creamy and light. Pour carefully into crumb crust and bake in 375° oven for 20-25 minutes. Remove from oven.

Continued on next page

TOPPING

1 pint sour cream	½ teaspoon vanilla
3 tablespoons sugar	

Beat together sour cream, sugar and vanilla. Spread over filling. Bake at 500° for 5 minutes. Let cool, in pan, on wire rack; refrigerate until thoroughly chilled before serving.

ALTERNATE TOPPING

1 can (1 lb.) pitted sour cherries, drained	2 tablespoons sugar
½ cup juice from cherries	2 teaspoons cornstarch
	Red food coloring

Blend cherry juice, sugar and cornstarch in saucepan. Cook, stirring constantly, until thickened and clear. Blend in a few drops of food coloring. Stir in cherries and let cool. Spoon cherry topping over filling and chill thoroughly before serving.

Mrs. Suzanne S. Braden (Suzanne Schmidt)

Pineapple Cheesecake

CRUST

2 cups graham cracker crumbs	½ cup sugar
	½ cup butter, melted

Combine all ingredients; mix well. Press onto bottom and sides of 9-inch spring-form pan. Do not bake.

FILLING

1 can (8½ oz.) crushed pineapple, drained	¾ cup sugar
2 large packages (8 oz. each) cream cheese, softened	2 eggs
	1 teaspoon vanilla

Spread pineapple carefully over crust. Beat cream cheese; add sugar gradually, mixing well. Add eggs, one at a time, beating well after each addition. Add vanilla and beat until creamy. Spread over pineapple. Bake at 375° for 20 minutes. Remove from oven.

TOPPING

1 pint sour cream	½ teaspoon vanilla
¼ cup sugar	

Combine all ingredients; mix well. Spread over filling and bake at 400° for 10 minutes. Let cool, in pan, on wire rack; then chill for at least 2 hours before serving.

Mrs. William B. Ward (Ellen Elkins)

Gingerbread

½ cup butter, softened	1 teaspoon ground ginger
½ cup sugar	1 teaspoon ground cloves
1 cup cane syrup	1 teaspoon cinnamon
2 eggs	2 teaspoons soda
2½ cups flour	1 cup boiling water

Grease and flour tube pan. Cream butter and sugar. Add syrup. Beat in eggs, one at a time. Sift flour, ginger, cloves and cinnamon together; add to creamed mixture. Dissolve soda in boiling water and stir into batter. Pour into prepared pan and bake in 350° oven for about 45 minutes. (This is a bread-type gingerbread.)

Mrs. James E. Snoddy, Jr. (Suzie Robertson)

Heirloom Gingerbread

1½ cups flour	1 egg, slightly beaten
1 cup sugar	2 tablespoons sorghum molasses
½ teaspoon ground ginger	1 teaspoon soda
1 teaspoon cinnamon	Scant teaspoon salt
½ cup shortening	1 cup buttermilk

Combine flour, sugar, ginger and cinnamon. Cut in shortening. Reserve 1/4 cup of this mixture for topping. Add egg to remaining flour mixture; stir in molasses. Dissolve soda and salt in buttermilk; add to molasses mixture and pour into greased 8-inch square pan. Sprinkle the reserved topping over batter and bake at 350° for about 30 minutes. Serve hot. (This is a coffee cake-type gingerbread.) Serves 8.

Mrs. Elbridge H. Gerry (Barbara Eisner)

Idabess's Old Fashioned Gingerbread

1 cup butter, softened	1 teaspoon ground cloves
1 cup sugar	1 teaspoon ground ginger
2 eggs, well beaten	1 cup dark molasses
2 cups flour	1 teaspoon soda
1 teaspoon cinnamon	1 cup boiling water

Cream butter and sugar. Add eggs, flour, cinnamon, cloves, ginger and molasses. Mix thoroughly. Dissolve soda in boiling water and add to batter. Mix well. Pour into greased 9" x 12" pan and bake at 375° for about 30 minutes. When cool, dust with powdered sugar. (This is a cake-like gingerbread.) Serves 12.

Mrs. Lewis A. Brown (Sidney Walsh)

Flaky Pie Crust

2¼ cups sifted flour　　　　½ cup shortening
¾ teaspoon salt　　　　　　⅓ cup ice water
¼ cup butter, softened

Sift flour and salt together. With pastry blender, cut butter into flour very finely. Add shortening and cut into mixture coarsely (until pea-sized). Sprinkle ice water, one tablespoon at a time, onto mixture, moistening only a small portion at a time. Push moistened dough to side of bowl. Continue until all flour mixture is moistened only enough to barely hold together. Form lightly into a ball, wrap in wax paper, and chill in refrigerator 20-30 minutes before rolling out on floured surface. Makes enough pastry for 9-inch, 2-crust pie.

Mrs. H. Edward Maddox, III (Donna Gray)

Hot Water Pie Crust

½ cup shortening　　　　　　½ teaspoon baking powder
¼ cup boiling water　　　　　½ teaspoon salt
1¾ cups flour

Put shortening in bowl. Add boiling water and beat until creamy and cold. Sift flour, baking powder and salt together; add to shortening mixture. Stir until dough forms a smooth ball. Wrap and chill until firm. Roll out between sheets of wax paper. Makes enough pastry for 9-inch, 2-crust pie.

Mrs. Henry P. Luckett (Evelyn Sanford)

Quick and Easy Pie Crust

1 cup sifted flour　　　　　　¼ cup salad oil
½ teaspoon salt　　　　　　　2 tablespoons cold milk

Combine flour and salt. Into a measuring cup, pour oil and milk (but do not stir together). Then pour liquids, all at once, into flour. Stir lightly with fork until mixed. Roll into ball; flatten slightly. Roll out between sheets of wax paper; gently fit into 9-inch or 10-inch pie pan. To bake, prick pastry all over with fork; bake at 475° for 8-10 minutes, until lightly browned.

Mrs. Roland M. Howard (Joan Lander)

Never Fail Pie Crust

1 cup flour	¼ cup corn oil
½ teaspoon salt	2½ tablespoons ice water

Sift flour with salt into bowl. **Slowly** dribble oil into flour, mixing with fork until coarsely blended. Sprinkle water over dough and mix. Form into a ball and roll out between sheets of wax paper. Peel off top piece of paper and fit crust into 9-inch or 10-inch pie pan. (If paper sticks to crust, chill in refrigerator a few minutes.) To bake pie shell, prick pastry all over with fork and bake at 425° for 10-12 minutes.

Mrs. James A. Baker, III (Mary Stuart McHenry)

Graham Cracker Crumb Crust

1⅔ cups graham cracker crumbs	⅛ teaspoon nutmeg
¼ cup sugar	5 tablespoons butter, melted
¼ teaspoon cinnamon	

Combine crumbs, sugar, cinnamon, nutmeg and melted butter; mix well. Press mixture evenly onto bottom and sides of 9-inch pie pan. If unbaked pie shell is desired, refrigerate until ready to fill. If baked pie shell is desired, bake at 375° for 8 minutes or until golden brown. Remove from oven, let cool on wire rack before filling. Makes one 9-inch pie shell.

Mrs. Richard R. McKay (Emily Ann Finch)

Meringues

3 egg whites	1 cup sugar
Pinch salt	1 teaspoon vanilla
Pinch cream of tartar	Food coloring, if desired

Beat egg whites with salt and cream of tartar until stiff and dry. Add 1/2 cup of the sugar. Beat until creamy; add vanilla and food coloring. Fold in remaining 1/2 cup sugar just until combined, being careful not to dissolve sugar. Grease cookie sheet and cover with brown paper. Spoon heaping tablespoons of meringue mixture onto paper to form mounds, 3 inches apart. With back of spoon, make a depression in each mound, shaping a shell to hold filling. Bake at 325° for 5 minutes. Turn heat off and leave meringues in oven 20 minutes longer, or until "dry." Cool completely before removing from paper. Makes 6 large meringues.

Mrs. Edward G. Pearson (Coggie Meyer)

Meringue Shells

6 egg whites
½ teaspoon salt

½ teaspoon cream of tartar
1 box (1 lb.) powdered sugar

Beat egg whites with salt and cream of tartar until very stiff. Gradually add powdered sugar, beating constantly. Beat at high speed for 20 minutes. Line cookie sheet with wax paper. Drop meringue mixture by large spoonfuls onto wax paper, allowing 3 inches between meringues. Using back of spoon, shape into shells. Bake at 350° for 10-15 minutes. Slip wax paper onto wet towel to loosen meringues. Fill with ice cream and top with fruit. Makes 12 large meringues or 18 medium ones.

Mrs. Robert J. Hogan (Mary Burke)

Apple Pie In-A-Paper Bag

1 unbaked deep, 9-inch pastry
    shell; or 1 unbaked, 10-inch
    pastry shell
2½ pounds baking apples

¾ cup sugar
2 tablespoons flour
1 teaspoon cinnamon
2 tablespoons lemon juice

½ cup sugar
½ cup flour
½ cup butter, softened

Pare, core and cube apples (approximately 7 cups cubed apples.) Combine with 3/4 cup sugar, 2 tablespoons flour and the cinnamon. Pile into prepared pastry shell and sprinkle with lemon juice.

To make topping, combine 1/2 cup sugar and 1/2 cup flour; cut in butter until mixture is crumbly. Sprinkle evenly over apples (pie will be high). Slide pie into heavy brown paper bag, large enough to cover pie loosely. Fold end of bag over and fasten with paper clips. Bake in 425° oven for 1 hour. (Bag will not burn.) Remove from oven, open bag with scissors, remove pie and cool on wire rack.

Mrs. William A. Bramley (Kay Borden)

Fresh Cranberry Pie

2 cups fresh cranberries	1 cup flour
1½ cups sugar	½ cup butter, melted
½ cup chopped pecans	¼ cup shortening, melted
2 eggs	Sweetened whipped cream for topping (optional)

Grease 10-inch pie pan generously. Spread cranberries in pan and sprinkle with 1/2 cup of the sugar and pecans. Beat eggs well; add remaining 1 cup sugar and blend thoroughly. Add flour, butter and shortening; beat well. Pour batter over cranberries. Bake in 325° oven for about 35 minutes, or until light brown. Serve warm. Top with whipped cream, if desired.

Mrs. Lorenzo B. Taylor (Marilyn Dubach)

Pear Pie

Pastry for 2-crust, 9-inch pie	¼ teaspoon nutmeg
4 cups peeled, cored, sliced hard pears	¼ teaspoon salt
2 tablespoons water	¼ teaspoon cinnamon
⅓ cup white sugar	2 tablespoons flour
⅓ cup brown sugar	¼ cup butter, melted
	2 tablespoons lemon juice

On lightly floured surface, roll out half of the pastry into an 11-inch circle. Use to line 9-inch pie pan. Do not bake. Refrigerate prepared pie shell and remaining pastry until ready to use. Combine pears, water and white sugar; boil for about 5 minutes. Remove from heat; add brown sugar, nutmeg, salt, cinnamon, flour, butter and lemon juice. Mix well. Pour into chilled pastry shell. Roll out remaining pastry into a circle; fit over filling. Fold edge of top crust under edge of bottom crust; press together with fingertips or fork to seal. Make several slits near center of pie for steam to escape. Bake in 450° oven for 10 minutes. Reduce heat to 350° and bake 35-45 minutes longer.

Mrs. Vernon L. Miller (Lois DuBose)

Orange Pie

Pastry for 2-crust, 9-inch pie
1¼ cups sugar
2 tablespoons cornstarch
½ teaspoon cinnamon
¼ teaspoon salt

3 cups fresh orange sections, drained
2 tablespoons butter, melted
Juice of 1 lemon or lime, if oranges are very sweet

Roll out half of pastry. Line 9-inch pie pan with bottom crust; do not bake. Mix together sugar, cornstarch, cinnamon and salt. Add orange sections, melted butter and lemon juice. Fill pastry shell and dot with a little more butter. Roll out remaining pastry; cut into strips. Use strips to make a lattice top for pie. Bake in 400° oven for 15 minutes. Reduce heat to 325° and bake until brown, about 45 minutes more. (Mandarin orange sections may be substituted for 1 cup of the fresh orange sections.)

Miss Nancy Woods

Blueberry Pie

1½ cups graham cracker crumbs
(11 double crackers)
¼ cup butter, melted
1 envelope unflavored gelatin
2 cans (1 lb. each) Monarch blueberries, drained
(reserve juice)

1 package (4 oz.) vanilla pudding mix
1½ teaspoons vanilla
1 cup whipping cream
Sugar

To make crust, combine graham cracker crumbs and butter. Toss with a fork and press into 9-inch pie pan. Bake in 350° oven for 10 minutes. Let cool. Soften gelatin in reserved blueberry juice; add vanilla pudding mix and cook in saucepan until thick, stirring constantly. Remove from heat; stir in 1 teaspoon of the vanilla. Allow to cool. Fold in blueberries. Pour into cooled, baked crumb crust. Whip cream, adding remaining 1/2 teaspoon vanilla and sugar to taste. Spread evenly over pie. Refrigerate until serving time.

Mrs. Edward W. Kelley, Jr. (Ellen Elizardi)

Cherry Cheese Pie

1 baked, 9-inch graham cracker pie shell
¾ cup sugar
1 large package (8 oz.) cream cheese, softened

1 teaspoon vanilla
1 cup whipping cream
1 can (1 lb., 5 oz.) cherry pie filling

Combine sugar, cream cheese and vanilla; beat well. Whip cream and fold in gently. Pour into prepared shell. Cover with cherry pie filling and refrigerate for several hours before serving.

Mrs. Jack S. Josey (Elva Johnson)

Creamy Lemon Cheese Pie

1 baked, 9-inch graham cracker crumb crust	2 eggs, beaten
	¾ cup sugar
3 small packages (3 oz. each) cream cheese, softened	1 cup sour cream
	1 tablespoon grated lemon peel
¼ cup lemon juice	1 tablespoon sugar

Combine cream cheese and lemon juice; blend well. Add eggs and 3/4 cup sugar; beat until fluffy. Spoon evenly into crumb crust and bake at 350° for 15 minutes. Remove from oven; let cool for 5 minutes. To make topping, mix together sour cream, lemon peel and 1 tablespoon sugar. Carefully spoon over pie filling. Return to 350° oven and bake an additional 10 minutes. Remove from oven; let pie cool, in pan, on wire rack. Then chill for at least 5 hours before serving.

Mrs. Richard R. Nelson (Marjorie Shepherd)

Strawberry Cheese Pie

1 baked, 9-inch pastry shell	2 tablespoons cream
4 cups fresh strawberries	2 tablespoons orange juice
1⅓ cups sugar	1 tablespoon grated orange rind
2 tablespoons cornstarch	
1 large package (8 oz.) cream cheese, softened	½ cup whipping cream
	1 tablespoon sugar

In saucepan, mash 2 cups of the strawberries. Combine 1 cup of the sugar and cornstarch; add to strawberries. Cook until thick, stirring constantly until glaze is clear. Mash through a strainer and let glaze cool. Combine remaining 1/3 cup sugar, cream cheese, cream, orange juice and orange rind; blend until creamy. Spoon into cooled, baked pastry shell. Cut 1-1/2 cups of the strawberries in half and arrange on filling. Carefully pour cooled glaze over strawberries. Whip cream with sugar; garnish pie. Decorate with remaining strawberries.

Mrs. Marvin V. Cluett (Lollie Lauderdale)

Strawberry Pie

1 baked, 9-inch pastry shell
1 small package (3 oz.) cream
  cheese, softened
Juice of ½ lemon
1 cup whipping cream

½ cup sugar
2 cups whole, fresh
  strawberries
1 scant cup Smucker's
  currant jelly

Mix cream cheese with lemon juice. Whip cream; add sugar gradually. Fold whipped cream into cream cheese mixture; spread into cooled, baked pastry shell. Arrange strawberries upright over whipped cream mixture. (If berries are very large, cut in half to completely cover top of pie.) Melt jelly and pour over strawberries. Refrigerate until set, at least 2 hours.

Mrs. Ralph S. O'Connor (Maconda Brown)

Frozen Strawberry Pie

1½ cups vanilla wafer crumbs
½ cup finely chopped walnuts
  or almonds
½ cup butter, melted
1 egg white

1½ cups sliced, fresh strawberries
1 cup sugar
2 tablespoons cointreau, kirsch,
  or strawberry liqueur
1 cup sour cream

Make crust by combining crumbs, nuts and butter; press into 10-inch pie plate. Bake at 350° for 6 minutes; let cool. With electric mixer, beat egg white, strawberries and sugar at medium speed, increasing to high speed as mixture thickens. Beat for 15 minutes, or longer. (Be patient; it **will** thicken.) When soft peaks form, fold in liqueur and sour cream. Spoon into cooled crumb crust; freeze at least 4 hours. If preferred, this filling may be frozen in paper baking cups placed in muffin tins. (Frozen strawberries may be substituted but if so, decrease sugar to 1/2 cup.)

Mrs. Richard M. Riggs (Katherine Grace)

Waverly Jeff Davis Pie

1 partially-baked 10-inch
  pastry shell
1 cup butter, softened
2 cups sugar

3 tablespoons flour
3 eggs
1½ teaspoons vanilla
1 cup milk

Cream butter. Combine sugar and flour; beat into butter. Add eggs; beat well. Add vanilla and milk; mix well. (Mixture will look curdled; do not worry.) Pour into cooled, baked pastry shell, being careful that filling is even with rim. Bake at 325° for about 60 minutes, or until filling is browned on top and firm. Remove from oven; let cool on wire rack.

Mrs. William N. Finnegan, III (Martha Ann Moore)

Pumpkin Ice Cream Pie

24 vanilla wafers
1 pint vanilla ice cream,
   softened
1 can (1 lb.) pumpkin
1¾ cups sugar
½ teaspoon salt
1 teaspoon cinnamon

½ teaspoon ground ginger
¼ teaspoon ground cloves
1 teaspoon vanilla
1 cup whipping cream
1 cup slivered almonds
Sweetened whipped cream for
   garnish or topping

Line 10-inch pie pan with whole vanilla wafers. Spread softened ice cream over cookies; freeze until firm. Mix pumpkin with 1-1/2 cups of the sugar, salt, cinnamon, ginger, cloves and vanilla. Whip cream until stiff; fold into pumpkin mixture. Spoon mixture over ice cream. Cover with foil and freeze until firm (about 4 hours). Meanwhile, combine almonds with remaining 1/4 cup sugar in small skillet. Stir over low heat until sugar begins to color. Remove from heat as soon as almonds are caramel-colored. Spread on wax paper to cool. When ready to serve, garnish or top pie with whipped cream and sprinkle with crushed caramelized almonds.

Mrs. Anne Neff (Anne Eastham)

Grasshopper Pie

20 chocolate Hydrox cookies,
   crushed
2 tablespoons butter, melted
24 large marshmallows

½ cup milk
¼ cup green creme de menthe
2 tablespoons white creme
   de cacao
1 cup whipping cream

(Reserve a small amount of cookie crumbs to sprinkle on top of finished pie.) Mix crushed cookies and butter together. Press into 9-inch pie pan to make crust. Melt marshmallows with milk in top of double boiler. Cool and add liqueurs. Whip cream and fold into marshmallow mixture. Pour into prepared crust and sprinkle with reserved crumbs. Freeze until just before serving.

You may vary this recipe to make "Pink Squirrel" or "Brandy Alexander" pie by substituting creme de noyaux or brandy for the creme de menthe.

Mrs. Robert E. Clemons (Grayson Reed Cecil)

Jamaican Rum Cream Pie

CRUST

1 box (5 oz.) Zwieback, crushed	½ teaspoon cinnamon
2 tablespoons sugar	½ cup butter, softened

Combine Zwieback crumbs, sugar, cinnamon and butter; mix well. Press into 10-inch pie plate. Set aside.

RUM FILLING

6 egg yolks	½ cup dark rum (Jamaican)
1 scant cup sugar	2 cups whipping cream
1 envelope unflavored gelatin	Semi-sweet chocolate curls
½ cup cold water	for garnish

Beat egg yolks until light; add sugar. In a small pan, soften gelatin in water; place over low heat and stir until gelatin is dissolved. Bring to a boil; pour over egg mixture, stirring briskly. Stir in rum. Whip cream until stiff and fold into rum mixture. Spoon into prepared pie crust; chill until firm. Sprinkle top generously with semi-sweet chocolate curls.

Mrs. J. Malcolm Horn (Helen Hargrove)

Cecile's Coconut Chiffon Pie

2 baked, 9-inch pastry shells	½ cup cold water
4 eggs, separated	Pinch salt
½ cup whipping cream	2 cups fresh grated coconut
1 cup sugar	1 teaspoon vanilla
1 envelope unflavored gelatin	Sweetened whipped cream
	for topping

In top of double boiler, beat egg yolks until light. Add cream and 1/2 cup of the sugar. Cook over hot water until thick, stirring constantly. Soften gelatin in water; then add to egg yolk mixture and stir until dissolved. Let cool. Beat egg whites with salt until soft peaks are formed. Gradually beat in remaining 1/2 cup sugar; continue beating until stiff peaks are formed. Fold beaten egg whites into cooled custard mixture. Fold in 1 cup of the coconut and vanilla. Pour into cooled, baked pastry shells and chill. Before serving, top with whipped cream and sprinkle each pie with remaining 1/2 cup coconut. Makes two 9-inch pies.

Mrs. Harold E. Daniels (Gayle Garth)

American Key Lime Pie

1 baked, 9-inch pastry shell
1 envelope unflavored gelatin
1 cup sugar
¼ teaspoon salt
4 eggs, separated
½ cup lime juice
¼ cup water

1 teaspoon grated lime peel
Green food coloring
1 cup whipping cream
Sweetened whipped cream
   for topping
Grated lime peel, grated
   pistachio nuts and thin lime
   slices for garnish

Thoroughly mix gelatin, 1/2 cup of the sugar and salt in saucepan. Beat together the egg yolks, lime juice and water; stir into gelatin mixture. Cook over medium heat until mixture begins to boil, stirring constantly. Remove from heat; stir in grated lime peel. Add food coloring, sparingly, to tint a pale green. Chill, stirring occasionally, until mixture mounds slightly when dropped from a spoon. Beat egg whites until soft peaks form; gradually add remaining 1/2 cup sugar. Continue beating until stiff peaks are formed. Fold into chilled gelatin mixture. Whip cream and fold into mixture. Pile into cooled, baked pastry shell. Chill until firm. Spread with additional whipped cream. Stand lime slices all around edge of pie; garnish with grated lime peel and pistachio nuts.

Mrs. Joe B. Ehresman (Kay Weeks)

Mile High Lemon Pie

1 baked, 9-inch pastry shell
1 envelope unflavored gelatin
1 cup sugar
5 eggs, separated

½ cup water
½ cup lemon juice
1 teaspoon grated lemon rind

Combine gelatin and 1/2 cup of the sugar in top of double boiler. Beat egg yolks slightly. Combine with water and lemon juice; add to gelatin mixture. Place over boiling water and cook, stirring constantly, until gelatin is dissolved and mixture is slightly thickened. Add lemon rind. Chill until mixture is slightly thicker than unbeaten egg white. Beat egg whites until stiff. Gradually add remaining 1/2 cup sugar; beat until very stiff. Slowly fold egg whites into gelatin mixture. Pile into cooled, baked pastry shell. Chill until firm.

Mrs. John H. Lindsey (Sara Houstoun)

Baked Lemon Chiffon Pie

1 baked, 9-inch pastry shell
3 eggs, separated
3 tablespoons hot water
¼ cup lemon juice

1 tablespoon grated lemon rind
1 cup sugar
Pinch salt

In top of double boiler, beat egg yolks. Add hot water, lemon juice, lemon rind, 1/2 cup of the sugar and salt. Cook over hot water until thickened, stirring occasionally. Remove from heat; allow to cool. Beat egg whites until soft peaks are formed. Gradually beat in remaining 1/2 cup sugar. Fold into cooled lemon mixture. Pour into cooled, baked pastry shell. Bake at 325° for 5-10 minutes. Let cool before serving.

Mrs. Thornton Greer (Ann Painter)

Lemon Angel Pie

MERINGUE CRUST

4 egg whites
¼ teaspoon cream of tartar

¾ cup sugar

Beat egg whites until frothy. Add cream of tartar; beat until soft peaks are formed. Add sugar gradually, beating until stiff peaks are formed. Spread over bottom and sides of buttered, 9-inch pie pan. Bake at 275° for 1 hour. Set aside to cool.

LEMON FILLING

4 egg yolks
½ cup sugar
3 tablespoons lemon juice

1 teaspoon grated lemon rind
1 cup whipping cream

In top of double boiler, beat egg yolks. Add sugar, lemon juice and lemon rind; cook over hot water 5-8 minutes, or until thickened, stirring constantly. Remove from heat and allow to cool. Whip cream until stiff. Fold half of the whipped cream into cooled lemon custard, blending gently. Pour into cooled meringue crust. Sweeten remaining whipped cream slightly and spread over filling. Refrigerate several hours before serving. This pie may be frozen, if desired.

Mrs. Douglas S. Craig (Alice Picton)

Kelley's Fabulous Lemon Icebox Pie

1 baked, 9-inch, graham
    cracker pie shell
4 egg yolks
1 egg white, stiffly beaten

1 can (15 oz.) Eagle Brand
    sweetened, condensed milk
¼ to ½ cup fresh lemon juice
Sweetened whipped cream for
    topping

Beat egg yolks until lemon colored; fold in egg white. Fold in condensed milk and slowly stir in lemon juice to taste. Pour into cooled, baked pie shell. (Do not cook pie.) Refrigerate for about 6 hours. Before serving, top with slightly sweetened whipped cream. (If preferred, top with meringue using remaining 3 egg whites, plus a little sugar.)

Mrs. Gordon R. West (Josephine Morrow)

Buttermilk Pie

1 unbaked, 9-inch pastry shell,
    chilled
1½ cups sugar
3 tablespoons flour
2 eggs, well beaten

½ cup butter, melted
1 cup buttermilk
2 teaspoons vanilla
1 teaspoon lemon extract

Combine sugar and flour; stir in eggs. Add melted butter and buttermilk; mix well. Stir in vanilla and lemon extract. Pour into chilled pastry shell and bake at 425° for 10 minutes. Reduce heat to 350° and bake 35 additional minutes. (Do not open oven door while baking.)

Mrs. Hughes Fleming (Mildred Hughes)

Chocolate French Silk Pie

1 baked, 9-inch pastry shell
½ cup butter
1 cup sugar
1 teaspoon vanilla

1½ ounces unsweetened chocolate,
    melted
2 eggs
1 cup whipping cream
Shaved chocolate

Cream butter and 3/4 cup of the sugar. Stir in vanilla and melted chocolate. Add eggs, one at a time, beating well after each addition. Pour into cooled, baked pastry shell. Add remaining 1/4 cup sugar to cream and refrigerate for 2-3 hours before whipping. Top pie with the sweetened whipped cream and decorate with shaved chocolate. Refrigerate until thoroughly chilled before serving.

Mrs. P. Michael Wells (Page Thomson)

Chocolate Angel Strata Pie

1 baked, 9-inch pastry shell	¾ cup sugar
2 eggs, separated	1 package (6 oz.) semi-sweet
½ teaspoon white vinegar	chocolate chips
¼ teaspoon salt	¼ cup water
½ teaspoon cinnamon	1 cup whipping cream

Combine egg whites with vinegar, salt and 1/4 teaspoon of the cinnamon; beat until soft peaks are formed. Gradually add 1/2 cup of the sugar; continue beating until stiff. Spread meringue over bottom and on sides of cooled, baked pastry shell. Bake at 325° for 15-18 minutes, or until lightly browned. Let cool and refrigerate. Melt chocolate chips and let cool. Mix slightly beaten egg yolks with water; stir into melted chocolate. Spread 3 tablespoons of this mixture over chilled meringue. Refrigerate remaining chocolate mixture. Combine remaining 1/4 cup sugar, remaining 1/4 teaspoon cinnamon and whipping cream. Beat until stiff. Spread half of the sweetened whipped cream over chocolate layer; chill. Blend remaining whipped cream with reserved chocolate mixture; spread over whipped cream layer. Chill pie at least 4 hours before serving.

Mrs. Lewis A. Brown (Sidney Walsh)

Hershey Bar Pie
COOKIE CRUST

6 tablespoons butter	½ teaspoon salt
17 Nabisco chocolate wafers	

Melt butter in skillet. Crush chocolate wafers into fine crumbs. Add crumbs and salt to melted butter; stir until well blended. Press into 9-inch pie pan. Bake in 275° oven for 10 minutes. Let cool.

HERSHEY FILLING

5 Hershey bars without almonds	½ cup milk
(⅞ oz. each)	2 cups whipping cream
16 large marshmallows, halved	Toasted almonds, chopped

Put Hershey bars, marshmallows and milk in top of double boiler; stir gently over hot water until melted and well blended. Remove from heat and let cool thoroughly. Whip cream and fold half of it into chocolate mixture. Spoon filling into cooled crust. Top with remaining whipped cream. Sprinkle with almonds. Refrigerate at least 6 hours before serving.

Mrs. George N. Allen, Jr. (Bonnie Blades)

Fudge Pie

½ cup butter
2 ounces unsweetened chocolate
2 eggs
1 cup sugar
¼ cup flour

¼ teaspoon salt
1 teaspoon vanilla
¾ cup chopped pecans
Ice cream or sweetened whipped
  cream for topping

Melt butter and chocolate over low heat. In a large bowl, combine all other ingredients and mix well. Stir in chocolate mixture and blend well. Pour into buttered, 9-inch pie pan. Bake in 350° oven for 30 minutes. Serve with ice cream or sweetened whipped cream, if desired. The outside is crusty—the inside is fudgy. Freezes beautifully—thaws quickly.

Mrs. Gleaves M. Love (Betsy Riggle)

Madeline's Fudge Pie

½ cup butter, melted
1 cup sugar
2 eggs
1 ounce unsweetened
  chocolate, melted
½ cup sifted flour

1 teaspoon vanilla
1 cup chopped pecans
1 baked, 9-inch pastry
  shell (optional)
Ice cream or whipped cream
  for topping

Mix butter and sugar. Add eggs, one at a time, beating after each addition. Add chocolate, flour, and vanilla. Stir in pecans; mix well. Pour into well-buttered, 9-inch pie pan or into baked, cooled pastry shell. Bake at 325° for 25-30 minutes. Let cool. Serve with topping of ice cream or whipped cream, if desired.

Mrs. Herbert E. Smith, Jr. (Barbara Hartung)

Almond Macaroon Pie

½ cup fine saltine cracker
  crumbs (10-12 crackers)
⅔ cup chopped pecans
3 egg whites
1 cup sugar

½ teaspoon baking powder
¼ teaspoon salt
1 teaspoon almond extract
1 cup whipping cream

Combine cracker crumbs and pecans; set aside. Beat egg whites until stiff. Combine sugar and baking powder; fold into egg whites. Fold in cracker crumbs and pecans, salt and almond extract. Pour into lightly greased 9-inch pie pan and bake in 325° oven for 20-30 minutes. Increase heat to 425° for the last few minutes of baking time. Several hours before serving, spread top of pie with sweetened whipped cream.

Mrs. Charles T. Niblack (Eleanor Allen)

Southern Pecan Pie

1 unbaked, 8-inch pastry
   shell
1 cup light brown sugar,
   firmly packed
½ cup white sugar
1 tablespoon flour
2 eggs

2 tablespoons milk
1 teaspoon vanilla
½ cup butter, melted (do not
   substitute)
1 cup pecans, chopped
Whipped cream or ice cream
   for topping (optional)

Mix brown sugar, white sugar and flour. Add eggs, milk, vanilla and melted butter; beat well. Fold in pecans. Pour into unbaked pastry shell. Bake in 375° oven for 40-50 minutes. Serve slightly warm. Top servings with whipped cream or ice cream, if desired.

Mrs. James J. Loeffler (Margo Meynier)

Yummy Yankee Pecan Pie

1 unbaked, 10-inch, pastry
   shell
½ cup butter, softened
½ cup sugar
¾ cup white corn syrup
¼ cup maple syrup

3 eggs, slightly beaten
1 teaspoon vanilla
2 cups pecans, broken but
   not chopped
Whipped cream for topping
   (optional)

Cream butter and sugar. Gradually stir in corn syrup and maple syrup. Add eggs and vanilla and blend well. Fold in pecans. Pour into unbaked pastry shell. Bake in 325° oven for 1 hour. Top servings with whipped cream, if desired.

Mrs. H. Edward Maddox, III (Donna Gray)

Exquisite Pie

2 unbaked, 9-inch pastry shells
1 cup butter
2 cups sugar
3 eggs, well beaten
2 tablespoons vinegar
½ teaspoon ground allspice

½ teaspoon cinnamon
½ teaspoon ground cloves
2 teaspoons vanilla
1 cup grated coconut
1 cup raisins
1 cup chopped nuts

Cream butter and sugar. Add eggs, then vinegar; mix well. Stir in allspice, cinnamon, cloves and vanilla. Fold in coconut, raisins and nuts. Pour into 2 unbaked pastry shells. Bake at 350° for 35-45 minutes. These pies may be frozen before baking.

Mrs. Terry H. Keith (Betty Ann Warner)

Funeral Pie

1 unbaked, 9-inch pastry shell
1 pint sour cream
1½ cups brown sugar
2 eggs, beaten
2 tablespoons cornstarch
½ teaspoon nutmeg

¼ teaspoon cinnamon
Pinch of ground cloves
¼ teaspoon salt
1 tablespoon lemon juice
½ cup raisins

Mix sour cream and brown sugar together. Stir in eggs. Combine cornstarch, nutmeg, cinnamon, cloves and salt; add to egg mixture. Stir in lemon juice; fold in raisins. Pour into unbaked pastry shell. Bake in 375° oven for 45 minutes, or until filling is firm.

Mrs. Lyon L. Brinsmade (Susannah Tucker)

Austrian Pastries

1 cup flour
Pinch salt
1 cup butter, softened
1 cup creamed cottage cheese

2 egg whites, slightly beaten
Strawberry preserves, or
currant jelly, for filling

Mix flour and salt; cut in butter. Mash cottage cheese through a sieve; add to flour-butter mixture and mix thoroughly. Refrigerate until well chilled. On lightly floured surface, roll pastry 1/8" thick and cut into small (1-2 inch) squares. Dip squares into egg whites, one at a time. Put a dab of preserves or jelly in center and seal with a second pastry square. Brush tops with additional egg white. Bake on cookie sheets in 450° oven for 10-12 minutes, until lightly browned. Makes about 2 dozen pastries, depending on size.

Mrs. Jack R. Winston (Martha Francis)

Party Pecan Nuggets

CREAM CHEESE PASTRY

½ cup butter, softened
1 cup flour

1 small package (3 oz.) cream
cheese, softened

Combine butter, flour and cream cheese, mixing well. Roll into small balls; pat to fit bottom and sides of **very small** muffin pans. Fill with Pecan Filling.

PECAN FILLING

1 egg
2 tablespoons butter, melted
⅛ teaspoon salt
¾ cup brown sugar

¼ cup white corn syrup
1 teaspoon vanilla
⅔ cup pecan halves
Candied cherries (optional)

Combine all ingredients, except pecans and cherries; beat until well mixed. Fold in pecans. Fill pastry shells and top each with a candied cherry, if desired. Bake in 325° oven for 30 minutes. Makes 24 nuggets.

Mrs. Robert F. Flagg (Nancy White)

DESSERTS

Hints

DESSERTS

TO SCALD MILK: Heat milk over very low heat, or over hot water in double boiler, until small bubbles form around edge of pan. (To keep milk from sticking to pan, and to make pan easier to clean, rinse pan in cold water before scalding milk.)

TO USE EXTRA EGG YOLKS: Substitute 2 egg yolks for 1 whole egg when making baked or boiled custards (or mayonnaise).

BEFORE MEASURING MOLASSES OR CORN SYRUP, grease measuring cup slightly.

TO MEASURE BROWN SUGAR: Always pack firmly. If brown sugar is lumpy, roll with rolling pin before measuring.

TO MAKE CHOCOLATE CURLS: Scrape unsweetened or semi-sweet chocolate with a vegetable peeler.

WHEN FREEZING ICE CREAM IN ICE-CREAM FREEZER: Let ice cream mix cool before pouring into freezer can; NEVER fill freezer can more than 2/3 full, to allow for expansion.

WHEN FREEZING ICE CREAM OR SHERBET IN REFRIGERATOR: Pour mixture into ice tray; freeze until mushy. Spoon into cool bowl and beat with electric or rotary beater until smooth. Return to cold ice tray and freeze until firm.

Bananas Foster

4 ripe bananas
¼ cup butter
½ cup brown sugar

4 dashes cinnamon
¼ cup banana liqueur
½ cup light rum

Peel bananas and slice in half lengthwise. Melt butter and brown sugar in flambe pan (shallow copper chafing dish). Add bananas and saute briefly over hot flame. Sprinkle with cinnamon. Pour liqueur and rum over bananas. Ignite and baste with flaming liquid until flame burns out. Serve with vanilla ice cream if desired. Makes 4 servings.

Mrs. Wallace M. Davis, Jr. (Barbara Sterrett)

Cherries Jubilee

2 large cans (1 lb. each) pitted
   Bing cherries
1 jar (10½ oz.) currant jelly
1 teaspoon cinnamon
¼ cup lemon juice

½ cup chopped, blanched
   almonds
12 large vanilla ice cream balls
1 cup whiskey (at least
   96 proof)

Drain cherries and pour into shallow casserole. Beat jelly until smooth; stir in cinnamon and lemon juice. Pour over cherries. Sprinkle almonds over all. Heat in 350° oven for 10 minutes. Place ice cream balls in serving bowls. Transfer cherries to copper chafing dish. Pour whiskey over cherries and flame. Spoon cherries and flaming sauce over ice cream. Serves 12.

Mrs. William M. Thorsell, Jr. (Martha Thompson)

Fresh Fruits in Grand Marnier

4 large navel oranges
Zest of 1 orange
½ cup juice from oranges
1 cup sugar

¼ cup Grand Marnier
2 cups sliced strawberries
2 cups honeydew melon balls
Mint

Grate off just the zest (the very outside rind) from 1 of the oranges. Peel and section oranges over a bowl to save juice. To make syrup, combine zest of orange, 1/2 cup juice from oranges and sugar in saucepan. Bring to a boil; boil 3 minutes. Allow to cool; then stir in Grand Marnier. Combine orange sections, strawberries and melon balls in serving bowl. Pour cooled syrup over fruit. Refrigerate several hours before serving to blend flavors. Garnish with mint. (Use only fresh fruits.) Serves 6-8.

Mrs. Paul F. McBride, Jr. (Pattie Cunningham)

Fresh Peach Dumplings

Enough pastry for 2-crust,
9-inch pie
6 fresh peaches, peeled but
left whole
¾ cup fresh blueberries
1 cup sugar
1 cup water

¼ cup melted butter
¼ teaspoon nutmeg
¼ teaspoon cinnamon
1 cup powdered sugar
¼ cup additional butter, melted
Juice of 1 lemon
Grated rind of 1 lemon

Roll pastry 1/8" thick on lightly floured surface. Cut into six 5-inch squares. Split peaches enough to remove seeds. Fill each seed cavity with 2 tablespoons blueberries. Place each peach in center of a pastry square and fold corners to the center over top of peach. Press edges together and prick with fork. Arrange close together in buttered, shallow casserole. Combine sugar, water, 1/4 cup melted butter, nutmeg and cinnamon; heat until sugar is dissolved. Pour mixture over dumplings. Bake in 375° oven for 40-45 minutes. To make sauce, combine powdered sugar, remaining 1/4 cup melted butter, lemon juice and lemon rind; beat until mixture is light and fluffy. Serve over warm dumplings. Serves 6.

Mrs. Lorenzo B. Taylor (Marilyn Dubach)

Crepes with Lemon Filling

CREPES

2 cups flour
¼ teaspoon salt
3 eggs, separated
¼ cup butter, melted and cooled

2 cups milk
1 tablespoon brandy
Additional melted butter

Sift flour and salt into bowl. Beat egg yolks lightly; blend in cooled butter, 1 cup of the milk and the brandy. Add gradually to flour. Beat until smooth. Stir in remaining cup of milk. Beat egg whites until fairly stiff and fold into batter. (Batter should be thin; it may be necessary to add a little additional milk.) Make crepes, one at a time, in hot, 5- or 6-inch crepe pan or heavy frying pan. Tilt pan and pour in 1 tablespoon batter; tip and turn so that batter covers bottom of pan. Place pan over medium-high heat. Brush a little melted butter around pan at edge of crepe. As soon as edges curl and bubbles form on top, turn crepe with spatula and brown other side. Continue making crepes until all batter is used. Fill crepes with Lemon Filling. Makes at least forty 5-inch crepes. (Prepared crepes may be filled immediately, refrigerated for several days, or frozen. If refrigerated or frozen, place wax paper or paper towling between crepes and wrap tightly. Crepes may also be filled with chicken, ham, cheese or any fruit filling.)

Continued on next page

LEMON FILLING

2 eggs
1 additional egg yolk
½ cup butter

⅔ cup sugar
Grated rind and juice of
1 large lemon

In a Pyrex or enameled saucepan, beat eggs and egg yolk. Add butter, sugar, lemon rind and lemon juice. Cook over low heat, stirring constantly, until thick. With crepes best side down, put 1-1/2 teaspoons of filling in center of each. Roll up and arrange crepes side by side in shallow baking dish. (Sauce will keep in refrigerator for several weeks and may be used on other desserts, such as pound cake.) Sprinkle crepes with sugar (preferably superfine). Bake in 300° oven for 10 minutes. Makes enough filling for 40 crepes. Cover with Macaroon Topping.

MACAROON TOPPING

¼ cup butter, melted
¾ cup crushed macaroons

Mix butter and macaroon crumbs together; spoon over crepes before serving. Crepes should be served warm, not hot.

Mrs. Wayne Weachman (Nina Perlitz)

Apple Crisp

8 medium cooking apples,
   peeled, cored and sliced
½ cup water
1 teaspoon cinnamon

¾ cup flour
1 cup sugar
½ cup butter

Put apples, water and cinnamon in shallow, greased, 2-quart baking dish; mix well. Combine flour and sugar; cut in butter until crumbly. Sprinkle over apple mixture. Bake, uncovered, in a 375° oven for 1 hour. Serve hot, topped with cream or ice cream if desired. Serves 8.

Mrs. Thomas G. Vandivier (Bettie Ebaugh)

Pears Vin Rouge

2 cups dry red wine	6 firm fresh pears
1½ cups sugar	2 tablespoons Grand Marnier
1 cinnamon stick	or Triple Sec liqueur
3 whole cloves	Sour cream
4 slices lemon	Ground cinnamon
4 slices orange	

In a saucepan, combine wine, sugar, cinnamon stick, cloves, lemon slices and orange slices; simmer for 5 minutes. Peel, halve and core pears; simmer in syrup for about 25 minutes, or until tender. Add Grand Marnier. Let pears cool in syrup; refrigerate until thoroughly chilled. Place pears with their syrup in serving bowl. Serve with sour cream flavored with ground cinnamon. Serves 6.

Mrs. Richard R. McKay (Emily Ann Finch)

Russian Plums

2 cans (1 lb. each) purple	2 pints sour cream
plums, seeded	Brown sugar

Drain nearly all juice from plums. Put 3 or 4 plums in individual dessert bowls. Cover each serving with sour cream. Sprinkle generously with sifted brown sugar. Chill 2-3 hours. This dessert may be made with other fruit as successfully as with plums. Serves 6.

Mrs. James Howard Park, III (Bette Naylor)

Scandinavian Cold Fruit Cup

1 package (10-12 oz.)	½ package frozen peaches
frozen raspberries	Whipped cream for topping

Chop fruits (still frozen) into pieces small enough to fit in blender. Add just enough water to enable the blender to puree; blend briefly until consistency of icy mush. Strain out raspberry seeds, if desired. Serve immediately in sherbet glasses; garnish with whipped cream. Can also be served as soup with finger sandwiches for a light summer luncheon. Serves 4.

Mrs. Scott Cahill (Betty Scott)

Blueberry Delight

¼ cup butter, softened
½ cup sugar
2 eggs, beaten
1 cup flour

1 teaspoon baking powder
¼ cup milk
1½ cups fresh blueberries (frozen
  blueberries may be used)

Cream butter and sugar; stir in eggs. Sift flour and baking powder together. Add to creamed mixture alternately with milk, beating well. Coat blueberries with small amount of additional flour (to assure even distribution of berries in cake); fold into batter. Pour into lightly greased 8- or 9-inch square pan. Bake at 350° for 30 minutes. Cut into squares. Top with following sauce. Serves 6-8.

SAUCE

¼ cup butter, softened
½ cup sugar
1 egg yolk, well beaten

¼ cup boiling water
Vanilla, to taste

Cream butter and sugar in top of double boiler. Blend in egg yolk and boiling water. Cook over hot water until mixture thickens, stirring frequently. Stir in vanilla. Spoon hot sauce over servings of Blueberry Delight.

Miss Ellen Ketchum

Blueberry Cobbler Cake

2 cups fresh blueberries
Juice of ½ lemon
3 tablespoons butter, softened
1¾ cups sugar
½ cup milk

1 cup flour
1 teaspoon baking powder
½ teaspoon salt
1 tablespoon cornstarch
1 cup boiling water

Grease 8-inch square pan. Put berries in pan and sprinkle with lemon juice. Cream butter and gradually blend in 3/4 cup of the sugar. Add milk, flour, baking powder and 1/4 teaspoon salt; beat until well combined. Spread batter over berries. Mix remaining 1 cup sugar, remaining 1/4 teaspoon salt and the cornstarch; sprinkle evenly over batter. **Very carefully** pour boiling water over all. Bake in 375° oven for 50-60 minutes, or until crust is light brown. Serve warm, with cream, for dessert; or serve as coffee cake for breakfast. Serves 6.

Mrs. Cullom E. Connely (Margaret Deuel)

Dewberry Cobbler

½ cup butter	¾ cup flour
2 cups sugar	¾ cup milk
3 rounded cups dewberries	2 teaspoons baking powder

Melt butter in 2-quart casserole. Sprinkle 1 cup of the sugar over dewberries and set aside. Mix remaining cup sugar, flour, milk and baking powder; stir into melted butter. Spoon berries on top of "crust" mixture. (Crust comes to the top during baking.) Bake at 300° for about 1 hour, or until crust is light brown. Serves 4-6.

Mrs. John H. Lindsey (Sara Houstoun)

Steamed Cranberry Pudding

1½ cups sifted flour	½ cup light molasses
2 teaspoons soda	½ cup hot water
1 teaspoon baking powder	2 cups fresh cranberries

Combine flour, soda and baking powder; stir in molasses and hot water. Fold in cranberries. Spoon into a 1-1/2 quart mold, about 2/3 full; cover mold tightly. Place on rack in large saucepan containing at least 1-1/2" water. Cover pan and steam over low heat for 2-1/2 hours. Serve warm with Vanilla Cream Sauce. Serves 8.

VANILLA CREAM SAUCE

| ½ cup butter | 1 cup sugar |
| ½ cup cream | Vanilla |

Combine all ingredients in top of double boiler. Place over hot water; heat until well blended and sugar is dissolved. Spoon sauce over individual servings of Steamed Cranberry Pudding. Makes about 2 cups.

Mrs. Henry T. Hilliard (Lydia Caffery)

Plum-Gingerbread Pudding

1 can (1 lb.) purple plums	½ teaspoon salt
with syrup	1 cup raisins
1 package (about 14 oz.)	
gingerbread mix	

Drain plums, reserving syrup for sauce. Remove seeds from plums and cut into small pieces. Prepare gingerbread mix according to package instructions. Stir in salt, raisins and plums. Pour into well-greased 2-quart mold. Bake, uncovered, in 375° oven for about 1 hour. Loosen edges with knife and turn out onto serving plate. Serve warm with Plum Sauce. Serves 10-12.

Continued on next page

PLUM SAUCE

Syrup from canned plums	**2 tablespoons cornstarch**
¼ cup sugar	**1 tablespoon lemon juice**

Add enough water to plum syrup to make 1-1/2 cups liquid. Combine sugar and cornstarch in small saucepan. Gradually stir in plum syrup. Cook over medium heat, stirring constantly, until mixture thickens. Let boil 1 minute, stirring until sauce is clear. Add lemon juice. Immediately spoon over warm pudding.

Mrs. W. Carter Grinstead, Jr. (Linda Ruth Rowe)

Steamed Plum Pudding

1 cup flour	1 pound pitted dates, chopped
1 tablespoon nutmeg	½ pound almonds, chopped
1 tablespoon ground allspice	1 large loaf (1½ lbs.) white
1 tablespoon cinnamon	bread, made into crumbs
1 tablespoon ground cloves	1½ pounds beef suet, finely
1 teaspoon salt	chopped
2 pounds raisins	2 cups sugar
2 pounds currants	6 eggs, well beaten
1 pound citron, chopped	2 cups bourbon or wine

Sift flour with nutmeg, allspice, cinnamon, cloves and salt. Mix in raisins, currants, citron, dates and almonds. Add bread crumbs and suet; mix well. Beat sugar and eggs together; stir in bourbon. Add to fruit mixture and mix well. Spoon into greased pudding molds, about 2/3 full. (Coffee cans may be used.) Cover molds tightly. Place molds on rack in large pan containing at least 1-1/2" water. Cover pan and steam pudding over low heat for about 6 hours. Unmold pudding, allow to cool, then wrap tightly in foil. Let season several days before serving. (Additional bourbon may be poured over pudding during seasoning, if desired.) Heat pudding thoroughly before serving. (Return pudding to mold and steam or wrap pudding tightly in foil and heat in moderate oven.) When ready to serve, sprinkle pudding generously with additional bourbon and ignite with match. Serve with Hard Sauce. Makes 2 large, or several small, puddings.

HARD SAUCE

1 cup butter, softened
1 cup sugar
1 teaspoon vanilla

Cream butter and sugar. Blend in vanilla. Serve with Plum Pudding. Makes about 2 cups.

Mrs. Dick H. Gregg (Katharine Parker)

Super Soft Custard

2½ cups milk
4 eggs, slightly beaten
⅔ cup sugar

¼ teaspoon salt
2 teaspoons vanilla

Scald milk in double boiler. Combine eggs, sugar and salt in bowl. Gradually stir hot milk into egg mixture; return to double boiler. Cook, stirring constantly, over hot (not boiling) water until mixture coats a metal spoon. Remove from heat immediately. Cool slightly; stir in vanilla. (If custard is lumpy, blend in blender for a few seconds.) Pour into custard cups. Chill. Serves 6.

Mrs. John H. Lindsey (Sara Houstoun)

Whipped Floating Island

4 cups milk
3 eggs, separated
1 cup sugar

¼ cup cornstarch
1 teaspoon vanilla
¼ cup sherry

Scald milk over low heat. In a bowl, combine egg yolks, sugar and cornstarch; beat well. Slowly add hot milk to mixture. Pour mixture into saucepan. Cook, stirring constantly, until custard thickens. Remove from heat and let cool. Mix in vanilla and sherry. Very gently, fold in stiffly-beaten egg whites. Chill before serving. (Custard will not keep overnight.) Serves 6-8.

Mrs. James Richard Gray (Betsy Bonnet)

Caramel Cup Custard Ebby

6 egg yolks
1 cup sugar
¼ teaspoon salt

Dash nutmeg
2 cups milk
½ teaspoon vanilla

Beat egg yolks until lemon-colored; add 1/2 cup of the sugar, salt and nutmeg. Scald milk and pour slowly into egg mixture, beating well. Stir in vanilla. In small iron skillet, rapidly heat remaining 1/2 cup sugar, stirring until lightly caramelized. (Do not cook too long.) Divide caramelized sugar into 6 individual ramekins or custard cups. When sugar is cool, pour custard into ramekins; place in baking pan containing 1″ hot water. Bake in 350° oven for 40-45 minutes. Chill before serving. Serve in the ramekins or unmold into dessert bowls. Serves 6.

Mrs. Wallace M. Davis, Jr. (Barbara Sterrett)

Caramel Custard

3 eggs, separated
1½ cups sugar
2 cups milk
½ cup butter

2 tablespoons flour
3 tablespoons additional milk
1 envelope unflavored gelatin
¼ cup cold water

In saucepan, beat egg yolks with 1/2 cup of the sugar. Stir in 2 cups milk. Place over low heat and cook, stirring constantly, until mixture thickens enough to coat a metal spoon. In a heavy skillet, stir remaining 1 cup sugar over medium heat until melted and lightly caramelized. Remove from heat and stir in butter; gradually blend into custard. Combine flour and 3 tablespoons milk to make a smooth paste; stir into custard. Soften gelatin in cold water and add to custard mixture. Return to heat and cook until thickened, stirring constantly. Remove from heat and allow to cool. Beat egg whites until stiff and fold into cooled custard. Spoon into 1-1/2 quart mold or into individual serving dishes. Serves 6-8.

Mrs. W. Meade Wheless, Jr. (Nancy Park)

Coconut Ring with Caramel Sauce

2 cups coffee cream
2 envelopes unflavored gelatin
½ cup cold water
1 cup sugar

Dash salt
1 teaspoon almond extract
2 cups shredded coconut
3 cups whipping cream

Scald coffee cream; remove from heat. Soften gelatin in water; stir into hot cream to dissolve. Add sugar and salt; mix well. Let cool. Stir in almond extract and coconut. Whip cream and fold in. Pour mixture into 2-1/2 quart ring mold. Chill until firm. Unmold onto serving plate and top with Caramel Sauce. Serves 8-10.

CARAMEL SAUCE

1 tablespoon butter
1 box (1 lb.) brown sugar
2 egg yolks, beaten

1 cup coffee cream
Dash salt
1 teaspoon vanilla

Combine butter and sugar in top of double boiler. Add egg yolks, cream and salt. Cook and stir over hot water until smooth and thick; let cool. Stir in vanilla. Serve with Coconut Ring. Makes about 3 cups sauce.

Mrs. Terry H. Keith (Betty Ann Warner)

371

Lemon Custard

¼ cup butter, softened	4 eggs, separated
1¾ cups sugar	5 tablespoons flour
½ cup lemon juice	1 cup milk
2 tablespoons grated lemon rind	

Cream butter and sugar. Add lemon juice and rind. Beat egg yolks; add to creamed mixture and mix well. Mix in flour and milk until thoroughly blended. Beat egg whites until stiff and fold in. Pour into baking dish. Place dish in pan of hot water; bake in 325° oven for 50 minutes. Let cool thoroughly before serving. Serves 6-8.

Mrs. Antone Wessendorff (Ann Garrow)

Sherry Pudding

8 eggs, separated	2 envelopes unflavored gelatin
2 cups sugar	¼ cup cold water
2 cups dry sherry	2 cups whipping cream

Beat egg yolks until lemon-colored; add 1-3/4 cups of the sugar, a small amount at a time, beating constantly. Stir in sherry. Heat mixture in double boiler. Soften gelatin in cold water. When sherry mixture is hot, add gelatin. Cook and stir until custard thickens. Beat egg whites until stiff and dry, beating in remaining 1/4 cup sugar. Pour hot sherry custard over egg whites, blending well. Chill in refrigerator for about 1 hour. Whip cream and fold into chilled custard; spoon into 2-quart ring mold. Refrigerate at least 6 hours before unmolding. Serves 8.

Mrs. Peter Elliman (Judy Cunningham)

Crème Brûlée

8 egg yolks	2 teaspoons vanilla
5 tablespoons sugar	2 tablespoons (or more)
4 cups whipping cream	brown sugar
	Raspberries

Beat egg yolks and sugar together. Scald whipping cream and pour slowly into egg yolk mixture, stirring constantly. Stir in vanilla. Pour into **shallow,** 2-quart baking dish (mixture should be no higher in dish than 1''); set baking dish in pan of hot water. Bake at 350° until set, about 1 hour. Remove from oven and sift brown sugar evenly over entire top of custard. Place under hot broiler long enough for sugar to melt and form a glaze, about 30-60 seconds. Allow to cool, then refrigerate until chilled. At serving time, spoon into small dessert dishes and top with raspberries if desired. Makes 8 servings.

Mrs. James D. McMurrey (Odette Hemenway)

Chocolate Pots De Crême

1 package (6 oz.) semi-sweet
chocolate chips
6 eggs, separated

2 teaspoons dark rum or brandy
Whipped cream, for garnish
Chocolate curls or slivered
almonds

Melt chocolate in top of double boiler over hot, not boiling, water, stirring until completely smooth. Let cool. Blend in beaten egg yolks. Add rum or brandy. Beat egg whites until stiff and fold into chocolate mixture. Spoon into chocolate pots or ramekins; chill. Garnish with whipped cream and sprinkle with chocolate curls or slivered almonds. Makes 6-8 servings.

Mrs. James Howard Park, III (Bette Naylor)

Instant Pots De Crême

1 package (6 oz.) semi-sweet
chocolate chips
2 tablespoons sugar
Pinch salt
1 egg

1 teaspoon vanilla
1½-2 teaspoons dark Jamaican
rum or 1 teaspoon powdered
instant coffee
¾ cup milk
Whipped cream, for topping

Combine chocolate, sugar, salt, egg, vanilla and rum in blender. Heat milk just to boiling. Pour over other ingredients. Cover and blend 1 minute. Pour immediately into chocolate pots or ramekins. Chill at least 1 hour. Serve with whipped cream. Serves 4.

Mrs. Mervyn Lea Rudee (Betsy Eager)

Chocolate Mousse

4½ ounces semi-sweet chocolate
2 tablespoons water
2 tablespoons powdered
instant coffee

5 eggs, separated
¼ cup sugar
1 cup whipping cream

In top of double boiler put chocolate, water and instant coffee. Cook over hot water, stirring until chocolate is melted and mixture is smooth. Remove from heat. Add egg yolks, one at a time, beating constantly; set aside. Beat egg whites, gradually adding sugar; continue beating until stiff. Fold into chocolate mixture. Whip cream and fold in. Spoon into dessert dishes and refrigerate for at least 3 hours. Serves 6-8.

Mrs. Harmon Whittington (Delores Welder)

Cold Chocolate Souffle

1 envelope unflavored gelatin
3 tablespoons cold water
2 ounces unsweetened chocolate
½ cup powdered sugar

1 cup milk
¾ cup granulated sugar
¼ teaspoon salt
1 teaspoon vanilla
2 cups whipping cream

Soften gelatin in water; set aside. Melt chocolate in top of double boiler over hot, not boiling, water. Stir in powdered sugar and blend until smooth. Scald milk; stir into chocolate mixture. Cook, stirring constantly, until mixture reaches the boiling point. (Do not boil.) Remove from heat and mix in softened gelatin, granulated sugar, salt and vanilla. Chill until slightly thickened. Beat until light and airy. Whip cream and carefully fold into chocolate mixture. Pour into souffle dish or serving bowl. Refrigerate 2-3 hours, or until firm. Serves 6-8.   *Mrs. Edward W. Kelley (Allie May Autry)*

Sunkist Chiffon Dessert

8 eggs, separated
1 cup sugar
Pinch salt
Juice and grated rind of
    2 oranges

Juice and grated rind of 2 lemons
1 envelope unflavored gelatin
½ cup cold water
24 lady fingers
Whipped cream for garnish

In top of double boiler, beat egg yolks; add sugar, salt, orange juice and rind, and lemon juice and rind. Cook over hot water, stirring until thickened. Soften gelatin in cold water; add to hot mixture and stir until dissolved. Let cool. Beat egg whites until stiff; fold into cooled custard mixture. Arrange halved lady fingers on sides and bottom of spring-form pan. Pour in custard and refrigerate for 3-4 hours. Turn out onto serving platter and garnish with whipped cream. Serves 12.
    Mrs. Burke Baker, Jr. (Betty High)

Sherry Lemon Jelly

1 cup boiling water
1 small package (3 oz.)
    lemon-flavored gelatin
1 cup dry sherry

½ cup whipping cream,
    for topping
Additional sherry
2 or 3 tablespoons chopped nuts

Add boiling water to lemon-flavored gelatin; stir to dissolve completely. Add sherry and mix well. Pour into shallow serving dish or into small dessert bowls; chill until set. Whip cream; sweeten with sugar and flavor with sherry. Fold in nuts. Serve as topping. Serves 6.

Mrs. R. W. Tidemann (Bettie Brewster)

Apricot Mousse

1 large can (1 lb., 14 oz.)
    apricots
1 cup syrup from apricots
1 small package (3 oz.) orange-
    flavored gelatin

10 large marshmallows
1 cup whipping cream
Additional whipped cream,
    for topping
Curacao

Bring apricot syrup to a boil; pour over orange gelatin. Add marshmallows, stirring until melted. Puree apricots and stir into gelatin mixture. Chill. When mixture is partially set, whip 1 cup cream and fold in gently. Pour into 1-1/2 quart mold or individual dessert dishes. Refrigerate until set. Flavor additional whipped cream with curacao and serve with Apricot Mousse. Serves 6-8.

Mrs. Rotan McGown (Charlotte Rotan)

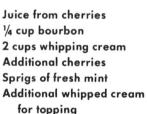

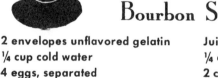

Bourbon Snow

2 envelopes unflavored gelatin
¼ cup cold water
4 eggs, separated
1 cup sugar
2 cups milk, scalded
1 jar (4 oz.) maraschino
    cherries, chopped

Juice from cherries
¼ cup bourbon
2 cups whipping cream
Additional cherries
Sprigs of fresh mint
Additional whipped cream
    for topping

Soften gelatin in water; set aside. In top of double boiler, beat egg yolks with sugar. Stir in scalded milk. Cook over hot water, stirring constantly, until mixture coats metal spoon. Remove from heat and add softened gelatin; stir until dissolved. Let cool. As mixture begins to set, beat with electric mixer. Add cherries, cherry juice and bourbon. Beat egg whites until stiff; fold in. Whip cream and fold in. Pour into lightly-greased, 2-quart mold; chill until firm. Garnish with whole cherries and mint. Serve with additional whipped cream. Serves 12.

Mrs. Macrery B. Wheeler, Jr. (Elma Landram)

Brandied Charlotte Russe

3 envelopes unflavored gelatin
1 cup water
1 cup milk
1 cup sugar
2 egg yolks, well beaten
¼ cup brandy

5 egg whites, stiffly beaten
1 cup whipping cream
Additional whipped cream,
  for topping
1 cup coarsely chopped pecans
Maraschino cherries

Soften gelatin in water. Stir milk and sugar together and bring to boiling point. Remove from heat; slowly add egg yolks and softened gelatin. Cook in double boiler for 10 minutes, stirring constantly. Remove from heat and let cool. When completely cool, stir in brandy. Fold in egg whites; whip 1 cup cream and fold in. Rinse a 2-1/2 quart mold in cold water; spoon mixture into mold. Chill until firm. To serve, cut in slices. Top each serving with additional whipped cream, pecans and a cherry. Serves 12.

Mrs. Hughes Fleming (Mildred Hughes)

Emerald Mint Mold

16 large marshmallows
⅔ cup green creme de menthe
2 cups whipping cream
Green food coloring (optional)
½ cup sugar

¼ cup cocoa
¼ teaspoon salt
1 cup boiling water
1 teaspoon vanilla
Toasted slivered almonds
  for topping

Place marshmallows and creme de menthe in saucepan over **very** low heat. Stir until marshmallows are melted. Remove from heat and chill. Whip cream and fold into chilled mixture. Color with green food coloring, if desired. Place in 1-quart mold and freeze. To make sauce, combine sugar, cocoa, salt and water; cook until thick. Remove from heat and add vanilla. To serve, unmold dessert onto serving plate. Pour chocolate sauce over dessert and sprinkle with almonds. Serves 6.

Mrs. David C. Campbell (Verlyn Miller)

Bavarian Cream with Raspberry Sauce

Lady fingers (about 14)
2 envelopes unflavored
  gelatin
¼ cup cold water
8 egg yolks

1 cup sugar
2 cups milk
2" piece vanilla bean
¼ cup Cointreau
2 cups whipping cream

Continued on next page

Line two 1-quart molds or souffle dishes with lady finger halves, covering bottom first, then standing them up around sides of mold. Soften gelatin in cold water. Combine egg yolks and sugar; beat well. Scald milk with vanilla bean; pour slowly over egg yolk mixture, stirring constantly. Cook over boiling water, stirring constantly, until custard is smooth and thick. Remove vanilla bean. Add softened gelatin and continue stirring until gelatin is completely dissolved. Strain through wire strainer and let cool, stirring occasionally to prevent a film from forming. When cool, add Cointreau. Whip cream and fold in carefully. Pour into prepared molds; chill at least 2 hours. Unmold onto serving platter and serve with Raspberry Sauce. Serves 8-10.

RASPBERRY SAUCE

½ cup Cointreau	1 cup whipping cream
1 package (10-12 oz.) frozen raspberries	2 tablespoons sugar

Add Cointreau to frozen raspberries; let thaw. Drain, reserving juice. Whip cream, fold in sugar and raspberries. Thin with a little reserved juice. Sauce may be served immediately or refrigerated until serving time. Serve in sauce boat with ladle, to be spooned over individual servings of Bavarian Creme. Makes about 2 cups sauce.

Mrs. Lorenzo B. Taylor (Marilyn Dubach)

Coffee Bavarian Cream

2 eggs, separated	½ teaspoon vanilla
½ cup sugar	½ cup black coffee
¼ teaspoon salt	1 cup whipping cream
½ cup milk	Additional whipped cream,
1 envelope unflavored gelatin	for topping
¼ cup cold water	Grated sweet chocolate

In top of double boiler, beat egg yolks; add 1/4 cup of the sugar and the salt. Slowly add milk. Cook over hot water, stirring constantly, until mixture begins to thicken. Soften gelatin in cold water; add to mixture, stirring until gelatin is dissolved. Stir in vanilla and coffee. Refrigerate until slightly thickened. Beat egg whites until stiff. Slowly add remaining 1/4 cup sugar, beating constantly. Whip cream and fold into gelatin mixture. Fold in stiffly beaten egg whites. Pour into 12 individual dessert cups; chill until firm. Top with whipped cream and grated chocolate. Serves 12.

Mrs. George V. Kane, Jr. (Alafair Benbow)

Strawberry Bavarian Creme

4 cups fresh strawberries	¼ cup cold water
1 tablespoon lemon juice	¼ cup hot water
¾ cup sugar	2 cups whipping cream
2 envelopes unflavored gelatin	Whole fresh strawberries, for garnish

Puree strawberries in blender. Add lemon juice and sugar; stir until sugar is dissolved. Soften gelatin in cold water; add hot water and stir until gelatin is dissolved. Fold gelatin into strawberry puree. Stir over ice until mixture begins to thicken. Whip cream and fold in. Pour into 1-1/2 quart mold and chill until firm. Garnish with whole strawberries. Serves 6.

Mrs. W. T. Hancock (Kano Mayo)

Sock Club Delight

6 eggs, separated	1 teaspoon vanilla
1 cup butter	2 cups vanilla wafer crumbs
1 box (1 lb.) powdered sugar	Whipped cream for topping
2 cups chopped pecans	Maraschino cherries (optional)
½ teaspoon almond extract	

Beat egg whites until stiff; set aside. Cream butter and powdered sugar together. Add egg yolks, one at a time, beating after each addition. Stir in pecans, almond extract and vanilla. Fold in egg whites. In buttered, large rectangular Pyrex dish, sprinkle half of the cookie crumbs. Carefully pour on half of the filling. Repeat layers, reserving small amount of crumbs to sprinkle on top. Refrigerate for 24 hours before serving. Cut into squares and top each serving with whipped cream and a cherry, if desired. Serves 16 generously.

Miss Janet Woods

English Toffee Squares

1½ cups vanilla wafer crumbs	1 cup powdered sugar
1 cup chopped nuts	1½ ounces unsweetened chocolate, melted
3 eggs, separated	½ teaspoon vanilla
½ cup butter	Whipped cream

Continued on next page

Combine vanilla wafer crumbs and chopped nuts; sprinkle half in buttered, 9-inch square pan. Beat egg whites until stiff; set aside. Cream butter and powdered sugar. Beat egg yolks and add to creamed mixture. Blend in melted chocolate and vanilla. Fold in egg whites. Pour mixture carefully over crumb layer and sprinkle with remaining crumbs. Refrigerate for several hours or overnight. Cut in squares and serve with whipped cream. Serves 6.

Mrs. Bruce E. Barnett (Ann Poyner)

Moonbeams

2 packages (4 oz. each) individual
   sponge cake dessert cups
1 envelope unflavored gelatin
¼ cup cold water
1 large can (13 oz.)
   evaporated milk

1 cup orange juice
3 tablespoons lemon juice
¾ cup sugar
2 tablespoons grated
   orange rind
Sweetened whipped cream

Crumble sponge cakes. Soften gelatin in water. Scald milk in double boiler; add 1 tablespoon of the softened gelatin. Chill in refrigerator until **very** cold. Heat orange juice and lemon juice. Add sugar, orange rind and remaining softened gelatin; chill until mixture starts to thicken. Whip milk until thick and fluffy. Fold into orange mixture. In a 9-inch spring-form pan, alternate layers of crumbled cake and filling (4 layers cake, 3 of filling). Refrigerate for at least 12 hours. Turn out and frost with sweetened whipped cream. Serves 8-10.

Mrs. W. S. Perkins (Sue Scott)

Ice House Cake

24 lady fingers
1 cup butter
1½ cups powdered sugar
6 eggs, separated

2 cups chopped almonds or
   pecans
1 teaspoon vanilla
1 pound almond macaroons,
   crumbled

Line sides and bottom of large spring-form pan with lady finger halves. Cream butter and sugar. Add well-beaten egg yolks. Stir in nuts and vanilla. Beat egg whites until stiff and fold in. Stir in crumbled macaroons. Pour mixture over lady fingers. Chill in "ice house" for at least 36 hours before serving. Serves 12.

Mrs. Glen E. Vague (Julia Finnell)

North Carolina Party Dessert

1 large angel food cake
(about 1 lb.)
4 eggs, separated
1 cup sugar
½ cup sherry

1 envelope unflavored gelatin
2 tablespoons cold water
3 cups whipping cream
½ cup broken pecans

Cut crust from cake. Tear cake into small (1/2") pieces; set aside. In top of double boiler, beat egg yolks until light, gradually adding 1/2 cup of the sugar. Stir in sherry; place over boiling water and cook until mixture thickens, stirring constantly. Set aside and let cool. Soften gelatin in cold water and dissolve over boiling water; let cool slightly. In a large bowl, whip 2 cups of the cream; fold in egg yolk mixture and pecans. Beat egg whites until stiff; add 6 tablespoons of the remaining sugar. Fold in gelatin and egg whites. In a large tube pan, place a layer of cake pieces and cover with a layer of custard. Repeat until all is used, making 3 layers of cake and 3 layers of custard. Refrigerate for at least 12 hours. Unmold onto serving plate. Whip remaining 1 cup cream, adding remaining 2 tablespoons sugar. Spread over top and sides of cake. Serves 10-12.

Mrs. Platt W. Davis, Jr. (Janet Houstoun)

Tipsy Pudding

1 quart milk
4 egg yolks
5 tablespoons sugar
2 tablespoons flour
Pinch salt
1 small angel food cake (10 oz.)

2 tablespoons (or more) sherry
1 cup whipping cream
1 teaspoon additional sugar
½ teaspoon vanilla
½ teaspoon almond extract
½ cup currant jelly

To make custard, scald milk in double boiler. Combine egg yolks, sugar, flour and salt. Gradually stir hot milk into egg mixture; return to double boiler. Cook over hot water, stirring constantly, until mixture thickens. Strain custard and let cool. (If a richer-looking custard is desired, add 2 drops yellow food coloring.) Break angel food cake into 1" chunks. Drizzle sherry over cake. Whip cream and add 1 teaspoon sugar, vanilla and almond extract. In crystal serving bowl, layer half of the cake, half of the custard and half of the whipped cream. Repeat layers. Dot with currant jelly. Refrigerate at least 4 hours (longer is better) before serving. Serves 8.

Mrs. Willis M. Powell, Jr. (Mary Wheless)

Chocolate Velvet Angel Cake

1 box angel food cake mix	¼ teaspoon salt
1 cup semi-sweet chocolate chips	2 cups whipping cream
1 large package (8 oz.) cream	2 tablespoons sugar
cheese, softened	3 tablespoons coffee liqueur
¾ cup maple syrup	Melted or grated chocolate,
½ teaspoon powdered instant coffee	for decoration

Prepare angel food cake batter according to package directions. Pour 6 cups of the batter into ungreased, 2-1/2 quart, round-bottomed ovenproof bowl. Bake at 325° for 30 minutes. (Use remaining batter for additional cake or cup cakes.) When done, invert cake and bowl on wire rack to cool. After cake is cool, but before removing from bowl, cut out center of cake, leaving a 1-1/2 inch thick shell. Loosen cake shell from sides of bowl, but do not remove; set aside. Melt chocolate chips over hot, not boiling, water. Using electric mixer, beat cream cheese at medium speed until light and fluffy. Slowly beat in maple syrup, instant coffee and salt. Fold in melted chocolate. Whip 1 cup of the cream and fold in. Pour into prepared angel cake shell. Cover with freezer wrap or heavy foil and freeze. Remove cake from freezer at least 2 hours before serving time. Let stand at room temperature for 15 minutes; then loosen sides of shell from bowl with a spatula. Invert onto serving plate. Sprinkle liqueur over top of cake. Whip remaining cup of cream, blend in sugar and use to frost cake. Decorate by drizzling melted chocolate over cake, or sprinkle with grated chocolate. Refrigerate until serving time. This dessert may be kept in freezer up to a week. (Cup cakes or loaf cake made with extra cake mix batter may be filled by this same method. Bake cup cakes only 20 minutes.) Makes 12-16 servings.

Mrs. Frank C. Smith, Jr. (Sally McQueen)

Chocolate Angel Dessert

2 packages (6 oz. each) semi-	2 cups whipping cream
sweet chocolate chips	1 small angel food cake
2 tablespoons sugar	(8-10 oz.)
5 eggs, separated	Slivered almonds for topping

Melt chocolate chips with sugar over hot, not boiling, water; blend until smooth. Remove from heat and stir in beaten egg yolks; let cool. Beat egg whites until stiff; whip cream. Fold egg whites and whipped cream into chocolate mixture. Break half of the cake into bite-sized pieces; layer in buttered 9-inch, spring-form pan. Cover with half of the chocolate mixture. Repeat layers. Chill for 6-8 hours, or overnight. Sprinkle slivered almonds on top and around sides before serving. Serves 12.

Mrs. James Howard Park, III (Bette Naylor)

Chocolate Icebox Cake

24 lady fingers	6 eggs, separated
3 bars (4 oz. each) German's sweet chocolate	1 tablespoon Grand Marnier, or vanilla
4½ tablespoons water	2 cups whipping cream
8½ tablespoons sugar	Grated unsweetened chocolate

Line sides and bottom of large spring-form pan with halved lady fingers. Melt sweet chocolate in top of a double boiler over hot water; add water and 4-1/2 tablespoons of the sugar, mixing until smooth. Add 2 tablespoons of the chocolate mixture to beaten egg yolks; return to double boiler and stir well. Cook, covered, over boiling water for 8 minutes; let cool. Stir in Grand Marnier. Whip cream; stir in remaining 4 tablespoons sugar. Reserve about 1/2 cup sweetened whipped cream for topping. Fold remainder of sweetened whipped cream into chocolate mixture. Very gently, fold in stiffly-beaten egg whites. Slowly pour half of the filling over lady fingers. Add a second layer of halved lady fingers; cover with remaining filling. Chill for 2 hours. Top with reserved whipped cream and sprinkle with grated chocolate. Chill for another 3 hours. Serves 10.

Mrs. Jack T. Currie (Dorothy Peek)

Chocolate Brandy Icebox Cake

24 lady fingers; or small angel food cake, cut into strips	2 tablespoons powdered instant coffee
8 tablespoons (or more) brandy	½ cup slivered almonds or chopped pecans
2 bars (4 oz. each) German's sweet chocolate	2 cups whipping cream
4 eggs, separated	

Butter a deep, round, 2-1/2 to 3 quart bowl; line sides and bottom with halved lady fingers or strips of cake. Sprinkle with 1 tablespoon (or more) of the brandy. Melt chocolate in top of double boiler; stir over hot water until smooth. Beat egg yolks; blend in melted chocolate. Add instant coffee and 6 tablespoons of the brandy. Add nuts, reserving a few. Fold in stiffly-beaten egg whites. Whip cream and fold half of it into the mixture. Spoon half of the chocolate mixture over lady fingers in bowl; sprinkle with reserved nuts. Top with second layer of lady fingers; sprinkle with remaining 1 tablespoon (or more) brandy. Spoon on remaining chocolate mixture. Top with another layer of lady fingers. Chill until thoroughly set. To serve, turn out cake onto serving platter and frost with remaining whipped cream. Cake may be frozen. Serves 10-12.

Mrs. John D. Staub (Alice York)

Butterscotch Icebox Cake

24 lady fingers
½ cup butter
2 cups powdered sugar
4 egg yolks
1 teaspoon vanilla

Coffee flavoring, or strong
coffee, to taste
2 cups whipping cream
1 package (8½ oz.) butterscotch
hard candy
1 cup chopped pecans

Line bottom and sides of large spring-form pan with lady finger halves. Cream butter, sugar and egg yolks. Stir in vanilla and coffee. Whip cream and fold in. Spoon half of mixture over lady fingers. Wrap candy in a linen towel and pound with wooden mallet to crush it coarsely. Combine candy with pecans; sprinkle half over whipped cream mixture. Cover with remaining lady finger halves; repeat layers of whipped cream mixture and candy. Refrigerate at least 3 hours. Serves 12.

Mrs. Robert Mosbacher (Jane Pennybacker)

Cabinet Pudding

2 envelopes unflavored gelatin
1½ cups cold water
1 cup sherry
6 eggs, separated
7 tablespoons sugar
½ cup chopped, candied
pineapple

1 cup broken pecans
1 cup toasted, crushed almond
macaroons
A few candied or maraschino
cherries, quartered
Sweetened whipped cream
Additional cherries for decoration

In saucepan, sprinkle gelatin into 1/2 cup of the water to soften. Add sherry and remaining cup water. Bring to boiling point. (Do not boil.) Beat egg yolks with sugar and slowly stir into sherry mixture. Return to boiling point, stirring constantly. Remove from heat, allow to cool; then refrigerate until slightly thickened. Beat egg whites until stiff; fold into sherry-custard mixture. Fold in pineapple, pecans, macaroon crumbs and quartered cherries. Rinse 1-1/2 quart mold with cold water; pour pudding into mold and refrigerate several hours, or overnight, before serving. Unmold onto serving plate. Arrange mounds of sweetened whipped cream around the pudding. Top each mound of whipped cream with a cherry. Serves 6-8.

Mrs. Anderson Brogniez (Burdine Anderson)

Forgotten Dessert

7 egg whites
1 teaspoon cream of tartar
Dash salt
½ cup sugar

1 cup whipping cream
Fresh or frozen strawberries or
  raspberries, for topping

Heat oven to 450°. Beat egg whites slightly. Add cream of tartar and salt; beat until very stiff. Continue beating, adding sugar gradually; beat until sugar is dissolved. Butter a 9" x 13" Pyrex dish. Spread mixture in dish; put in oven and turn off heat. Leave dessert in oven overnight. (Do not peek.) Next day, whip cream and spread over top of meringue. Refrigerate at least 4 hours before serving. To serve, cut into squares and top with sweetened strawberries or raspberries. Serves 12.

Mrs. Theodore J. Haywood (Nancy Ferguson)

Irish Trifle

1 loaf pound cake
Sweet orange marmalade
Chopped toasted almonds
1 cup sherry
½ cup sugar
4 egg yolks, beaten

1 teaspoon cornstarch
1¾ cups milk, scalded
1 tablespoon vanilla
Whipped cream
Maraschino cherries

Slice cake, lengthwise, 1/2" thick. Spread each slice with marmalade and arrange in single layer in large rectangular Pyrex dish. Sprinkle with chopped almonds. Sprinkle sherry over all and refrigerate for at least 12 hours. To make custard sauce, combine sugar, egg yolks and cornstarch in saucepan; slowly add scalded milk. Cook and stir over moderate heat until mixture coats a metal spoon. Remove from heat and stir in vanilla. To serve, divide cake onto 8 individual dessert plates. Pour custard sauce over each serving; garnish with whipped cream and a cherry. Serves 8.

Mrs. Mavis P. Kelsey (Mary Wilson)

Rich Reward

1 envelope unflavored gelatin
½ cup cold water
3 eggs, separated
1 cup milk
½ cup white sugar
½ cup brown sugar

2 cups whipping cream
2 tablespoons bourbon (optional)
36 chocolate Hydrox cookies,
  crushed
Grated chocolate, or additional
  cookie crumbs, for topping

Continued on next page

Soften gelatin in cold water. In double boiler beat egg yolks; add milk, white sugar and brown sugar. Add gelatin and cook over hot water, stirring frequently, for 10-15 minutes, or until mixture thickens and coats a metal spoon. Remove from heat; let cool completely. Beat egg whites very stiff and fold into cooled custard. Whip cream; stir in bourbon. Fold into custard. Layer half of the crushed cookies in large rectangular Pyrex dish (about 9" x 13"). Pour on half of the filling. Repeat layers. Decorate with shaved chocolate, or additional cookie crumbs; allow to chill for several hours or overnight. Cut into squares to serve. Serves 12-15.

Mrs. James Marshall Shatto (Rebecca Crowder)

Chocolate Calories

4 eggs	¼ cup Droste's cocoa
1 cup butter, melted	4½ tablespoons flour
2 teaspoons vanilla	1 cup coarsely chopped pecans
2 cups sugar	1 cup whipping cream

Beat eggs well; add melted butter and vanilla. Sift together sugar, cocoa and flour; add to egg mixture. (Batter will be thin.) Stir in pecans. Pour batter into large rectangular (9" x 13") Pyrex dish. Set dish in pan of water (use roaster or broiler pan) and bake at 325° for 45 minutes. (Cake may not look "done," but it is. Do not overcook. It will be chewy.) When cool, cut into squares. Top each serving with whipped cream. Serves 10-12.

Mrs. Richard M. Riggs (Katherine Grace)

Chocolate Party Special

1 cup flour	1 teaspoon vanilla
¾ cup sugar	½ cup chopped pecans
¼ teaspoon salt	½ cup additional sugar
2 teaspoons baking powder	5 tablespoons additional cocoa
1½ tablespoons cocoa	1 cup hot water
½ cup milk	Ice cream or whipped cream
2 tablespoons butter, melted	

Sift together flour, 3/4 cup sugar, salt, baking powder and 1-1/2 tablespoons cocoa. Stir in milk, melted butter, vanilla and pecans. Pour into well-greased large rectangular Pyrex dish. Make topping by mixing 1/2 cup sugar, 5 tablespoons cocoa and hot water; pour over batter. Bake at 350° for 40 minutes. Cut into squares; invert onto dessert plates so that sauce is on top. Top with ice cream or whipped cream. Serves 8-10.

Mrs. Kemerton Dean (Ada Dodge)

Chocolate Intrigue

½ cup margarine	¼ teaspoon soda
½ cup shortening	1 cup milk
2 cups sugar	½ teaspoon vanilla
4 eggs	¾ cup Hershey's
3 cups sifted flour	chocolate syrup
½ teaspoon salt	2 teaspoons baking powder

Grease bottom only of 9" x 13" pan. Cream margarine, shortening and sugar. When light and fluffy, add eggs, one at a time, beating well after each addition. Sift together flour, salt and soda. Add to creamed mixture alternately with milk, beginning and ending with dry ingredients. Blend thoroughly after each addition. Beat in vanilla. Spread 2/3 of the batter in prepared pan. To remainder, add chocolate syrup and baking powder. Mix well. Spread chocolate batter over white batter, being careful not to mix the two. Bake in 350° oven for about 1 hour and 15 minutes. Let cake remain in pan. Cut in squares and serve warm. Serves 12.

Mrs. Ford Hubbard (Julia Shepherd)

Chocolate Roll

6 eggs, separated	1 tablespoon flour
½ cup sugar	1 cup whipping cream
3 tablespoons cocoa	Chocolate sauce, for topping

Beat egg yolks; beat in sugar, cocoa and flour. Beat egg whites until stiff and fold into chocolate mixture. Line jelly roll pan with wax paper. Spread batter in pan. Bake at 350° for 30 minutes. While warm, turn out on damp linen towel, remove wax paper, roll up in towel and refrigerate. Whip cream; unroll cake and spread with whipped cream. Roll cake up again and cut into slices to serve. Top with chocolate sauce. Serves 6-8.

Mrs. William E. Davis, Jr. (Margaret Tomlinson)

Fresno Pudding

1 cup flour	½ cup milk
⅔ cup white sugar	2 cups water
1 ½ teaspoons baking powder	1 cup brown sugar
¼ teaspoon salt	2 tablespoons butter
1 cup raisins	Whipped cream or ice cream, for topping

Continued on next page

Sift together flour, white sugar, baking powder and salt. Combine raisins and milk; mix into dry ingredients. Spread batter in buttered, 1-1/2 quart baking dish. Combine water, brown sugar and butter in saucepan. Heat, stirring constantly, until syrupy. Pour syrup over batter. Bake at 350° for 30-40 minutes. Serve warm, topped with whipped cream or ice cream. Serves 4-6.

Mrs. Mervyn Lea Rudee (Betsy Eager)

Pumpkin Date Torte

½ cup pitted, chopped dates
½ cup chopped pecans
2 tablespoons flour
¼ cup butter, melted
1 cup brown sugar
⅔ cup canned pumpkin (or cooked mashed fresh pumpkin)
1 teaspoon vanilla

2 eggs
½ cup sifted flour
½ teaspoon baking powder
½ teaspoon cinnamon
½ teaspoon nutmeg
¼ teaspoon ginger
¼ teaspoon soda
Whipped cream

Mix dates, pecans and 2 tablespoons flour; set aside. Blend melted butter and brown sugar. Stir in pumpkin and vanilla. Beat in eggs, one at a time. Sift together 1/2 cup flour, baking powder, cinnamon, nutmeg, ginger and soda. Add to pumpkin mixture and blend thoroughly. Stir in floured dates and nuts. Turn into greased, 9-inch, round cake pan. Bake in 350° oven for 25-30 minutes. Serve warm with whipped cream. Serves 8.

Mrs. Ralph Bowen, Jr. (Sheila Smith)

Dandy Date Loaf

2 cups vanilla wafer crumbs
1 cup pitted, chopped dates
½ cup chopped pecans

½ cup Eagle Brand sweetened condensed milk
2 teaspoons lemon juice
Whipped cream

Combine vanilla wafer crumbs, dates, pecans, condensed milk and lemon juice. Knead mixture by hand and shape into a roll 3'' in diameter. Wrap in wax paper and chill at least 3 hours. Cut into slices and serve with whipped cream. Keeps well in refrigerator. Serves 6-8.

Mrs. James Marshall Shatto (Rebecca Crowder)

Blueberry Torte

2 cups graham cracker crumbs
(16 double crackers)
⅓ cup butter, melted
1 cup sugar

1 large package (8 oz.) cream
cheese, softened
2 eggs
1 can (1 lb. 6 oz.) blueberry
pie filling

To make crust, mix graham cracker crumbs with melted butter and 1/2 cup
of the sugar. Press firmly over bottom of 8-inch square pan; set aside. With
electric mixer, blend cream cheese and remaining 1/2 cup sugar until creamy
and smooth. Add eggs, one at a time, beating well after each addition. Pour
over crumb crust and bake at 350° for 25-30 minutes. Allow to cool; then
gently spread blueberry pie filling over all. Chill overnight. Cut into squares
to serve. Serves 6-8.

Mrs. W. K. King (Rosalie Meek)

Coconut Torte

4 egg whites
1 cup sugar
1 cup graham cracker crumbs
½ cup coconut, shredded or flaked

½ cup chopped nuts
¼ teaspoon salt
1 teaspoon vanilla or rum
Coffee ice cream

Beat egg whites until stiff; fold in sugar and beat until glossy. Combine graham cracker crumbs, coconut, nuts and salt; fold in egg whites and vanilla.
Spoon into greased 9-inch pie pan; bake at 350° for 30 minutes. Serve in
wedges topped with coffee ice cream. Serves 8.

Mrs. William C. French, Jr. (Frances Griggs)

Food For The Gods

6 eggs, separated
2 cups sugar
10 tablespoons saltine
cracker crumbs

1 tablespoon baking powder
1 pound pitted dates, chopped
1 pound English walnuts, broken
1 cup whipping cream

Beat egg whites until stiff; set aside. Beat egg yolks; add sugar, and beat
well. Mix in cracker crumbs, baking powder, dates and walnuts. Fold in
the egg whites. Bake in greased 8-inch square pan at 375° for 45 minutes.
Serve with whipped cream. Serves 8.

Mrs. Robert L. Reese (Alice Moore)

Coffee Almond Tortoni

1 egg white
Pinch salt
6 tablespoons sugar
1 cup whipping cream
1 tablespoon powdered
  instant coffee
½ teaspoon vanilla
½ cup (or more) toasted
  slivered almonds
Shaved chocolate, for
  topping

Beat egg white until stiff; add salt and 4 tablespoons of the sugar. Whip cream and fold in remaining 2 tablespoons sugar and instant coffee. Fold in egg white, vanilla and almonds. Spoon into 6 paper baking cups or individual ramekins. Sprinkle with shaved chocolate. Freeze thoroughly. This dessert may be made several days before needed. Serves 6.

Mrs. E. H. Thornton, Jr. (Ramona Meyers)

Bourbon Breeze

4 egg yolks
¼ cup bourbon
2 cups whipping cream
24 almond macaroons, crushed
Additional whipped cream
(optional)

Beat egg yolks until light; stir in bourbon. Whip cream and fold in. Gently fold in macaroon crumbs. Freeze in ice tray for at least 2 hours. Cut into squares and top with additional whipped cream, if desired. Serves 6.

Mrs. Paul S. Ache, Jr. (Betsy Evans)

German Chocolate Freeze

1 bar (4 oz.) German's
  sweet chocolate
3 eggs, separated
1 cup powdered sugar
1 cup chopped pecans
2 cups whipping cream
1 pound vanilla wafers, crushed

Melt chocolate in top of double boiler. Beat egg yolks and add to chocolate. Stir in powdered sugar. Cook and stir until slightly thickened. Remove from heat and let cool. Stir in pecans. Beat egg whites until stiff and fold into chocolate mixture. Whip cream and fold in. Put 1/3 of the mixture into 9-inch square dish. Sprinkle with 1/3 of the vanilla wafer crumbs. Repeat layers twice, ending with crumbs. Freeze for several hours. Cut into squares to serve. Serves 8.

Mrs. James Marshall Shatto (Rebecca Crowder)

Lemon Delight

3 eggs, separated
¼ cup lemon juice
1 teaspoon grated lemon rind
⅛ teaspoon salt

½ cup sugar
1 cup whipping cream
1 tablespoon additional sugar
1½ cups vanilla wafer crumbs

In top of double boiler, beat egg yolks. Stir in lemon juice, lemon rind, salt and 1/2 cup sugar. Cook over hot water until thick, stirring constantly; let cool. Whip cream; set aside. Beat egg whites until stiff; add 1 tablespoon sugar. Fold egg whites into whipped cream. Combine whipped cream mixture and lemon mixture; fold just enough to blend. Sprinkle a generous layer of vanilla wafer crumbs into 1-1/2 quart Pyrex dish. (Reserve small amount of crumbs for topping.) Pour in lemon mixture and sprinkle with reserved crumbs; freeze. Cut into squares to serve. Serves 8.

Mrs. Charles B. Williams (Bobbie Ruth Richardson)

Frozen Maple Mousse

3 egg yolks
1 cup maple syrup
1 envelope unflavored gelatin
2 tablespoons cold water

1 cup miniature marshmallows
6 almond macaroons, crumbled
1 cup chopped nuts
2 cups whipping cream

In double boiler beat egg yolks and maple syrup together. Cook until thickened. Soften gelatin in cold water; add to maple mixture and stir to dissolve gelatin. Remove from heat and beat until cool. Add marshmallows, macaroon crumbs and nuts. Whip cream and fold in gently. Spoon into 2-quart mold; freeze until ready to serve. Makes 8 servings.

Mrs. Pete Gardere (Nancy Penix)

Angel Food Strawberry Delight

1 package (3¼ oz.) slivered
  almonds
1 tablespoon butter
1 angel food cake (8-10 oz.)
  cubed

2 quarts vanilla ice cream,
  softened
2 packages (10-12 oz. each)
  frozen strawberries, thawed
¼ cup rum

Brown almonds in butter; set aside. In a 9" x 12" baking dish, make layers in the following order: half the cake pieces, 1/3 of the ice cream, half the strawberries and half the almonds. Repeat layers. Stir rum into remaining 1/3 of the ice cream and spread it over the top. Freeze for 24 hours. Cut into squares. Serves 10-12.

Mrs. Victor F. Grima (Chlotille Cole)

Individual Baked Alaska with Whiskey Sauce

1 small angel food loaf cake (8-10 oz.)	Pinch salt
	6 egg whites
1 quart coffee ice cream, softened	⅛ teaspoon cream of tartar
	¾ cup sugar

Cut cake into 6 slices about 3/4" thick. Arrange slices about 4" apart on cookie sheet. On cake slices, spread layer of ice cream about 1" thick. Place in freezer while preparing meringue. To make meringue, add salt to egg whites; beat until frothy. Add cream of tartar and beat until stiff, but not dry. Gradually beat in sugar. Completely cover cake-and-ice-cream slices with meringue; return to freezer. (This much can be prepared early in the day.) At serving time, bake frozen Alaskas in 450° oven for 5 minutes. Serve immediately with Whiskey Sauce. Serves 6.

WHISKEY SAUCE

3 egg yolks	4 or 5 tablespoons bourbon
6 tablespoons powdered sugar	1 cup whipping cream

Beat egg yolks; stir in powdered sugar and bourbon. Whip cream and fold in. (Sauce may be made early in the day and refrigerated.) Serve with the Baked Alaskas.

Mrs. Frank J. McGurl (Mary Martin)

Coffee Spumoni

1 gallon coffee ice cream	¼ cup bourbon
1 cup broken pecans	Whipped cream
2 tablespoons butter	Pecan halves
2 dozen almond macaroons, crumbled	

Let ice cream soften. Toast pecans lightly in butter. Butter two 9-inch square pans. Sprinkle macaroon crumbs in each pan, reserving some crumbs for topping. Mix bourbon into ice cream. Spread half of the ice cream over crumbs. Sprinkle with toasted pecans. Spread remaining ice cream over pecans and sprinkle with remaining crumbs. Freeze. Cut into squares to serve. Top each serving with whipped cream and a pecan half. Makes 18 servings.

Mrs. R. Henry Lake (Fredrica Lanford)

Mary's Apricot Torte

1 can (1 lb., 14 oz.)
   peeled apricots, drained
   and chopped
½ cup sugar
2 tablespoons lemon juice

2 tablespoons apricot brandy
1 cup whipping cream
1 cup almond macaroon crumbs,
   (about 12 cookies)
Apricot halves for garnish
   (optional)

Combine apricots with sugar, lemon juice and apricot brandy. Whip cream and fold in. Sprinkle half of the macaroon crumbs in 1-1/2 quart dish. Gently spoon apricot mixture over crumbs. Sprinkle remaining crumbs on top. Freeze at least 5 hours, or until firm. Remove from freezer about 30 minutes before serving. Cut into squares. Garnish with additional rum-soaked apricot halves, if desired. (A variation of this dessert may be made using 2 cups diced, fresh peaches or strawberries. If fresh fruit is used, use a little more sugar. Vary liqueur to compliment fruit choice.) Serves 6-8.

Mrs. James A. Baker, Jr. (Bonner Means)

Ozark Pudding

1 egg
¾ cup sugar
3 tablespoons flour
1¼ teaspoons baking powder
Pinch salt

1 teaspoon vanilla
½ cup chopped nuts
½ cup peeled, chopped apples
1 quart coffee, or Irish coffee
   ice cream, softened

Beat egg, add sugar. Sift flour, baking powder and salt together; blend into egg mixture. Stir in vanilla, nuts and apples. Pour into buttered 9-inch pie pan. Bake at 350° for 25-30 minutes. Let cool, then crumble. Sprinkle half of crumbled mixture into 8" square pan lined with wax paper. Spread ice cream over top. Sprinkle with remaining crumbled mixture. Freeze. Serves 6-8.

Mrs. William A. Bramley (Kay Borden)

Grape Ice Cream

4 cups grape juice
2 cups cream
2 cups milk

2 cups sugar
Juice of 1 lemon

Combine all ingredients; mix well. Freeze in ice trays, stirring occasionally. Makes about 2-1/2 quarts.

Mrs. Thomas E. Berry (Joan Jester)

Rainbow Compote

1 quart pistachio ice cream
3 cups sliced, fresh peaches,
   slightly sweetened
1 quart raspberry sherbet

2 cups fresh or frozen blueberries
1 quart vanilla ice cream
2 cups fresh strawberries,
   slightly sweetened

Chill in freezer a large brandy snifter or other deep glass dish. Let ice cream and sherbet soften. Layer ingredients in frosted brandy snifter in the following order: pistachio ice cream, peaches, raspberry sherbet, blueberries, vanilla ice cream, strawberries. Return to freezer until firm. (Two packages, 10-12 oz. each, frozen peaches, thawed and drained, may be substituted for fresh peaches.) Serves 18.

Mrs. Terry H. Keith (Betty Ann Warner)

Peppermint Ice Cream Pie

1 package (6 oz.) semi-sweet
   chocolate chips
2 tablespoons butter, softened
2 tablespoons powdered sugar

1 quart peppermint ice cream,
   softened
Chocolate shavings for topping

Line 9-inch pie pan by pressing a 12-inch square of heavy aluminum foil on bottom, sides, and over rim. Sprinkle chocolate chips evenly on foil liner. Put in 250° oven for 5 minutes, absolutely no longer. Blend butter into softened chocolate. Add powdered sugar; blend again until mixture thickens slightly. Spread mixture thinly over bottom and up sides of foil liner. Refrigerate 30 minutes for chocolate shell to harden. Peel foil from shell and return shell to pie pan. Fill with softened ice cream; decorate with shaved chocolate. Store in freezer until ready to serve. Serves 6-8.

Mrs. Charles W. Dabney, Jr. (Julia Vinson)

Lime Ice Cream

1½ cups sugar
1½ cups water
¼ teaspoon salt
1 quart cream

1 cup lime juice (8-15 fresh
   limes)
1 teaspoon vanilla
Few drops green food coloring

Boil sugar and water until syrupy. Add salt; allow to cool. Stir in cream, lime juice, vanilla and food coloring. Pour into container of ice cream freezer; cover tightly. Pack with ice and ice-cream salt. Freeze until firm. Makes about 3 quarts.

Mrs. Bass C. Wallace (Julia Picton)

Aunt Mab's Lemon Ice Cream

3 lemons

1 ½ cups sugar

1 teaspoon unflavored gelatin

2 cups milk

2 cups whipping cream

Squeeze the juice from 2-1/2 lemons; slice remaining half lemon very thin. Combine lemon juice and lemon slices; cover with sugar and set aside. Soften gelatin in a little cold water; dissolve over hot water. Add gelatin to milk. Stir in lemon mixture and put into container of ice-cream freezer. Cover tightly. Pack with ice and ice-cream salt. Freeze until mushy. Whip cream. Remove cover of freezer and fold in whipped cream. Freeze until firm. Allow to stand at least 1 hour before serving. Makes about 2 quarts.

Mrs. Ben G. Sewell (Elizabeth Hall)

Mango Ice Cream

2 cans (14 oz. each)

mangoes, drained

1 ½ cups sugar

⅓ cup lemon juice

1 pint whipping cream

1 pint coffee cream

Puree mangoes in blender or mash through sieve; add sugar and lemon juice. Stir in whipping cream and coffee cream. Pour into container of ice cream freezer; cover tightly. Pack with ice and ice-cream salt. Freeze until firm. Let stand several hours before serving, to enhance flavor. Makes about 3 quarts.

Mrs. J. Harvey Suttles, Jr. (Lida Picton)

Peach Ice Cream

2½ cups sugar

14 large, ripe peaches,

peeled and sliced

Pinch salt

Juice of 1 lemon

1½ pints whipping cream

1½ pints coffee cream

Sprinkle sugar over peaches; let stand at least 1 hour, stirring occasionally until syrup is formed. Mash through sieve or food mill. Add salt, lemon juice, whipping cream and coffee cream. Mix well. Pour into container of ice cream freezer; cover tightly. Pack with ice and ice-cream salt. Freeze until firm. Makes about 4 quarts.

Mrs. Douglas S. Craig (Alice Picton)

Strawberry Ice Cream

6 pints fresh strawberries
2 cups sugar
1½ pints whipping cream

1½ pints coffee cream
Pinch salt

Cover strawberries with sugar. Let stand at least 1 hour, stirring occasionally, until syrup is formed. Put through sieve or food mill. Add remaining ingredients and mix thoroughly. Pour into container of ice-cream freezer; cover tightly. Pack with ice and ice-cream salt. Freeze until firm. Makes about 4 quarts.

Mrs. Douglas S. Craig (Alice Picton)

Fresh Fruit Ice Cream

2 cups (or more) mashed
   fresh fruit
¾ cup sugar

Juice of 1 lemon
¼ teaspoon almond extract
1 pint whipping cream

Combine fruit and sugar; refrigerate overnight. Stir in lemon juice and almond extract. Freeze to a mush. Whip cream and fold into icy fruit. Spoon into 2 ice trays and freeze until firm. Makes about 1-1/2 quarts.

Mrs. R. W. Tidemann (Bettie Brewster)

Old Fashioned Vanilla Ice Cream

6 eggs, separated
2 cups sugar
2 tablespoons flour

2 quarts milk
1 pint whipping cream
2 tablespoons vanilla

In large saucepan, beat egg yolks well; add sugar, flour and 1 quart of the milk. Mix well. Heat to scalding, stirring constantly. Remove from heat; add cream, vanilla and remaining quart of milk. Mix thoroughly. Beat egg whites until stiff, but not dry. Fold into cream mixture. Pour into container of 6-quart ice cream freezer; cover tightly. Pack with ice and ice-cream salt; freeze. When ice cream is semi-firm, or almost frozen, 4 cups sweetened fresh fruit (peaches or strawberries) may be added if desired. Makes 4-5 quarts.

Mrs. LaMar W. Lee (Mary Louise Townes)

Vanilla Ice Cream

6 eggs	4 cups coffee cream
2¾ cups sugar	6 cups milk
¼ teaspoon salt	2⅓ tablespoons vanilla

Beat eggs well; add sugar, salt, cream, milk and vanilla. Mix thoroughly. Pour into container of 6-quart ice-cream freezer; cover tightly. Pack with ice and ice-cream salt; freeze until firm. Makes about 5 quarts.

Mrs. R. Henry Lake (Frederica Lanford)

Watermelon Ice

4 cups diced watermelon
Juice of 2 lemons
½ cup sugar

Put all ingredients in blender. Blend well; pour into 1-1/2 quart ice tray. Freeze until firm. Makes about 1 quart.

Mrs. J. Malcolm Horn (Helen Hargrove)

Apricot Sherbet

2 cups sugar	1 can (6 oz.) apricot nectar
1 cup water	1 cup whipping cream
Juice of 2 lemons	1 cup milk
Juice of 4 oranges	

Combine sugar and water; heat until sugar is dissolved. Add lemon juice, orange juice and apricot nectar. Stir in cream and milk. Freeze in ice trays, stirring occasionally until frozen. (May also be frozen in ice-cream freezer.) Makes about 2-1/2 quarts.

Mrs. Joe C. Walter, Jr. (Elizabeth Ann Cowden)

Orange Ice

4 cups water	2 cups sugar
2 cups orange juice	Grated rind of 2 oranges
Juice of 4 lemons	

Combine water, orange juice and lemon juice; stir in sugar. When sugar is completely dissolved, add grated orange rind. Freeze in ice trays. Stir frequently until thoroughly frozen. Makes about 2 quarts.

Mrs. J. L. Mosle (Eleanor Thompson)

Lemon Milk Sherbet

6 lemons
1 cup boiling water

3 cups sugar
2 quarts milk or cream

Squeeze lemons. Pour boiling water over rinds. Add lemon juice and sugar to lemon rind mixture; let stand until syrupy. Strain syrup and chill. Stir in milk or cream (depending on richness desired). Pour into container of ice-cream freezer; cover tightly. Pack with ice and ice-cream salt. Freeze until firm. Makes about 3-1/2 quarts.

Mrs. Peter Elliman (Judy Cunningham)

Orange - Lemon Sherbet

1 large (12 oz.) and 1 small
(6 oz.) can frozen orange
juice concentrate
1 can (6 oz.) frozen lemon
juice concentrate

3 cups sugar
1 can (13 oz.) evaporated milk
2½ to 3 quarts homogenized
milk

Thaw orange juice and lemon juice; add sugar and mix well. Refrigerate for at least 1 hour. Pour into container of 6-quart ice-cream freezer. Pour evaporated milk into container; mix well. Add enough homogenized milk to fill container 2/3 full; mix thoroughly. Cover tightly. Pack with ice and ice-cream salt. Freeze until firm. Makes about 5-1/2 quarts.

Mrs. A. J. Hurt, Jr. (Patty Parrish)

Three Fruit Ice

¾ cup sugar
1 cup water
1 teaspoon unflavored gelatin
2 tablespoons cold water

1 cup lemon juice
1 cup orange juice
3 bananas, peeled and mashed
1 egg white, stiffly beaten

Combine sugar and 1 cup water in saucepan; boil for 5 minutes. Soften gelatin in 2 tablespoons cold water; stir into hot syrup. Stir in lemon juice, orange juice and bananas; mix well. Refrigerate until cold. Fold in stiffly beaten egg white. Freeze in 1-1/2 quart ice tray, stirring every 30 minutes, until frozen. Makes about 1-1/2 quarts.

Mrs. Richard Whittington (Lettalou Garth)

Mango Sherbet

1 can (14 oz.) mangoes with juice	1 teaspoon unflavored gelatin
1 cup sugar	½ cup cold water
	1¾ to 2 cups orange juice

Drain mangoes, reserving juice. Add enough water to juice to make 1 cup. Add sugar to juice and heat. Soften gelatin in cold water; stir into hot syrup. Puree mangoes; stir in orange juice and hot syrup. Pour into ice trays and freeze, stirring occasionally. Makes about 1-1/2 quarts.

Mrs. Lyon L. Brinsmade (Susannah Tucker)

Mama Julia's Vanilla Sauce

½ cup sugar	2 tablespoons butter
3 tablespoons flour	½ cup (approximately) cream
½ cup water	1 teaspoon vanilla

Mix sugar and flour in saucepan. Add water and blend well; then add butter. Cook over low heat until thick, stirring frequently. Add enough cream to thin to desired consistency. Stir in vanilla. Serve warm over gingerbread or plain cake. Makes about 2 cups.

Mrs. George H. Black, Jr. (Carolyn Cave)

Blue Ribbon Chocolate Sauce

½ cup butter	1 box powdered sugar, sifted
4 ounces unsweetened chocolate	1 large can (13 oz.) evaporated milk

Melt butter and chocolate in double boiler; remove from heat. Add powdered sugar alternately with milk, stirring constantly; mix well after each addition. Return to heat and cook in double boiler for 30 minutes, stirring frequently. Store in refrigerator. When ready to use, heat in double boiler, and if necessary, add a little water. Sauce keeps well in refrigerator or may be frozen. Makes about 4 cups sauce.

Mrs. Thomas E. Berry (Joan Jester)

Easy Chocolate Sauce

½ cup sugar
1 egg yolk, beaten
6 tablespoons cream

2 ounces unsweetened
chocolate
½ teaspoon vanilla

Combine all ingredients in top of double boiler; cook over hot water until very thick. Serve over ice cream. Makes about 1 cup.

Mrs. George H. Lane (Joan Bagby)

Vassies Secret Fudge Sauce

2 pounds unsweetened chocolate
2½ pounds (5 cups) sugar
1 quart whipping cream

Melt chocolate over low heat. Dissolve sugar in cream in another double boiler, stirring constantly. Pour melted chocolate into the sugar and cream mixture. Continue stirring until thick. Pour into jars and refrigerate. When ready to use, thin with coffee cream. (This sauce hardens on ice cream.) Makes about 5-1/2 pints.

Mrs. George A. Hill, III (Gloria Lester)

Lemon Butter Sauce

6 eggs
Grated rind and juice of 4 lemons

2 cups sugar
1 cup butter

In top of double boiler, beat eggs with lemon juice and sugar. Add lemon rind and butter; cook over hot water, stirring constantly, until mixture thickens. Serve on pound cake or gingerbread. Makes about 5 cups sauce.

Mrs. William G. Godfrey (Dineen Schuhmacher)

Steamed-Pudding Sauce

½ cup butter
1 cup powdered sugar
¼ cup cream

Few raisins
Pecan halves
1 teaspoon vanilla, rum,
brandy or whiskey

Cream butter and sugar in top of double boiler; stir in cream. Cook over hot water for 2 hours over low heat, stirring occasionally. Add raisins and pecans; and continue cooking 30 additional minutes. Stir in flavoring. Serve **hot** over steamed pudding. Makes about 2 cups sauce.

Mrs. Glen E. Vague (Julia Finnell)

Weights and Measures

3 teaspoons—1 tablespoon
1 ounce—2 tablespoons
4 tablespoons—1/4 cup
5 tablespoons plus 1 teaspoon—1/3 cup
8 tablespoons—1/2 cup
4 ounces—1/2 cup
16 tablespoons—1 cup
8 ounces—1 cup

1 cup—1/2 pint
2 cups—1 pint
16 ounces—1 pound
2 pints—1 quart
4 cups—1 quart
4 quarts—1 gallon (liquid)
8 quarts—1 peck (dry)
4 pecks—1 bushel

THE FOLLOWING EQUAL ONE POUND

2 cups liquid
2 cups butter or shortening
2 cups granulated sugar
4-4-1/2 cups powdered sugar, sifted
2-1/2 cups brown sugar, packed
4 cups sifted flour
4-3/4 cups sifted cake flour
4 cups cocoa
3 cups cornmeal
4 cups grated cheese

4 cups shelled pecans
5 cups dry, shredded coconut
3 cups raisins or currants
9 average sized eggs
2 cups crabmeat
4 small tomatoes
3 large onions
3 medium potatoes (2-1/3 cups sliced)
3 medium apples (3 cups sliced)
3 medium bananas (2-1/2 cups sliced)

OTHER EQUIVALENTS

1 stick butter—1/2 cup
1 square chocolate—3 tablespoons grated chocolate
8-10 egg whites—1 cup
1 cup whipping cream—2 cups whipped cream
22 saltines, crushed—1 cup crumbs
1 medium lemon—1 tablespoon grated rind, 3 tablespoons juice
1 medium orange—2 tablespoons grated rind, 1/3 cup juice
1 dozen medium oranges—4 cups juice

INGREDIENT SUBSTITUTIONS

1 ounce (1 square) unsweetened chocolate—3 tablespoons cocoa plus 1 tablespoon butter
1 teaspoon baking powder—1/2 teaspoon cream of tartar plus 1/4 teaspoon soda
1 tablespoon cornstarch—3 tablespoons flour
1 cup milk—1/2 cup evaporated milk plus 1/2 cup water
1 cup buttermilk (or sour milk)—1 cup fresh milk mixed with 1 tablespoon vinegar or lemon juice
1 cup honey—3/4 cup sugar plus 1/4 cup liquid
1 cup cake flour—1 cup all-purpose flour, less 2 tablespoons
1 egg—2 egg yolks (in custards, mayonnaise)

Index

INDEX

INDEX

INDEX

NOTES

NOTES

NOTES

NOTES

NOTES